school-age children

school-age children
Development and Relationships

Mollie S. Smart / Russell C. Smart

Department of Child Development and Family Relations
University of Rhode Island

THE MACMILLAN COMPANY, NEW YORK
Collier-Macmillan Limited, London
1973

Copyright © 1973, The Macmillan Company

Printed in the United States of America

All rights reserved. No part of this book may be reproduced or
transmitted in any form or by any means, electronic or mechanical,
including photocopying, recording, or any information storage and
retrieval system, without permission in writing from the Publisher.

Reprinted with modifications from *Children: Development and Relationships*,
Second Edition, by Mollie S. Smart and Russell C. Smart, copyright © 1967
and 1972 by The Macmillan Company and *Readings in Child Development and
Relationships*, by Russell C. Smart and Mollie S. Smart, copyright © 1972
by The Macmillan Company.

The Macmillan Company
866 Third Avenue, New York, New York 10022

Collier-Macmillan Canada, Ltd., Toronto, Ontario

Library of Congress catalog card number: 72–75853

Printing: 1 2 3 4 5 6 7 8   Year: 3 4 5 6 7 8 9

contents

v

4. Social Development and Interpersonal Relationships 197

5. An Overview of Human Life and Growth 269

introduction

Almost all cultures take some notice of the child's entering a new phase of life at 6 or 7 years of age. Although there are no general stages that are unique wholes, age 6 or 7 marks a shift in important processes of development. The fact that formal education is begun at this time in so many different cultures indicates widespread perception of such a shift. Likewise, writers from Shakespeare to Erikson have made use of this age in dividing life into portions that can be studied. We begin our discussion of this segment of life at 6 or 7 years and end it at the point where the pubescent growth spurt starts, an average age of 10, but a point which occurs within a wide range of years. The beginning of the school-age is marked by faster, more flexible, and more accurate thinking. Instead of being limited by his own point of view, the schoolchild can inquire and imagine himself into the places of other people, which he does in much of his social inter-action. His broader backlog of experience and his previous achievements with concepts supplement his emerging ability to consider several aspects of the situation before coming to a conclusion.

The loss of his preschool cuteness is not serious to the schoolchild. While an occasional child may mourn the passing of the days when adults thought him perfectly adorable just because he was a young child, most reports of such feelings of regret are from adults looking far backward toward early childhood. By the time he enters first grade, the healthy child has achieved enough trust, autonomy, and initiative that he wants to become involved with a private world of children, where adults are often unwelcome. Adults are, of course, necessary at times. He loves his parents and cares what they think, but his appetite for sitting on laps and being petted is definitely diminished. Teachers and club leaders are important, too, but in limited time and space. It seems as though the child withdraws most into his private sphere of peers and self at the very time (around 10) when he is least attractive to adults—most gangly, least cuddly, restless, dirty, teeth missing, and speaking a language of childhood that is not completely comprehensible to adults.

Building on all that has gone before, the child interacts with a widening world to create new and more complex behavior patterns. Instead of being confined to family, home, and neighborhood, the child is on his own in the school. Warm and acceptant as his teacher may be, he is not special to her, as he is to his mother. He is one of many, and as such must live with a kind of objectivity which he has not experienced before. Instead of playing with only little boys and girls who are the children of his parents' friends and neighbors, he plays and works with a variety of children. Meeting children from a social class different from his own, he may be surprised to find some of his schoolmates cleaner or dirtier, rougher or gentler, more or less interested in doing well at school than he. Playing in the homes of new friends, he discovers parents, behavior, houses, and yards unlike those he has known. Joining Cubs, Brownies, Bluebirds, or a similar organized group, the child embraces a new culture of symbolic pins, handclasps, and reflecting pools which symbolize his belongingness. His religious connections will expand, too. He may make his first communion or begin the study of Hebrew. The public library will enlarge his literary world by conferring the privilege of taking books out. If he lives in a community which sponsors children's concerts, he will be eligible to go to them. Thus he will interact directly with many aspects of the culture which formerly influenced him only through his family.

Privacy is a kind of freedom much enjoyed by the school-age child. Because he is able to take basic physical care of himself and his room, he is often able to keep mother and others out of his room, out of the bathroom, and out of his most secret transactions. Privacy means freedom to take his bath just the way he likes it, to make funny faces in the mirror, to devise messages, signals, codes, club rules, to visit alone with friends. Reading books means freedom to roam in a vast world of thought and imagination. Fast-growing competency in language and thought means greater facility in dealing with all of his private world.

Industry is the name Erikson gives to the stage of personality development of the schoolchild. He has also called it *duty and accomplishment*. This is the time when jobs get done, in contrast to the stage of initiative, when they got started but rarely finished. Having explored all sorts of possibilities for action, the child settles down to learn how to do things and to do them well. He becomes involved in the technology of his culture, whether it stresses fishing and making canoes, or reading, writing, and electronics. Withdrawing from home, mother, and the emotional situations involved in them, he turns to the objects, tools, and techniques of the society in which he lives. Most cultures make provisions for this changeover. Literate societies provide schools where teachers begin the long process of teaching reading and writing. Even in simpler cultures, teachers usually help the children learn the appropriate aspects of technology. Often boys learn farming from their fathers and girls homemaking from their mothers. In American culture, an astonishing number of specialists teach such extracurricular subjects as music, dancing, painting, bird watching, star gazing, first aid, camping, and skiing. Recreation workers and youth leaders teach not only these subjects and more but also concern themselves with group dynamics, character, values, leadership, community service, and so on. It is possible for a child to spend all of his hours left over from eating, sleeping, and physical care on lessons of one sort or another.

There are aspects of industry and duty which are better accomplished with other children (in the peer group) and alone, however, than in an onslaught of lessons. Take baseball, for instance. To be a real American boy, you practically have to know how to play it. As a girl, you have to know at least the rules of the game and preferably you can play softball. It takes thousands of practice throws to get to be a good pitcher and as many catches to be a baseman. Where could one do all this except in the neighborhood play lot with friends? There are many more games with rules and coordinations to be learned. During the school years children are willing, even eager, to practice and practice and practice—batting a ball, jumping, skating, jumping rope, singing and chanting the ditties of childhood, sewing doll clothes, cutting out cookies, playing cards and other games, identifying specimens and arranging collections. There are social skills to develop, too—making and keeping close friendships and being a club member.

Success in the stage of industry results in the child's knowing the pleasure and satisfaction of a job well done. He enjoys being a part of a productive situation. He knows that he can produce, achieve, and accomplish in certain areas, and in those situations he feels adequate. There are enough of them to give him a general feeling of being an adequate person. There are some places where he does particularly well and others where he just gets by. This knowledge is incorporated into his picture of himself.

A sense of *inferiority and inadequacy* is the result when development does not go well at this time of life. Since time of entrance to school is usually fixed rigidly, the child who is not ready to enter into the stage of industry is at a great disadvantage in personality development. Failure in the beginning work is disastrous to his concept of himself as an adequate person.

The final chapter is a general one about human life and growth. It deals with the various ways in which children interact with the physical and social surroundings, thereby changing, developing, and restructuring their bodies, minds, and personalities. Some principles of development are stated. Different ways of learning and maturing are discussed. The readings for the final chapter were chosen in order to show man as part of an ecosystem and to introduce the reader to the thoughts and styles of the great developmentalists.

Chapter 1

Merrill-Palmer Institute by Donna J. Harris

Physical Characteristics and Skills

Slow growth is typical of the period of middle childhood. In both size and proportions, these children change relatively little from year to year. The period of slow growth ends several months before menarche in the girl and a corresponding point of sexual maturity in the boy. Although the period of rapid growth, known as the pubescent growth spurt is discussed primarily in regard to adolescence, it is important to realize that some children in the elementary school are already in the pubescent growth spurt. Growth in height begins to pick up speed, on the average,

1

at about age 9 in girls and 11 in boys. A few girls, however, begin the spurt as early as age 8 and boys at 10. Most girls grow at top speed during their twelfth or thirteenth year, boys during their fourteenth or fifteenth year. A seventh grade classroom is sure to include a wide variety of sizes and stages of maturity. It is safe to generalize that children grow slowly during the early elementary school years.

The middle years are healthier than the preschool period. With growth needs and the burdens of illness claiming less of his energy than they did in an earlier stage of life, the schoolchild has more of himself to invest in relationships, problem solving, and acquiring of skills and knowledge. Now he works to develop and perfect many motor coordinations, enjoying the sense of adequacy which grows from successful performance. His concepts of himself and his body reflect the interactions of his body with the world and also reflect his perceptions of people's reactions to him.

Physical Growth

Growth can be described in terms of the large, general measurements of height and weight and also in terms of various parts of the body. A third way of considering it has to do with interrelationships of various aspects of growth.

Growth in Height and Weight

Percentile tables are available for white and black American children from 5 to 18 years of age, in grades 1 through 11 [50]. These tables (1–1 through 1–8) are based on measurements of 8480 children, an 8 percent sample of the children in school in Cincinnati. Age was defined by the student's last birthday. Measurements, recorded to the nearest inch or pound, were made without shoes, outdoor clothing, and sweaters. There are no consistent differences in median height or weight between whites and blacks. Nor do sex differences in height show up clearly in these tables. Evidence from most research indicates, however, that, on the average, males are taller than females excepting during the pubescent growth spurt [16, p. 548]. When physiological maturity rather than chronological age is taken into account, males are considerably taller than females.

Table 1–1 Percentile Distribution of Height in Inches for White Males (Age Defined at Subject's Last Birthday)

Age	N (Total = 2973)	Percentile						
		3RD	10TH	25TH	50TH	75TH	90TH	97TH
5	143	41	42	44	45	47	48	51
6	250	42	44	45	46	48	50	51
7	268	45	46	47	49	50	52	54
8	261	47	49	50	51	54	56	58
9	259	48	50	51	53	55	57	61
10	221	50	52	53	55	57	59	62

Source: Reprinted by permission from J. L. Rauh, D. A. Schumsky, and M. T. Witt, "Heights, Weights, and Obesity in Urban School Children," *Child Development*, 38, 515–530. Copyright © 1967, The Society for Research in Child Development, Inc.

Table 1–2 Percentile Distribution of Height in Inches for Nonwhite Males (Age Defined at Subject's Last Birthday)

Age	N (Total = 1208)	Percentile						
		3RD	10TH	25th	50TH	75TH	90TH	97TH
5	69	40	42	43	45	47	49	50
6	110	43	44	46	47	49	51	51
7	115	45	47	48	49	51	52	56
8	128	47	49	50	52	54	55	59
9	121	48	51	52	53	55	56	69
10	89	50	51	54	55	57	60	63

SOURCE: Reprinted by permission from J. L. Rauh, D. A. Schumsky, and M. T. Witt, "Heights, Weights, and Obesity in Urban School Children," *Child Development*, **38**, 515–530. Copyright © 1967, The Society for Research in Child Development, Inc.

Table 1–3 Percentile Distribution of Height in Inches for White Females (Age Defined at Subject's Last Birthday)

Age	N (Total = 3010)	Percentile						
		3RD	10TH	25TH	50TH	75TH	90TH	97TH
5	152	38	42	43	44	46	47	49
6	264	42	43	45	46	48	49	51
7	251	43	45	47	49	50	52	54
8	260	45	47	49	50	53	54	57
9	247	47	49	51	53	54	56	59
10	268	49	51	53	55	57	59	62

SOURCE: Reprinted by permission from J. L. Rauh, D. A. Schumsky, and M. T. Witt, "Heights, Weights, and Obesity in Urban School Children," *Child Development*, **38**, 515–530. Copyright © 1967, The Society for Research in Child Development, Inc.

Table 1–4 Percentile Distribution of Height in Inches for Nonwhite Females (Age Defined at Subject's Last Birthday)

Age	N (Total = 1289)	Percentile						
		3RD	10TH	25TH	50TH	75TH	90TH	97TH
5	80	41	42	44	45	46	49	50
6	132	42	44	45	47	48	50	54
7	132	44	46	48	49	51	53	57
8	137	46	48	50	51	53	56	59
9	108	46	50	51	53	55	58	60
10	88	50	53	55	57	59	61	64

SOURCE: Reprinted by permission from J. L. Rauh, D. A. Schumsky, and M. T. Witt, "Heights, Weights, and Obesity in Urban School Children," *Child Development*, **38**, 515–530. Copyright © 1967, The Society for Research in Child Development, Inc.

Table 1–5 Percentile Distribution of Weight in Pounds for White Males (Age Defined at Subject's Last Birthday)

Age	N (Total = 2973)	Percentile						
		3RD	10TH	25TH	50TH	75TH	90TH	97TH
5	143	37	40	42	46	50	54	59
6	250	38	41	45	48	52	58	67
7	268	42	46	50	53	58	63	77
8	261	44	50	55	61	67	75	83
9	259	51	54	60	66	74	87	98
10	221	54	62	66	73	82	96	110

SOURCE: Reprinted by permission from J. L. Rauh, D. A. Schumsky, and M. T. Witt, "Heights, Weights, and Obesity in Urban School Children," *Child Development*, **38**, 515–530. Copyright © 1967, The Society for Research in Child Development, Inc.

Table 1–6 Percentile Distribution of Weight in Pounds for Nonwhite Males (Age Defined at Subject's Last Birthday)

Age	N (Total = 1208)	Percentile						
		3RD	10TH	25TH	50TH	75TH	90TH	97TH
5	69	34	36	41	44	49	53	54
6	110	36	41	44	49	53	59	62
7	115	43	47	50	55	60	65	69
8	128	45	51	56	61	68	75	82
9	121	51	56	59	66	72	81	89
10	89	52	58	66	72	81	94	110

SOURCE: Reprinted by permission from J. L. Rauh, D. A. Schumsky, and M. T. Witt, "Heights, Weights, and Obesity in Urban School Children," *Child Development*, **38**, 515–530. Copyright © 1967, The Society for Research in Child Development, Inc.

Table 1–7 Percentile Distribution of Weight in Pounds for White Females (Age Defined at Subject's Last Birthday)

Age	N (Total = 3010)	Percentile						
		3RD	10TH	25TH	50TH	75TH	90TH	97TH
5	152	35	37	40	43	48	55	60
6	264	35	39	43	47	52	56	61
7	251	37	43	46	52	58	65	72
8	260	42	47	52	57	65	76	89
9	247	47	51	57	63	75	87	99
10	268	51	56	62	70	84	98	116

SOURCE: Reprinted by permission from J. L. Rauh, D. A. Schumsky, and M. T. Witt, "Heights, Weights, and Obesity in Urban School Children," *Child Development*, **38**, 515–530. Copyright © 1967, The Society for Research in Child Development, Inc.

Table 1–8 Percentile Distribution of Weight in Pounds for Nonwhite Females (Age Defined at Subject's Last Birthday)

Age	N (Total = 1289)	3RD	10TH	25TH	50TH	75TH	90TH	97TH
					Percentile			
5	80	33	36	37	41	46	51	57
6	132	34	38	42	46	50	54	67
7	132	39	44	48	51	58	63	86
8	137	42	47	52	58	67	76	84
9	108	46	53	58	65	76	89	104
10	88	51	58	67	78	89	116	131

SOURCE: Reprinted by permission from J. L. Rauh, D. A. Schumsky, and M. T. Witt, "Heights, Weights, and Obesity in Urban School Children," *Child Development*, **38**, 515–530. Copyright © 1967, The Society for Research in Child Development, Inc.

The weight tables shown here indicate that males are heavier than females between ages 5 and 10 or 11. At 11 for whites and 10 for blacks, the female weights exceeded the male, indicating the earlier pubescent growth spurt in girls. When the sexes are compared at the maturity level, however, males are heavier than females and when fat-free weight is compared, the difference is even greater [16, p. 548].

Girls' earlier entrance into the pubescent growth makes them temporarily taller and heavier. Although the average difference is small (an inch at 12 and 13 years), a fast-maturing girl towers above a slow-growing boy, a discrepancy which causes agony if children between 11 and 15 are pushed into dancing, dating, and other situations where their heights are compared. At all points in the growth cycle, girls are closer to maturity than boys, since they do not have to grow so far to reach it. For instance, 75 percent of adult height is attained by the average 9-year-old boy and by the average 7-year-old girl.

Height increases more steadily than weight, since it is influenced less by environmental changes. Both measurements are, of course, products of the organism's interaction with the environment, but since height depends almost entirely on the linear measure of skeletal growth, and since length of the skeleton is relatively resistant to short-term environmental pressures, progress in height is quite regular. It has been demonstrated that the bones do record such traumas as illnesses and malnutrition, but they do it in terms of bone scars, which can be detected only by X ray. Retarded growth and resulting small stature represent a general result of malnutrition, infections, and stress. Weight, in contrast to height, is a sensitive indicator of malnutrition or overnutrition. Weight is related to volume, which is the product of three linear measures. All types of body tissue, skeleton, muscles, fat, blood, and all the rest, contribute to weight. Thus although the skeleton is not shortened by illness or malnutrition, the soft tissues of the body may be reduced.

Cross-Culture Comparisons. Eight-year-old children from many regions of the world have been compared in physical measurements in a study using 300 samples [43]. Mean heights of the various groups varied from 106 centimeters in Bihar, India, to 129 centimeters in Norway, a range of about 9 inches. The shortest groups were mainly in Southeast Asia, Oceania, and South America, the tallest mainly in northern and central Europe, eastern Australia, and the United States. Five samples were taller than the United States white group, while only the Norwegian average was greater than that of the black sample from the United States. Weight

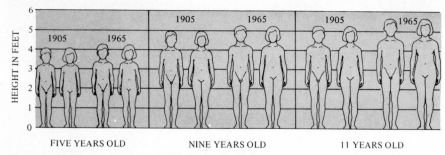

Figure 1–1. Increased size of children stems mainly from earlier maturation. A boy and girl aged 5 in 1965, and of average economic circumstances, were taller by about 2 inches than their counterparts of a half-century ago; 9-year-olds of 1965 averaged some 3 inches taller, and 11-year-olds nearly 4 inches taller. The figures are based on measurements made in the United States and Europe.

averages varied from 17 kilograms to 27 kilograms, a range of about 25 pounds. The average weight of the Norwegians was 50 percent greater than that of the East Pakistanis. The largest children live in parts of the world where nutritious food is abundant and where the infectious diseases are well controlled or largely eliminated.

Secular Changes. A growth trend continuing over a long time is evident in the prosperous parts of the world. Children have been growing taller and heavier. For example, between 1880 and 1960 the average North American white 8-year-old increased 9 centimeters in height and 4 kilograms in weight [42]. The trend was noted in France as early as 1835 [16, p. 532]. American, British, and Swedish data indicate that the average gain for 5- to 7-year olds between 1880 and 1950 was about 1.5 centimers per decade [69, p. 95]. Japanese children have increased greatly in height and weight since the end of World War II, according to a report from the Japanese National Institute of Nutrition [47]. The official linked the gains in growth with changes in the Japanese diet, such as a twentyfold increase in per capita milk consumption over the past 20 years and a doubled intake of animal protein. He commented that if the trend continues as expected, doorways and ceilings will have to be built higher and that, already, clothing and furniture manufacturers have had to revise their specifications. Along with the increase in height and weight there are changes in proportions, with legs growing longer and slimmer and trunks less chunky. The secular increase is now tapering off for the most privileged children, suggesting that some groups are reaching their maximum possible height [28, 64]. Privileged children from different parts of the world have remarkably similar growth patterns [24, 28]. For example, a comparison of heights and weights of high socioeconomic groups in the United States, Guatemala, and Panama showed no significant differences [24].

Changes in Children of Immigrants. Children of immigrants to America show great increases in height when compared with children born and reared in the country from which the immigrants came. The children and grandchildren of immigrants duplicate in one or two generations changes that might have taken five or more generations in the mother country [16, p. 533]. The change from Naples to Boston or Tokyo to San Francisco has entailed abrupt improvements in caloric intake, quality of food, disease prevention, and prenatal and infant care.

Table 1–9 Fels Multipliers for Stature Prediction of Boys and Girls of Average Parental Stature

Multiplier BOYS	Age	Multiplier GIRLS
1.47	7	1.35
1.40	8	1.29
1.35	9	1.23
1.29	10	1.17
1.24	11	1.12
1.19	12	1.07

SOURCE: Reprinted by permission from S. M. Garn, "Body Size and its Implications," in L. W. Hoffman and M. L. Hoffman (Eds.), *Review of Child Development Research*, Vol. II, pp. 529–561. Copyright © 1966, Russell Sage Foundation.

Predicting Adult Height. Final stature can be predicted fairly well from measurements in childhood. Table 1–9 gives the multipliers to use for boys and girls whose mid-parent height is average or slightly above average, or close to 169–172 centimeters.

Anyone interested in keeping longitudinal records on one or more children is advised to order copies of a height–weight interpretation chart for boys and girls from the National Education Association or the American Medical Association. The table in this book can be used for making rough predictions of future height, since children tend to remain in the same channel as they grow.

Proportions

Compared with preschool children, school-age children are graceful. With a relatively lower center of gravity, longer legs, and slimmer proportions, the older child is steadier on his feet. The photographs on these pages show typical proportions during the elementary school years as well as preschool and adolescent figures with which to compare the figures of middle childhood. (See Figures 1–2, 1–3, and 1–4.) Each new or refined coordination added to the child's motor schemas increases his poise. He fits better into adult furniture, even though it is still too big for him. He has grown out of a crib. Although his feet dangle at the table, he spurns a high chair. His new proportions make for excellent climbing, since longer arms and legs can reach more distant branches and a lower center of gravity steadies him. Similarly with bicycle-riding. Changes in growth rates also show up in facial changes. Relatively large at birth, the brain case is still large at 5. Then the face begins to catch up. The ratio of face to cranium is about 1:3 at 6 and 1:2 at 18 [5].

The changes in body configuration which take place during the years from 4½ to 7½ have been studied in some detail, since this is the period when the child is changing from a preschooler to a schoolchild, from a preconceptual thinker to one who can deal with concrete operations, from one concerned with the sense of imagination to one involved in problems of the sense of industry. In a search for some physical indications of sufficient maturity for assessing school readiness,

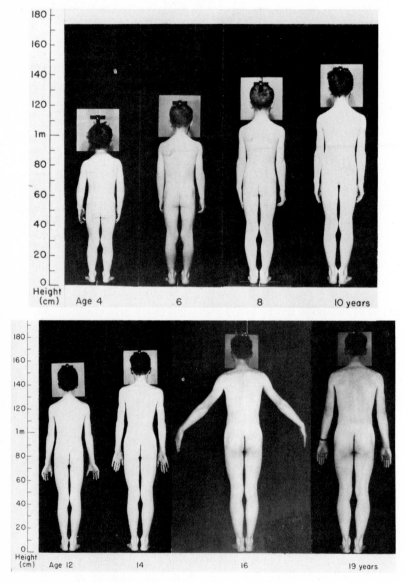

Figures 1–2 and **1–3.** A typical boy's growth from early childhood to adulthood.

SOURCE: Reprinted from *Growth Diagnosis*, by L. M. Bayer and N. Bayley, by permission of The University of Chicago Press. Copyright © 1959, The University of Chicago Press.

AGE IN YEARS

HEIGHT IN FEET

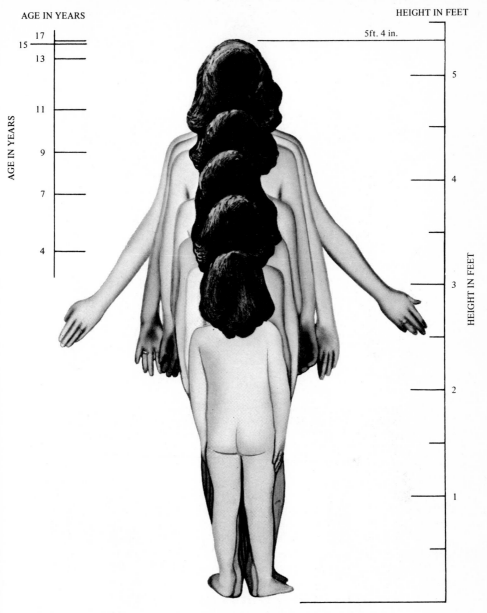

Figure 1–4. A typical girl's growth from early childhood to adulthood.

Source: Reprinted from *Growth Diagnosis*, by L. M. Bayer and N. Bayley, by permission of The University of Chicago Press. Copyright © 1959, The University of Chicago Press.

three types of body configuration were distinguished in photographs of boys and girls [58]. Schematic drawings of the figures are shown in Figure 1–5. Judges estimated maturity in terms of both face and body. After the judges of the photographs had agreed on which ones showed the various types of proportions, measurements and relationships between measurements were studied in order to

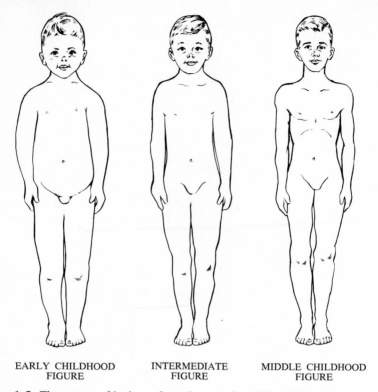

EARLY CHILDHOOD   INTERMEDIATE   MIDDLE CHILDHOOD
FIGURE   FIGURE   FIGURE

Figure 1–5. Three types of body configuration seen in middle childhood.

SOURCE: Reprinted from M. D. Simon, "Body Configuration and School Readiness," *Child Development*, **30,** Figure 1. Copyright © 1959, The Society for Research in Child Development, Inc.

find out which indicated the three stages of maturity. Results showed a general slimming down at the beginning of the middle childhood period, making boys and girls quite similar for a while. Then the girls became more typically feminine (rounded). Several indices proved useful in showing increasing maturity: head circumference to standing height (decreasing), waist circumference to height (decreasing), and leg length to height (increasing). Head circumference to leg length (decreasing) was found to be a good indication of maturity of proportions. The typical early childhood ratio was 86 for boys and 85 for girls, intermediate figures were 85 and 81, and middle childhood 81 and 81. Maturity of body configuration was found to be associated with success in first grade, and immaturity with failure. Apparently physical maturity, as indicated by proportions, tells something about the child's readiness for meeting the demands of school. There are, in addition to proportions, other useful physical indicators of maturity as related to success in school. Achievement in fifth grade was found to be correlated with size in relation to age and also with gross and fine motor coordination [40].

Tissues and Organs

Certain physiological and anatomical characteristics are especially typical of middle childhood. Those mentioned in the following description contribute to the child's appearance or to his behavior or both. *Fat* diminishes gradually and changes in distribution patterns. School-age children look much thinner than preschool children and adolescents. Girls have more fat than boys and it is placed differently, giving them softer contours at all ages after the first year [15]. The *skin* becomes less delicate. *Hair* may darken. While the *muscles* grow in size and in strength of connections with bones, they are still immature in function as compared with an adolescent's muscles. Muscles of school-age children are more readily injured by strain. For example, Little League pitchers are prey to "Little League Elbow," a muscular injury due to overuse. A brief observation in any first grade classroom will demonstrate how difficult it is for 6- and 7-year-olds—especially boys—to immobilize their muscles.

The *digestive* system shows added maturity by having fewer upsets and by retaining food for a longer time. Thus the school-age child does not have to be fed so carefully, so often, and so promptly as the preschool child. Because growth is slow, calorie needs, in relation to the size of the stomach, are not so great as they were earlier and as they will be during the coming growth spurt. The danger at this time is that the child will fill up on empty calories, foods which do not promote growth, such as sugar, starches, and excess fats. With relatively low calorie needs, it is important to eat foods that are high in proteins, minerals, and vitamins. The combination of freedom to move out from his mother's supervision, plus a bit of money in his pockets, may result in an excessive intake of soft drinks and candy.

Children vary widely in *bladder* capacity, boys having less than girls. There are individual differences in frequency of urination, and difference in one individual from one time to another, due to temperature, humidity, time of day, emotional state, fluids ingested, and so on.

Respiration grows slower, deeper, and more regular, changing from 20 to 30 inhalations per minute in the preschool period to 17 to 25 in the school age [68, p. 259]. Infections and disturbances of the respiratory system are fewer and milder than in the early years.

The *heart* grows slowly between 4 and 10 years. During that time it is smaller in relation to the rest of the body than at any other period of life [6]. This fact of growth is one of the reasons why strongly competitive sports are dangerous for school-age children. As the child grows toward maturity, his heartbeat slows down and his blood pressure goes up. Between 6 and 12, he reaches the average adult heart rate of 70–100 per minute. Blood pressure, at an average of 105 mm, is still below the adult norm.

Ears are less likely to become infected than they were during the preschool years. With the growth of the lower part of the face, the Eustachian tube, leading from the throat into the middle ear, grows longer, relatively narrower, and slanted. Thus it is harder for disease organisms to invade. With fewer respiratory infections too, there are fewer invading organisms in the child. Although studies on children's hearing have yielded a variety of results, they usually show increasing acuity with age [33]. There is some indication that the average child has greater acuity in the right ear than in the left.

The *eye* changes shape with growth, resulting in farsightedness until about age 6. Studies of visual acuity yield a wide range of results, one showing 20/20 vision to be typical at age 7, another study placing 20/20 vision at age 4 and yet another at 11 to 13 [11]. Thus there is some doubt as to the age when 20/20 vision is normally achieved. It is after 7 when the eyeball gains its full weight and several

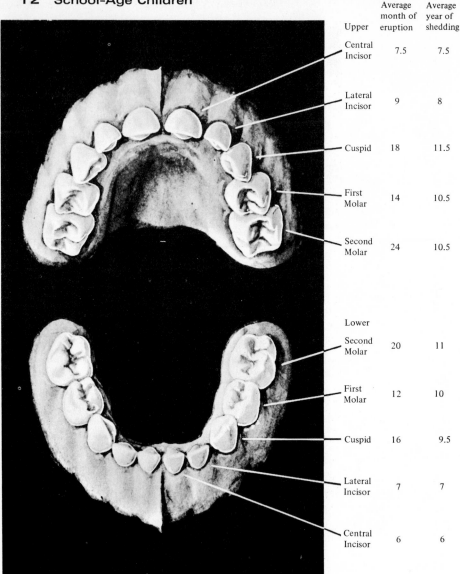

Upper	Average month of eruption	Average year of shedding
Central Incisor	7.5	7.5
Lateral Incisor	9	8
Cuspid	18	11.5
First Molar	14	10.5
Second Molar	24	10.5
Lower		
Second Molar	20	11
First Molar	12	10
Cuspid	16	9.5
Lateral Incisor	7	7
Central Incisor	6	6

Figure 1–6a. The primary (deciduous) teeth.

SOURCE: From "Dental Health Factors for Teachers." Copyright 1966 by the American Dental Association. Reprinted by permission.

years later that full development is completed. Binocular vision is usually well developed at 6 or shortly afterward, although not in all children. Large print is recommended for children throughout the school years [6]. A study of elementary school children showed 59 percent to have visual defects [25]. The defects increased from 17 percent in first grade to 82 percent at the end of the elementary years. Adequate physical care must include attention to signs of visual difficulties and regular eye examinations.

In adults, the right and left hemispheres of the *brain* are specialized for sound

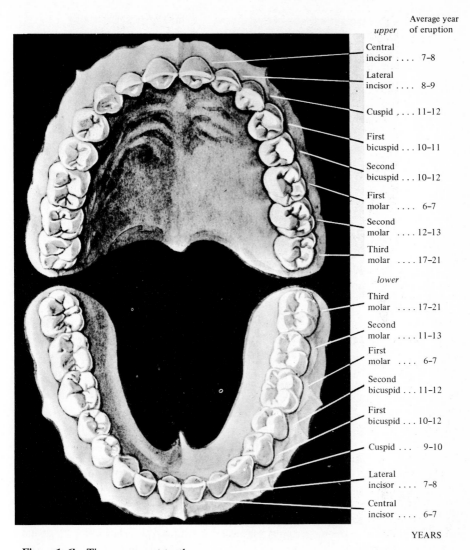

upper	Average year of eruption
Central incisor	7–8
Lateral incisor	8–9
Cuspid	11–12
First bicuspid	10–11
Second bicuspid	10–12
First molar	6–7
Second molar	12–13
Third molar	17–21
lower	
Third molar	17–21
Second molar	11–13
First molar	6–7
Second bicuspid	11–12
First bicuspid	10–12
Cuspid	9–10
Lateral incisor	7–8
Central incisor	6–7
	YEARS

Figure 1–6b. The permanent teeth.

SOURCE: From "Dental Health Factors for Teachers." Copyright 1966 by the American Dental Association. Reprinted by permission.

perception and interpretation. The speech center is normally in the left temporal lobe. Nonverbal sounds are processed primarily by the right hemisphere [34]. By 5 years of age, children show functional differentiation between the hemispheres. Before 10, the speech center can be reestablished on the right side if anything happens to damage the left temporal lobe [49]. If such an accident should occur after 12 years, the speech center cannot be organized on the right side, since the cortex involved has by that time become committed to the interpretation of experience. Thus the school age is a vital time for organization of the brain into laterally specialized functions. Boys do better in perceiving nonverbal sounds (such as dripping water, animal noises, a typewriter) and in spatial perception, whereas

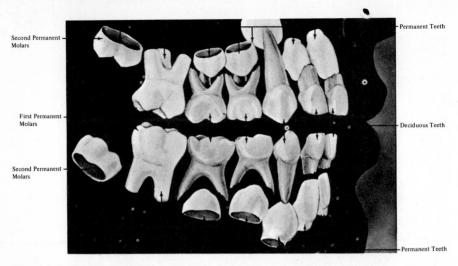

Second Permanent Molars

First Permanent Molars

Second Permanent Molars

Permanent Teeth

Deciduous Teeth

Permanent Teeth

Figure 1–7. Dentition of 6-year-old child.

SOURCE: From "Dental Health Factors for Teachers." Copyright 1966 by the American Dental Association. Reprinted by permission.

girls usually do better than boys in language. These findings suggest that boys' right hemispheres mature more rapidly than girls', as far as the lateral organization is concerned, and that probably girls' left hemispheres exceed boys' in lateral specialization [34].

The *skeleton* continues to ossify, replacing cartilage with bone. Since mineralization is not complete, the bones resist pressure and muscle pull less than more mature bones do. Good hygiene includes chairs, desks, and shoes that fit, frequent moving around, and caution in carrying heavy loads. For example, if a pack of newspapers is to be slung from one shoulder, it should be changed often from one shoulder to the other.

The skeleton is a useful maturity indicator, since its level of development is closely tied to progress toward sexual maturity. A child who is advanced in bone development will reach puberty at an earlier age than the average child. Not only is there this general relationship between the two kinds of development, but individual bones in the hand and wrist have a constant time relationship to sexual maturity. For instance, the sesamoid (a smaller round bone at the joint at the base of the thumb) appears within two to two and a half years before menarche [14, p. 107]. In the group of normal girls whose skeletal development was studied during puberty, menarche usually occurred soon after fusion of the epiphyses and shafts of the bones at the tips of the fingers [21, p. 11].

These are important years for *teething*, since most of the changes from deciduous to permanent teeth take place. At almost any time, a child has a gap or two in his jaw, a loose tooth, or one just popping through the gum. Nutrition, including sufficient fluorides, oral hygiene, and dental care are very important in assuring healthy teeth. Speech, nutrition, appearance, and body image are all affected by the soundness of teeth. Figure 1–6 shows the complete set of 20 baby teeth and the complete set of 32 adult teeth, indicating the replacements and additions which transform a young child's jaws into mature jaws. Figure 1–7 shows the two sets of teeth in place, the deciduous ones in the process of losing their roots through resorption, which prepares them to shed, leaving room for permanent teeth, since they exceed the number of baby teeth.

Since first permanent teeth to erupt in most children do not replace deciduous teeth, they are likely not to be recognized as permanent teeth. These teeth are the first molars, which appear just behind the second deciduous molars. As is the case with the deciduous teeth, there are some differences in the times of eruption when corresponding teeth in the two jaws are compared. There are also sex differences. The times of eruption of girls' teeth are earlier than those of boys'. This is in line with the faster rate of maturation of girls, but, comparing tooth for tooth, girls are further ahead in the eruption of some teeth than they are for others [63, p. 70].

Health and Safety

Fewer American children die than ever before. A recent report on the average annual death rate for children 5 to 14 years of age placed it at less than 6 in 10,000 for boys and less than 4 in 10,000 for girls [45]. A comparison of two decades showed a decline in mortality of about one third for school-age children. In the year when the United States had a death rate of 43.5 per 100,000 for children between 5 and 14, the rate in Denmark was 35.5. Death rates lower than the American were recorded in at least seven countries [57, p. 358]. Between ages 5 and 9, mortality rates in very poor countries are from five to nine times as great as the rates in the most prosperous countries. At 10 to 14 years, the rates in poor countries are three to five times those in wealthy countries. Thus the differential in the mortality rate in children decreases with age, since these figures represent a huge reduction from the situation at ages 1 to 4, when the death rate in poor countries is 20 to 40 times that in prosperous ones [57, p. 206].

Child health needs throughout the world are tremendous. Even in the United States, where health is improving from the standpoint of reduction of accident rates and communicable diseases, there are many areas in which child health could be improved. Malnutrition, disease, injuries, and environmental pollution, including crowding, all continue as threats to children.

Illnesses

School-age children have fewer illnesses than preschool children do [66]. Respiratory and gastrointestinal upsets decrease considerably, although they continue to be the most frequent types of illness, with respiratory the leading cause. After age 10 there is a further decrease in number of illnesses. The variety of major illnesses is greater during ages 6 to 10 than during all other ages studied, between birth and 18. The list of illnesses at 6 to 10 includes, for example, nephritis, septicemia, meningococcemia, and tuberculosis [66]. Figure 1–8 shows the distribution of the various types of illnesses between ages 5 and 14. According to a national health survey, children in this age group averaged 7.8 days in bed during one year, and 16.4 days of restricted activity, due to illness [37]. Schooldays lost due to illness averaged 5.3 days, with about three fifths of that time due to respiratory diseases [44]. The average number of acute illnesses was three per child. Medical attention was given to children for 54 percent of their illnesses.

The communicable diseases (including measles, chicken pox, mumps, whooping cough, and scarlet fever) are much less threatening to American children than

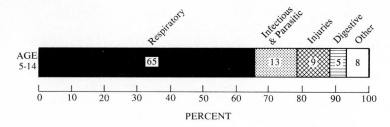

Figure 1–8. Frequency of occurrence of various types of illness in childhood.

SOURCE: From Chart B on page 18, "Problems of Youth," Legislative Reference Service, U.S. Government Printing Office, Washington, 1964.

they were in former years. In a longitudinal study of 67 boys and 67 girls, 50 girls and 45 boys had at least one communicable disease and over half of them had two [66]. No child had more than four. Death rates from these diseases declined by 70 percent to 80 percent in one decade, reaching the low figures of between two and seven deaths per million children between 5 and 14 [37].

It has been shown that most illnesses can be prevented by careful health supervision. Table 1–10a shows diseases that are controlled in the United States by routine immunization. Table 1–10b shows diseases still prevalent in the United States and not yet controlled by immunization. The disease situation is different, of course, in other parts of the world. Constantly increasing travel and communication in the world means that almost any disease might appear in a new location. Therefore, anyone who works with children needs a comprehensive handbook on communicable diseases, not in order to replace the physician who must diagnose and treat, but to be able to observe, refer, and cooperate with medical personnel. Such a handbook [3] is available free from many state health departments. The American Medical Association and the American Academy of Pediatrics provide a summary of facts about the communicable diseases of childhood and a vaccination schedule.

Many illnesses can be prevented by careful health supervision, carried out under the direction of a physician. Immunizations prevent most of the communicable diseases, as shown in Table 1–10. Optimal nutrition, rest, and exercise help the child to build his body's natural resistance to disease. Protection from extreme stress, both physical and mental, prevents the breakdown of the child's own resources for coping with disease. During middle childhood, one of the competencies to be learned is that of self-care, along with some knowledge of basic physiology and nutrition and of how disease organisms operate. Many children receive inadequate care during convalescence from an illness. Certain effects of an illness linger even after the temperature has returned to normal. And some parents do not even realize that the temperature is usually subnormal for a day or so after being elevated. Under the influence of stress, whether it be from infection, trauma, or psychological causes, the body tends to withdraw amino acids from muscles and other tissues and to use them for mobilization to meet the immediate crisis. After the acute part of an illness is over, therefore, the withdrawn materials must be returned to the raided parts of the body and be incorporated into their tissues [56]. This process requires rest and extra nutrients, especially protein. Muscles are likely to be flabby after an illness. Fatigue and poor posture may result if the convalescent child returns to a normal schedule too soon. Appetite is likely to

Table 1–10

A. Diseases controlled in the United States by routine immunizations, in order of initial usage of immunization

Smallpox	1796	Polio (Sabin)	1962
Diphtheria	1923	Measles	1964
Whooping cough	1933	Mumps	1968
Tetanus	1936	German measles	1969
Polio (Salk)	1954		

B. Diseases still prevalent in the United States

Chickenpox	Pinworm disease
Cold (common)	Pneumonia
Gonorrhea	Staphylococcal disease
Hepatitis (viral)	Streptococcal disease
Influenza	Syphilis
Mononucleosis	Tuberculosis
Pediculosis	

Prepared by Lucile Votta, R.N., from Rhode Island State Department of Health, *Recommendations, 1970*, and Franklin Top (Ed.), *Report of the Committee on Infectious Diseases, 1970*, Evanston, Illinois: American Academy of Pediatrics.

decrease. Lowered emotional control tends to go along with diminished vigor. Therefore, it is wise to arrange a gradual return to normal activity after an illness. Some pediatricians suggest that their patients stay in bed one day after the temperature has returned to normal and that they stay home from school the following day.

Special Health Problems. Although certain physical conditions are not considered illnesses, they have harmful long-range effects upon children's health. Dental caries is outstanding as this type of problem. (Many people do not consider it a disease, and since it is not incapacitating, it is rarely accorded the status of illness.) One child in four, at the 5 to 14-year range, has never been to a dentist [44]. A national health survey indicated that about half of the children in this age bracket had had no dental care during the preceding year. When children were divided as to family income, it was found that 5 to 14-year-olds, living in families of less than $4000 income, averaged 0.8 dental visits annually, and those in families of income above $4000 went to the dentist 2.4 times. Some progress toward dental health is being made in fluoridation of water supplies and in treating children's teeth with fluoride.

Long-range problems also include nutrition and fitness. Obesity is becoming more frequent among American children, with its prognosis of increasing obesity in adulthood. Obesity involves psychological problems, as well as physical. Fat children are less accurate than normal or thin children in identifying their own body shapes from photographs [17]. This finding suggests either lack of clarity in body image or denial of fatness, or both [38].

While some children are eating too many calories, others are not getting enough. And even more widespread than the problem of insufficient calories is poor quality of diet. Some children are thin and short because of poor quality and some are obese because of eating poor-quality food while having too many calories.

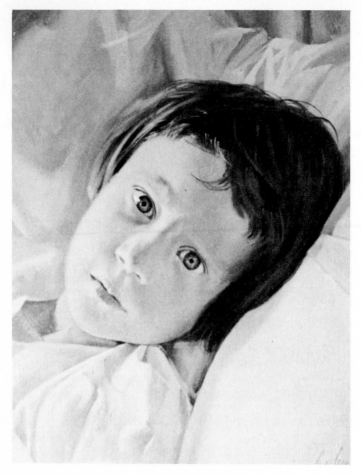

Figure 1-9. Stress shows in the face of this ill child.
Source: Reprinted by permission from *Nutrition Today*, 1970, **5**:1.

Accidents

Accidental injuries account for about half of the deaths of boys between 5 and 14 and for about one third of the deaths of girls the same age [45]. A comparison of present rates with those of a decade ago shows a substantial decrease in death rate from accidents (about 20 percent). As Table 1-11 shows, motor vehicles are the leading cause of accidental death, killing about twice as many boys as girls. Many of these fatalities occur when children are playing on streets and when they cross streets and highways. Among boys, drowning is second to motor vehicles as a cause of death. About 6700 children die from accidents each year in the United States. The number injured is about 12 million. Nearly one third of the people between 6 and 16 years of age are injured seriously enough to require medical attention or at least one day of restricted activity. About two fifths of the nonfatal injuries occur in or near the home.

Studies on accidents during the preschool years indicate that certain personality characteristics are typical of children who have many accidents. An extensive study

Table 1–11   Children's Deaths from Different Types of Accidents

| | Death Rate Per 100,000 | | | | | |
| | MALES | | | FEMALES | | |
Type of Accident*	Ages 5–14	Ages 5–9	Ages 10–14	Ages 5–14	Ages 5–9	Ages 10–14
All Types	25.1	22.9	27.5	10.9	13.1	8.5
Motor vehicle	10.4	10.5	10.3	5.2	6.1	4.3
Drowning †	5.5	4.8	6.3	1.2	1.1	1.3
Firearm	1.8	0.9	2.7	0.3	0.3	0.3
Fire and explosion	1.7	2.2	1.1	2.3	3.5	1.0
Falls	0.8	0.8	0.9	0.3	0.3	0.2

* According to rank among males.
† Exclusive of deaths in water transportation.
SOURCE: Basic data from Reports of the Division of Vital Statistics, National Center for Health Statistics. Reprinted by permission from *Statistical Bulletin*, Metropolitan Life Insurance Company, September 1964.

[39] on 684 children between 4 and 18 years of age compared groups with high, intermediate, and low accident liability. From school records and interviews with mothers, results showed accident liability to be associated with extraversion, daring, roughhousing, poor discipline, aggressiveness toward peers, impulsivity, carelessness, and unreliability. For girls, attention-seeking was also related to likelihood of accidents.

Oriental (Chinese and Japanese) children in California are injured less frequently than white and black Americans [36]. In traditional Oriental families, children are carefully supervised and sheltered and discouraged from exploration and initiation of activities. It follows logically that Oriental children would be exposed to fewer hazards than would average Americans in the same physical environment. Accident rates depend not only upon the dangers present in the environment but upon the protection offered by adults and also upon the behavior patterns of the child himself.

Chronic Illnesses and Impairments

Over 2 million children under 14 years of age must live with disabilities which are permanent or of indefinite duration. Figure 1–10 shows how these defects are distributed, with orthopedic defects most frequent, then speech, then hearing and visual defects, in that order [37]. The Children's Bureau, during a year when its crippled children's program gave aid to nearly 340,000 children under 21, reported that congenital malformations accounted for more than a quarter of these patients. About one fifth of the children under care had diseases of the bones and organs of movement. Cerebral palsy accounted for 8 percent, polio 7 percent, eye conditions 6 percent, impaired hearing 7 percent, and impairments from accidents 5 percent 44].

Chronic diseases and long-term disabilities may affect growth adversely. They certainly limit some of the child's activities. Conditions likely to retard growth include chronically infected tonsils and adenoids, intestinal parasites, rheumatic fever, and diabetes [6, pp. 53–56]. Good physical care can alleviate some of these conditions and even in cases where the condition cannot be cured, good care may result in normal growth.

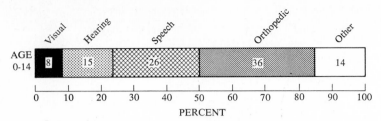

Figure 1–10. Frequency of occurrence of various types of impairments and defects in children.

SOURCE: From Chart C on page 19, "Problems of Youth," Legislative Reference Service, U.S. Government Printing Office, Washington, 1964.

Psychological Effects of Handicaps

The disabled child suffers not only the discomfort of diagnostic and treatment procedures. He also misses out on some of the activities which normal children have as part of everyday life. Requiring more physical care, he actually receives more nurturance from his mother and often from the whole family. He has a narrower social and interpersonal experience. Parents and often teachers give him less work to do, less responsibility to carry [52].

Different types of handicaps, of course, produce different reactions in the children burdened with them and in the social environments in which the children live. For example, when asked to rank five disabilities in order of preference, Jewish children judged confinement to a wheelchair as worse than obesity, and obesity as worse than facial disfigurement [19]. The normative group of children, drawn from a wide selection of environments, ranked obesity as most undesirable, facial disfigurement as next to obesity, and confinement to a wheelchair as the least undesirable of these conditions. Italian children ranked the handicaps in another order. A similar study done on a large number of children in Israel found socio-economic status related to attitude toward disability [7]. Children from poorer neighborhoods considered a physical disability (wheelchair necessary, amputated hand, leg in brace) worse than a cosmetic disability (obesity, facial disfigurement). Children from more prosperous neigborhoods thought the cosmetic handicap was worse than the physical. Thus it can be seen that a child's handicap is interpreted to him according to the particular value system of the people close to him. In studying children's perceptions of other children's handicaps, young children were asked questions about pairs of drawings in which one child was wearing leg braces and the other child was identical except for wearing no braces [30]. Five-year-olds were likely to reject the drawings of the handicapped child, but younger children showed no differences in responses to pictures of handicapped and normal children. While this study does not prove that preschool children are unaware of handicaps in others, it suggests that rejection of handicapped children may be more marked in school-age children than in younger ones.

The specific restrictions required by various handicaps differ from one to another. For example, the dietary requirements for diabetics are very embarrassing to some children, who often try to hide their condition from other children.

Even though there are some specific reactions to handicaps, certain general effects have been found, too. The self concepts of a wide selection of handicapped children were investigated in a summer camp situation, by asking these children and a group of normal children to describe themselves and others [52]. The children's conversations were analyzed into categories, so as to find out which topics were important to them and which, of these topics, were most significant. In general the handicapped children showed realistic facing of life by talking more about "handicap" than did the normal children. The handicapped boys discussed "health" and "physical ability" less, possibly reflecting awareness of the cultural demand that boys should be active and aggressive. "Spatial location" was discussed less by the handicapped, probably because these children had had limited spatial experiences, being unable to move around so freely on their own and not having been taken places by adults as much as normal children are taken. Handicapped girls talked more than normal girls and more than handicapped boys about "giving aid," suggesting the importance to them of receiving aid, as well as the fact that it is easier for girls to accept aid than it is for boys. Comments of the handicapped children indicated that they had fewer interactions with people, with the exception of interactions with mothers. This interpersonal impoverishment probably accounts for their greater use of egocentric comments and expression of self-depreciation and lack of confidence.

As the emotional and developmental situation of the handicapped child becomes understood, it is possible for parents and other adults to help him more effectively. For instance, knowing that handicapped children's spatial experiences are likely to be limited, the adults could plan more carefully to change the child's location and position often and, whenever possible, to take him on expeditions with the rest of the family instead of leaving him home with Mother. Knowing that his feelings of adequacy will be threatened, wise adults will help a handicapped child to develop competencies in the fields where he can operate. The task of broadening his interpersonal contacts is not easy, but constant awareness of it will bring more results than ignoring the matter.

Motor Coordination

Children's delight in vigorous motor play seems to be universal. Ball games, tag, running, chasing, and jumping games are to be found where children are. The motor skills which a society teaches to its children, however, reflect the values and economic level of that culture.

The Influence of Cultural Values on Motor Skills

In order to highlight the affluent American culture, consider the Asian society in which many a boy squats at the far end of a loom, assisting a skilled weaver and gradually acquiring his fine coordinations. Other boys do the rough outlining of ivory figures, which men finish and inlay into boxes and tabletops. Little girls struggle to embroider tiny mirrors onto skirts and bags. The aim is excellence in the vocational pursuits of weaving, ivory inlaying, and mirror embroidery. In America, vocational excellence has little place in the motor coordinations which children strive to learn. Their parents' aim is more all-round competence than specialized excellence. In fact, as far as girls are concerned, moderate skill may be preferred to excellence. The bureaucratic, other-directed middle-class society described by social observers of the 1950s [46, 54] would logically try to produce children who could fit into whatever kind of athletic recreation their peers were enjoying. These children would be able to make a fourth at tennis, would know an allemande-left from a right-hand-to-your-partner, and a figure eight from an outside edge, would stick on a horse, and be able to dive neatly from the low board, if not the high board.

Wanting moderate competence in many coordinations, American society offers many organized learning opportunities to children. Rarely do families teach such skills as dancing and swimming. Of 1008 parent–child contacts occurring in the water at two beaches, only 82 were instances of parents instructing children in swimming [60, 61]. (Most of the teaching which did occur was in upper-middle-class rather than lower-middle or lower-class families.) Instead of the informal family instruction of a simpler society, modern arrangements include dancing teachers sponsored by schools, the PTA, or community centers, and swimming teachers hired by the state, community, or club. Standards for teachers are set and controlled by the Red Cross. The water safety manual delineates levels of achievement in swimming and giving children specific goals for various coordinations. By requiring the child to be 12 years old before trying the Junior Lifesaving examination, the Red Cross implies that children under 12 can pass the beginner's, advanced beginner's, and intermediate tests. Thus much of what used to be learned informally, in the way of motor skills, has become formalized, standardized, and, in some instances, commercialized. Children still play, however. And perhaps more self-expression and immediate pleasure is in the trend of the future, with standards of competence in motor performance growing less important to parents. When the youth who have rejected middle-class values become parents of school-age children, we might expect changes in parental hopes and demands.

Play Activities

The average 6-year-old has acquired the motor skills basic to school-age play. He can throw, bounce, and catch a ball, although he does not do so very smoothly [23]. For many years, he will practice and seek to perfect games which use balls and similar objects for throwing, catching, hitting, bouncing, and carrying. By 6 years of age, a distinct sex difference in ball throwing is easily seen. Boys use a mature pattern of throwing, in which greater power is exerted by changing the weight to the right foot during the preparatory phase and to the left foot during delivery, the left foot having moved forward and the trunk having rotated [12, p. 125]. Girls use a less mature pattern, and some never succeed in pitching overhand.

Able to run and climb well, the child plays games of chase, such as tag and hide-and-seek, his interest in these games increasing steadily from 6 to 9 [62]. Running is basic to skipping, dancing, and skating. Most 6-year-olds can skip and jump rope, and 7-year-olds roller-skate [23]. With these skills, as with ball play, the youngster ventures into new games and coordinations, practicing as he goes in order to achieve competence in a variety of movements. Sometimes he plays follow-the-leader, gaining ideas and courage from a model who knows a little more about the skill than he does. Sometimes he jumps, skates, or bounces by himself, apparently thoroughly enjoying the process of developing motor skills.

The average 9-year-old is interested in a greater variety of play activities than he has been before or will be again [62]. When a group of children between 9 and 10 are asked to check their interests on a large list of activities, everything suggested is

Table 1–12 Activities Boys Reported Especially Enjoying

Bandits	Marbles
Bows and arrows	Making model airplanes
Boxing	Shooting
Building forts	Soldiers
Cars	Spacemen
Cops and robbers	Throw snowballs
Darts	Toy trains
Football	Use tools
Hunt	Wrestling

SOURCE: Reprinted by permission from B. G. Rosenberg and B. Sutton-Smith, "A Revised Conception of Masculine-Feminine Differences in Play Activity," *The Journal of Genetic Psychology*, **96**, Table 1, p. 167. Copyright © 1960, The Journal Press.

Table 1–13 Activities Girls Were Particularly Fond of Playing

Blind man's buff	Jacks
Building snowmen	Jump rope
Cartwheels	Leap frog
Clue	London bridges
Cooking	Mother, may I
Crack the whip	Mulberry bush
Dance	Musical chairs
Doctors	Name that tune
Dolls	Pick up sticks
Dressing up	Puzzles
Drop the handkerchief	Red rover
Farmer in the dell	Ring around the rosy
Follow the leader	Scrapbook making
Fox and geese	See saw
Hide the thimble	Sewing
Hopscotch	School
Houses	Simon says "thumbs up"
Huckle buckle beanstalk	Statues
In and out the window	Stoop tag
I've got a secret	Store

SOURCE: Reprinted by permission from B. G. Rosenberg and B. Sutton-Smith, "A Revised Conception of Masculine-Feminine Differences in Play Activity," *The Journal of Genetic Psychology*, **96**, Table 1, p. 167. Copyright © 1960, The Journal Press.

likely to be checked by someone. Tables 1–12, 1–13, and 1–14 represent a partial list of items which 50 percent or more of a group of fourth, fifth, and sixth graders said they liked to do [55]. About 70 percent of these activities are strongly motor, with large muscle coordinations chosen more than four times as often as fine coordinations. Breadth of interest varies from one child to another, some engaging in fewer than ten activities a week and others playing in over 100 different ways [62].

Table 1–14 Play Activities Enjoyed by Both Boys and Girls

Basketball	Tug-o-war	I spy
Bowling	Wall dodge ball	Monopoly
Cowboys	Clay modeling	Scrabble
King of the mountain	Draw or paint	Spin the bottle
Racing	Gardening	Tag
Soccer	Hide and seek	Tail on the donkey
Walk on stilts	Fly kite	Make collections
Dominoes	Ghosts	Hiking
Shuffleboard	Black magic	Raise pets
Baseball	Dodgeball	Stunts in gym
Boating	Tiddle di winks	Swimming
Fish	Cards	Horses
Camping	Checkers	Wood tag
Climbing	Pingpong	Kick dodge
Ball tag	Horse shoes	Bingo
Pool	Tennis	Tic tac toe
Post office	Skating	Dog and bone
Chess	Horse riding	Volleyball
Seven up	Bicycle riding	Roller skating

SOURCE: Reprinted by permission from B. G. Rosenberg and B. Sutton-Smith, "A Revised Conception of Masculine-Feminine Differences in Play Activity," *The Journal of Genetic Psychology*, 96, Tables 2 and 3, p. 168. Copyright © 1960, The Journal Press.

Components of Motor Ability

One analysis of the various kinds of motor abilities yields these classes: strength, impulsion, speed, precision coordination, and flexibility [22]. Strength, of course, refers to the amount of force the individual can exert. Impulsion is a measure of the rate at which movements are initiated from stationary positions, whereas speed is the rate of movements which have been begun. Precision is the accuracy with which a position is maintained (static precision) or with which a movement is directed (dynamic precision). Flexibility is freedom to bend and otherwise move the body. These components of motor ability can be studied in relation to different parts of the body, and sometimes in relation to the whole body.

Strength. Although strength can be measured in legs, shoulders, and back, or in practically any voluntary muscle, most of the research on increase in strength has been in terms of hand grip. Grip is measured by a dynamometer, an instrument which registers amount of pressure. Measurements of grip strength show a steady increase throughout the school years, boys showing greater strength than girls at each grade level measured (third, sixth, ninth, and twelfth), and Latin American groups being consistently weaker than Anglo American and Afro American. Afro girls were significantly stronger than Latin or Anglo girls at all grade levels [20]. Trunk strength is measured by performance of such exercises as the abdominal pivot (pushing the body around with hands on floor and back arched), push-ups, and leg raising while in sitting position [22]. Limb strength is estimated by dips (squatting and rising), chinning, rope-climbing, and push-ups.

Impulsion. Reaction time, or time required to respond to a stimulus, is one measure of impulsion. Reaction time may also be considered a measure of speed. Speed of reaction time increases steadily throughout the school age, with boys reacting slightly faster than girls [18]. Other measures include limb thrust, as shown in jumping, shot-put, short dash, and bar vault. A third measure is tapping, turning small objects, removing, and placing pegs. Girls tend to excel in measures of this type, as shown in a test of making dots alternately in two small circles [9]. Children's speed improved with age between 6 and 9, and at each level, girls were faster than boys.

Speed. Speed of movement can be measured for the whole body or for various parts, such as arms, hands, and fingers. Such skills as running and hopping show a steady increase in speed throughout the elementary school years. The gap between the sexes begins to widen at 11 or 12 years of age, after which time boys continue to gain while girls tend to taper off [12, pp. 157–158].

Precision. Balance, steadiness, and aiming are all aspects of precision. They are tested by such feats as standing on one foot, walking a line, tracing, threading, jumping and balancing, pursuit aiming, and placing dots in circles. Coordination of the whole body and dexterity of hand and fingers can also be considered as precision.

Flexibility. Ease of moving, bending, and stretching contributes to most motor skills. Flexibility is extremely important in dancing and in most sports. Flexibility depends largely on the looseness of the joints and also upon the ease with which the muscles stretch and relax.

Tests of Motor Ability

Two examples of motor tests will be mentioned here, the Lincoln–Oseretsky Motor Development Scale [59] and the Kraus–Weber Test [35]. The Lincoln–Oseretsky Scale is an individual test for children between 6 and 14 years of age. It consists of 36 items, shown in the sample score sheet reproduced in Table 1–15. The test samples a wide variety of motor skills, including gross bodily coordination, activities of trunk, legs, arms, and hands, finger dexterity, and eye–hand coordination. Although the various components of motor ability, strength, impulsion, speed, precision, and flexibility are all called into play by the various items, no separate scores are given. The child's score is for total or overall level of motor development. By means of percentile tables, the child can be compared with all children his age and with children his age and sex.

The Kraus–Weber Test is concerned with flexibility and strength of large muscles. The test will not delineate the upper limits of strength and flexibility. Rather, it was designed in order "to determine whether or not the individual has sufficient strength and flexibility in parts of the body upon which demands are made in normal daily living." Six simple items make up the Kraus–Weber Test. Each of the six items must be passed in order to pass the test as a whole. No score is given other than passed or failed. The results can, however, be broken down into flexibility and weakness failures.

The Kraus–Weber Test, from which an excerpt is given in Figure 1–11, was given widely throughout Europe and the United States as a measure of physical fitness. Over 4000 American children were compared with Austrian, Italian, and Swiss children. Figure 1–12 shows the incidence of American failures and European failures at all ages from 6 to 16. The European children show up ever so much better than Americans at all ages. What is more, the Americans gave poorer

Table 1–15 Sample Score Sheet for the Lincoln–Oseretsky Motor Development Scale

	Description	R-L	Trials Pts.	Notes
1	Walking backwards, 6 ft.		2	
2	Crouching on tiptoe		2	
3	Standing on one foot	R/L	2/2	/
4	Touching nose		1	
5	Touching fingertips	R/L	2/2	/
6	Tapping rhythmically with feet and fingers		1	
7	Jumping over a rope		1	
8	Finger movement		3	
9	Standing heel to toe		2	
10	Close and open hands alternately		3	
11	Making dots		2	
12	Catching a ball	R/L	5/5	/
13	Making a ball	R/L	2/2	/
14	Winding thread	R/L	1/1	/
15	Balancing a rod crosswise	R/L	3/3	/
16	Describing circles in the air		1	
17	Tapping (15″)	R/L	2/2	/
18	Placing coins and matchsticks		1	
19	Jump and turn about		1	
20	Putting matchsticks in a box		1	
21	Winding thread while walking	R/L	1/1	/
22	Throwing a ball	R/L	5/5	/
23	Sorting matchsticks	R/L	1/1	/
24	Drawing lines	R/L	2/2	/
25	Cutting a circle	R/L	1/1	/
26	Putting coins in box (15″)	R/L	1/1	/
27	Tracing mazes	R/L	1/1	/
28	Balancing on tiptoe		1	
29	Tapping with feet and fingers		1	
30	Jump, touch heels		1	
31	Tap feet and describe circles		1	
32	Stand on one foot	R/L	1/1	/
33	Jumping and clapping		1	
34	Balancing on tiptoe	R/L	1/1	/
35	Opening and closing hands		1	
36	Balancing a rod vertically	R/L	3/3	/

SOURCE: Reprinted by permission from William Sloan, "The Lincoln–Oseretsky Motor Development Scale," *Genetic Psychology Monographs*, **51**, Table 5, p. 247. Copyright © 1955, The Journal Press.

performances as they advanced in age. The authors attributed the difference in Americans and Europeans to the mechanization of life in America, especially to riding in cars instead of walking. The reports on Kraus–Weber findings stirred up considerable interest in "fitness," even in the White House. Television programs, community recreation and fitness programs, and PTA's rose to the challenge. There has not been complete agreement as to the meaning of "fitness" and as to how serious a matter it was that American children and youth were outclassed by Europeans on the Kraus–Weber Test. Some constructive steps have been taken to improve American youth.

Kraus-Weber Tests for Muscular Fitness
(There should not be any warm-up prior to taking the tests.)

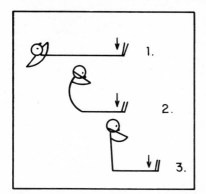

TEST 1.

Purpose: Tests the strength of the abdominals and psoas.

Designation: "Abdominals plus psoas" or A+.

Position of Person Being Tested: Lying supine, hands behind neck. The examiner holds his feet down on the table.

Command: "Keep your hands behind your neck and *try to roll up* into a sitting position."

Precaution: If the person being tested is unable to perform this movement at first try, it may be because he has not understood the directions. Help him a little and then let him try again. Watch for a "stiff back sit-up." This may indicate that either he has not understood you and needs a further explanation with emphasis on "rolling up," or that he has *very* poor abdominals and is doing most of the work with his psoas.

Watch also for a twist of the upper body as he sits up. This may be due to unequal development of the back muscles.

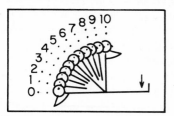

Marking: If the person being tested cannot raise his shoulders from the table, the mark is *0*. If unaided, he is able to reach a sitting position, the mark is *10*. If the examiner must help him halfway to the sitting position, the mark would be *5*. The distance from supine to sitting is marked from *0* to *10*.

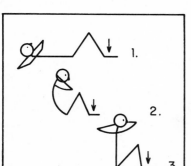

TEST 2.

Purpose: Further test for abdominals.

Designation: "Abdominals minus psoas" or *A−*.

Position of Person Being Tested: Lying supine, hands behind neck and knees bent. Examiner holds his feet down on the table.

Command: "Keep your hands behind your neck and *try to roll up* into a sitting position."

Precaution: The precautions are the same as for Test 1.

Figure 1–11. Two items from the Kraus–Weber Test are given here to illustrate how the tests for muscle strength and flexibility were conducted.

SOURCE: Reprinted by permission from H. Kraus and R. P. Hirschland, "Minimum Muscular Fitness Tests in School Children," *Research Quarterly*, **25**, 178–185. Copyright © 1954, American Association for Health, Physical Education, and Recreation, Washington, D.C.

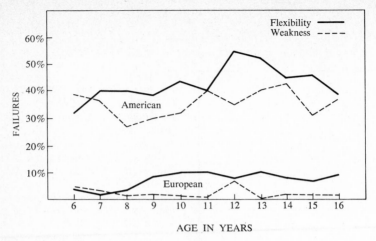

Figure 1–12. American children and youth compared with their European age-mates on tests of strength and flexibility, showing many more failures among Americans.

SOURCE: Reprinted by permission from H. Kraus and R. P. Hirschland, "Minimum Muscular Fitness Tests in School Children," *Research Quarterly*, **25**, 178–185. Copyright © 1954, American Association for Health, Physical Education, and Recreation, Washington, D.C.

Motor Problems

When a child enters school, the ability to sit down and keep still becomes important. From a practical point of view, it is a great help to the teacher if her pupils can inhibit motor activity sufficiently for her to maintain a quiet, orderly classroom, where she can be heard by all. There has been some difference of opinion on how much physical immobility matters for the child's learning his lessons, some teachers maintaining that children can accomplish more while quiet, others believing that bodily activity is an aid to learning, even though inconvenient for the teacher. When normal second grade boys were given tests of impulse control and conceptual thinking, a low correlation was found between impulse control and cognitive level [32].

Relationships between motor inhibition and intellectual behavior have been explored in studies of cognitive style, which will be discussed further in the following chapter. It seems worth mentioning these studies in connection with motor control, also, since a relationship has been found between ability to be still and tendency to form analytic concepts [31]. When children were divided into groups, according to the type of concepts which they formed most readily, the analytic children, as compared with nonanalytic, tended to be less impulsive, less distractible, more able to concentrate, and more able to inhibit motor acts. Observation suggests that more boys than girls show extremes of motor behavior, including impulsive, disorganized outbursts. In another study adult men were rated for involvement in intellectual mastery [31, p. 109]. An analysis (by another rater) of their childhood records showed that inability to inhibit motor activity during the childhood years was predictive of future avoidance of intellectual activities. Further corroboration came from the ratings on attention span of 46 fourth grade children. For boys, but not for girls, an analytic conceptual style was correlated with attention span. Thus childhood motor control was shown to be related to analytic conceptualization in childhood and intellectual involvement in manhood.

It is not certain that motor inhibition is basic to the analytic attitude; it may be that the analytic person inhibits motor activity more easily or that both conditions have a common source. Among kindergarten boys and girls, reflective and impulsive children were compared for their reactions to self-given commands [41]. Tested for inhibiting movement to the self-command "don't push," there was little or no difference between impulsives and reflectives when "don't push" was said aloud. When the self-command was said silently to himself, however, the impulsive child was more likely to push than was the reflective. Thus, at least at kindergarten age, reflective children showed greater inhibition under covert self-direction. Restless, impulsive children are often helped by a routine which gives legitimate opportunities for frequent moving around, combined with calm, firm reminders to reflect before answering. An experiment with hyperactive 9-year-old boys was successful in reducing their distractibility and impulsiveness on maze tests [48]. The boys were trained to give themselves verbal commands, such as *stop*, *listen*, *look*, and *think*, before beginning tasks and answering them. A successful physical educator [10] helps hyperactive children by providing a distraction-free setting with learning experiences that are stimulating and interesting, encouraging relative immobility. When normal fifth and sixth graders were given an excellent, broad program in physical education, their *academic* achievement was significantly better than that of controls who had only free play for exercise [27].

Gestures Inappropriate for Sex Role. In Smart and Smart, *Preschool Children* (Macmillan, 1973), it was mentioned that preschool children reinforce each other for sex-appropriate behavior, as shown by taking part in activities and playing with toys preferred by one sex or the other. Physical educators have found that boys who have problems with sex typing often adopt feminine gesture patterns [10, pp. 121–122]. Peers tend to reject such boys, consistent with the facts that boys reinforce boys, and boys reinforce for masculine behavior. Boys with feminine gestures can be taught quite readily to move in masculine ways, thus discarding patterns which irritate their peers and their parents. However, such treatment of symptoms may not be sufficient for coping with the basic problem, which usually lies in the child's relationships with his parents.

Laterality. Preference for one hand, foot, eye, or other organ over its opposite, as well as discrimination between right and left sides, all are aspects of laterality or sidedness. Thus laterality is not basically a problem, but it may become one. Left-handedness can be a severe handicap or it may not be. Confusion between left and right can also make trouble for a child.

The topic of hand preference is considered in depth, in terms of its establishment during the first years of life. During the elementary school years, a practical question concerns the changing of a preference already established. Since research possibilities are greater with older children, more data have been collected on school-age children and more is known about the relation of handedness to other questions concerning right and left. Laterality, or sidedness, includes all of the body, feet and eyes as well as hands. Laterality includes the individual's uses, preferences, and orientations to his own body and to left and right in other people, objects, and situations. Cultures define laterality through language and customs. For example, consider the implications in the Latin words *sinister* and *dexter* for left and right, the French *gauche*, which means awkward, and the fact that both English and German use the word *right* to refer to hand and to being correct. The custom of shaking hands is rigidly prescribed as for the right hand. A child

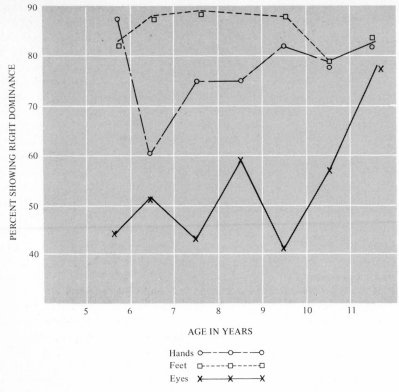

Figure 1–13. Percentage of children with established right lateral dominance in hands, eyes, and feet.

Source: L. Belmont and H. G. Birch, "Lateral Dominance, Lateral Awareness and Reading Disability." *Child Development*, 1965, **36**, 57–71.

grows up, therefore, with all sorts of meanings, implications, restrictions, and requirements attached to right and left.

Laterality in schoolchildren has been studied in terms of hands, eyes, and feet [1]. Preferences were determined by asking the child to show how he would throw a ball, turn a doorknob, cut with scissors, and write with a pencil. Eye preference was tested by asking the child to look through a kaleidoscope, sight a rifle, and look at the examiner through a hole in a paper. Foot preference was determined by noting which foot was used for kicking, estimating which foot kicked more skillfully. Figure 1–13 shows lateral preferences for hands, eyes, and feet at each year of age from 5 through 11. In each area, some children made mixed choices, showing that preference was not definitely established. Mixed preferences occurred more often at the younger ages, showing that the development trend toward laterality continues through the elementary school years. The table also shows that lateral preference was stronger for feet than for hands and weakest for eyes. Twenty-six percent of the children showed no clear-cut preference for eyes, whereas 14 percent showed none for hands, and only 4 percent for feet. About half the children were consistent in lateral preferences, and the others showed either crossed or mixed preferences. With increasing age, there was increasing use of the hand and eye on the same side.

Awareness of right and left also increased with age. The children were tested to see when they knew right and left on their own body parts. All questions were answered correctly by 70 percent of 5-year-olds, by 68 percent at 6, 89 percent at 7, 95 percent at 8, 94 percent at 10, and 100 percent at 11. Right–left awareness of own body is achieved about two years before hand preference is established. The authors suggest that the functions of lateral awareness and lateral preference are not closely related to each other.

The ability to make right–left discriminations in regard to the self develops before the ability to do so in regard to other persons and objects. The latter ability begins around 5 years of age and is well developed by 10 [4]. The ability to imitate a model while facing him is more complicated than merely telling right from left, although it includes right–left discrimination. It also involves transposing both the hand and the object acted upon. Success in such a test probably requires taking the other person's point of view and representing to oneself the way objects look and the way the body feels from within the other person. This ability has been found, through a series of tests, to increase with age from 8 to 18 years. Transposition responses increased most markedly between 12 and 14 years of age [67].

Further study on the question of lateral dominance, lateral awareness and reading difficulties has been done with 200 boys selected from the total number of 9- and 10-year-old boys in school in one community [2]. One hundred and fifty of these boys were the poorest readers in the age group, the others serving as a control group. Neither left-handedness nor mixed-handedness was found to be related to poor reading, but a definite relationship was found between left–right awareness and reading. Boys who were confused in identifying their own left and right body parts were more likely to be poor readers than boys who showed normal left–right awareness. Another investigation found a relationship between reading and directional awareness in the first grade but not in the fourth grade [8].

Laterality is also related to electrochemical processes in the body. During childhood, the right hand tends to show a higher galvanic skin response (conducts electricity better) than the left [13]. Boys below 11 years of age showed greater sensitivity to touch in the dominant thumb, as contrasted with the opposite thumb. Another group of children were classified by the number of errors they made in localizing their fingers which had been touched without the subjects being able to see them [51]. At age 10, children with a predominance of errors in locating fingers on the right hand were poorer readers than those who made more errors on the left hand. Six-year-olds showed no relation between reading and finger location errors. Therefore it seems that the source of finger location errors is related to the development or proficiency in reading but not to acquisition or beginning skills in reading.

The effects of forced lateral conversion have been studied by an ingenious method which keeps heredity factors constant while exploring results of differences in experience [70]. In Italy, left-handedness incurs considerable disapproval, and left-handed children are forced to write with the right hand, while in the United States, such coercion is not generally practiced. Left-handed children were selected by testing in Italy and in Italian American populations in Boston. They were compared with right-handed children and with each other. Boston children showed no significant personality differences between right-handed and left-handed groups but Italians were different from one another and from the Boston children. Left-handed

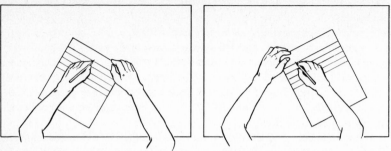

Figure 1–14. Recommended writing positions for left-handed and right-handed children.
SOURCE: Reprinted by permission from G. Hildreth, "The Development and Training of Hand Dominance: I. Characteristics of Handedness," *Journal of Genetic Psychology*, **75**, 197–220. Copyright © 1949, The Journal Press.

Italians were more demanding, impatient, subjective, dependent, and hypochondriacal. These characteristics indicate hypersensitivity and heightened self-preoccupation. The results of this research suggest that for healthy personality development it is best not to interfere with a definitely established preference for the left hand.

Left-handed children often need help in arranging the environment. A survey of practices of 19 commercial systems of handwriting gives a summary of present-day techniques for teaching the left-handed children to write [26]. The companies were concerned most with the position of the paper and the position of the arm, hand, and writing instrument. Figure 1–14 shows the recommended positions for left-handed and right-handed children. The left-handed child was thought to profit from help in assuming a certain position at the blackboard and a position while seated. A special kind of pencil has been designed for the purpose of letting the left-handed child see a word as he is writing it. Ordinarily, his hand tends to cover the word as he is writing, thus preventing visual feedback. An experimental group of left-handed children showed significant improvements in spelling when using this pencil, largely due to correcting reversals and omissions [65].

The left-handed child can use adult help in other situations, too, although probably none is so important as that of writing. He can be placed at the dinner table in such a way that his hand preference will not interfere with other people. He will need certain kinds of special equipment, such as left-handed scissors. If adults accept his special laterality casually, he will most likely avoid being embarrassed over it himself and hence will be less inclined to be awkward. Advantages can be appreciated, too, such as those accruing on the baseball diamond and tennis court.

Summary

Growth is relatively slow during middle childhood. Wide individual differences exist at the end of the elementary school period, however, since the onset of the pubescent growth spurt occurs then in some children and not in others. Boys are, on the average, slightly taller and heavier than girls, except for the years from 11 to 13, when girls are bigger because of being farther along in the pubescent growth spurt. Height increases more steadily than weight, since weight is more responsive to environmental changes.

The largest children in the world live in the most prosperous countries. The largest group is 23 centimeters taller and 10 kilograms heavier than the smallest. In prosperous countries there has been a recent decrease or even termination of the trend for children to grow bigger in each successive generation.

School-age children's bodily proportions contribute to their growing grace and agility. Facial proportions change, too, with the lower portion of the face growing more rapidly than the upper part. Different stages of bodily maturity can be distinguished during the middle years.

Certain aspects of physiological and anatomical maturing are especially significant. Fat decreases and changes somewhat in its distribution pattern. Muscles, although more firmly connected than in the preschool child, are still immature and easily strained. The digestive system is less prone to upsets than in a younger child. In relation to the size of the stomach, calorie needs are small. Bladder capacity varies, girls having a greater average capacity than boys. Respiration becomes slower and deeper. The heart is small in relation to the rest of the body. Growth of the face results in a change in the orientation of the Eustachian tube, which becomes more resistant to invasion by disease organisms. Visual defects increase throughout the school years. The skeleton matures, replacing cartilage with bone. As revealed by X rays, the skeleton is a useful maturity indicator. The baby teeth are replaced by permanent teeth, and additional permanent teeth erupt, the jaw growing to accommodate them.

Although child health has improved in the United States, children continue to face many health problems here and throughout the world. As is true during the preschool years, respiratory disturbances are the most frequent type of illness. The communicable diseases have declined in seriousness and incidence, due largely to immunization. Illness is prevented also by good nutrition, rest, exercise, protection from physical and mental stress, and cleanliness. Health is promoted also by good convalescent care and by teaching children principles and practices of self-care. Special health problems include dental caries and malnutrition, both of which are related to poverty.

Accidents are an important cause of death and injury of children, affecting more boys than girls. Chronic illnesses or impairments affect over 2 million children under 14. Growth is sometimes but not always adversely affected by chronic diseases and long-term disabilities. Certain activities are limited, resulting in handicapped children growing up in environments which differ significantly from those of normal children. Psychological effects of handicaps vary with the type of handicap and with the cultural and family environment of the child.

Many kinds of vigorous motor play, such as ball games, running, chasing, and jumping, are almost universal. Special motor skills reflect the values of the culture in which the child grows up. American parents tend to want their children to be moderately competent in many areas, often turning to experts for instruction for their children. School-age children build upon the basic motor skills learned in preschool years, practicing diligently and achieving a variety of competencies and interests.

The components of motor ability include strength, impulsion, speed, precision coordination, and flexibility. Various tests can be employed to measure these components, either as overall characteristics or as characteristics of certain parts of the body. General motor ability can be measured by a test which places the child in relation to other children his age. A test which measures flexibility and strength, used to compare Americans with Europeans, indicated that American children are inferior in these aspects of motor coordination. The ability to inhibit movement is important for getting along well in school. Impulsive movement is related to style of thinking.

Laterality includes preference for using one hand rather than the other, preference for one eye or for one foot. Cultures define laterality as right or wrong, good or bad, acceptable or not. Certain functions are reserved for one hand or the other. The child who does not fit into such rules and customs is handicapped, both through the attitudes of other people and because tools and arrangements are awkward for him. With some children, the nonpreferred hand can be brought into dominant use, often without noticeable harmful effects. When the child persists in using the unconventional hand, he needs special help in writing and other manual skills. Reading difficulties seem to be associated more with left–right confusion than with lateral dominance.

References

1. Belmont, L., & Birch, H. G. Lateral dominance and right–left awareness in normal children. *Child Devel.*, 1963, **34**, 257–270.
2. Belmont, L., & Birch, H. G. Lateral dominance, lateral awareness and reading disability. *Child Devel.*, 1965, **36**, 57–71.
3. Benenson, A. S. (Ed.). *Control of communicable diseases in man* (11th ed.), New York: American Public Health Association, 1970.
4. Boone, D., & Prescott, T. Development of left–right discrimination in normal children. *Percept. Motor Skills*, 1968, **26**, 267–274.
5. Breckenridge, M. E., & Murphy, M. N. *Growth and development of the young child* (8th ed.). Philadelphia: Saunders, 1969.
6. Breckenridge, M. E., & Vincent, E. L. *Child development* (5th ed.). Philadelphia: Saunders, 1965.
7. Chigier, E., & Chigier, M. Attitudes to disability of children in the multicultural society of Israel. *J. Health Soc. Behavior*, 1968, **9**, 310–317.
8. Cohen, A., & Glass, G. C. Lateral dominance and reading ability. *Reading Teacher*, 1968, **21**, 343–348.
9. Connolly, K., Brown, K., & Bassett, E. Developmental changes in some components of a motor skill. *Brit. J. Psychol.*, 1968, **59**, 305–314.
10. Cratty, B. J. *Perceptual-motor behavior and educational processes*. Springfield, Ill.: Charles C Thomas, 1969.
11. Eichorn, D. H. Biological correlates of behavior. In H. W. Stevenson (Ed.), *Child psychology*. The Sixty-second Yearbook of the National Society for the Study of Education, Part I. Chicago: University of Chicago, 1963, pp. 4–61.
12. Espenschade, A. S., & Eckert, H. M. *Motor development*. Columbus: Charles E. Merrill, 1967.
13. Fisher, S. Developmental sex differences in right–left perceptual directionality. *Child Devel.*, 1962, **33**, 463–468.
14. Flory, C. D. Osseous development in the hand as an index of skeletal development. *Mono. Soc. Res. Child Devel.*, 1936, **1**:3.
15. Garn, S. M. Fat weight and fat placement in the female. *Science*, 1957, **125**, 1091.

16. Garn, S. M. Body size and its implications. In L. W. Hoffman & M. L. Hoffman (Eds.), *Review of child development research. Vol. 2* New York: Russell Sage Foundation, 1966, pp. 529–561.
17. Gellert, E., & Girgus, J. S. Children's awareness of their bodily appearance. A developmental study of factors associated with the body percept. New York: Hunter College 1970. (Mimeo).
18. Goodenough, F. L. The development of the reactive process from early childhood to maturity. *J. Exper. Psychol.*, 1935, **18**, 431–450.
19. Goodman, N., Richardson, S. A., Dornbusch, S. M., & Hastorf, A. H: Variant reactions to physical disabilities. *Am. Sociol. Rev.*, 1963, **28**, 429–435.
20. Goss, A. M. Estimated versus actual physical strength in three ethnic groups. *Child Devel.*, 1968, **39**, 283–291.
21. Greulich, W. W., & Pyle, S. I. *Radiographic atlas of skeletal development of the hand and wrist* (2nd ed.). Stanford, Calif.: Stanford University Press, 1959.
22. Guilford, J. P. A system of the psychomotor abilities. *Am. J. Psychol.*, 1958, **71**, 164–174.
23. Gutteridge, M. V. A study of motor achievements of young children. *Arch Psychol.* 1939, No. 244.
24. Guzmán, M. A. Impaired growth and maturation in malnourished populations. In N. S. Scrimshaw & J. R. Gordon (Eds.), *Malnutrition, learning and behavior.* Cambridge, Mass.: M.I.T. Press, 1968, pp. 42–54.
25. Harmon, D. B. Some preliminary observations on the developmental problems of 160,000 elementary school children. *Woman's Medic. J.*, 1942, **49**, 75–82. Cited in Breckenridge & Vincent [6].
26. Herrick, V. E. *Comparison of practices in handwriting advocated by nineteen commercial systems of handwriting instruction.* Madison: Committee on Research in Basic Skills, University of Wisconsin, 1960. (Mimeo.)
27. Ismail, A. H., & Gruber, J. J. *Integrated development: Motor aptitude and intellectual performance.* Columbus, Ohio: Merrill, 1967.
28. Jackson, R. L. Effect of malnutrition on growth of the preschool child. In National Research Council. *Pre-school child malnutrition*, Washington, D.C., National Academy of Sciences, 1966, pp. 9–21.
29. Johnson, W., & Fretz, B. Changes in perceptual-motor skills after a children's physical developmental program. *Percept. Motor Skills*, 1967, **24**, 610.
30. Jones, R. L., & Sisk, D. A. Early perception of orthopedic disability. *Exceptional Children*, 1967, **34**, 42–43.
31. Kagan, J., Moss, H. A., & Sigel, I. E. Psychological significance of styles of conceptualization. In J. C. Wright & J. Kagan (Eds.), Basic cognitive processes in children. *Mono. Soc. Res. Child Devel.*, 1963, **28**:2, 73–111.
32. Kahana, B., & Kahana, E. Roles of delay of gratification and motor control in the attainment of conceptual thought. *Proceedings, 78th Annual Convention, Am. Psychol. Assoc.*, 1970, 287–288.
33. Kidd, A. H., & Kidd, R. M. The development of auditory perception in children. In A. H. Kidd & J. L. Rivoire (Eds.), *Perceptual development in children.* New York: International Universities Press, 1966, pp. 113–142.
34. Knox, C., & Kimura, D. Cerebral processing of nonverbal sounds in boys and girls. *Neurophyschologia*, 1970, **8**, 227–237.
35. Kraus, H., & Hirschland, R. P. Minimum muscular fitness tests in school children. *Res. Quart.*, 1954, **25**, 178–185.

36. Kurokawa, M. Acculturation and childhood accidents among Chinese and Japanese Americans. *Genet. Psychol. Mono.*, 1969, **79**, 89–159.
37. Legislative Reference Service. *Problems of youth.* Washington, D.C.: U.S. Govt. Printing Office, 1964.
38. Lerner, R. M., & Gellert, E. Body build identification, preference, and aversion in children. *Devel. Psychol.*, 1969, **1**, 456–462.
39. Manheimer, D. I., & Mellinger, G. D. Personality characteristics of the child accident repeater. *Child Devel.*, 1967, **38**, 491–513.
40. Medinnus, G. R., & Robinson, R. Maturity as a predictor of school achievement. Paper presented at the meeting of the Society for Research in Child Development, Santa Monica, Calif., March 29, 1969.
41. Meichenbaum, D., & Goodman, J. Reflection-impulsivity and verbal control of motor behavior. *Child Devel.*, 1969, **40**, 785–797.
42. Meredith, H. V. Change in the stature and body weight of North American boys during the past 80 years. In L. Lipsitt & C. Spiker (Eds.), *Advances in child development and behavior.* Vol. 1. New York: Academic, 1963, pp. 69–114.
43. Meredith, H. V. Body size of contemporary groups of eight-year-old children studied in different parts of the world. *Mono. Soc. Res. Child Devel.*, 1969, **34**:1.
44. Metropolitan Life Insurance Company. Health of the school-age population. *Stat. Bull.*, 1961, **42**:8, 1–3.
45. Metropolitan Life Insurance Company. Accident hazards of school-age children. *Stat. Bull.*, 1964, **45**:9, 3–5.
46. Miller, D. R., & Swanson, G. E. *The changing American parent.* New York: Wiley, 1958.
47. *New York Times. Japanese taller as diet improves.* May 25, 1969.
48. Palkes, H., Stewart, M., & Kahana, B. Porteus maze performance of hyperactive boys after training in self-directed verbal commands. *Child Devel.*, 1968, **39**, 817–826.
49. Penfield, W. The uncommitted cortex, the child's changing brain. *Atlantic*, 1964, **214**(1), 77–81.
50. Rauh, J. L., Schumsky, D. A., & Witt, M. T. Heights, weights and obesity in urban school children. *Child Devel.*, 1967, **38**, 515–530.
51. Reed, J. C. Lateralized finger agnosia and reading achievement at ages 6 and 10. *Child Devel.*, 1967, **38**, 213–220.
52. Richardson, S. A., Hastorf, A. H., & Dornbusch, S. M. Effects of physical disability on a child's description of himself. *Child Devel.*, 1964, **35**, 893–907.
53. Richardson, S. A., & Royce, J. Race and physical handicap in children's preference for other children. *Child Devel.*, 1968, **39**, 467–480.
54. Riesman, D., Glazer, N., & Denny, R. *The lonely crowd.* New Haven: Yale University Press, 1950.
55. Rosenberg, B. G., & Sutton-Smith, B. A revised conception of masculine–feminine differences in play activities. *J. Genet. Psychol.*, 1960, **96**, 165–170.
56. Scrimshaw, N. S. The effect of the interaction of nutrition and infection on the preschool child. In National Research Council, *Pre-school and malnutrition.* Washington, D.C.: National Academy of Sciences, 1966, pp. 63–73.
57. Shapiro, S., Schlesinger, E. R., & Nesbitt, E. L. *Infant, perinatal and childhood mortality in the United States.* Cambridge, Mass.: Harvard University Press, 1968.

58. Simon, M. D. Body configuration and school readiness. *Child Devel.*, 1959, **30**, 493–512.

59. Sloan, W. The Lincoln–Oseretsky motor development scale. *Genet. Psychol. Mono.*, 1955, **51**, 183–251.

60. Smart, S. S. Personal communication, 1964.

61. Smart, S. S. Social class differences in parent behavior in a natural setting. *J. Marr. Fam.*, 1964, **26**, 223–224.

62. Strang, R. *An introduction to child study* (4th ed.). New York: Macmillan, 1959.

63. Tanner, J. M. *Growth at adolescence* (2nd ed.). Oxford: Blackwell, 1962.

64. Tanner, J. M. Earlier maturation in man. *Sci. Am.*, 1968, **218**(1), 21–27.

65. Ure, D. Spelling performance of left-handed school children as affected by the use of a pencil modified to increase visual feedback. *J. Exper. Child Psychol.*, 1969, **7**, 220–230.

66. Valadian, I., Stuart, H. C., & Reed, R. B. Studies of illnesses of children followed from birth to eighteen years. *Mono. Soc. Res. Child Devel.*, 1961, **26**:3.

67. Wapner, S., & Cirillo, L. Imitation of a model's hand movements: Age changes in transposition of left–right relations. *Child Devel.*, 1968, **39**, 887–894.

68. Watson, E. H., & Lowrey, G. H. *Growth and development of children* (5th ed.). Chicago: Year Book, 1967.

69. Whipple, D. V. *Dynamics of development: Euthenic pediatrics*. New York: McGraw-Hill, 1966.

70. Young, H. B., & Knapp, R. P. Personality characteristics of converted left handers. *Percept. Motor Skills*, 1966, **23**, 35–40.

Readings in
Physical Characteristics and Skills

Children grow taller, wider, and heavier. Some children change more rapidly in these dimensions than others. Children move their bodies, and parts of their bodies, some more skillfully than others. These statements hardly need formal proof. Even though physical and motor growth are obvious, it does not follow that they can be taken for granted. To understand child development fully, one needs to know the antecedents and consequences of physical and motor growth. This chapter contains two reviews of literature and two studies, one of each from each of the two related areas.

Tables of average heights and weights of children are useful not because they show what any given child should weigh, although they are sometimes misused in that way, but because they make it possible to see a child in relation to a group of children. To be of greatest use the averages should be of a group composed of children like the child whose growth is being assessed, but such norms are only occasionally available.

In the article reprinted from a longer article by Stanley M. Garn are given "Parent-specific Size Standards." These are the average heights of sons and daughters of short, average, and tall parents. Genetic factors for stature are therefore controlled, at least roughly. Other factors which influence children's heights are not controlled for in these tables. Elsewhere in the same article Garn reviews research on other antecedents and consequences of body size in children.

Anna Espenschade, in the second article, reviews some of the research that has been done on children's motor development. The figures quoted by Espenschade show the increasing skill which school children show in basic motor skills. The leveling off of girls' performance in adolescence may be due, at least in part, to a decrease in girls' motivation to perform well in these kinds of tasks, as Espenschade points out.

The third article, by Harben Young and Robert Knapp, is an interesting piece of research into the effects of making left-handed children use their right hands. Young and Knapp make use of culturally defined attitudes toward left-handedness by comparing boys of similar racial stock brought up in Italy and in the United States. The tests of lateral dominance are ones which beginning students of child development can use if they are interested in determining lateral dominance in children. The personality measures used by Young and Knapp are not so easily duplicated.

The Correlates of Body Size

Stanley M. Garn
THE FELS RESEARCH INSTITUTE

Body size from infancy through adolescence carries with it a variety of physiological, developmental, and behavioral correlates. For constant age, taller individuals have a larger basal oxygen consumption and in consequence they eat more because they need more. Taller children, like taller adults, have larger bones and in consequence their needs for calcium and phosphorous during growth must be proportionately larger. Taller children are also slightly but consistently advanced in a variety of developmental measures. Skeletal age tends to be advanced in taller children. Taller children are also slightly but consistently advanced in the number of teeth present at a given age (Cattell, 1928) and in the extent of calcification of the teeth as radiographically determined (Garn, Lewis, and Kerewsky, 1965).

Why the developmental correlates of size exist is not totally clear. To some extent they are a function of social stratification and socioeconomic group differences such that the more favored are both taller and developmentally advanced. To some extent, even within family lines, it can be shown that the physiologically more mature children are taller *because* they are more mature. Further, the mechanisms connecting tallness to dental development are by no means clear, particularly since the formation and eruption of the permanent dentition are to the very largest extent unrelated to most environmental influences.

THE CAUSE OF VARIATIONS IN SIZE   It should be pointed out here that there is no consistent explanation for variations in size in adulthood, nor is there as yet a satisfactory explanation for the mechanisms responsible for size variations in childhood. Granting that superior nutrition results in greater growth, the *mechanisms* by which this occurs are not known. Granting the genetic nature of stature, the mechanisms by which the genes make for variations in the length of the body and the size of its individual components are still not known.

One theory is that bigness is achieved through greater secretion of the growth-stimulating hormone (GSH) of the anterior pituitary. This is a reasonable theory, and it is in partial accordance with observational data. Hypopituitary children, lacking or partially lacking the growth stimulating hormone, do fail to grow. Hyperpituitary children do in fact achieve giantism. At the present time, however, there is no adequate measure of normal variations in growth hormone levels, either in the blood or in the urine nor are indirect indicators as alkaline phosphatase adequate for the purpose. With progress in the immunological approach to the measurement of growth-stimulating hormone, the possible relationship between variations in growth-stimulating

Reprinted from Stanley M. Garn, "Body Size and Its Implications," in L. W. Hoffman and M. L. Hoffman (Eds.), *Review of Child Development Research*, Vol. II, pp. 540–561. Published by Russell Sage Foundation, 1966. By permission.

hormone and statural differences may become clearer (Rimoin, Merimee, and McKusick, 1966).

Alternatively, differences both in size and in rate of growth may be a function of the bones *themselves* rather than in the amount of stimulating or trophic hormone. This is technically referred to as the target-organ theory. It refers to the notion (supported by observations on certain kinds of dwarfism) that variations in response of the target-organ, or end-organ, rather than the stimulating hormone are involved. Clearly, there is a pressing need for an understanding of the mechanisms through which variations in size are attained and through which ultimate size attainment is determined.

BODY SIZE AND BEHAVIORAL CORRELATES   In addition to the more obvious developmental, metabolic, and endocrine correlates of body size during the growing period, a large number of mental and behavioral correlates have also been reported (Abernethy, 1936; Ljung, 1965; Tanner, 1960, 1962). Though the magnitude of the correlations is generally low, for the most part they are systematically in the expected direction. Taller children tend to walk earlier (Norval, 1947). Boys and girls with a larger lean body mass tend to be advanced in gross motor development. A variety of studies report that "reading readiness" is positively correlated with stature. And most measures of "intelligence" appear to be loosely associated with body size during the growing period. Differences in nursery school behavior similarly relate in part to variations in the fat-free or lean body mass. (See Douglas, Ross, and Simpson, 1965; Ljung, 1965.)

Explanations for the behavioral correlations with body size are both numerous and varied and it is unlikely that all of the reported behavioral correlations have a common causal basis. A random sample of children represents a wide range of socioeconomic classes involving variations in caloric adequacy, medical care, parental attention, and parental encouragement. In the more complex behaviors, as represented by the introversion-extroversion continuum or dominance-submission scales, it is not improbable that larger body size gives a child initial advantage that he may then capitalize upon. Typed as a strong man, or leader, the large child may incorporate such successes into the system of devices he utilizes to deal with the world.

Nevertheless, there is reason to believe that some of the size-behavior correlates are in fact developmental in nature, representing a faster rate of behavioral development in those children who are ahead physically. More recent studies show a residual correlation between stature and test scores of children in Great Britain even among children of the same sex, age, stage of sexual development, social class, and size of family. However, to quote Douglas and his associates (1965), ". . . the correlation is not simply explained by an advancement in physical development being associated with an advancement in intellectual development."

THE PUBERTAL SPURT IN SIZE AND INTELLIGENCE   As long ago as 1922, Murdock and Sullivan advanced the notion of an adolescent "spurt" in the rate of mental growth, analogous to the well-known adolescent spurt in stature. In more recent years, this idea has been advanced by Tanner (1962) and investigated in England, Scotland, Canada, and Sweden. Boyne and Clark (1959) have reported secular changes in *both* stature and intelligence; and their British data are in accordance with Canadian reports (Binning, 1958) and a recent Swedish monograph by Ljung (1965) who studied "practically all the pupils in their respective year group in Sweden."

The rationale behind an adolescent spurt in "intelligence" paralleling the spurt in stature is not clear. The fact that there is a spurt in stature in almost all boys and in the majority of girls does not of itself indicate that the brain must behave like the bones. Indeed, it may be observed that intellective potential is not diminished in the panhypopituitary dwarf, nor is there any present evidence that intellectual activity is increased in the hyperpituitary child, or in the sexual precocities.

Granting that there is an adolescent spurt in intelligence, paralleling the spurt in stature and possibly involving changes in the brain itself, there remains to be seen whether this has a steroidal basis or not. Testosterone-treated boys and estrogen-treated girls would help to answer this question.

MUSCLE MASS AND AGE AT WALKING   As an example of the complexity of relationships between physical and behavioral variables, one may report a relationship between leg muscle mass and age at walking. Infants with large leg muscle masses (as determined radiographically) stand up and walk earlier. Infants with small leg muscle masses stand up and walk later (Garn, 1962b, 1963). This overall relationship is partially independent of body size per se as it is also independent of other Gesellian parameters at the same age level. While it might be argued that the relationship between leg muscle mass and walking or standing is the simple result of physical activity, the fact that muscle mass at six months is *predictive* of walking versus nonwalking or standing versus nonstanding at one year suggests that the relationship is developmental rather than directly causal in nature.

TWO-GENERATIONAL STUDIES OF SIZE AND BEHAVIOR   Most relationships between size and behavior in infancy and childhood pose the inevitable cart-or-horse problem, the same problem that attends relationships between size and maturation. Are more muscular boys bigger simply because they are more mature (hence, developmentally older) or do genes for earlier maturation also make for bigger size? Are correlations between size and behavior purely developmental, or are genes for size actually involved? Would parents of different sizes, within the same socioeconomic class, produce progeny who differ in the rates of psychomotor or intellective development?

It is possible to circumvent this problem by going back one full generation, categorizing the parents in terms of various parameters of size, and then examining the behavioral progress of the children so sorted. This is a classic approach in the genetics of animal behavior as extensively reviewed by Fuller and Thompson (1960). It can be applied to numerous parental size parameters, among them the familiar measurement of stature and the less familiar measurement of the bony chest breadth (representing the lean body mass).

Considering parental stature first, there is evidence for a relationship between parental stature and the psychomotor behavior of their progeny at six, twelve, and eighteen months. Taking fathers and mothers first separately, and then together (the combined-parent or "midparental" stature) and some 91 items in the total of the Gesell spectrum, the number of significant point biserial correlations is close to twice expectancy. There is some evidence, therefore, that taller parents, within a particular socioeconomic group, have infants who are slightly advanced in specific Gesell items (Hull, 1966).

Alternatively, taking the bony chest breadth of the parents (as measured on postero-anterior chest radiographs), it is clear that the parental bony chest breadth relates to Gesell, Merrill-Palmer, and even early Binet performance. Where both parents are above average in bony chest breadth, the progeny are not only notably larger from birth on, as characterized by greater body weight and far larger lean body mass, but they are systematically advanced in psychomotor, form board, and even language proficiency (Garn et al., 1960; Kagan and Garn, 1963).

It is not implied that the children of taller parents are "smarter" at six, twelve, or eighteen months; nor is it to be claimed that the progeny of parents with large fat-free masses are inherently more "intelligent" as reflected by their Gesell, eighteen-month Merrill-Palmer, or thirty-six-month Binet scores. The indication simply is that greater body size in either the horizontal or the vertical direction is attained through a faster rate of growth, and this faster rate of physical growth is associated with more rapid acquisition of the skills and abilities measured by the tests in question. So apart from nutrition, social experience, and parental stimulation, size per se does relate to behavioral development, in part because greater body size is attained by a higher rate of growth.

PARENT-SPECIFIC SIZE STANDARDS

Returning to size per se, it should be obvious that all massed-data "average" size standards, whether group-specific or not, or contemporary or not, suffer from the same major disadvantage. They are scarcely child-specific, that is, they do not apply well to individual children. Children come from a variety of parental mating types, and it is obvious that the children of tall parents and the children of short parents will be but poorly fitted by average values that fail to take parental size into account.

Though this statement is self-evident, it is best given substance by picturing two children from the Fels Longitudinal Studies. One, a girl (subject 356), is the child of very tall parents. Father and mother taken together average 181 cm —well above the nationwide male average of 175 cm. The other child (subject 371) is a boy, the child of very short parents. Together they average 164 cm— below the nationwide average for women alone. One might expect the girl to exceed the female norm and the boy to fall well below the age-size norm for the boys.

As shown in Figure 1, these children grow exactly as might be expected. The daughter of tall parents (subject 356) greatly exceeds the normative median for girls at all ages. Parent-specific size values are clearly needed for her. The boy, subject 371, the son of short parents, is well below the average for boys. His size has been a source of some concern to his physician since he was a

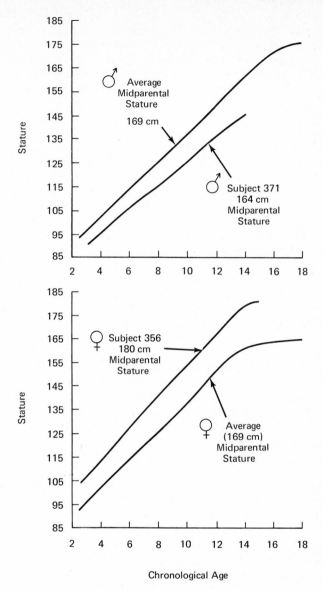

FIGURE 1.   *Statural growth of the children of extreme parental size. The boy, shown in the upper part of Figure 1, is the progeny of two parents of short stature, with a midparental average of 164 cm. This subject (Fels No. 371) is short for his age, far below the average. On the other hand, subject No. 356, the daughter of tall parents, is well above the age-size average for girls. These two cases exemplify the need for parent-specific age-size standards. Where parental size is known, such standards are a vast improvement over the conventional average approach. See also Garn and Rohmann (1966).*

tot, even though the physician is himself an outstanding authority on child growth, and an early contributor to *Child Development*. For subject 371, parent-specific size standards for statural growth would have been distinctly useful. Clearly, there is a large proportion of children, the progeny of tall parents and the progeny of short parents, for whom conventional age-size standards are inappropriate and, in fact, deceptive.

Preliminary Parent-Specific Age-Size Standards   Despite the obvious need for parent-specific age-size standards for boys and girls, such have not been previously available. A parent-specific age-size table broken down into but two or three parental size categories would require a minimum of 200–300 boys and girls measured at each age, and 400–600 parents measured too. Given two sexes, 36 half-year age intervals, and the above minimum sample size at each age, at least 14,400 boys and girls would have to be measured and 28,800 mothers and fathers. Since the task of collecting and measuring over 14,000 boys and girls and the nearly 29,000 parents would be formidable in a purely cross-sectional context, the nonexistence of parent-specific age-size standards for children up to now is rather readily understood.

However, the longitudinal approach in this instance comes to our rescue. Having stature data on children taken at exact age intervals within narrow tolerance limits (Garn and Shamir, 1958), and having parental size data as well, it is a comparatively simple matter to sort the prepunched size data of children categorized according to parental size, and so to produce parent-specific age-size standards for growing children.

A part of such a table, newly constructed for the purposes of this review, is given in Table 2. Parental size here refers to the midparent value (the average of the paternal and maternal statures) as originally suggested by Galton eighty years ago. Parental stature here refers to stature measured early in the fourth decade; only three midparent size categories are tabulated, for reasons of simplicity. These are the 163 cm (short) midparent value, the 169 cm (median) midparent value, and the 175 cm (tall) midparent value.

As shown in Table 2, the use of parental size adds an important new parameter to age-size standards for children. Even at one year of age, the children so categorized are a centimeter or more apart. At age eighteen the difference is 2.4 cm (approximately one inch) or more. Were extreme parental size categories included as in the original tabulation from which this table is abridged, the differences would be even more dramatic. But the sample size is insufficient to justify including the extreme parental size categories here.

Further Applications of Parent-Specific Size Standards   While the parent-specific size standards for children given in Table 2 are applicable to American-born children of the middle socioeconomic classes (lower middle to upper middle) of Northwestern European ancestry and well nourished, as judged from subcutaneous fat measurements, the applicability of these standards is potentially wider. In field situations, as in nutritional surveys, where stature standards do not yet exist, the values given in Table 2 offer the possibility of being child-appropriate to a degree not conventionally possible. They have been applied, retrospectively, to several groups, including

TABLE 1

Parent-Specific Age-Size Tables for Boys and Girls of Three Selected Midparent Values

	BOYS PARENTAL MIDPOINT				GIRLS PARENTAL MIDPOINT		
AGE	163 CM	169 CM	175 CM	AGE	163 CM	169 CM	175 CM
1–0	73.1	75.1	77.1	1–0	73.0	74.0	74.6
2–0	85.4	87.4	88.9	2–0	84.0	85.5	88.2
3–0	93.2	96.0	98.3	3–0	90.4	93.8	96.5
4–0	99.5	103.1	106.3	4–0	96.8	103.9	103.8
5–0	105.6	110.0	112.7	5–0	103.5	109.1	111.0
6–0	110.9	115.4	118.7	6–0	110.2	115.0	117.3
7–0	116.2	121.3	124.6	7–0	116.5	120.2	124.0
8–0	121.6	126.8	130.4	8–0	122.4	125.8	130.2
9–0	126.9	131.9	136.0	9–0	128.6	131.4	136.6
10–0	132.5	137.4	141.5	10–0	135.1	136.9	143.1
11–0	138.5	143.0	146.8	11–0	141.6	143.4	149.6
12–0	144.7	148.4	152.4	12–0	147.8	150.3	155.8
13–0	151.0	154.9	159.6	13–0	154.2	157.0	161.7
14–0	158.8	161.6	167.8	14–0	158.8	160.4	165.9
15–0	165.8	167.9	174.7	15–0	159.8	162.2	168.4
16–0	169.4	172.8	176.6	16–0	160.5	163.4	169.7
17–0	170.9	175.4	177.8	17–0	160.8	164.0	170.9
18–0	171.5	176.2	178.6	18–0	161.0	164.3	171.8

The values shown are based on fully longitudinal analyses of the statural growth of more than 500 children representing in excess of 12,000 observations in all. The midparent value, here the average of paternal and maternal statures, refers to parental size at age thirty. To use, determine the midparent stature and present age of the child in question, reading out in the sex-appropriate column.

SOURCE: Fels Parent-Specific Size Tables for Midparent Categories shown smoothed and arranged by James Eagen. See Garn and Rohmann (1966).

the Aleut of Umnak and Atka in the Aleutians, for whom parental stature is individually available. For the Aleut children stature estimates based on parental size and using the appropriate Fels midparental size categories came remarkably close to observed individual size data.

New parent-specific size standards for children based on contemporary cross-sectional data and with parental size carefully measured (not reported) would be the ideal solution. It would be an immense undertaking, however, as mentioned above. A practical expedient might be to combine data from extant longitudinal studies (Harvard, Fels, Denver).

SIZE, CHROMOSOMES, AND SEX

At nearly all ages, as shown in Table 2, the human male is taller than the female, a point misconstrued in some elementary texts. At equal maturity levels, holding physiological age constant, sex difference in stature is even greater. Males are considerably taller than females at comparable levels of maturation and the fat-free weight is then far greater in the male (Fomon, 1966;

Owen et al., 1966). The 7 per cent sexual dimorphism in body size that may be seen after sexual maturity, the 3 per cent to 5 per cent sex difference in tooth size, and the 30 per cent sexual dimorphism in the adult lean body mass have their beginnings well before birth.

Final differences in size have their origin in pituitary timing and in the type and amount of steroid mediation. The male continues to grow for a longer time than the female, and the magnitude of the steroid-mediated adolescent growth spurt is generally larger. The total muscle mass and particularly the muscles of the upper back and shoulders are disproportionately responsive to androgenic (masculinizing) steroids. But many size differences, such as those in the size of the permanent teeth, which form in the jaws prepubertally, owe nothing to the later mechanisms of hormonal differentiation.

The sexual dimorphism in body size prior to puberty most likely has its origin in the Y chromosome, that small chromosome which apparently contains little but genes affecting size and sex. Y-containing chromosomal types, the normal XY and XXY, and to some extent the XXXY, appear to be taller than the non-Y chromosomal types, the XO, the normal XX, the XXX, and so on. Thus it is reasonable to believe that the difference between the normal XY (male) and the normal XX (female) has to do with genes on the Y chromosome. However, it also may be observed that the XO chromosomal type (Turner's syndrome) is generally smaller than the normal XX even in prepubertal life. To some extent, as suggested by a recent paper of Gorlin, Redman, and Shapiro (1965), early maturation and abnormalities of development increase with the number of chromosomes (XXX, XXXY, etc.).

Contrasting the long legs, narrow shoulders, and broad hips of subjects with Klinefelter's syndrome (XXY) with the short legs, broad shoulders, and narrow hips of Turner's syndrome (XO), Shimaguchi and associates (1964) suggest that the X chromosome includes genes affecting body build and body length. Tanner and his colleagues (1959) comment on the role of the X and Y chromosomes in skeletal maturation and therefore final size. However, the haploid XO is more than just a subject who never matures. There are multiple developmental defects wherever the number of sex chromosomes is less than or greater than two. So the extent of X and Y determination of the sexual dimorphism in size and development can only partially be ascertained by comparing the haploid XO with the XX and XY and those diploid chromosomal types with the polyploid XXY, XXXY, etc.

PARENT–CHILD SIZE SIMILARITIES AND THEIR CHROMOSOMAL BASES   Apart from the sexual dimorphism in size, which currently may be attributed to the Y chromosome in part, it is possible to estimate the extent to which sex chromosomes are involved in the determination of normal body size from various parent-child and sibling size correlations. Father–son and brother–brother stature correlations represent a test of Y-linkage. Father–daughter and sister–sister correlations provide a test of X-linkage (for fathers and daughters have the paternal X chromosome in common).

However, viewing complete parent–child size correlations, such as are given in Table 3, it would appear that the bulk of variance in stature is determined by autosomal genes, that is, genes on the 22 pairs of chromosomes that

Table 2
Parent–Child Stature Correlations

	FA–DA		FA–SO		MO–DA		MO–SO		M–P–DA		M–P–SO	
	N	r	N	r	N	r	N	r	N	r	N	r
Birth	115	.14	135	.14	128	−.06	146	.15	114	.05	134	.18
0.12	147	.12	163	.17	162	−.01	176	.13	146	.07	161	.19
0.25	151	.24	169	.05	171	.16	184	.08	150	.25	167	.07
0.50	161	.29	171	.33	181	.14	187	.26	160	.28	170	.38
0.75	160	.32	169	.07	182	.29	185	−.02	159	.38	168	.04
1.00	165	.34	177	.36	186	.23	194	.27	164	.34	175	.42
1.50	161	.36	173	.09	180	.22	188	.15	161	.37	170	.14
2.00	158	.36	168	.37	179	.28	183	.30	158	.40	166	.45
2.50	158	.42	161	.39	175	.35	175	.33	158	.49	160	.47
3.00	153	.20	167	.37	172	.13	182	.32	152	.21	166	.45
3.50	149	.38	162	.41	165	.34	173	.37	149	.46	161	.51
4.00	150	.38	163	.36	166	.30	172	.36	150	.44	162	.48
4.50	143	.38	166	.40	157	.35	172	.36	143	.47	165	.50
5.00	141	.35	163	.38	158	.33	172	.35	141	.44	162	.48
5.50	135	.38	160	.37	150	.36	167	.37	135	.47	158	.49
6.00	136	.36	162	.36	150	.32	169	.36	136	.44	160	.49
6.50	126	.37	158	.36	141	.32	163	.40	128	.45	156	.51
7.00	127	.39	155	.34	140	.28	161	.34	127	.43	153	.47
7.50	121	.38	152	.38	134	.29	155	.36	121	.43	150	.50
8.00	116	.39	146	.39	129	.27	151	.35	116	.42	145	.50
8.50	107	.40	146	.37	119	.25	151	.34	107	.42	145	.48
9.00	108	.40	142	.37	119	.24	148	.34	108	.42	141	.48
9.50	106	.36	134	.36	116	.22	138	.33	106	.38	133	.46
10.00	105	.34	130	.36	114	.19	134	.35	105	.35	129	.47
10.50	106	.30	121	.38	113	.16	126	.35	106	.34	121	.48
11.00	100	.30	115	.39	107	.11	118	.33	100	.28	114	.48
11.50	99	.31	112	.40	104	.10	116	.35	99	.29	112	.49
12.00	95	.33	110	.40	100	.15	144	.31	95	.32	110	.46
12.50	91	.35	110	.38	95	.20	114	.29	91	.35	110	.45
13.00	91	.37	105	.36	96	.21	109	.28	91	.38	105	.42
13.50	87	.40	102	.35	91	.32	106	.25	87	.45	102	.40
14.00	85	.37	100	.34	89	.34	104	.27	85	.45	100	.41
14.50	82	.40	95	.31	86	.40	99	.34	82	.50	95	.42
15.00	80	.40	94	.32	84	.43	99	.36	80	.51	94	.43
15.50	74	.49	87	.33	77	.48	91	.33	74	.59	87	.41
16.00	76	.46	84	.34	79	.48	87	.36	76	.58	84	.45
16.50	69	.48	85	.37	73	.49	89	.45	69	.59	85	.50
17.00	69	.47	80	.33	73	.49	83	.41	69	.58	80	.46
17.50	64	.48	75	.35	67	.50	79	.46	64	.60	75	.47
18.00	65	.49	77	.33	69	.51	80	.38	65	.61	77	.46

This table which summarizes like-sexed and unlike-sexed parent-child correlations at half-year intervals through eighteen years is based upon complete serial-longitudinal size data from the Fels studies. The fact that father-son correlations do not exceed mother-son correlations argues against Y-linked inheritance, and the fact that father-son correlations are of the magnitude that they are represents evidence against X-linkage. Taken together, it appears that size is largely determined by autosomal genes and that somewhat less than 50 per cent of size variance is accounted for by genes held in common by the child and both parents. For details, see text. See also Fisher (1918) and Hewitt (1957).

have nothing to do with sex. Father–son correlations are not uniformly higher than mother–son correlations, and so on. There is a suggestion, in the shifting magnitude of correlations after puberty, that X-mediation may perhaps be involved in part but autosomal inheritance is still largely indicated. (See also Garn and Rohmann, 1966.)

In other parameters of human physical development, notably ossification timing and tooth calcification, the X chromosome seems to be disproportionately involved (Garn et al., 1965; Garn and Rohmann, 1962). Tanner and associates (1959) have compared normal males (XY), Turner's syndrome (XO), and Kleinfelter's syndrome (XXY) in an attempt to ascertain the role of the X and Y chromosomes in maturational timing.

However, the data newly presented in detail in Table 3 show the difficulty of demonstrating other than autosomal mediation of normal variations in stature at the present time. While the fact that father–daughter correlations exceed father–son correlations after age thirteen would implicate the X chromosome in part, exactly the same trend holds for the mother. That is, the mother–daughter correlations also exceed the mother–son correlations after age thirteen, and here the maternal contribution (an X chromosome in either case) is presumably equal. Accordingly, then, it is reasonable to say that the bulk of genes affecting stature within a sex are located on the autosomes, but that some measure of X-mediation appears to be superimposed. (See also Fisher, 1918; Hewitt, 1957.)

THE NUTRITIONAL MODIFICATION OF BODY SIZE

The proposition that body size can be modified by nutrition during growth needs scarce qualification today. It can be documented from the prenatal period through the completion of epiphyseal union. It can be shown experimentally in laboratory animals (Dickerson and McCance, 1961; Platt and Stewart, 1962) and it can be shown by a multitude of natural experiments, including famines, in man. It can be shown in relation to nutritional status, rating separately the caloric intake, the protein intake, and intake of fat-soluble vitamins. It can be shown in relation to socioeconomic status, where such status reflects the caloric reserve. The nutritional modification of stature and body size can also be demonstrated in malabsorption syndromes, where available nutrients are unable to pass through the gut. Regulating the amount of food available, within broad limits, regulates body size (Acheson, 1960).

Prenatally, body size can be modified by maternal nutrition up to a point. In famine situations, the body size of the newborn is reduced if the maternal caloric intake falls below 1,500 calories per day (Antonov, 1947; Smith, 1947a,b). Neonates in starvation areas and where protein-calorie malnutrition is common are smaller than are the newborn in Northwest Europe, the United States, New Zealand, and Australia. Still, depriving the mother has relatively less effect on her baby than might be suspected because of the peculiarly "parasitic" nature of the maternal-fetal relationship (Smith, 1947b).

Knowing this, the inability to control fetal size by adjusting the maternal caloric intake during pregnancy is better understood. There was a time when we tried to prevent overly large babies by dietary control measures. We established the twenty-pound rule, which is, that the mother should not gain more than twenty pounds during any single pregnancy. We now know that the twenty-pound rule has a cosmetic effect (keeping the mother from gaining excess fat during pregnancy) but it does not materially reduce the size of the infant at birth.

But if limited dietary attempts to manipulate birth size are relatively ineffective, intrauterine control of prenatal nutrition can still be demonstrated. Twins, particularly those monozygotic (single-egg) twins sharing a common placenta, are individually smaller than might be expected for their gestation length. Both monozygotic and dizygotic (separate-egg) twins compete for nutrients prenatally: in one sense twins are "starved" newborn. The same may be shown in some developmentally mature but extremely small full-term infants whose placental growth has been restricted and thus incapable of providing a full flow of nutrients. That such prenatal nutritional limitations may have a permanent effect is suggested when the smaller monozygotic twin at birth remains the smaller twin throughout life, i.e., the "runt" effect.

After birth and through the time of weaning there are numerous limitations on body size. In underdeveloped areas undergoing acculturation, the bottle-fed baby may be at a major disadvantage, for the "milk" is often highly diluted reconstituted milk and sanitary measures are nonexistent. The infant may thus be deprived nutritionally and subject to multiple diarrheas. In overdeveloped nations, on the other hand, the bottle-fed baby may become bigger than the breast-fed baby, the milkman having an endless supply compared with the mother. Now the point here is not bottle feeding versus breast feeding, but rather that the nutritional quality of the infant's diet affects the rate of growth. At the same time, we must consider the complex interaction of nutrition and infection (Scrimshaw and Béhar, 1961; Scrimshaw, Taylor, and Gordon, 1959). Growth of infants in many countries today is inhibited by diarrheas and other infections. At the same time, infants with suboptimal nutrition, particularly infants deprived of good quality protein, are more subject to diarrheas and other infections. So size in infancy is both directly influenced by nutrition and indirectly influenced by the diseases that malnutrition breeds.

Today, malnutrition and especially protein-calorie malnutrition (PCM) inhibit the growth of millions of preschool children in Central Asia, South America, Africa, Asia, India, and the Middle East (May, 1965). It is not infrequent in nutrition surveys to discover that such children in protein-calorie malnutrition areas average below the fifth percentile by recent American or English size standards or even below the first percentile. Such malnutrition has an economic basis, where calories and especially quality protein are in short supply. However, the problem is cultural as well. There may be excessive dependence upon a single cereal or root crop such as corn, manioc, or rice, each with its own characteristic limiting amino acids. Or, even where legumes and other crops abound, nutritional knowledge may be defective so that children are not given readily available foods that are necessary for their growth. In making the transition from the agricultural village to the industrial town, weaning may be premature, depriving the infant of good quality human milk protein and substituting a thin gruel of corn or a highly diluted watered "milk" with sugar added for calories. Vitamin-rich and protein-rich foods may be withheld from the preschool child under the mistaken notion that such "strong" foods are harmful. Small wonder that in such cultures and subcultures infant mortality is excessively high, those who survive are stunted and small, and both infants and children are particularly prone to infection, as described in the recent National Academy of Sciences conference on malnutrition in the preschool child (1966) and in the earlier conference volume on tropical health (National Academy of Sciences, 1962).

MALNUTRITION, SIZE, AND BEHAVIORAL DELAY   Recent studies on protein-calorie malnutrition (PCM) have suggested behavioral delay as well as delayed maturation and inadequate size attainment as a consequence. Children from protein-malnutrition areas of Central and South Africa are comparable to American children in psychomotor development during their first six months of life, or even ahead, but they tend to fall behind thereafter (Dean, 1954; Geber and Dean, 1957). Such behavioral delay is particularly pronounced in acute protein-calorie malnutrition, in the diseases known as *kwashiorkor* and *marasmus*. As studied in Mexico City and in Guatemala City, the degree of psychomotor delay is proportional to the degree of retardation in size. Some authorities have viewed this delay in the motoric, manipulative, and language development as indicative of major central nervous system impairment (Brown, 1965; Dean, 1954; Geber and Dean, 1957; Scrimshaw and Béhar, 1961; Stoch and Smythe, 1963).

Now behavioral abnormalities may be produced in experimental animals by giving them a diet deficient in quality protein (Moore et al., 1964). So the facts are clear enough. Attainment of various items on the Gesell schedule—creeping, crawling, standing, walking, drawing, using three words, pointing to parts of the body, and following the geometrical forms—may be delayed in geographical areas where protein malnutrition is common. Viewing a ward full of children hospitalized with kwashiorkor, one is impressed with their lethargy and their behavioral retardation. But the question is whether the behavioral delay is a simple function of the lethargy and malaise associated with acute illness, where the child has no real interest in his environment. Or it may be possible that the children with protein-calorie malnutrition are suffering from very real brain damage. It is possible that there is delayed cerebral growth in early kwashiorkor and marasmus. It is suggested, though by no means proven, that the consequences of protein-calorie malnutrition are both statural and psychological retardation, even persisting through adulthood (Stoch and Smythe, 1963) and involving deficient brain growth (Brown, 1965).

NUTRITION AND SIZE AT MATURITY

There is a jump in years from the preschool infant to the adolescent, and from malnutrition to overnutrition, but the same general principles apply. The poorer the state of nutrition, the smaller the size, the later the onset of sexual maturity, and the later the completion of growth. Thus, size and sexual maturity tend to be advanced in the higher socioeconomic groups and delayed in the lower. Similarly, menarche is earlier in fatter girls, in some cases by two or

three years or more. Demonstrably, overnutrition as measured by obesity results
in acceleration of the maturational process in both sexes. Fat children are more
mature and bigger earlier (Garn and Haskell, 1960; Quaade, 1955; Wolff,
1955). While children can be stuffed into early maturity, as they can be starved
into late maturity, it is not known how broadly these generalizations apply.
Early maturing children are certainly bigger earlier, but they stop growing
sooner. Starved children are late to mature but obviously may grow for a
longer period of time. While there is compensatory growth, it has its limits;
otherwise well-nourished and starved populations would tend to be alike in
adult stature (Howe and Schiller, 1952).

The effects of nutrition on size are complicated. In man, malnutrition
is rarely just a restriction in calories. Many of the malnourished populations
of the world are short on fats and especially short on animal protein. In the
several Guatemalan villages we have studied in conjunction with INCAP, the
caloric intake in four-year-old children is approximately a third less than that
of age-matched children in the Fels Longitudinal series. (See Figure 2.) On
the other hand, protein intake in these Guatemalan villages ranges below 50
per cent of what comparable children in Ohio have to eat. And finally, as shown
in Figure 2, the intake of *animal protein* is particularly restricted in these Guatemalan Indian villages so that the children from the villages of Santa Maria and

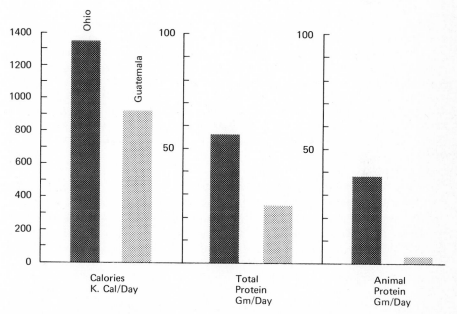

F I G U R E 2.   *Comparative daily intakes of calories, protein, and animal protein in four-
year-old children from southwestern Ohio and from two Mayan villages in Guatemala. The Mayan
Indian children consume 30 per cent fewer calories, 50 to 60 per cent less protein, and 90 to 95 per cent
less animal protein. These data, abridged from cooperative studies by the Institute of Nutrition of
Central America and Panama (INCAP) and the Fels Research Institute, provide a dramatic example
of how nutritional parameters restrict body size. Here animal protein becomes the limiting factor,
not just for growth but for actual survival (see text).*

Santa Cruz average less than 10 per cent as much animal protein as do the children from Southwestern Ohio. It is the quality protein of animal origin much more than the caloric intake as a whole that appears to be the growth-limiting factor, and, along with being growth-restricting, protein deficiency predisposes the children in these areas of malnutrition per se. A program of protein-calorie supplementation now being carried out in the village of Santa Catarina promises to effect a "secular trend" in short order. (See *Federation Proceedings*, 1964, p. 338.)

NUTRITION AND SIZE   While it is dangerous to overgeneralize about growth mechanisms and the mechanisms that control body size, limited generalizations can be made. Caloric deficiency on the part of the mother, below levels we ordinarily find in our country, can reduce the size of newborn. Even with an adequate supply of mother's milk, infections during the nursing period can limit growth. Limited quantity and poor quality of the post-weaning diet, combined with parasitic infestations and recurrent infections thereafter, limit growth through the adolescent period and beyond. On the other hand, supernutrition certainly promotes maximum body size and early sexual maturation. Our children have virtually unlimited access to calories; their avenues for caloric expenditure have become limited; and childhood diseases and infections have far less impact because of immunizations, antibiotics, and superior medical care.

So in man we are now able to view both nutritional extremes as they affect body size. We can measure the impact of undernutrition and consequent infection on size in much of the world. In exploring the effects of malnutrition, and in the analysis of growth improvement following nutritional supplementation, we have a partial understanding of the mechanism of secular change in size. At the same time, we can document the auxogenic or growth-promoting effects of overnutrition and of supernutrition on our own children and adolescents, and we have begun to wonder whether greater body size and earlier maturation has been purchased at the expense of predisposition to cardiovascular and atherosclerotic diseases.

SUMMARY AND CONCLUSIONS

Despite methodological considerations, which favor recumbent length, and theoretical considerations (which view stature as a complex of independent axial and appendicular segments), stature—standing height—continues to be the most used measure of body size. In infancy and childhood, as in adolescence, stature has multiple correlates with physiological, metabolic, psychomotor, and intellective performances not all of which are simply "developmental" in nature.

Over the past century, excepting wartime and depression periods, stature has increased, the more so for the least favored groups. As shown by nutritional experiments, this "secular" trend may be attributed to an increase in caloric intake, an improvement in nutritional quality, and a decrease in childhood diseases, including those associated with malnutrition. Today, areas of protein-calorie malnutrition are areas of statural stunting, apparent developmental delay, and (possibly) permanent brain damage.

The use of stature as a reference parameter is predicated upon the availability of appropriate norms or standards. Unfortunately, many such standards are twenty to fifty years out of date, and (for much of the world) rarely group-specific. In stature prediction, the use of "bone age" rather than chronological age greatly improves results. For individuals, parent-specific stature standards constitute a methodological advancement, especially for the children of tall parents and the children of short parents. A new parent-specific age-size table is given in this paper.

Apart from nutritional modifications, stature has an obvious genetic parameter, as shown from midparent versus child correlations approximating .5. Present data suggest that most of the genes affecting stature are located on the autosomes. The Y chromosome, however, appears to be responsible for the sex difference in stature and the far larger sex difference in the lean body mass. The mechanism of genetic mediation of stature is not known, though a timing effect (regulating the duration of growth) can be isolated as one determinant.

Of major interest to the behavioral sciences is the extent to which genetic and nongenetic factors affecting stature attainment directly and indirectly affect behavior.

References

ABERNETHY, E. M. Relationships between mental and physical growth. *Monogr. Soc. Res. Child Develpm.*, 1936, **1**, No. 7.

ACHESON, R. M. Effects of nutrition and disease on human growth. In J. M. Tanner (Ed.), *Human growth.* Oxford: Pergamon Press, 1960.

ANTONOV, A. N. Children born during the siege of Leningrad in 1942. *J. Pediat.*, 1947, **30**, 250–259.

BINNING, G. Earlier physical and mental maturity among Saskatoon public school children. *Canad. J. Publ. Hlth.*, 1958, **49**, 9–17.

BOYNE, A. W. & CLARK, J. R. Secular change in the intelligence of 11-year-old Aberdeen schoolchildren. *Hum. Biol.*, 1959, **31**, 325–333.

BROWN, R. E. Organ weight in malnutrition, with special reference to brain weight. Paper read at International Congress of Pediatrics, Tokyo, November 7–13, 1965.

CATTELL, P. Dentition as a measure of maturity. *Harvard Monogr. Educ.* Cambridge: Harvard Univ. Press, 1928, No. 9.

DEAN, R. F. A. Standards for African children and the influence of nutrition. *J. Trop. Med.*, 1954, **57**, 283–289.

DICKERSON, J. W. T. & McCANCE, R. A. Severe undernutrition in growing and adult animals: 8. The dimensions and chemistry of the long bones. *Brit. J. Nutr.*, 1961, **15**, 567–576.

DOUGLAS, J. W. B., ROSS, J. M., & SIMPSON, H. R. The relation between height and measured educational ability in school children of the same social class, family size and stage of physical development. *Hum. Biol.*, 1965, **37**, 178–186.

Federation Proceedings, 1964, **24**, No. 2, Part I.

FISHER, R. A. The correlation between relatives on the supposition of Mendelian inheritance. *Trans. Roy. Soc. Edinb.*, 1918, **52**, 399–433.

FOMON, S. Body composition of the infant. Part I: The male reference infant. In F. Falkner (Ed.), *Human Development.* Philadelphia: W. B. Saunders, 1966.

FULLER, J. L. & THOMPSON, W. L. *Behavior genetics.* New York: Wiley, 1960.

GARN, S. M. Determinants of size and growth during the first three years. *Mod. Prob. Pediat.*, 1962, **7**, 50–54.

———. Human biology and research in body composition. *Ann. N. Y. Acad. Sci.*, 1963, **110**, 429–446.

———. The applicability of North American growth standards in developing countries. *Canad. med. Ass. J.*, 1965, **93**, 914–919.

———. Malnutrition and skeletal development in the pre-school child. In *Pre-school child malnutrition—primary deterrent to human progress*. Washington: National Research Council—National Academy of Sciences, 1966.

———, CLARK, A., LANDKOF, L., & NEWELL, L. Parental body-build and developmental progress in their offspring. *Science*, 1960, **132**, 1555–1556.

——— & HASKELL, J. A. Fat thickness and developmental status in childhood and adolescence. *Amer. J. Dis. Child.*, 1960, **99**, 746–751.

———, LEWIS, A. B., & KEREWSKY, R. S. Genetic, nutritional, and maturational correlates of dental development. *J. dent. Res.*, 1965, **44**, 228–242.

——— & ROHMANN, C. G. X-linked inheritance of developmental timing in man. *Nature*, 1962, **196**, 695–696.

——— & ROHMANN, C. G. Interaction of nutrition and genetics in the timing of growth and development. *Pediat. Clin. N. Amer.*, 1966, **13**, 353–379.

——— & SHAMIR, Z. *Methods for research in human growth*. Springfield, Ill.: Charles C Thomas, 1958.

GEBER, M. & DEAN, R. F. A. Gesell test on African children. *Pediatrics*, 1957, **20**, 1055–1065.

GORLIN, R. J. REDMAN, R. S., & SHAPIRO, B. L. Effect of X-chromosome aneuploidy on jaw growth. *J. dent. Res.*, 1965, **44**, 269–282.

HEWITT, D. Some familial correlations in height, weight and skeletal maturity. *Ann. Hum. Genet.*, 1957, **22**, 26–35.

HOWE, P. E. & SCHILLER, M. Growth responses of the school child to changes in diet and environmental factors. *J. Appl. Physiol.*, 1952, **5**, 51–61.

HULL, E. I. Unpublished data on Fels subject material, 1966.

KAGAN, J. & GARN, S. M. A constitutional correlate of early intellective functioning. *J. genet. Psychol.*, 1963, **102**, 83–89.

LJUNG, B.-O. The adolescent spurt in mental growth. *Stockholm Stud. in Educ. Psych.* Uppsala: Almquist & Wiksell, 1965.

MOORE, A. U., BARNES, R. H., POND, W. G., MACLEOD, R. B., RICCIUTI, H. N., & KROOK, L. Behavioral abnormality associated with a kwashiorkor-like syndrome in pigs. *Fed. Proc.*, 1964, **23**, 397.

MURDOCK, K. & SULLIVAN, L. R. Some evidence of an adolescent increase in the rate of mental growth. *J. educ. Psychol.*, 1922, **13**, 350–356.

National Academy of Sciences-National Research Council. *Tropical health: Publication 996*. Washington: NAS-NRC, 1962.

National Academy of Sciences-National Research Council. *Pre-school child malnutrition—primary deterrent to human progress*. Washington: NAS-NRC, 1966.

NORVAL, M. A. Relationship of weight and length of infants at birth to the age at which they begin to walk alone. *J. Pediat.*, 1947, **30**, 676–678.

OWEN, G. M., FILER, L. J., JR., MARESH, M., & FOMON, S. J. Body composition of the infant. II. Sex-related difference in body composition in infancy. In F. Falkner (Ed.), *Human Development*. Philadelphia: W. B. Saunders, 1966.

PLATT, B. S. & STEWART, R. J. C. Transverse trabeculae and osteoporosis in bones in experimental protein-calorie deficiencies. *Brit. J. Nutr.*, 1962, **16**, 483–495.

QUAADE, F. *Obese children*. Copenhagen: Danish Science Press, 1955.

RIMOIN, D. L., MERIMEE, T. J., & MCKUSICK, V. A. Growth-hormone deficiency in man: An isolated, recessively inherited defect. *Science*, 1966, **152**, 1635–1637.

Scrimshaw, N. S. & Béhar, M. Protein malnutrition in young children. *Science*, 1961, **133**, 2039–2047.

———, Taylor, C. E., & Gordon, J. E. Interactions of nutrition and infection. *Amer. J. Med. Sci.*, 1959, **237**, 367–403.

Shimaguchi, S., Ashizawa, K., Endo, B., & Sakuro, H. An anthropometrical approach to the Turner's syndrome. *Zinruigaku Zassi*, 1964, **72**, 29–50.

Smith, C. A. Effect of wartime starvation in Holland upon pregnancy and its product. *Amer. J. Obst. & Gynec.*, 1947, **53**, 599–608 (a).

———. Effects of maternal undernutrition upon the newborn infant in Holland. *J. Pediat.*, 1947, **30**, 229–243 (b).

Stoch, M. B. & Smythe, P. M. Does undernutrition during infancy inhibit brain growth and subsequent intellectual development? *Arch. Dis. Child.*, 1963, **38**, 546–552.

Stoudt, H. W., Damon, A., & MacFarland, R. A. Heights and weights of white Americans. *Hum. Biol.*, 1960, **32**, 331–341.

Tanner, J. M. (Ed.). *Human growth.* Oxford: Pergamon Press, 1960.

———. *Growth at adolescence.* (2nd ed.) Oxford: Blackwell Scientific Publications, 1962.

———, Prader, A., Habich, H., & Ferguson-Smith, M. A. Genes on the Y chromosome influencing rate of maturation in man: skeletal age studies in Klinefelter's (XXY) and Turner's (XO) syndromes. *Lancet*, 1959, **2**, 141–144.

Wolff, O. H. Obesity in childhood: a study of the birth weight, the height, and the onset of puberty. *Quart. J. Med.*, 1955, **24**, 109–123.

Fundamental Motor Skills

Anna Espenschade
UNIVERSITY OF CALIFORNIA

Running, jumping, and throwing are common elements in active games. Throughout the growing years boys and girls have opportunities for frequent participation in these and so develop these capacities. Thus performance in running, jumping, and throwing may be used as an indication of motor ability, although it must be recognized that experience and training, interest and attitude play increasingly important parts in achievement. Since these are the same basic activities that are important indicators of motor development in early and middle childhood, it is possible to study age changes and sex differences over a wide age range. Two measures of jumping have been consistently used— the standing broad jump and the jump and reach. Although techniques have differed slightly in some cases, the number of comparable records is considerable. Running events have been given less frequently probably due to space limitations or safety factors. Then, too, the distances vary by age and sex. However, the number of yards per second can be computed from available records and

From pp. 430–437 (including figures and References) in "Motor Development" by Anna Espenschade from *Science and Medicine of Exercise and Sports* edited by Warren R. Johnson. Copyright © 1960 by Warren R. Johnson. Reprinted by permission of Harper & Row, Publishers, Inc.

so the data may be made roughly comparable. In throwing, the event commonly selected is a distance throw but the size and weight of ball and measurement of records differ somewhat from study to study. In so far as possible, comparable scores have been obtained. The results are presented in Table 1 and Figures 1, 2, 3, and 4. Norms in many cases are given according to classification by age, height, and weight, so the actual scores selected from these tables are those of the "average" boy or girl.

All studies agree in showing increase in scores by age for boys from the earliest measures made in childhood to those taken in the last year of high

TABLE 1

Age Changes in Motor Performance

Age	Run Yards per sec	Standing Broad Jump (inches)	Jump and Reach (inches)	Brace (score)	Distance Throw (feet)
		Boys			
5	3.8	33.7	2.5		23.6
6	4.2	37.4	4.0	5.5	32.8
7	4.6	41.6	6.1	7.5	42.3
8	5.1	46.7	8.3	9.0	57.4
9		50.4	8.5	10.0	66.6
10	5.9	54.7	11.0	11.0	83.0
11	6.1	61.0	11.5	11.1	95.0
12	6.3	64.9	12.2	12.7	104.0
13	6.5	69.3	12.5	13.1	114.0
14	6.7	73.2	13.3	14.5	123.0
15	6.8	79.5	14.8	15.2	135.0
16	7.1	88.0	16.3	16.2	144.0
17	7.2	88.4	16.9	(15.9)	153.0
		Girls			
5	3.6	31.6	2.2		14.5
6	4.1	36.2	3.5	5.5	17.8
7	4.4	40.0	5.7	7.5	25.4
8	4.6	45.9	7.7	9.0	30.0
9		51.3	8.7	10.0	38.7
10	5.8		10.5	10.5	47.0
11	6.0	52.0	11.0	11.1	54.0
12	6.1		11.2	11.8	61.0
13	6.3	62.1	11.0	11.8	70.0
14	6.2	62.7	11.8	11.9	74.5
15	6.1	63.2	12.2	11.5	75.7
16	6.0	63.0	12.0	11.8	74.0
17	5.9				

Source: References 2, 3, 4, 6, 7, 8, 9, 10, 12, 13, 14, 15, 17, 19, 20, 21, 25, 26. Scores presented are averages from available reports.

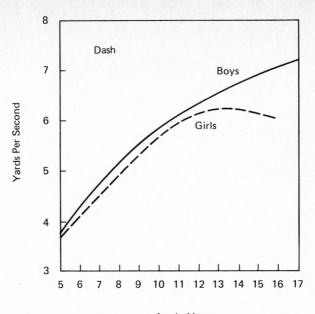

FIGURE 1.   *Running.*

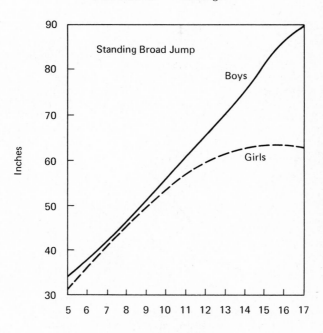

FIGURE 2.   *Standing broad jump.*

57

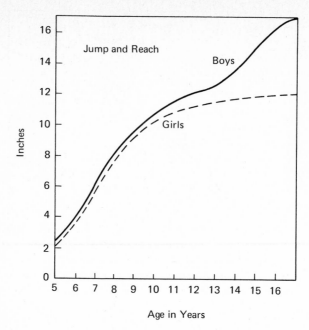

FIGURE 3.   *Jump and reach.*

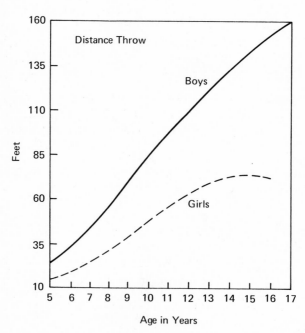

FIGURE 4.   *Distance throw.*

school. Girls show improvement throughout the early school years but scores reach their maximum as early as 13 years of age in running and jumping and show little change after 13 in distance throwing. Physical size and strength measures continue to increase well beyond this age level so this cessation of change cannot be due to attainment of physical maturity. Some authors have attributed it to adolescent changes in build and development of secondary sexual characteristics. However, there is considerable evidence of loss of interest due to cultural influences. An explanation in terms of capacity seems less tenable than one in terms of motivation.

Sex differences are present in all events at almost all age levels, but, due to the changing inflection of the curves for boys and for girls after 13 years, differences increase markedly after this time. Times in the 40- or 50-yard dash are quite close for boys and girls aged 11 and 12, but boys are consistently superior. In jumping and especially in throwing, the boys excel at every age level. The magnitude of the difference in throwing is remarkable and is out of proportion to those in any other physical measure. This difference is confined to distance throwing, however, and does not apply to target throwing at short distances. Differential practice seems insufficient to account for these results but certainly no other reasons have been advanced to date to throw light on these facts.

The relation between pubescence and performance in these basic activities has been studied on several occasions. In 1925, Atkinson (2) published an analysis of records from 9000 Philadelphia high school girls in six events. When the data were grouped according to those who had not yet reached the menarche, those who were one year beyond and so on up to seven years, no marked deviations in mean scores were found from those by chronological age. However, a study of the best performances showed that they were made by the developmental extremes. In jumping, throwing for distance, and basketball goal shooting, girls maturing very late excelled. In the running events, and in ropeclimbing, the early maturing girls excelled.

In the California Adolescent Study (8) it was possible to group the girls according to age deviation from menarche but there were very few cases studied as early as a year before this time. When chronological age was held constant, correlations between physiological maturity and performance in most events was negligible.

The picture for boys is different, however, and resembles more closely the findings in relation to strength. McCloy (15) investigated the influence of pubescence on performance and found it of some significance but discarded it as a factor in classification because of the difficulty in assessing stage of pubescence and the fact that its influence extends over a limited age range.

More recently Nevers (19) has shown the relationship between a combined score in five track events (running, jumping, shot put) and the McCloy classification index, for each of three pubescent groups. Pre- and postpubescent boys improve steadily at each class but pubescent boys of all classes seem to score approximately the same number of points. The rate of gain and the actual scores are greater for postpubescents at all overlapping indices. These results differ from those obtained by the same author in strength measures, especially in regard to performance of the pubescent group.

The determination of physiological maturity in the California Adolescent Study was on a different basis, and three phases or zones of pubescence were tentatively identified. When the several motor tests were correlated with this estimate of physiological maturity (chronological age held constant) the highest relationship was found to be with the distance throw, the lowest with the broad jump. Percentage change in performance according to zones of maturity was of especial interest as it appeared that boys in Zones II, III, and in early maturity each improved approximately equal amounts in the dash, whereas in both jumps, the largest proportion of change occurred in Zone II and in the distance throw in Zone III. Thus the pubescent boy gains steadily in running, rather abruptly and early in jumping and somewhat later in throwing (8). This is in accord with the physical growth sequence in which legs lengthen and hips widen earlier than shoulder girdle development occurs.

Each of these basic activities differs from the others not only in developmental pattern but in qualities required for performance. This is readily seen when test scores are intercorrelated. It is true, of course, that errors of measurement must be considered in studying relationships found. In running events, stop-watch timing even when carefully done is subject to considerable error. This is especially true in the case of records for young children when the distance run is only 35 or 40 yards. The additional problems in testing children—of simple, clear directions which the child surely understands, of attention span, of interest and effort, may all contribute to error. Experienced experimenters, however, have obtained reliabilities in running events of .88 (10) for 4–6-year-olds, and coefficients of the order of .9 are frequently reported for older children.

Jumping can be measured still more accurately, especially the broad jump. Reliability coefficients range from .82–.89 for elementary school children to .95 or above for senior high school boys. Throwing tends to be highly reliable when reasonable care in procedures is maintained. Coefficients of the order of .9 to .98 may be obtained.

It should be noted that measurement in these events is least consistent in young children and in girls and in the case of older boys is especially reliable. Quite possibly motivation is a factor here. Certainly reliability may be expected to influence the intercorrelations computed between the several events. Actually, very few studies are available on young children in which this interrelationship has been studied. Indeed, the literature does not yield many studies at any ages in which exactly the same events have been interrelated. Since standard track and field events for boys ordinarily include a shot-put and it has been considered easier to administer than a throw for distance, many studies on boys have selected this event. McCloy (15) has shown that either a distance throw or a shot-put may be used in combination with running and jumping to predict "total points" on a larger number of track and field events for boys. The majority of physical activity programs for girls do not include a shot-put, however. As the technique of performance must be learned, this event ordinarily cannot be used as a test for girls.

Intercorrelations between the dash, broad jump, jump and reach, and indoor baseball (softball) throw for distance as reported by a number of investigators are given in Table 2. Certainly no consistent trends are evidenced. There does seem to be a tendency for relationships between events for boys to be

TABLE 2
Intercorrelations Reported by Various Investigators

	DASH WITH BROAD JUMP			DASH WITH DISTANCE THROW	
AGE	BOYS	GIRLS	REF.	BOYS	GIRLS
49–78 mo.	.53		(10)	.36	
1st 3 grades	.475	.576	(5)	.244	.442
10–14 yr.		.61	(16)		.43
10–13 yr.	.665		(unpub.)	.502	
Jr. H.S.	.642		(22)	.545	
	.787		(23)		
	.64	.61	(8)	.38	.51
	.67	.64	(8)	.48	.44
Sr. H.S.	.44		(15)		
	.76		(15)		
	.58	.60	(11)		
	.48	.45	(8)	.38	.41
	.49		(8)	.24	.23
		.57	(20)		

	BROAD JUMP AND DISTANCE THROW			BROAD JUMP WITH JUMP AND REACH	
AGE	BOYS	GIRLS	REF.	BOYS	GIRLS
49–78 mo.	.41		(10)	.53	
1st 3 grades	.311	.441	(5)	.401	.547
8 year	.58	.35	(24)	.63	.62
10–13 yr.	.53		(unpub.)		
10–14 yr.			(16)		.49
Jr. H.S.	.721		(22)		
	.39	.45	(8)	.42	.30
	.60	.51	(8)	.45	.37
Sr. H.S.	.46	.48	(8)	.65	.56
	.47	.42	(8)	.51	.64
			(1)	.604	

greater at the junior high school level than before or after this time. In the case of the girls, however, correlations are of approximately the same order at all age levels. Those between dash and broad jump are approximately .6 while those between dash and distance throw and between distance throw and broad jump average more nearly .4. More investigators have reported figures for boys and less consistency appears among these. It would certainly be premature in the light of the available evidence to draw conclusions in regard to the organization of motor abilities in children of 6–18 years.

Nor are factor analysis studies adequate to throw real light on this subject.

Analyses of this type have been made for the most part on data from college men. Selection of tests given and resulting emphasis in factors extracted has been different in the different studies. Although strength or power and speed or velocity are identified in practically all cases, these two factors are not adequate to account for all components underlying performances in running, jumping, and throwing. And the relative importance of even these factors is not firmly established.

In tracing the course of development of postural-locomotor control from infancy through adolescence, two basic concepts emerge. Structure and function are found to be closely interrelated at all times; there are wide individual differences in rate of maturation, but the over-all pattern of development is the same for all. In infancy, developing neural structures especially seem to bring about rapid changes in motor behavior. Sex differences in rate of maturation may be observed in childhood in the earlier age at which girls perform such activities as hopping and skipping in comparison to boys. At puberty, a marked change in rate of development is again evident. In boys, the postpubescent period is one of continuing development in motor performance; in girls little change appears after puberty. It must be recognized that the marked sex differences at adolescence are due in part to experience and training, interests and attitudes, as well as to capacity.

Motor performances dependent upon strength and power are closely related to size and build at all ages. Balance and coordination show little relationship to physique or strength at any one time but do increase with age. There is some evidence to show retardation in growth in balance during the period of most rapid physical growth, at puberty. In spite of these differing growth patterns, measures of coordination, of running, jumping, and throwing are substantially intercorrelated at all ages, 4–17. It is possible, that the cross-sectional data, including as they do a range of maturity levels, may obscure the true picture here as is true for the curves of growth. It may be that maturity itself operates as a factor to increase the size of the intercorrelations.

Extensive data on the same children over this entire age span are needed to answer fully the questions raised in this review, but a variety of investigations of smaller scope may make substantial contributions to this field.

References

1. ANDERSON, THERESA, & McCLOY, C. H. The measurement of sports ability in high school girls. *Res. quart.*, 1947, **18**, 2–11.
2. ATKINSON, R. K. A motor efficiency study of eight thousand New York City high school boys. *Amer. Phys. Educ. Rev.*, 1924, **29**, 56–59.
3. ———. A study of athletic ability of high school girls. *Amer. Phys. Educ. Rev.*, 1925, **30**, 389–399.
4. BLISS, J. G. A study of progression based on age, sex, and individual differences in strength and skill. *Amer. Phys. Educ. Rev.*, Jan & Feb. 1927, **32**, 11–21; **32**, 85–99.
5. CARPENTER, AILEEN. Tests of motor educability for the first three grades. *Child Develpm.*, 1940, **11**, 293–99.
6. COZENS, F. W., CUBBERLEY, HAZEL, & NEILSON, N. P. *Achievement scales in physical education activities for secondary school girls and college women.* New York: Barnes, 1937.

7. ———, Trieb, M. H., & Neilson, N. P. *Physical education achievement scales in activities for boys in secondary schools.* New York: Barnes, 1936.
8. Espenschade, Anna. Motor performance in adolescence. *Soc. Res. in Child Develpm. Monogr.*, 1940, **5**, 1.
9. ———. Development of motor coordination in boys and girls. *Res. quart.*, 1947, **18**, 30–43.
10. Hartman, Doris M. The hurdle jump as a measure of the motor proficiency of young children. *Child Develpm.*, 1943, **14**, 201–211.
11. Hutto, L. E. Measurement of the velocity factor and of athletic power in high school boys. *Res. quart.*, 1938, **9**, 109–128.
12. Jenkins, L. M. *A comparative study of motor achievements of children five, six and seven years of age.* New York: Teachers College, Columbia University, Contribution to Education, no. 414, 1930.
13. Kane, R. J., & Meredith, H. V. Ability in the standing broad jump of elementary school children 7, 9, and 11 years of age. *Res. quart.*, 1952, **23**, 198–208.
14. Latchaw, Marjorie. Measuring selected motor skills in fourth, fifth and sixth grades. *Res. quart.*, 1954, **25**, 439–499.
15. McCloy, C. H. *Measurement of athletic power.* New York: Barnes, 1932.
16. McCraw, L. W. A factor analysis of motor learning. *Res. quart.*, 1949, **20**, 316–335.
17. Neilson, N. P., & Cozens, F. W. *Achievement scales in physical education activities.* Sacramento: State Dept. of Education, 1934.
18. Nelson, Caroline E. The effect of motor ability and previous training upon the achievement and learning of sport skills in the ninth grade. Unpublished M.A. thesis, Univ. of California, 1950.
19. Nevers, J. E. The effects of physiological age on motor achievement. *Res. quart.*, 1948, **19**, 103–110.
20. Physical performance levels for high school girls. *Education for Victory*, 1945, **3**, 1–4.
21. Poole, Margaret. Physical performance levels for high school girls. Unpublished M.A. thesis, Univer. of California, 1946.
22. Powell, Elizabeth, & Howe, E. C. Motor ability tests for high school girls. *Res. quart.*, 1939, 10, 81–88.
23. Ragsdale, C. E., & Brechenfeld, I. J. The organization of physical and motor traits in junior high school boys. *Res. quart.*, 1934, **5**, 47–55.
24. Seashore, H. G. The development of a beam walking test and its use in measuring development of balance in children. *Res. quart.*, 1947, **18**, 246–259.
25. Seils, L. G. The relationship between measures of physical growth and gross motor performance of primary-grade school children. *Res. quart.*, 1951, **22**, 244–260.
26. Temple, Andree. Motor abilities of white and negro children of 7, 8, and 9 years of age. Unpublished M.A. thesis, Univer. of California, 1952.

Personality Characteristics of Converted Left Handers*

Harben Boutourline Young
HARVARD SCHOOL OF PUBLIC HEALTH

Robert Knapp
WESLEYAN UNIVERSITY

Summary.—*Left-handed children in Italy are subjected to social opprobrium and in school are forced to forego their natural disposition in favor of right handedness. Italian-American children, on the other hand, are free from such coercion. In this study three samples of Italian children are compared with a sample of Italian-American children on personality source traits taken from Cattell's High School Personality Questionnaire. Left-handed Italian children show a consistent and statistically very secure elevation on Factor I of the Cattell scale, a finding unparalleled in the data from the American sample. While the interpretation of this particular finding is not entirely clear, it does suggest that left-handed children show a higher degree of sensitivity and self-centeredness in consequence of their forced lateral conversion.*

The prevalence of left handedness has been estimated as varying from .5 to 13 per cent in different populations (Verhaegen & Ntumba, 1964; Belmont & Birch, 1963). The figure undoubtedly varies not only because of genetic influences but also according to the criteria used for determining left lateral dominance. For example, if writing with the left hand were used as the criterion, it might be that in the Northeastern United States the true figure would be somewhat raised whereas in Italy there would be apparently zero prevalence of left handers. In a cross-cultural study of young Americans of Southern Italian descent and Southern Italians in Italy we found for the United States resident population that all left handers wrote with the left hand and there was even one basic right hander who had joined them. In Italy although the true prevalence was the same as in America (about 10 per cent) not one *S* was a left-handed writer.

History demonstrates that considerable pains have been taken to show the inferiority of left handers. The Concise Oxford Dictionary gives among others the following meanings of left handed: "awkward, clumsy, ambiguous, double-edged, of doubtful sincerity or validity, ill-omened, sinister." Roget's Thesaurus adds for good measure, "gauche, gauchipawed, unskillful." The dominant note of pity becomes tinged with alarm as one examines further the meaning of "sinister:" of evil omen, ill-looking, of villainous aspect, wicked.

Reprinted with permission of author and publisher: Young, H. B., and Knapp, R. H. Personality characteristics of converted left handers. *Perceptual and Motor Skills*, 1966, *23*, 35–40.

* The financial support of the Grant Foundation, 130 E. Fifty-ninth Street, New York, and the Wenner-Gren Foundation for Anthropological Research, 14 E. Seventy-first Street, New York, is gratefully acknowledged.

However, one by one the old ideas have had to yield. Left handers are neither less intelligent, nor lower achievers, nor more clumsy (Clark, 1957; Ihinger, 1963). There is not a higher proportion of left lateral dominants among children with reading disability (Belmont & Birch, 1965). The swing of the pendulum has presented some interesting hypotheses still to be tested, e.g., are left handers different in relation to originality and creativity? But it is an over-all impression that left lateral dominants do not differ from right handers, at least in tolerant cultures. This is a contrast to evidence that ambilaterality may be associated with poor ego strength and more maladjustment (Palmer, 1963).

The problem of the effects of forced change was presented to us by the situation described in the first paragraph of this paper where the entire population of Italian resident left handers (48 boys in a population of 724) were obliged to convert to the right side. In America no opprobrium attaches to left handedness, children are not required to "convert," and this quality is even often considered an advantage in various sports. The left-handed person in America suffers few penalties if any. In Italy, it is quite otherwise. Left handedness is considered both a moral and personal defect and regarded with widespread suspicion. The term "sinister" means both "left" and "dangerous" in Italian. As a result of this the left handed in Italy are subject to a peculiar and frequently painful personal experience not shared by their American counterparts. We were drawn to explore possible differential effects upon their development in their differing circumstances.

METHOD

SUBJECTS Ss were all males in the age range 13 to 15. Each S from Boston, Rome, and Palermo had four grandparents from the South of Italy (defined as the regions comprising Mezzogiorno, excluding Sardegna). The Boston boys were second-generation born. The Florence boys were students at the junior and middle high schools. They were distributed as follows:

CITY	N_{tot}	LEFT LATERAL DOMINANT	
		N	%
Boston	95	11	12
Rome	127	10	8
Palermo	108	11	10
Florence	489	27	6
Total	819	59	7

TESTS OF LATERAL DOMINANCE AND PERSONALITY SOURCE TRAITS   Clark's (1957) tests of laterality were employed.

(a) *Handedness* was determined from three tests. (1) *Clark No. 18, Throwing.* —A small box was placed on a chair. The boy stood at about 2 yards distance with the ball on the table in front of him. He was requested to pick up the ball and throw it into the box. (2) *Clark No. 12, Reaching.*—The boy was seated with his arms hanging down. The tester stood behind him holding a cylinder over his head almost out of reach but in an equally favorable position for either side. The boy was asked to reach up and take the tube. (3) *Clark No. 1, Manual rotation.*—Here a small screw-top bottle, filled with colored counters, was used. The task was to remove the top, take the counters, arrange them, put them back and then replace the top. The task was performed on three occasions and note was made of which hand was used for manipulation of the top and the counters.

(b) *Foot* preference was based on three tasks. (1) *Clark No. 5, Kicking.*—A rubber ball was placed three yards from a chair. The boy was asked to kick the ball between the legs of the chair. (2) *Clark No. 17, Hopping.*—The boy stood with his back against the wall and his feet together. He was instructed on command to commence hopping to the far side of the room. (3) *Clark No. 8, Stepping.*—The boy stood with his back against the wall and his heels touching it. On the command go he was to take two steps out from the wall.

Each of the above tests was performed three times. Ss were not informed that these were tests for lateral dominance and were left with the impression that the examiner was interested in motor skills and agility. Three tests for ear dominance and four for eye dominance were also performed, but these will not be reported here since eye and ear dimensions are not subject to coercive correction in Italy.

In order to adhere to Clark's findings as to the relative importance of these tests, a double weighting was accorded to throwing and kicking. Ss were then classified as marked right (R2), moderate right (R1), ambidextrous (0), moderate left (L1), and marked left (L2). In each of the four centers, Boston, Palermo, Rome, and Florence, a group of left handers was selected from the available samples. A control group of right handers, in every instance twice the number of left-handers, was selected from the remaining Ss in each city. In all three cities the right-handed control group was selected in such a fashion that their average Raven Progressive Matrix score (Raven, 1956; Tesi & Young, 1962) was equated with that of the left-handed Ss. The Ss then answered the High School Personality Questionnaire (Cattell & Beloff, 1957; Cattell, et al., 1961), a factor scaled instrument designed to measure personality source traits.

RESULTS

The composite score for lateral dimensions for the hand and foot tests yielded a Pearson correlation of .79 among the boys included in this study. Table 1 gives the mean raw scores for each factor of the High School Personality Questionnaire for right- and left-handed boys in each center. Between right and left handers there are no significant differences in Boston. A significant difference on Factor A (Schizothymia vs. Cyclothymia) for Palermo (left handers are more schizothymic) is not sustained in Rome or Florence. A significant difference on Factor C (ego strength) for Palermo (left handers have less ego strength) is not sustained in Rome or Florence. On Factor E (submissiveness vs. dominance) the Florence left handers are significantly more submissive but there is a reverse trend (neither significant) in Palermo and Rome. On Factor F (desurgency vs. surgency) the left-handed Palermo Ss are significantly less

TABLE 1

Raw Factor Scores on the HSPQ for Right and Left Handers in Four Cities

City	N	A	B	C	D	E	F	G	H	I	J	O	Q²	Q³	Q⁴
Boston L	11	5.5	6.7	6.1	4.7	4.8	5.4	5.9	5.3	3.8	5.6	4.5	6.6	4.9	4.3
Boston R	22	5.8	6.6	5.2	5.0	5.2	5.5	6.0	5.7	4.0	5.3	4.2	5.9	5.0	4.1
		$p = .05$		NS $p < .01$									NS		
Palermo L	11	3.9	6.3	4.2	4.8	5.3	4.6	6.0	6.2	4.8	5.1	5.9	5.6	4.2	4.6
Palermo R	22	4.9	6.4	5.8	5.1	4.5	6.2	6.1	6.2	3.4	5.2	4.9	6.0	4.5	4.9
		$p = .05$		$p < .01$			$p < .02$			$p = .02$		$p < .10$ $> .05$			
Rome L	10	4.7	7.6	5.5	4.2	5.2	5.9	6.2	5.4	4.6	4.6	5.8	6.7	5.0	4.9
Rome R	20	5.2	6.7	5.8	4.5	4.7	5.6	6.4	6.1	3.3	4.9	5.3	6.6	5.0	4.8
										$p < .10$ $> .05$					
Florence L	27	5.4	8.4	5.3	4.3	4.2	5.6	5.9	5.4	4.1	5.2	5.8	6.4	4.8	5.0
Florence R	49	5.5	7.6	5.5	5.1	5.3	5.4	5.5	5.2	3.0	5.1	5.9	6.2	4.3	4.9
						$p < .01$				$p < .02$					

enthusiastic and happy-go-lucky, but this is not sustained in the other two Italian centers. Only on Factor I (harria vs. premsia) is there a marked consistent trend in all three centers. The left handers are consistently more premsic, that is, more demanding, impatient, subjective, dependent, hypochondriacal. Accordingly, it will be seen that only Factor I yields consistent differences in all three Italian cities between right and left handers. The differences on Factors A, C, and F observed in the Palermo sample are not sustained in the other two cities. There is reason to believe that the cultures of Sicily and Southern Italy imposed greater penalties upon the left-handed child than those of Central, and especially of Northern Italy. But we shall not attempt here to advance any conclusive explanation of the special findings applying to the Palermo sample.

TABLE 2

Mean Scores on Cattell's Factor I for Right and Left Handers in Three Italian Cities

		ROME	PALERMO	FLORENCE
Left	N	10	11	27
	M	4.60	4.73	4.15
Right	N	20	22	49
	M	3.35	3.41	2.98

$$F_{handedness} = 14.88, \text{df} = 1/135, p = .01$$
$$F_{cities} = 1.13, \text{df} = 1/135, \text{n.s.}$$

Table 2 presents an analysis of variance which confirms the overall significant association of left lateral dominance with high score on Factor I, significant beyond the .001 level of confidence.

DISCUSSION

The results seem perfectly clear but not so the cause. It is tempting to attribute the difference to the forced conversion, but apart from such conversion there is still the relatively more hostile environment to assess.

It is our impression that since World War II much of the opprobrium associated with left handedness has dissolved, at least among upper social classes in Italy. On the other hand, it still remains the practice to require left-handed children to convert in school to right handedness in writing. Were opprobrium and not conversion the prime source of elevation on Factor I, we might expect this factor to be lower among Ss from high social classes. This proves on inspection not to be the case, suggesting that the duress of forced conversion in school may be the primary determinant of our finding.

Factor I is regarded by Cattell as having an association with neuroticism but not with anxiety. There is evidence that it is associated with over-protective treatment in early childhood. But there is also evidence of association with insecurity in the child (Cattell, personal communication, 1965). Cattell considers this factor as being strongly affected by the environment. It is clear, in any event, that the personal qualities associated with this factor must be related to hypersensitivity and heightened self-preoccupation. It was striking that the separation of right- and left-handed Ss on Factor I so incisive in Italy is not confirmed in our sample of Boston children.

Clark (1957) has presented suggestive evidence that Ss who had been forcibly converted from left to right did less well on achievement tests than right handers paired for intelligence. Sielicka, et al. (1963) have observed a high proportion of neurotic symptoms in 83 left-handed children who had been forcibly converted. It must be concluded that attention should be given to the psychological fate of left-handed children, especially in those cultures which, through opprobrium or forced conversion in school, force them to abandon their natural disposition or face the disadvantage of social penalties.

References

BELMONT, L., & BIRCH, H. G. Lateral dominance and right-left awareness in normal children. *Child Develpm.*, 1963, 34, 257–270.

———, & BIRCH, H. G. Lateral dominance, lateral awareness and reading disability. *Child Develpm.*, 1965, 36, 57–71.

CATTELL, R. B., & BELOFF, J. *The High School Personality Questionnaire.* Champaign, Ill.; Institute for Personality and Ability Testing, 1957.

———, BELOFF, J., & COAN, R. W. *The High School Personality Questionnaire.* (Translation and adaptation into Italian language and culture by the Harvard Florence Research Project in collaboration with the Psychological Division of the Italian National Research Center) Florence: Organizzazioni Speciali, 1961.

CLARK, M. M. *Left handedness.* London: Univer. of London Press, 1957.

IHINGER, R. F. Some relationships among laterality groups at three grade levels in performances on the California Achievement Tests. In California Association of School Psychologists and Psychometrists, *Towards a professional identity in school psychology.* Los Angeles: Author, 1963. Pp. 70–74.

PALMER, R. D. Hand differentiation and psychological functioning. *J. Pers.*, 1963, 31, 445–461.

RAVEN, J. C. *Guide to using Progressive Matrices 1938.* (Revised Order 1956). London: Lewis, 1956.

SIELICKA, M., BOGDANOWICZ, I., DILLING-OSTROWSKA, E., SZELOZYNSKA, K., & KAC-ZENSKA, M. [Forced use of the right hand in lefthanded children as a cause of neurosis.] *Pediat. Polska*, 1963, 38, 405–408.

TESI, G., & YOUNG, B. H. [A standardization of Raven's Progressive Matrices 1938 (Revised Order 1956).] *Arch. Psicol. Neurol. Psichiat.*, 1962, 23, 455–464.

VERHAEGEN, P., & NTUMBA, A. Note on the frequency of left-handedness in African children. *J. educ. Psychol.*, 1964, 55, 89–90.

Chapter 2

Courtesy Education Development Center

Intellectual Development

The central problem of the school age, the development of the sense of industry, requires the child to solve intellectual problems and to develop intellectual skills, along with the motor coordinations and social skills which also contribute to his adequacy. Intellectual development proceeds through growth in three main modes: thinking, imagination, and language. These three activities are intimately related and dependent on one another.

Characteristics of Thinking During Middle Childhood

As was true during the preschool period, an important part of cognition is the taking in of information and processing it into meaningful and useful form. Information and experience are stored as memories, to be tapped when needed. When memories are in the form of words, they are likely to be more easily available. The outstanding cognitive developments during this period are increased freedom and control in thinking and increased understanding of relationships between events and/or symbols. The child takes satisfaction in his feeling that there exists a systematic, productive way of thinking about experience and in his conviction that he can think thus [42, p. 139].

Flexibility of Thought

While the preschool child reacts rather promptly to his perceptions of the moment, the school-age child can delay his response while he takes several aspects of the situation into account. His thoughts range back and forth in various directions, dealing with more than one perception at a time, comparing them, considering them in relation to past experience and knowledge. Thus he shows more control, as well as flexibility. With his increasing store of memories, his past becomes more and more useful for evaluating and interpreting the present. The preschool child is egocentric or centered in his thinking, limited in such a way that he cannot consider and weigh several pertinent factors at one time; the school-age child is less egocentric or more decentered in his thinking. Another aspect of the immobility of preschool thinking is that the child is centered on his own point of view. With his growing flexibility of thought, the older child can look at situations from the points of view of other people.

The child's increasing mobility of thought enters into everything that he does: his classifying, ordering, and dealing with numbers, his language, his social relationships, and self concepts. His thinking is limited in flexibility, however. He tends to think about concrete things rather than about abstractions.

Reversibility is one aspect of the flexible and controlled thinking which emerges during middle childhood. Reversibility has two meanings, both of which apply. First, the child can think an act and then think it undone. He can think himself partway through a sequence of action, return to the first of it, and then start out in another direction. In contrast to thoughts, motor acts and perceptions are irreversible, since they cannot be undone. Reversibility is one of the most important differences between thought and action. When the child can try out different courses of action mentally, instead of having to touch and see in order to believe, he has the advantage of a quicker and more powerful control over his environment and himself.

The second meaning of reversibility is that any operation can be canceled by an opposite operation. For example, the operation of subtracting 3 from 5 is canceled by the operation of adding 3 to 2. $5 - 3 = 2$ is canceled by $2 + 3 = 5$. Another example is this: all children minus all girls equals all boys; all boys plus all girls equals all children. Also: hemisphere minus torrid zone minus frigid zone equals temperate zone; temperate zone plus frigid zone plus torrid zone equals hemisphere. The child learns that there are certain kinds of things which can be taken apart and put back together again into their original form and that he can do this dissembling and reassembling in his thoughts.

Concrete Operations

The name that Piaget gives to the stage of cognition which lasts from about 7 to 11 is the period of concrete operations. At this time, the child understands and uses certain principles of relationships between things and ideas. In this understanding and using, he operates on (does something to) objects, ideas, and symbols. As was true in infancy, "to know an object is to act on it" [44, p. 8]. But now the action is interiorized. The child adds and subtracts. He classifies and orders. He applies rules to social situations. Each operation fits into a system, and the systems fit together. The operation two-plus-two-equals-four fits into a system of addition, which is part of a system of arithmetic.

The infant's cognitive behavior is sensorimotor, concerned with simple adjustments to the immediate present, symbolic behavior being completely absent. The preschool child begins to use symbols in some kinds of representational thought. Beginning at around 7 years, children can use symbols consistently to perform acts of cognition which are abstracted and freed from complete dependence on sensory stimulation. In this stage of concrete operations, the child mentally performs acts which he formerly really carried out physically. The adolescent can think in more abstract terms than the child, however. During the years between 7 and 11, the child makes great strides in understanding principles of relationships and in his use of symbols for manipulating or operating on experience. Developing certain logical rules in dealing with his experiences, he performs two important operations: classifying and ordering.

Classifying. Although children in the preoperational period are dominated by their immediate perceptions in their grouping of objects, children in the stage of concrete operations can reflect upon and choose the qualities by which they group. From the experience of picking out a group of objects with something in common, the child internalizes (creates a mental structure of) the common quality into a concept of a class. Strolling along the beach, he collects small, hard objects into his pail, squats down and sorts them into a pile of shells and a pile of stones. From these activities, he comes to think of shells and of stones. He builds a concept *shell* and a concept *stone*. From more experiences on the beach, he can build concepts of bivalves and univalves, of clams and scallops, of marine life and terrestrial life. An important aspect of his understanding of classes is that he can also think of subclasses. Suppose our shell collector, in the stage of concrete operations, has his bivalves sorted into a pile of six scallop shells and ten clam shells. Ask him, "Do you have more clam shells or more shells?" He will know that he has more shells. His preschool brother, however, who knows full well the difference between clams and scallops, will most likely answer, "More clam shells." The younger child cannot compare a part with the whole which includes the part; the older child can. When the younger child thinks of the clam shells (the subclass), it seems as though he takes them out of the shells (the class), leaving the scallop shells (the other subclass), with which he then compares the clam shells. It has been found that if a child who is close to the maturity necessary for solving a class inclusion problem is presented with it verbally, he is more likely to succeed than if he has a visual presentation [72]. For example, a verbal presentation was "Suppose I had six jackets and two hats. Would I have more jackets or more things to wear?" The corresponding visual presentation shows six jackets with two hats. The younger child, seeing the pictures, tends to compare hats with jackets instead of jackets with the total number of objects. When the strong influence of perception is removed, it

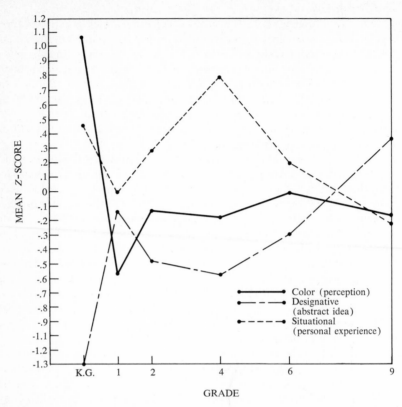

Figure 2–1. Age changes in the use of three different bases for classifying objects. Younger children use personal experience and perception more and abstract ideas less than older children.

Source: Adapted from A. E. Goldman and M. Levine, "A Developmental Study of Object Sorting," *Child Development*, **34**, 649–666.

seems, the child on the brink of concrete operations has a better chance with this problem.

A very cherished activity of children in the elementary school years is collecting. Children collect stamps, butterflies, coins, matchbooks, trading cards, evergreen cones, rocks, and so on. Although some of the motivation for collecting may be imitation of peers or receiving a stamp book for Christmas, the main push comes from classifying as an emergent ability. Just as the youngster thrilled to riding his tricycle after he mastered the pedals, he now enjoys collecting for the sake of collecting. And just as he first splashed colors onto his nursery school easel without planning ahead, he starts out as a rather indiscriminate collector. Any stamps— any cones—will do. Crude classifying is satisfying at first. Then finer classifications are made as the child grows in his ability to conceptualize more and more complicated classificatory systems. As the child matures, he classifies more and more on the basis of abstract ideas and less on the basis of perception or personal experience. The results from a test of sorting objects, given at several age levels from kindergarten through college, and also to adult scientists, proves these points [19]. Figure

2–1 shows the prevalence of three different bases for classifying, as they occurred at the various levels of maturity. Classifying on basis of perception is illustrated by the line for color, which drops sharply between kindergarten and first grade and remains fairly constant after second grade. Situation, as a basis for classifying, represents personal experience, as, for example, when the subject explains his selection by saying, "You buy them all in a hardware store." This rationale for sorting is high in the early grades, dropping steadily after fourth grade. Classification in terms of an abstract idea occurs seldom in the kindergarten and frequently in the higher grades.

Relations and Ordering. From the experience of arranging things in order, the child internalizes concepts of relations. A little girl arranges her dolls so that they can watch her dance for them, the tallest doll on the bottom step, the next tallest on the second step, and so on up to the shortest doll on top. The child's activities are preparing her to have concepts of decreasing and increasing size, concepts of relations. The place where the term *relations* is commonly used, in regard to family members, is a true example of concepts of relations. Many experiences must go into building the concepts on which family trees hang.

Ordering activities occur often in children's play. Objects collected can be ordered inside their classes—all the coins arranged in order of their minting dates, the evergreen cones according to length. Children may line each other up, using height as a criterion, for the purpose of taking turns. Just as they enjoy using their newly developed ability to classify, so do they enjoy ordering the world in terms of various relations.

Children find the world ordered for them, too. The kindergarten teacher lines them up for going to the bathroom and getting morning milk. Perhaps she helps them to order sounds in terms of high to low or colors from light to dark. Early in the school career, the child meets that remarkable ordering device, the alphabet. An ever-widening collection of symbols called words, he finds, can be ordered in terms of their structure and its relation to the alphabet. He learns that many other kinds of relations and orders exist and that it is his job to learn them. Relations of events in time are called history. Relations of places in space are called geography. (Relate time relations and space relations and you get geology and astronomy, but these come later in school. The child in the stage of concrete operations is aware of them, however.)

Numbers are concepts derived from the operations of classifying and ordering. A cardinal number is a class. *Four* means a group of four apples or four auto-mobiles or four abracadabras. An ordinal number is a relation. Fourth is related to third and fifth in size and position. A real understanding of *four* requires an understanding of *fourth*, and vice versa. Thus classifying and ordering are interlocking and essential processes in the development of number concepts. Understanding of the principle of conservation of quantity is basic to development of the concept of number [45, p. 23].

Ordering Space. The infant has early experiences in space. Through looking, touching, manipulating, and moving, he discovers that he is a separate object in space and that he has an inside and an outside. Bodily experience continues to be a source of discovery and of material for building concepts of space. Lateralization is a body-based way of ordering in space which is important in communication and in thinking. The development of laterality has already been considered in the previous chapter, since it related so closely to the body. (See pages 29–32.) When

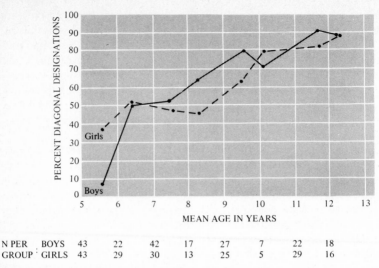

N PER   BOYS 43   22   42   17   27   7   22   18
GROUP GIRLS 43   29   30   13   25   5   29   16

Figure 2–2. Percent diagonal designations in self-drawings by sex and age.

SOURCE: Reprinted by permission from E. Gellert, "Children's Lateralizations of Human Figures: Analysis of a Developmental Transition," *The Journal of Psychology*, **67**, 107–126. Copyright © 1967, The Journal Press.

children first attribute sidedness to another person, they act as though the other person were a mirror image. Thus the right hand of the other person is the hand directly opposite the child's own right hand. Children between 5 and 13 were asked to make drawings of themselves and then to indicate in the drawing which hand would be used for writing [17]. Transposing orientation, the assigning of right and left to the sides diagonally opposite, increased quite steadily with age, as can be seen in Figure 2–2. The majority of 5-year-olds lateralized mirror-wise, with the girls considerably less likely to do so than boys. By 12 years, about 90 percent transposed. A probable explanation is that transposition occurred as the children grew less egocentric and more able to put themselves into the place of another person.

Measuring of space is done at first with the body and later with an independent measuring tool, when the child discovers that the whole is composed of a number of parts which can be taken apart and added together and that one unit can be substituted for another. Piaget demonstrates the child's understanding of measurement by showing him a tower of blocks on a table and asking him to build another, just like it, on a lower or higher table, of blocks of a different size [43]. The pre-operational child builds his tower to the visual level of the model, comparing the two by stepping back and sighting them. A slightly more mature child lays a rod across the tops of the two towers. The next step in appreciation of the problem is to notice that the bases are not the same and to suggest moving his tower to the table where the model is. Since this is not permitted, he then looks for a measuring instrument. He most likely uses his own hands, placing one at the top and the other at the bottom of his tower and moving to the other tower. Then he may line up a point on his own body with the tower. When the idea of a measuring tool, probably a third tower, finally occurs to him, it indicates logical reasoning. He has reasoned that if the measuring instrument is the same as his tower, then it is the same as the model, and the two towers are the same. That is, $B = C$ and $B = A$. Therefore $A = C$. Still later he realizes that he can use a longer rod and mark the point of his tower's height and then later that he can use a shorter rod by counting the number of times he applies it.

Ordering Time. When children were asked to reproduce brief intervals of time, they did not show improvement between 6 and 12 years of age [16]. As adults do, they too overestimated time presented aurally more than they did time presented visually. When asked to reproduce rhythms, results were different. Auditory rhythms were reproduced more accurately than visual. Also, errors in both modalities decreased with age. It may be that hearing is more basic than seeing for perception of rhythm.

Age-related improvements occur in estimating and conceiving of long periods of time. For example, a large number of students in elementary school, high school, and college were asked to estimate ages of adults [55]. Sudden increases in accuracy were noted at the fourth grade level and in college. While an appreciation of historical time is still developing throughout the school-age span, and formal thinking about history is impossible until around 16 [35], children profit from learning about past events and earlier cultures. They can eventually order such knowledge in time as they become able to handle more complex time concepts.

Conservation

As cognitive structures develop, the child builds a more and more permanent, stable, and inclusive picture of the world, the people in it, himself and their inter-relationships. As a baby, he learned about the permanence of objects, that things continued to exist even when he could not perceive them. As a preschool child, he began to form concepts of space, relations, time, and number, but he was dominated by his perceptions. As concepts become more organized the child achieves the idea of constancy. He realizes that certain properties are invariant (remain the same) in spite of transformations (changes) in other properties. Substance, quantity, and number are seen as permanent. Conservation of number, for example, means that the child realizes that 7 is always 7, whether it consists of $3 + 4$, $5 + 2$, :::., ...:.., ****, or any other arrangement.

Conservation of substance means that the child realizes that the amount of material stays the same if nothing is added or taken away, even though the shape and/or position of the material change. One of Piaget's methods of exploring a child's conservation of substance is with two equal balls of clay. After the child has agreed that they contain equal amounts, the examiner rolls one ball into a sauage and asks, "Which has more clay?" The child in the stage of concrete operations will say that they are the same, while the child who has not achieved conservation of substance will reply either that the ball is larger (because it is fatter) or the sausage is larger (because it is longer). A variation on this test is to break one ball into little bits and ask whether the ball or the heap of bits contains more clay. If the child cannot conserve, he will say that the bits contain less (because they are smaller) or that they contain more (because there are more pieces). Conservation of substance can be demonstrated with liquid, starting with the same amounts of lemonade in two identical glasses and then pouring the contents of one glass into a thinner or a fatter glass. Or liquid from one glass can be poured into two and questions asked about whether the amount is the same. When the clay ball and sausage test was

Table 2–1 Percentage of Children at Each Year in the Junior School (Ages 7 through 11) in Various Stages of Understanding Conservation of Amount

No. of Children	Stage 3 Conservation %	Stage 2 Transition %	Stage 1 Non-Conservation %
1st year (83)	36	33	31
2nd year (65)	68	12	20
3rd year (99)	74	15	11
4th year (75)	86	9	5

SOURCE: Reprinted by permission from K. Lovell, *Growth of Basic Mathematical and Scientific Concepts in Children* (New York: Philosophical Library, Inc., 1962), Table 1, p. 63.

given to 322 English children between 7 and 12, results showed how conservation ability was distributed [36]. In stage 1, nonconservation, the child denied conservation. In stage 2, he sometimes admitted it, sometimes denied it. In stage 3, he was firmly convinced of conservation.

The idea of conservation is by no means an all-or-none notion which the child either has or does not have. One investigator [76] cautions that conservation should not be thought of as a particular concept but as "an index of a set of semi-inter-related cognitive attitudes." Conservation of number of kindergarten and first grade children was found to be highly related to their success in making differentiations between the magnitudes width versus depth, length versus thickness, height versus width, and age versus height. The mastery of these distinctions occurred before development of conservation of number. As can be seen by Table 2–1, there is a transition stage for the conservation of amount. Research shows that for different situations that have to do with *amount*, conservation is achieved at different times [34]. For example, many children recognized that there was the same amount of rubber in a rubber band before and after stretching before they appreciated conservation in the clay ball and sausage experiment. Furthermore, some of the nonconservers of the ball and sausage situation were able to conserve when liquid was poured into a glass of different shape. Conservation is not achieved at the same time for the different ways of ordering, as, for example, amount and weight. The children who were tested for conservation of amount were tested for conservation of weight also [36]. They were shown two balls of clay, the smaller one weighted so as to make it heavier. After the child had agreed that the smaller ball was heavier than the larger one, the latter was rolled into a sausage and questions asked about the weights of the sausage and ball. Table 2–2 shows the distribution of children at each stage of conservation. Comparing it with Table 2–1, it can be seen that weight conservation, as shown by this experiment, developed more slowly than conservation of amount. Conservation of volume is acquired after conservation of weight. No matter which material was used for testing, conservation of amount, weight, and volume were achieved in that order [62]. However, the times at which the child went through the amount-weight-volume sequence varied from one material to another. On a conservation task involving numbers and length, number conservation was achieved earlier than length conservation [21].

That conservation develops at different times in regard to different situations is an argument for the importance of experience in building mental structures.

Table 2–2 Percentage of Children at Each Year in the Junior School (ages 7 through 11) in Various Stages of Understanding Conservation of Weight

Year	Stage 3 Conservation %	Stage 2 Transition %	Stage 1 Non-Conservation %	No. of Children Tested
1st year	4	5	91	57
2nd year	36	36	29	73
3rd year	48	20	32	66
4th year	74	13	13	168
				364

SOURCE: Reprinted by permission from K. Lovell, *Growth of Basic Mathematical and Scientific Concepts in Children* (New York: Philosophical Library, Inc., 1962), Table 2, p. 71.

As the child interacts with his environment, he learns first here, then there, and finally everywhere, that substance, weight, length, area, and numbers remain the same throughout changes in arrangement and position. The following investigation underlines the role of practical experience in the speed with which weight conservation is learned [34]. Children who were not conservers in regard to amount of sausages and balls of clay were asked, "What would happen to the weight of a piece of butter if it hardened?" and "What would happen to the weight of a lump of clay plasticine if it got harder?" Many more children conserved with the weight of butter than the weight of plasticine. These children had had frequent experience in shopping for butter by weight and in seeing it soften and harden under different conditions at home. They knew from many experiences that the weight of the butter stayed the same under varying conditions of shape and texture. With plasticine, though, the weight had rarely if ever been a matter of any practical importance.

Attempts to teach children conservation have generally met with indifferent success, especially when children were younger than the age at which it is normally learned. Using subjects between 6 years 5 months and 7 years 8 months, with an average age of 6 years 11 months, a successful experiment was carried on [66]. Children who failed tests of conservation were divided into two groups, one of which received instruction and the other of which did not. The instruction was based on the idea that the understanding of reversibility contributes heavily to the appreciation of conservation. Using dolls and doll beds, the experimenter and child went through a standard series of situations in which the child put the dolls into the beds and took them out with, for example, the dolls close together, the dolls closer together and a bed removed, the dolls farther apart, and the dolls farther apart and a bed added. The experimenter would question the child each time in such ways as, "Do you think we can put a doll in every bed now?" Each situation was repeated until the child predicted correctly and confirmed his prediction. All subjects but one succeeded, after training, in demonstrating conservation, and the whole control group showed no change. What is more, the trained children transferred the notion of conservation to a test which used checkers and cards instead of dolls and doll beds.

Another successful experiment in teaching conservation was done with 20 gifted 5-year-olds [49]. The inquiry method, used for nine 20-minute sessions, dealt with classification, multiple classification, seriation, and reversibility. To teach classification, for example, the teacher asked questions which led the children to observe, verbalize, and discuss differences and similarities. Multiple classification was learned by acting out, trying out, and discussing. For instance, with a pile of objects in the center of the table, each child was told to collect items that belonged together. One was to take everything red, another everything that writes. Of course both reached for the red pencil, which led to verbalizing the fact that the pencil belonged in two groups, and to generalizing that an object can be two things at the same time and then to verbalizing other examples of multiple classification. After the experimental group had had these experiences in thinking, they did significantly better than a control group on tests of conservation. The investigators agreed entirely with Piaget's belief that children build their own mental structures through their own activity. "In the area of logico-mathematical structures, children have a real understanding only of that which they invent themselves, and each time that we try to teach them something too quickly we keep them from reinventing it themselves" [46, p. vi]. The experiments with the gifted 5-year-olds were an attempt to let children invent and discover in situations offering maximum opportunities for developing their thought processes.

Conservation is related to many other measures. Transitivity tests might be expected to correlate more highly with conservation tests, and this was indeed the case [53]. (Concrete transitivity was shown when a child, after seeing that stick *A* was longer than stick *B* and that stick *B* was longer than stick *C*, concluded that stick *A* was longer than stick *C*.) Among children 4 to 10 years of age who were tested for both conservation and transitivity, most of those who showed transitivity also showed conservation, and most of those who did not show transitivity did not show conservation [53]. A child's ability to conserve can be measured by a conservation scale based on a variety of conservation tasks [20]. Performance on the scale is correlated with school grades, high verbal ability, low scores on a lie scale, favorable ratings by teachers and peers, and lack of dominating attitudes in mothers. Among young children who were developing conservation, there was a tendency for those with higher IQs to achieve conservation earlier [2]. The complexity of the task also makes a difference as to whether young children conserve amount. Success in conservation tests was somewhat related to success on a stencil design test, picture vocabulary, reading, and measurement [2]. Thus the development of conservation seems to be influenced by and connected with many aspects of the child's life, both cognitive and emotional.

Cognitive Style

Children use their mental structures in a variety of ways. To say that two children have the same IQ or the same mental age is not to imply that they think in the same ways or that they will achieve the same products. Nor does it mean similarity of cognitive behavior if two children develop conservation and transitivity at the same time. To get at some of the differences in the ways in which children behave intellectually, the concept *cognitive style* is useful.

There are different ways of organizing perceptions and classifying and finding solutions to problems. The particular ways preferred by an individual are called his *cognitive style*. Kagan and associates [26] have found that some children analyze the environment much more minutely than do others in forming concepts and producing answers. "Some children are splitters, others are lumpers," they say. The tendency to differentiate the stimulus environment, in contrast to re-

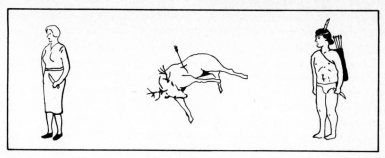

Figure 2–3. An example of the stimuli used in the test for conceptual style for children. The child was asked to choose two figures which "were alike or went together in some way."

SOURCE: From J. Kagan, H. A. Moss, and I. E. Sigel, "Psychological Significance of Styles of Conceptualization," *Monographs of The Society for Research in Child Development*, **28**, Figure 2. Copyright © 1963, The Society for Research in Child Development, Inc. Used by permission.

sponding to the stimulus-as-a-whole, they call "an analytic attitude." To test cognitive style in children, they used a set of stimuli, each containing three drawings. The child was asked to select two figures which "were alike or went together in some way." Since the drawings could be grouped in two or three ways, the child's first choice was considered his preference. An analytic response would be choosing the two figures holding knives in Figure 2–3. A relational or thematic response would be choosing the hunter and the dead deer. Other tests used were word association tests, word lists to be learned, and figure sorting tests, all of which gave indications as to the child's preference for conceptualizing by analytical, relational, or inferential concepts. (Inferential concepts involve making an inference about the items grouped together, not on objective description. For instance, the two figures would be chosen not as holding knives but as killers.)

A relational style at age 6 was found more often in children who had, as 2-year-olds, been rated high on seeking contact and high on oral behavior, such as licking, drooling, sucking, and mouthing [41]. The inferential-categorical style was related positively to directed sustained activity (autonomy) at 2 and negatively related to contact-seeking and oral behavior. In this study, analytic style did not show a relation to behavior ratings at 2 years, but other research has found analytic style to be a significant variable.

An analytic style is based on two fundamental tendencies, both of which are quite stable in the individual: the tendency to analyze visual presentations, and reflectivity [28]. Reflectivity refers to one of the characteristics of school-age thought which was discussed in the first part of this chapter, under the heading "Flexibility of Thought," the delaying of a response while considering various aspects of the situation, mentally trying out different solutions before deciding on the answer. Impulsive children answer problems faster and make more errors than do reflective children [27]. Reflectivity does *not* mean the delaying of response because of fear or inability to think of solutions. The opposite of reflectivity is impulsivity which involves responding quickly without first thinking of alternative solutions. Impulsivity-reflectivity seems to be a general and pervasive measure, since an individual's performance was found to be consistent across different tests, given under different conditions [68]. Impulsive and reflective children have been compared in the search strategies they use for solving visual comparison problems [52]. The behavior of impulsive and reflective 9-year-old boys was analyzed as to frequency, duration, and sequence of observing responses to pictures from the Matching Familiar Figures Test. In this test, the child has to pick a figure identical to a model out of six similar pictures. For example, a teddy bear sitting on a chair must be matched. The five wrong choices include a chair that sticks up too far, a bow on the other side of the teddy's neck, and a head tilted upward. The two groups of boys were found to differ not only in the greater length of time spent by reflectives before responding, but in the way they went about solving the problem. The reflective children spent less time looking at the standard and more time looking at the alternatives. They appeared to compare alternatives and then to consult the standard for verification, selection, or rejection. The impulsive children apparently compared the standard globally with one alternative at a time, thus making six decisions in terms of *the same* or *different*. Details were likely to escape them, and while their response was quicker, it was less accurate.

A similar experiment analyzed the scanning behavior of children between 3 and 10 years of age [64]. When required to tell whether two drawings were the same or different, children under 6 tended to look at only a few details of each stimulus and to answer before gathering sufficient information. The majority of children over 6 used an adequate scanning strategy. Thus reflectivity is seen to be age-related; a finding also mentioned by other experimenters [26].

Figure 2–4 shows the increase in analytic responses from Grade 1 through Grade 6. Although there is, on the average, no sex difference in reflectivity, the extremes do show a difference between boys and girls [25]. There are more very reflective boys than girls and more very impulsive boys than girls. Impulsivity is expressed in motor behavior as well as in cognitive behavior. Perhaps the motor impulsivity is basic to the cognitive impulsivity, but in any case, there are more boys than girls who show extreme lack of motor inhibition. The student can easily verify this statement by observing a few times in a kindergarten or grade school, where he will be almost sure to see one or more little boys unable to sit still for more than a few moments. These youngsters wriggle in their chairs, sharpen their pencils often, throw things in the wastebacket, get frequent drinks of water, drop things on the floor, poke their neighbors, and pay attention to all sorts of extraneous stimuli. Understandably, it is likely to be hard for very impulsive children to learn to read. Not only does their motor activity preclude sitting still long enough to concentrate; the beginning reader who responds very quickly is likely to give the wrong answer. Without pausing to look at it long enough or to reflect on whether the letter is *b* or *d* or *p*, for example, the child encounters many sources of error. It has been found that the impulsive child is more likely to make a mistake in the latter part of the word rather than the first part [26].

Now let us examine the other of the two fundamental tendencies which contribute to analytic style the tendency to analyze visual presentations. A significant sex difference is usually found when this area is investigated, with boys and men superior [26, 37, 71]. For example, in Kagan's previously mentioned study, boys would be more likely than girls to group the two figures holding knives, while girls would be more likely than boys to place together the hunter and the deer. There are, of course, girls and women who are analytic in their concept formation, and there are boys and men who prefer relational concepts. Differences exist between individuals, regardless of sex.

The sources of differences in regard to analytic thinking have been sought by

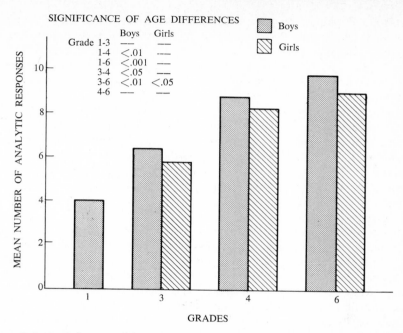

SIGNIFICANCE OF AGE DIFFERENCES

Grade	Boys	Girls
1-3	—	—
1-4	<.01	—
1-6	<.001	—
3-4	<.05	—
3-6	<.01	<.05
4-6	—	—

Boys
Girls

MEAN NUMBER OF ANALYTIC RESPONSES

GRADES

Figure 2–4. Analytic responses of boys and girls to conceptual style test, grades 1 through 6.

SOURCE: Reprinted by permission from J. Kagan, H. A. Moss, and I. E. Sigel, "Psychological Significance of Styles of Conceptualization," *Monographs of The Society for Research in Child Development*, **28**:3. Copyright © 1963, The Society for Research in Child Development, Inc.

Maccoby [37], who attributes an important role to the child's assumption of initiative, responsibility, and independence. Since analytic concepts are important for success in mathematics and of less use in language tests, it is pertinent to investigate the child-rearing methods of mothers of analytic and nonanalytic children, and of children with high or low mathematical ability. Overprotected boys, whose mother babied them at age 10 or 11 by taking them to school and helping them to dress, were very poor in math but good in language [32]. Autonomous 2-year-olds had higher nonverbal IQs at age 6 than did children who had shown more dependency at 2 [41].

A comparison of girls who were high in math and low in verbal, with girls whose talents were the opposite, showed that the mothers of the former tended to leave their daughters alone to solve problems. Girls who were high in verbal tests and low in math were likely to have mothers who intruded when their daughters worked on problems, praising, criticizing, and offering suggestions [4]. Further evidence comes from a study in which boys were tested for whether they saw visual presentations as wholes or whether they easily analyzed for details. Interviews with the mothers of these children revealed that the analytic youngsters had been given considerable freedom to explore the environment and to use their initiative, while the nonanalytic children had been kept closely tied to their mothers who were intolerant of self-assertion and who often talked about the dangers of the environment.

More detailed studies of analytic, differentiated children have confirmed earlier findings in regard to the mother's influence on the cognitive development of her child [11]. The investigators were interested in children who had distinct self concepts and who structured and analyzed their experiences. They found a relationship between these characteristics in children and tendencies in the mothers to permit or encourage their children in responsible activities, such as walking to school alone, going to camp, doing homework, keeping appointments, and taking care of pets. Children tended to see mothers with these characteristics as supportive to them.

Advantages of Analytic and Nonanalytic Styles. While the analytic style is more useful in certain fields, such as mathematics and physics, other styles can be more productive in other areas. A very strong reflective attitude may be a disadvantage in the humanities, arts, and social sciences [28]. It has been suggested that good memory for faces is more common among people who experience situations globally than among those who react analytically [74, p. 121]. Research [31] shows that while an analytic style is efficient in learning analytic concepts, a different approach gives quicker results with relational concepts. Third grade boys were tested to see how quickly they learned, for example, that *ces* (a nonsense syllable) stood for objects with a missing leg, as shown by pictures of a table, boy, and bird, and that *hib* (another nonsense syllable) meant objects related to school, as shown by teacher, crayons, and globe. Boys with analytic style learned the first concept more quickly. To learn analytic concepts, the analytic boys took an average of 20.3 trials, while the nonanalytic boys required 38.7 trials. For the relational concepts, analytic boys had 35.4 trials and the nonanalytic boys 27.9. Thus the speed with which concepts were learned was related to the cognitive style of the subjects, with each style having an advantage and a disadvantage in the array of tasks presented.

Cognitive Integration

As the child makes use of his different senses for perceiving, he has the task of putting together the various kinds of information into useful form. He develops more and more effective ways of exploring his environment [13] and of integrating what he finds out about it. When given a choice of attending to information from one sensory modality or another he tends to choose the one most useful for the task [18].

Age-related changes have been shown in the ways in which children examine objects with both eyes and hands [1]. With the task of matching through touching and looking, 3-year-olds made clutching and catching-like movements, using their palms considerably on the objects they were examining. Four-year-olds made the same movements but added more exploration. Five-year-olds used both hands more cooperatively, but not until 6 years did children systematically trace the shape of the figure. By about 9, fingertips were used almost exclusively for exploration, but between 6 and 9, palms and fingertips both were used. Eye movements underwent similar refinement, increasing with age in number and in tendency to sweep across the figure and trace its outlines. Accuracy in matching shapes presented in one modality, such as vision, increases throughout the preschool and school years.

The patterning of intersensory integration can be studied by having children match a pattern of events in one modality with a pattern of events in another. Matching through vision and touch, as described above, is one such type of task. Matching information from listening and looking is another, a type of task which has implications for learning to read. Good readers usually perform better than poor readers in matching auditory and visual patterns [47]. A comparison of normal and learning-disordered children, 8 to 15 years of age, demonstrated a difference in the processes used by the two groups in dealing with auditory and visual material [51]. Stimuli from both modalities were presented simultaneously in the form of a spoken digit and a digit on a card. Three such presentations were made and the subjects asked to report them. Children in the normal group were more likely than the other group to recall the digits in pairs, one seen and one heard, whereas the learning-disordered children were more likely than normals to recall in terms of one modality or in a mixed fashion. Older children recalled in pairs more than younger. Thus the ability to integrate the auditory and visual material was greater in normal children than in learning-disordered, and in older children rather than younger.

Other interrelations between different kinds of sensory modalities have also been found to mature throughout childhood, but at varying times and to varying degrees [9]. For example, visual-touch was better integrated than visual-kinesthetic (muscular sense) or kinesthetic-touch at each age.

The brain functions involved in intersensory integration are depressed by malnutrition [9]. Tests across several sensory modalities were given to Guatemalan village children who had probably suffered early malnutrition and to economically favored urban children. In the village, the taller children did better than shorter ones on tests of intersensory integration, while in the city group, height and intersensory integration were not related. In a malnourished population, short stature indicates the probability of malnutrition during the early months of life, the time when the brain is growing rapidly. Apparently, the function of intersensory integration is depressed by early retardation in brain growth.

The synthesizing of symbolic information includes such tasks as putting together visual symbols, words, and actions. Such integrating involves intersensory systems which probably operate in different ways under different conditions. A task of map-making was used to explore the synthesizing of symbolic information in black and white boys and girls in ghetto, working-class, and middle-class settings [14]. The child made string patterns to match symbols. He was told that a certain pattern was supposed to be a river and others were roads and bridges. He then used the symbols to "Make a bridge going across a river with a road on each side." Both sex and social class were significant factors in success on this test of synthesizing. White middle-class boys scored highest, probably due to their environment rich in mechanical toys and encouragement in their use. Black girls exceeded black boys in working-class and middle-class districts. The author suggests that the girls profited from homemaking responsibilities, such as setting the table, with instruction from their mothers. Black boys in the ghetto excelled over black boys in the working-class districts and middle-class suburbs. These boys were used to taking care of themselves in a dangerous environment. They knew how to use perceptual signals, such as soul-brother signs, and how to run and hide. Thus the success on maplike tasks seemed to result from strengths in different systems for the three groups which excelled.

Cultural Variations in Intellectual Performance

When various intellectual abilities are measured, some children are found to vary in their strengths and weaknesses and in their overall ability patterns. Differences

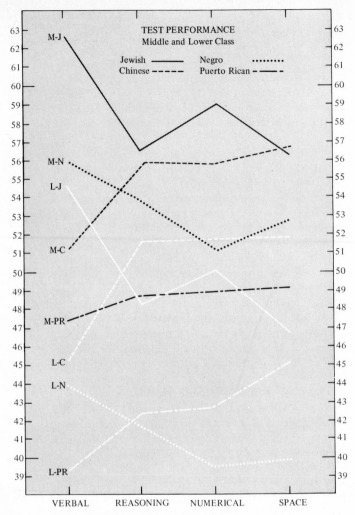

Figure 2–5. Mean test profiles of lower- and middle-class first grade children of four ethnic groups. Each profile is the average performance of 20 boys and 20 girls. The tests were specifically constructed to measure these specific abilities at this age level.

Source: Reprinted from G. Fifer, "Social Class and Cultural Group Differences in Diverse Mental Abilities." In *Proceedings of the 1964 Invitational Conference on Testing Problems*. Princeton, N.J.: Educational Testing Service, 1965. Used by permission.

can be seen by comparing children in different countries or in different ethnic or class groups in the same country.

Mexican–American differences were derived from repeated testing of city children from Grades 1 through 12 [23]. The Mexicans were more likely to be passive in coping with tasks and to respond in terms of immediate sensory experience. Americans tended to be more highly differentiated perceptually and cognitively, more venturesome, more willing to risk failure, freer with fantasy, and more direct in approach. Another American–Mexican comparison was concerned with class differences, as well as national [77]. Advantaged and disadvantaged first, second, and third grade children in both countries were given the Matrix Test, which explores classifying activities. Social class differences were observed in both countries but in the United States, the class difference was greater. American children were more successful on the test, the disadvantaged American group being similar to the Mexican advantaged group.

Ethnic group differences are reported in the next two studies, one in the United States and one in Africa. Figure 2–5 shows the results of comparing mental abilities of first grade children from four ethnic groups, each of which was divided by social class. The comparison was made on the basis of scores from tests designed to measure verbal, reasoning, numerical, and spatial abilities. The ethnic groups varied considerably in patterns of abilities. In each group, the lower and middle class showed the same pattern, although they differed in amount of ability [15].

Perceptual discrimination was tested in middle-class African and European children in Kenya, using coeducational, integrated primary schools [5]. Although Europeans did slightly better than Africans, the sex difference was much greater than the ethnic difference, boys being superior to girls.

Class differences in tests of intelligence, achievement, cognition, and language are almost always reported to favor the middle-class over lower socioeconomic groups, as occurred in the study reported above. Critics often question the validity of such tests, however, saying that they are based on the experience of the middle-class child and that they do not measure the strengths of the lower-class child. An object-sorting task was devised to measure how well children could classify objects when no verbal communication was required, in contrast to coding a verbal label [30]. The subjects were 12 middle-class and 12 lower-class boys at four age levels: 6, 8, 10, and 12. (Unfortunately, race differences were not controlled and nearly all of the lower-class boys were black.) As might be expected, the middle-class boys scored higher on making classifications verbally. When objects were classified with no talking required there was no class difference. At 6 years the lower-class boys were below, but by 8 they were above the middle-class boys, and after that, both performances were about the same. These results suggest that middle-class children have developed more efficient conceptual organization before they start to school but that the school experience may stimulate such development in lower-class children. Consistent with these results, another class comparison shows disadvantaged fifth and sixth graders to be ahead on a test of visual fluency [50]. These children produced more visual symbols than an advantaged group and did just as well on tests of esthetic judgment and originality. Thus we see again that when verbal performance is not required, poor children are not always at a disadvantage.

Cognitive Limitations

During the stage of concrete operations, the child can reason from assumptions and hypotheses, but often he confuses assumptions and hypotheses with factual evidence. That is, he thinks of an explanation and then assumes that it is right. Then he looks for evidence to support it and ignores evidence that contradicts it. This behavior is the *egocentrism* of the concrete operational period. Whereas the preschool child was centered on his own perceptions and viewpoints, the schoolchild is stuck with his own hypotheses. One result of this situation is what Elkind calls *cognitive conceit* [12]. When the child first makes the discovery that adults, usually represented by one of his parents, do not know everything, he assumes that they know very little. If the adult is wrong in one thing, the child figures, then he must be wrong in nearly everything, and if the child is right in one thing, he must be right in nearly everything. Cognitive conceit underlies some of the antipathy that children feel for growing up. It is also basic to the jokes children most enjoy and to many favorite children's stories, such as *Peter Pan* and *Tom Sawyer*, and their fantasies, such as believing that one is adopted and is really the child of royal and/or wealthy parents.

Language

Intimately associated with cognitive development, language is both a product of intellectual growth and a contributor to it. The school-age child masters more of the mechanics of his language, articulating more clearly, using longer and more complicated sentences, and doubling his vocabulary, both spoken and understood, between first and sixth grade [54]. Vocabulary continues to increase throughout adolescence and into adulthood. Not until the child reaches eighth grade level does his reading vocabulary equal his listening vocabulary [10]. That is, he can understand more words if they are spoken to him than he can by reading them to himself.

Normative Examples

Level of abstraction and facility in using *words* can be traced in intelligence tests. To give an idea of the average abilities at each year, the following examples are presented from the Stanford–Binet test [58].

Year 6. Defines six words such as *orange, envelope, puddle.*
Opposite analogies. ("A bird flies, a fish . . .)
Describes or interprets a picture.

Year 7. Tells what is foolish in an absurd picture.
Tells how two things are alike (an apple and a peach).
Answers questions of comprehension. (What makes a sailboat move ?)
Opposite analogies. (The rabbit's ears are long ; the rat's ears are . . .)

Year 8. Defines eight words, such as *gown, roar, eyelash.*
Recalls a story.
Explains verbal absurdities
Gives similarities and differences. (A baseball and an orange.)

Year 9. Makes rhymes. (A color that rhymes with head.)

Year 10. Defines 11 words, such as *juggler, scorch, lecture.*
Defines two of : pity, curiosity, grief, surprise.
Gives reasons. (Why children should not be too noisy in school.)
Names 28 words in a minute.

Year 11. Explains absurdities.
Defines three of : *connection, compare, conquest, obedience, revenge.*
Gives similarities between three things. (Snake, cow, sparrow.)

Socialized speech becomes more frequent as the child grows beyond egocentrism into the stage of concrete operations. More able to look at situations from another person's point of view, he tries to convey meaning, to understand what the other person is telling him, and to give and take through words. (In egocentric speech, the child is not concerned with exchanging meaning with someone else but only with expressing himself.) Through socialized speech, he checks his perceptions and interpretations of reality with other people's. Egocentric speech decreases in observable form as the child learns to speak to himself silently. Egocentric speech thus becomes the tool of thinking, problem solving, and self-regulation. Language continues to be useful as an aid in learning and remembering. Children who showed that they used mediation in problem solving were able to make more use of verbal labeling for learning through observation [63].

Freed from the dominance of moment-by-moment experience, the child can sit back and reflect. He has many more real choices of behavior open to him, since he can delay action while thinking. Having more possibilities for different kinds of action means that he is a more differentiated person, more of an individual. And because of being more truly an individual, there are more ways in which he can relate to other people. Thus the development of speech and thought contribute to the child's development as an individual and a social being.

Articulation

Normative studies show that most 7-year-olds can articulate all English phonemes satisfactorily. At 5, however, some children do not produce all English sounds adequately. About 75 percent of 1500 children tested after entering kindergarten had at least one misarticulation [56]. Articulation tests and others were given to nearly 500 children in the kindergarten and the tests repeated at six-month intervals for four years [56]. The children with the lowest scores in the kindergarten were also the poorest articulators when they reached second grade. By fourth grade, they still had a number of articulation problems.

Several practical findings resulted from this study. Kindergarten teachers, without using tests, identified the children with the lowest articulation scores, an indication that teachers' reports would be very helpful in identifying the children who will need speech therapy. The most common misarticulations were with *s, l*, and *r*, but patterns vary from one child to another.

Well-developed articulation is correlated with ability to apply the rules of morphological change [57]. In addition to articulation tests, the children in kindergarten, first, and second grades were also tested for ability to change words into plurals, possessives, different tenses, and so on. At each age level, children who made the largest number of errors in articulation were also the children who performed poorly on the morphology test, while the best articulators were also superior in morphology.

Language and Concept Formation

The formation of a concept does not take place by memorizing a word and attaching it to objects. Rather the formation of a concept is a creative process which solves a problem [65, pp. 54–58]. A word is the mediating sign for the concept, helping in its formation, and then coming to stand for it. When a child first uses language, he employs words which stand for concepts, words given him by adults. He communicates with adults using these words which stand for approximations of the concepts for which adults use them. For Bobby, *teacher* means any one of the four ladies who run the four-grade school that he attends. For Bobby's father, *teacher* means any person who stands in an educational relationship to another person, in the past, present, or future, anywhere in the universe. As children progress toward the stage of formal operations, they become capable of forming concepts which are more and more abstract.

The ways in which children learn words through verbal context were examined by Werner and Kaplan in one of the first studies to deal with this process [29, 70]. They show how concepts emerge as products of problem solving, whereas words come to stand for the concepts gradually, during their emergence. The subjects were between 8 and 14 years of age. The task was to find the meaning of 12 artificial words each of which appeared in six different contexts. For example, *lidber* (gather) was presented thus:

1. All the children will lidber at Mary's party.
2. The police did not allow the people to lidber on the street.
3. The people lidbered about the speaker when he finished his talk.
4. People lidber quickly when there is an accident.
5. The more flowers you lidber, the more you will have.
6. Jimmy lidbered stamps from all countries.

Under 10 or 11 years of age, children often indicated that they did not differentiate between the word and its context. Word–sentence fusion was apparent in their answers, as where one little boy said that Jimmy collected stamps from all countries, and then stated, "The police did not permit people to collect stamps on the street." The word *collect* had fused with a word from sentence 6, to make *collect stamps* instead of *collect*.

The younger children's responses often showed a tendency to include more in a word meaning than an older person does and also to perceive a sentence as an undifferentiated whole. For instance, a child of 9 responded to the sentence *People talk about the bordicks* [faults] *of others and don't like to talk about their own*. He said, "People talk about other people and don't talk about themselves, that's what bordick means." Then, when trying to fit his interpretation of bordick into the sentence *People with bordicks are often unhappy*, he said, "People that talk about other people are often unhappy . . . because this lady hears that someone is talking about her and she'll get mad." Thus he took more meaning from the first sentence than an adult would ascribe to *bordick* and tried to fit almost all of the context of the first sentence into the second. He could not isolate the meaning of *bordick* out of the first sentence in order to fit it into the second.

The 9-year-olds gave correct responses to only 6.7 percent of the sets of sentences, whereas the 13-year-olds succeeded with 47.7 percent. The younger children tended not to see the necessity for integrating the cues of all six contexts, but with increasing age, children tried harder and more successfully to integrate. Younger children tended to change the context of sentences to fit with their solutions, whereas older ones showed more respect for the context as given. Throughout the age range studied, there was a growing appreciation of the sentence as a stable grammatical structure. Children between 5 and 14 have been found to increase with age in the ability to abstract and then apply language rules [33]. This process can be facilitated by having children imitate a model and by rewarding correct responses.

Throughout the childhood years the use of compound and complex sentences increases in relationship to the use of simple sentences. Figure 2–6 shows the frequencies of various types of sentences between ages 8 and 14, as calculated from children's written compositions. The language of middle childhood has a

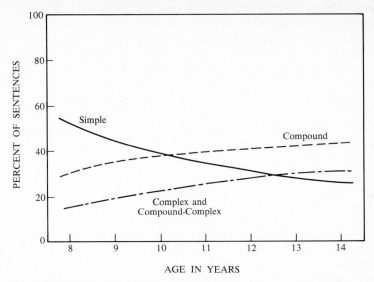

Figure 2–6. Frequencies of simple, complex, compound, and complex-compound sentences in written compositions of children ages 8 through 14.

SOURCE: From G. A. Miller, *Language and Communication*, 1951. Used by permission of McGraw-Hill Book Company.

very distinctive flavor. In fact, it has been said that childhood has its own culture, consisting of behavior patterns which are passed from one generation of children to the next, without benefit (or contamination) of adult intervention. An extensive collection [40] of English children's language humor traces jokes and stories historically and geographically, revealing some connections with European and Middle Eastern children's language productions. Children's humor is shown to have broad, deep, and ancient sources, connecting each generation of children with the past. Children apparently teach their rhymes and riddles to one another, initiating the younger ones, leaving the treasure with them and then almost forgetting it.

Word Magic. Words give power over reality. The chants of childhood combine names with other magic-making words in order to induce certain feelings or behavior in playmates. For example: Cry, Billy, cry / Stick your finger in your eye / And tell your mother it wasn't I. The name-calling of childhood is half in earnest, half in play. Sometimes it is an imaginative attempt to produce a new verbal pattern, sometimes an effort to control or change reality. Mike, in a burst of annoyance at Chris, shouted "You're a cringing crustacean." The result, a cowed and silent Chris, strengthened Mike's belief in word magic, for had not his words changed his friend?

Word magic, the power of words to change reality, is used more by children than adults, but it is not the exclusive property of children.

Star light, star bright   What goes up the chimney?
First star I've seen tonight   Smoke.
I wish I may, I wish I might   May your wish and my wish
Have the wish I wish tonight.   Never be broke.

If you say RABBITS for your first word on the first morning of the month, you'll have good luck all month. If two people say the same word together spontaneously, each will get a wish if he keeps quiet until asked a question. This is the simple word magic of childhood, so appealing that adults often engage in it "just for fun." (Our family says RABBITS.) Having only recently discovered the very real power of words, it is understandable that children attribute even more power to them than they actually have. It is hard to check reality in this respect. How can we possibly know that it did no good to say RABBITS this month? We have had pretty good luck. It surely did no harm. It was no trouble to say. We'll continue to say RABBITS when we remember. Eventually, of course, the educated person develops intellectually to the point where he rejects word magic from most of his life. Not in his grade school years, however. The less sophisticated person may continue to use word magic often throughout his life.*

Humor. Characteristic of the very creative human being, humor is the joint product of thinking, language, and imagination, but especially of imagination. Since humor is a way of solving problems and reducing tensions, it is functionally related to each stage of life. The available cognitive processes determine the level of joke which can be made and/or appreciated.

A new phase in humor begins with the beginning of the school age, in keeping with the *industry* stage of personality development and the *concrete operations* of cognitive development. Long, rambling stories are no longer extremely funny. A joke has to be concise, with a surprise ending or punch line. Jokes are funniest and most enjoyed when they are close to but not beyond the upper level of understanding of the child [75]. Children use ready-made jokes or invent jokes similar to them [73]. With more realistic, objective thinking, the child does not permit himself the free-flowing fantasy of his preschool days, his stage of developing initiative and imagination. Although he still expresses his wishes, fears, aggression, and anxiety, they are further down in his unconscious. They appear in more stylized form, like other people's, as the standard jokes of childhood. The "little moron" jokes are especially appropriate to the school-age child [73]. These children, concerned with industry, duty, and accomplishment, with being smart, with adequacy, find the stupid behavior of the moron tension-relieving. The moron in their jokes is definitely not a child like themselves. He is an older person. The jokes disparage parents, teachers and the silly answers they give children. They reassure children that it is all right not to know the things they do not know and cannot find. Jokes that belittle adults also express cognitive conceit, a result of the egocentrism of the stage of concrete operations [12].

The following selection of typical American jokes comes from a book [22, p. 229]† on middle childhood. Too crude to amuse adults and yet possessing the surprise which a real joke requires, these examples show what is funny and tension-releasing to someone halfway between the preschool age and adulthood.

What is black and white and read all over?
A newspaper.
No. A sunburned zebra.

* A highly sophisticated person, too, may use word magic throughout life if he is a very creative person. Such people have extremely complex and flexible cognitive powers [3, p. 193]. An extremely creative adult can assume a childlike viewpoint temporarily, giving his imagination rein to work naive magic, as did Lewis Carroll.
† From *Behavior and Development from Five to Twelve* by Glen R. Hawkes and Damaris Pease. Copyright © 1962 by Glenn R. Hawkes and Damaris Pease. Reprinted by permission of Harper & Row, Publishers.

What was the president's name 35 years ago?
Franklin Roosevelt.
No. Richard Nixon. His name doesn't change just because he is older.

What do ghosts eat for breakfast?
Ghost toasties and evaporated milk.

What does the mother ghost say to the baby ghost?
Don't spook until spooken to.

Teacher: How would you punctuate this sentence: *I saw a five-dollar bill in the street.*
Jimmy: I would make a dash after it.

Linda: Do you know I don't have all my toes on one foot?
Debbie: No! How did it happen?
Linda: I have five on one foot and five on the other.

What did one eye say to the other?
Just between you and me something smells.

What's twelve and twelve?
Twenty-four.
Shut your mouth and say no more.

What's eight and eight?
Sixteen.
Stick your head in kerosene.
Wipe it off with ice cream.
And show it to the king and queen.

Imagination

The school-age child can and does use all the modes of imaginative expression in which the preschool child engages—fantasy, dreams, the performing arts, and the producing arts. As it does throughout life, imagination is linked with controlled thinking and language to form the complex system with which human beings think, communicate, solve problems, and create. The balance of these three links is, in middle childhood, a little different from what it was during the preschool years. Controlled thought and language have become more powerful instruments for dealing with the environment.

Some of stored experience is immediately accessible or conscious, some is inaccessible or unconscious, some is preconscious or available but not immediately or perhaps not completely. With increasing control of thought, the older child becomes more and more able to concentrate his attention on a task or on a narrow range of stimuli when he wishes. He can also let his attention wander, daydream, fantasy. In this relaxed attitude of openness to thoughts, memories, ideas, and stimuli, he may be in touch with preconscious material which, with an attitude of strict control, he would not experience. Developing his sense of industry, he feels impelled to learn the accepted practices of his culture, the tried-and-true ways of producing, the techniques of work which adults and older children offer to him. But he is also capable of creative behavior, producing what is new, unique, or original by combining ideas and things in new ways.

Measuring Creativity. Some individuals are more creative than others. It is not too difficult to pick out some very creative adults, since they are known, or can be rated and chosen on the basis of original work they have done. Since few children ever produce things or ideas that can be rated in the work world, their creativity has to be assessed in other ways, if it is to be studied. Observation suggests that children vary widely in creativity. Many investigators have tried to distinguish between creativity and intelligence as measured by standardized tests. Success in separating the two processes came through assuming that creativity includes these two elements: abundant production of unique associations; a playful, permissive attitude [67]. Children were tested individually for amount and uniqueness of production in a relaxed atmosphere of playing games, with no pressures of time and few restrictions. Number of unique responses and total number of responses were measured in verbal and visual situations. The three verbal "games" were instances, alternate uses, and similarities. *Instances* included naming all the round things the child could think of, all the things that make a noise, all the square things, and all the things that move on wheels. *Alternate uses* involved telling all the different ways one could use a newspaper, knife, automobile tire, cork, shoe, key, and chair. *Similarities* consisted of telling all the ways in which a potato and a carrot are alike, a cat and a mouse, a train and a tractor, and several other such pairs. Visual tests were giving meanings or interpretations for a number of abstract patterns and lines. Figure 2–7 shows examples of the drawings used.

All the children in a fifth grade class were given the creativity tests and the Wechsler Intelligence Scale for Children, as well as ability tests, achievement tests. Behavior ratings were made. Since creativity and intelligence varied independently, subjects could be placed above or below the mean for each. The investigators were able to divide the subjects into four groups for each sex: high IQ with high creativity, low IQ with high creativity, high IQ with low creativity, and low IQ with low creativity. Many significant differences between various groups were seen.

Girls high in both dimensions were highly self-confident, interested in academic work, and able to concentrate well. Sought after by peers, they also sought and enjoyed companionship. They were also disruptive in the classroom, seeking attention and possibly eager to propose new ideas and activities in order to relieve boredom.

Girls high in creativity but low in intelligence were at the greatest disadvantage of all groups. Cautious, hesitant, lacking in self-confidence, they deprecated their own work, had a hard time concentrating, and disrupted classroom procedures in a protesting fashion. Other girls avoided them and they avoided others.

Girls low in both dimensions apparently compensated for poor academic performance by social activity. Compared with the high creative, low IQ girls, the low-low girls were more self-confident, less subdued, and more outgoing.

The high IQ, low creative girls were self-confident and assured, able to concentrate, fairly hesitant about expressing opinions, and unlikely to be disruptive. While other girls sought her companionship, this type of girl was aloof socially, hesitant to overextend herself or to commit herself.

Only the intelligence and not creativity was pertinent to the behavior ratings for boys in the classroom. The highly intelligent boy was self-confident, interested, and able to cope and to concentrate. The low IQ boys were more likely to be withdrawn, self-deprecating, and self-punishing.

Conceptualizing in boys was related to both creativity and IQ. High IQ, low creativity boys were least likely of all groups to give *thematic* or relational responses (see page 81) when asked to group objects together and tell why they grouped as they did. An example of a thematic response was "getting ready to go out," given by a child who put together a comb, lipstick, watch, pocketbook, and door. Boys high in creativity switched flexibly between the two styles of organizing: thematic and inferential-conceptual. Further testing showed that the high IQ, low

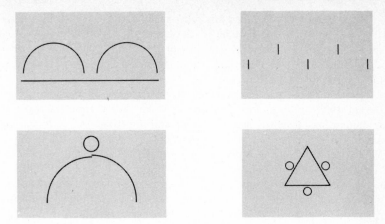

Figure 2–7. Stimulus materials for visual part of creativity test.

SOURCE: From *Modes of Thinking in Young Children: A Study of the Creativity-Intelligence Distinction*, by Michael A. Wallach and Nathan Kogan. Copyright © 1965 by Holt, Rinehart and Winston, Inc. Reprinted by permission of Holt, Rinehart and Winston, Inc.

creative boys could use thematic grouping if they were asked to do so. When they were given free choice, however, they did not use themes. These results, along with further evidence on girls' acceptance or rejection of unconventional picture labels, leads to this conclusion: the high IQ, low creativity child is likely to be intolerant of unlikely hypotheses about the world, reluctant to "stick his neck out," afraid of being wrong. Anxiety level is low in this group. It looks as though this type of child is attuned to what succeeds in the ordinary classroom.

Creativity seems to be associated with moderate levels of anxiety. The most creative child is not necessarily the happiest. He may well be sensitive to sadness and pain. High creativity involves not only a playful contemplation of the possible but most likely also requires high persistence and concentration, "an obsessive, task-centered reluctance to put a problem aside" [67].

Intelligence and Achievement as Revealed through Tests

Most schoolchildren are tested many times as part of academic procedure. Teachers give tests or examinations in order to see how much children have learned and, upon this basis, to give them grades or credits. Intelligence tests, achievement tests, and diagnostic tests are given in various contexts in order to achieve a variety of aims.

Among the several intelligence tests used for children, the Stanford–Binet and the Wechsler Intelligence Test for Children are pointed out as those used most often for individual examinations. Both tests yield IQs. The Wechsler also gives a percentile rating, showing how the child stands in relation to a representative 100 children. Verbal and nonverbal scores are a further advantage of the Wechsler, which is the test most often used with school-age children. When an individual test is administered, a qualified psychologist carries out carefully designated procedures in a room alone with the child. In addition to giving the items in standardized ways, the psychologist pays special attention to the child's comfort, alertness, motivation, and any other such factors which might conceivably contribute to his doing the best he is capable of. The psychologist makes and records observations on the total behavior of the child, in addition to recording passes and failures on tests. Thus an individual intelligence test can yield valuable qualitative information, as well as scores.

For every individual test given, many group tests are administered. Teachers give the informal tests, quizzes, and exams which they themselves make up, as well as standardized tests which are made up and sometimes scored by nationwide test bureaus. A group test is a rough instrument, as compared with an individual test. When a child is one of a group, his own particular feelings, attitudes, and needs cannot be taken into consideration to any degree. No qualitative observation can be made. The result is only a score which is an indication of how one child stands in relation to the group. Such tests are useful for revealing characteristics of the group and for pointing out children who need further study.

Prediction of Success

Intelligence tests correlate significantly with success in school, as measured by grades. Third and fourth grade children, tested on the Stanford–Binet test and on the California achievement tests, showed these correlations: IQ and arithmetic, 0.59 for girls and 0.50 for boys; IQ and reading, 0.57 for girls and 0.66 for boys [8]. Since the correlations are far from perfect, this table shows that academic success is based upon more than IQ but that IQ is an important factor. The Stanford–Binet and most other intelligence tests are adaptations and refinements of Binet's original procedures, which were devised in order to predict academic success.

There are many different ways of judging success. If the criterion of originality or production of new ideas is considered, then IQ tests are of limited usefulness. Correlations between IQ and some tests of creative thinking are fairly high (from 0.11 to 0.73) if the subjects have a wide range of IQs [48]. For a group of uniformly low, average, or high IQs, however, correlations with tests of creative thinking are generally low (0.00 to 0.45).

Intelligence tests tend to sample the kinds of intellectual processes which produce *the* right answer to each question, whereas creativity tests sample processes which produce unusual, new, original, often multiple answers. The former type of thinking is called convergent, the latter divergent. It is reasonable, then, that if success is being defined in terms of creative production, IQ tests may not be sufficient for predicting it. High IQ is, however, correlated with many other superior characteristics, as will be seen below. British children between 8 and 12, who scored above 140 IQ on the WISC, were studied by means of tests for creativity, logical thinking, mathematics, and personality [35]. These children scored high on mathematics tests, but they had not attained the stage of formal thought to any great degree. Although largely in the stage of concrete thought, as are most children their age, these gifted children were very flexible in thinking and were able to use their schemas in a greater variety of situations than could children of average IQ. A factor analysis revealed that their general intelligence contributed to their success on creativity tests, but that creativity was also dependent on other factors, including logical thinking and abilities measured by verbal and mathematical creativity tests. These children, like American gifted children [69], were generously endowed with desirable personality characteristics and were popular with their peers. A positive relationship was found between creativity and reversibility in operations of classifying when Canadian children were examined with creativity tests and some of Piaget's tests [39].

Success in adult life is more difficult to define than success in school, where grades are easily used as a measure. Many adults can point to at least one former schoolmate who has achieved status and success in business, a profession, or the arts and who used to be a poor student in school. There is, however, some relation beween intelligence at school age and performance as an adult. Children who tested at the low and high ends of the scale and a group of average scorers have been studied as adults. The various criteria of their success include earnings, status, degrees, publications, family behavior, and survival rates. All criteria are shown to have some relation to childhood IQ by the two studies which follow.

Terman and his associates [59] have published four volumes of *Genetic Studies of Genius* in which over 1000 gifted children were studied, between 1921 and 1945. The distribution of Stanford–Binet IQs was between 135 and 200, with a mean of 151. Various criteria of success were used to appraise the subjects 25 years after their selection as gifted children, showing the widespread superiority of these people as adults. Half the men and over half the employed women were in professional occupations. This ratio was nine times the proportion of professional men in the general Californian population. Eighty percent of the men were in the two highest groups, as contrasted with 14 percent in the general professional population. Seventy percent were college graduates, as contrasted with 7 percent for the population of corresponding age. Twenty-five percent of the college graduates were elected to Phi Beta Kappa or Sigma Xi. Twenty-nine percent took graduate degrees. A random selection of people would probably contribute less than 5 percent of the doctors and lawyers produced by the gifted group. The subjects received a proportionately large number of scholarships, assistantships, and fellowships. The gifted group earned significantly more money than the average, even though they were below the age for maximum earning capacity. The group had published 90 books and 1500 articles. Nearly 100 patents had been granted.

Marriage and divorce rates and age at marriage were the same as in the general population, but for the gifted college graduates, as compared with all college graduates, incidence of marriage was higher, age of marriage lower, and the divorce rate lower. The married gifted group showed a slightly higher score on a marital happiness tests than did a group of less gifted subjects. The mean IQ of the 384 offspring tested was 128, with fewer than expected below 80 IQ and those above 150 being 28 times as numerous as in the general population. The death rate was 4.0 percent, significantly lower than that of the general population the same age.

At the other end of the distribution of IQs were 151 adults who had, as schoolchildren, been judged mentally deficient, because of IQs below 70, placement in special classes for a year or more, and teachers' and psychologists' evaluations [6]. The subjects' average age was 42. Only nine of them were institutionalized. All but seven of those not in institutions had at least part-time jobs. About 83 percent were self-supporting part of the time. The range of occupations included all categories from managerial to unskilled labor. The most common occupations were laborer for males, and housekeeper for females. The higher-placed subjects included a business manager and a bookkeeper. The subjects were tested with the Wechsler Intelligence Test, on which scores are expected to be a little higher than on the Stanford–Binet.

The results, however, averaged 23 points higher, an increase greater than the difference in the two tests would explain. IQs ranged from 56 to 104. Improvement in performance scores was greater than in verbal scores.

About a third were entirely self-sufficient, less than half had some assistance from public relief funds, and the remainder lived in institutions or with their parents. Types of dwellings ranged from filthy shacks to costly new houses. Eighty percent of the group were married, with a marriage rate slightly below the general population. Divorce rates were about average. About 80 percent of those married had children, most of whom were making average progress at school. The children's average IQ was 95, with a range from 50 to 138.

Higher than the national average, the death rate was 15 percent, with twice as many males as females deceased. Nearly a third of the deceased had died violently, a much greater percentage than the national average for violent deaths.

In all these measures of success, even in the global one of staying alive, the high IQ group greatly exceeded the low IQs. And while the low IQs did better than might have been expected in several measures, they were below average in most criteria. Overwhelming evidence points to the lifelong advantages of having a high IQ. Table 2–3 summarizes the comparison between the groups.

Table 2–3 Comparison of High and Low IQ Groups on Criteria of Success in Life

Success Criterion	Terman's Gifted Group			Charles' Retarded Group		
	ABOVE AVERAGE	SAME	BELOW	ABOVE AVERAGE	SAME	BELOW
Occupational status	X					X
Education	X					
Income	X					X
Publications	X					
Marriage rate		X				X
Divorce rate		X			X	
Marital happiness	X					
Children's intelligence	X				X	
Height & weight	X					
Death rate			X	X		

Adult outcomes of average childhood IQs are rather surprising. Twenty-five subjects who had tested average (a mean IQ of 100) at age 6 were retested at an average age of 33, when the mean IQ of the group was 107 [7]. At age 6, the range of IQs was 96 to 104; at age 33, IQs ranged from 90 to 132. Changes in IQ ranged from −8 to +29. Thus, a group of children who had tested average at age 6 were scattered all the way from the lower end of the average category to the superior level. In occupational classification, the subjects ranged from unskilled labor to professional, with a wide variety of jobs represented. Educational attainment ranged from eighth grade to graduate school. The results of the study suggest that IQ in the early elementary school years is an inadequate basis on which to predict future achievement and from which to make educational plans for children who test average.

Estimating Readiness for Educational Experiences

Although IQ accounts in part for academic success, another important influence is the child's readiness to learn from the situation presented. Readiness is a function of the child's stage of maturation and of his "set" or motivation toward the particular kind of learning involved [24, p. 392]. Maturation is tested by physical-motor tests, most of which are appropriate for the infant and preschool child. The Lincoln–Oseretsky test (mentioned in the previous chapter) is an example of a physical-motor test designed for the school-age child. Subject matter-readiness tests are often used upon school entrance and during the early grades, in order to place the child in a class or group where the level and type of work are suited to his maturity and interests. The most frequently used readiness tests are those of reading readiness, which correlate highly (around 0.75) with progress in first grade reading [24, p. 424]. Arithmetic readiness tests are also used. Tests for aptitudes, such as artistic and musical talent, are readiness tests in the sense that they predict whether the child will profit greatly from education in these fields. Aptitude tests do not imply that everyone will eventually reach a state of readiness, however, since specialized talents are distributed quite unevenly throughout the population. Reading tests correlate highly with intelligence tests. It is estimated that a mental age of $6\frac{1}{2}$, as measured by the Stanford–Binet, is necessary for learning to read [24, p. 420]. Reading tests typically explore the following: visual discrimination of differences and similarities in letters, words, phrases, or pictures; auditory discrimination of words, linking them to pictures; motor control in such activities as maze tracing, placing dots in circles, and drawing lines; understanding numbers and relations; remembering and reproducing a story; vocabulary, naming objects, and classifying; reproducing pictures; giving information, by answering questions of common knowledge; laterality, through hand- and eye-preference tests.

Measuring Achievement Level and Diagnosing Deficiencies

Measures of achievement show what a child has learned and what he can do in the field in question. The ordinary classroom tests and examinations are usually achievement tests, used as a basis for giving marks and grades. Standardized achievement tests are used quite widely, often to reveal how a particular class, school, or area stands in relation to children throughout the country as a whole. The California Achievement Tests [60] are an example of this type of test. Through their use, a child can be compared with a large, carefully selected sample of children. Weaknesses, as well as strengths, can be diagnosed through the use of achievement tests, especially standardized ones. The California Achievement Tests, for example, can serve as a rough diagnostic test, since they consist of a battery. The arithmetic section includes four groups of tests, addition, subtraction, multiplication, and problems. A deficiency in any particular area can point to the need for further diagnostic study and then to definite remedial measures.

Research

All types of tests are used for research purposes. Sometimes research programs require the giving of tests which are valuable to the individuals involved. Often, however, the investigator has to get information which benefits neither the child nor his parents. The experimenter may be developing his own tests, using the children's performances as the basis of standardizing tests, which will eventually be useful for individual diagnosis. Or he may be testing theories and generating hypotheses. Research can also be done on test data that were originally collected in order to give information about children as individuals.

Summary

The school-age child feels a necessity to develop intellectual skills as part of a whole network of competencies which contribute to his sense of industry. His thinking increases in both flexibility and control. He can delay his response to the experience of the moment, taking account of several aspects of the situation, weighing them, bringing in past experience, and even considering the future. The points of view of other people are realities which enter into his deliberations and influence his actions. While considering which response to make, the child can think an act and think it undone, thus trying out various courses of action mentally. He also learns that there are certain kinds of processes or operations of thought and of nature which can be done and undone, or reversed.

The child thinks about experiences and symbols in systematic ways. He is not likely to think about pure abstractions, however. In his classifying, he can understand relations between classes and subclasses and between parts and wholes. He relates objects to each other, ordering them in terms of size, age, sound, or some other criterion. Number concepts are built from the combined operations of classifying and ordering. During this period of cognitive development, the child becomes convinced of certain constancies in the environment. He comes to realize that substance, weight, length, area, volume, and numbers remain the same (are conserved) even when changes are made in arrangements and positions. The notion of conservation, like other cognitive achievements, is built through interaction with the environment.

Cognitive style refers to the ways in which an individual characteristically perceives, organizes his perceptions, and seeks solutions to problems. Some children analyze experiences minutely; others respond more to the event-as-a-whole or to the object-in-relation. An analytic style is based on two fairly stable characteristics: the tendency to analyze visual arrays, and the tendency to reflect before responding. At both extremes of reflectivity, very reflective and very impulsive, there are more boys than girls. Analytic thinking seems to be related to child-rearing practices, especially to the promotion of independence, responsibility, and initiative.

Language develops in intimate relationship with thought and with social interaction. The ability to talk silently to oneself increases, contributing to problem solving and self-regulation and opening more avenues of behavior from which to choose. Language development and concept formation contribute to one another. Concepts, and the words attached to them, emerge gradually, as the words become differential from the context in which they appear. As the child matures, he shows increasing understanding of the sentence as a stable grammatical structure.

Imagination continues to be used in problem solving and self-expression, although there is some indication that the school-age child uses imagination less than does the preschool child. A large part of the imaginative expression of middle childhood is through language and humor, which create the distinctive culture of childhood. Language play takes the form of magic-making formulas, verses, and chants which are handed down from one generation of children to another, and riddles reflect the child's preoccupation with adequacy.

Intelligence, achievement, and special abilities are often tested and meas at this time of life. Most testing is done in groups, at school, in order to assign credit for what the child has learned. The child may be compared with his classmates or with a broader group, even a national sample. Intelligence tests correlate with achievement in school and with success in later life, as measured by many criteria. Although group performance can be predicted fairly well from intelligence tests, such tests tell little about what a given child will achieve. IQ tests and creativity tests tap different intellectual functions. Readiness tests are used to explore various aspects of maturity which are necessary before a child can profit from certain educational experiences. Reading readiness tests are widely used. Diagnostic tests reveal areas where children need remedial help. All types of tests are used for research purposes.

References

1. Abravanel, E. The development of intersensory patterning with regard to selected spatial dimensions. *Mono. Soc. Res. Child Devel.*, 1968, **33**:2.
2. Almy, M., Chittenden, E., & Miller, P. *Young children's thinking.* New York: Teachers College Press, 1966.
3. Barron, F. *Creativity and psychological health.* Princeton: Van Nostrand, 1963.
4. Bing, E. Effect of childrearing practices on development of differential cognitive abilities. *Child Devel.*, 1963, **34**, 631–648.
5. Bowden, E. A. F. Perceptual abilities of African and European children educated together. *J. Soc. Psychol.*, 1969, **70**, 149–154.
6. Charles, D. C. Ability and accomplishment of persons earlier judged to be mentally defective. *Genet. Psychol. Mono.*, 1953, **47**, 3–71.
7. Charles D. C., & James, S. T. Stability of average intelligence. *J. Genet. Psychol.*, 1964, **105**, 105–111.
8. Crandall, V. J., Dewey, R., Katkovsky, W., & Preston, A. Parents' attitudes and behaviors and grade school children's academic achievements. *J. Genet. Psychol.*, 1964, **104**, 53–66.
9. Cravioto, J., & Licardie, E. R. Intersensory development of school-age children. In N. S. Scrimshaw & J. E. Gordon (Eds.), *Malnutrition, learning and behavior.* Cambridge, Mass.: M.I.T. Press, 1968, p. 252–268.
10. Durrell, D. D. Listening comprehension versus reading comprehension. *J. Reading*, 1969, **12**, 455–460.
11. Dyk, R. B., & Witkin, H. A. Family experiences related to the development of differentiation in children. *Child Devel.*, 1965, **36**, 21–55.
12. Elkind, D. Cognitive structure in latency behavior. Paper presented at the conference on "Origins of Individuality." Madison: University of Wisconsin, Sept. 26–27, 1969.
13. Elkind, D., & Weiss, J. Studies in perceptual development. III: Perceptual exploration. *Child Devel.*, 1967, **38**, 553–561.
14. Farnham-Diggory, S. Cognitive synthesis in Negro and white children. *Mono. Soc. Res. Child Devel.*, 1970, **35**:2.
15. Fifer, G. Social class and cultural group differences in diverse mental abilities. Princeton, N.J.: Educational Testing Service, 1965.

16. Gardner, D. B. Children's perception of time and rhythm: Intersensory determinants. Paper presented at the annual convention of the Rocky Mountain Psychological Association, Denver, May 9, 1968.

17. Gellert, E. Children's lateralization of human figures: Analysis of a developmental transition. *J. Psychol.*, 1967, **67**, 107–126.

18. Gliner, C. R., et al. A developmental investigation of visual and haptic preferences for shape and texture. *Mono. Soc. Res. Child Devel.*, 1969, **34**:6.

19. Goldman, A. E., & Levine, M. A developmental study of object sorting. *Child Devel.*, 1963, **34**, 649–666.

20. Goldschmid, M. L., & Bentler, P. M. The dimensions and measurement of conservation. *Child Devel.*, 1968, **39**, 787–815.

21. Gottfried, N. W. The relationship between concepts of conservation of length and number. *J. Genet. Psychol.*, 1969, **114**, 85–91.

22. Hawkes, G. R., & Pease, D. *Behavior and development from five to twelve.* New York: Harper, 1962.

23. Holtzman, W. H., Diaz Guerrero, R., Swartz, J. D., & Tapia, L. L. Cross-cultural longitudinal research on child development: Studies of American and Mexican schoolchildren. In J. P. Hill (Ed.), *Minnesota symposia on child psychology, Vol. 2.* Minneapolis: University of Minnesota Press, 1969, pp. 125–158.

24. Horrocks, J. E. *Assessment of behavior.* Columbus, Ohio: Merrill, 1964.

25. Kagan, J. Development and personality differences in problem-solving. Paper presented at the Wheelock College Institute for the Exploration of Early Childhood Education. Boston, November 6, 1964.

26. Kagan, J., Moss, H. A., & Sigel, I. E. Psychological significance of styles of conceptualization. In Wright [74], pp. 73–111.

27. Kagan, J., Pearson, L., & Welch, L. Conceptual impulsivity and inductive reasoning. *Child Devel.*, 1966, **37**, 583–594.

28. Kagan, J., Rosman, B. L., Day, D., Albert, J., & Phillips, W. Information-processing in the child: Significance of analytic and reflective attitudes. *Psychol. Mono.*, 1964, **78**:1.

29. Kaplan, E. The acquisition of word meanings: A developmental study. *Mono. Soc. Res. Child Devel.*, 1952, **15**:1.

30. Kaplan, M. L., & Mandel, S. Class differences in the effects of impulsivity, goal orientation, and verbal expression on an object-sorting task. *Child Devel.*, 1969, **40**, 491–502.

31. Lee, L. C., Kagan, J., & Rabson, A. Influence of a preference for analytic categorization upon concept acquisition. *Child Devel.*, 1963, **34**, 433–442.

32. Levy, D. M. *Maternal Overprotection,* New York: Columbia University Press, 1943.

33. Liebert, R. M., Odom, R. D., Hill, J. H., & Huff, R. L. Effects of age and rule familiarity on the production of modeled language constructions. *Devel. Psychol.*, 1969, **1**, 108–112.

34. Lovell, K. *The growth of basic mathematical and scientific concepts in children.* New York: Philosophical Library, 1961.

35. Lovell, K. Some recent studies in cognitive and language development. *Merrill-Palmer Quart.*, 1968, **14**, 123–138.

36. Lovell, K., & Ogilvie, E. A study of the conservation of substance in the junior school child. *Brit. J. Educ. Psychol.*, 1960, **30**, 109–118. Cited in [34].

37. Maccoby, E. E. Woman's intellect. In S. M. Farber & R. H. L. Wilson (Eds.), *The potential of woman*. New York: McGraw-Hill, 1963, pp. 24–39.
38. Neale, J. M. Egocentrism in institutionalized and noninstitutionalized children. *Child Devel.*, 1966, **37**, 97–101.
39. O'Bryan, K. G., & MacArthur, R. S. Reversibility, intelligence, and creativity in nine-year-old boys. *Child Devel.*, 1969, **40**, 33–45.
40. Opie, I., & Opie, P. *The lore and language of school children*. Oxford: Clarendon, 1959.
41. Pedersen, F. A. & Wender, P. H. Early social correlates of cognitive functioning in six-year-old boys. *Child Devel.*, 1968, **39**, 185–193.
42. Piaget, J. *The psychology of intelligence*. London: Routledge & Kegan Paul, 1950.
43. Piaget, J. How children learn mathematical concepts. *Sci. Am.*, 1953, **189**, 74–79.
44. Piaget, J. Cognitive development in children: The Piaget papers. In R. E. Ripple and V. N. Rockcastle (Eds.), *Piaget rediscovered*. Ithaca, N.Y.: School of Education, Cornell University, 1964, pp. 6–48.
45. Piaget, J. *The child's conception of number*. New York: Norton, 1965.
46. Piaget, J. Foreword to M. Almy, E. Chittenden, & P. Miller, *Young children's thinking*. New York: Teachers College Press, 1966.
47. Pick, A. D. Some basic perceptual processes in reading. *Young Children*, 1970, **15**, 162–181.
48. Ripple, R. E., & May, F. B. Caution in comparing creativity and IQ. *Psychol. Reports*, 1962, **10**, 229–230.
49. Roeper, A., & Sigel, I. E. Finding the clue to children's thought processes. In W. W. Hartup and N. L. Smothergill (Eds.), *The young child: Reviews of research*. Washington, D.C.: National Association for the Education of Young Children, 1967.
50. Rogers, D. W. Visual expression: A creative advantage of the disadvantaged. *Gifted Child Quart.*, 1968, **12**, 110–114.
51. Senf, G. M. Development of immediate memory for bisensory stimuli in normal children and children with learning disorders. *Devel. Psychol. Mono.*, 1969, **1**, No. 6, Part 2.
52. Siegelman, E. Reflective and impulsive observing behavior. *Child Devel.*, 1969, **40**, 1213–1222.
53. Smedslund, J. Development of concrete transitivity of length in children. *Child Devel.*, 1963, **34**, 389–405.
54. Smith, M. K. Measurement of the size of general English vocabulary through the elementary grades and high school. *Genet. Psychol. Mono*, 1941, **24**, 311–345.
55. Stevenson, H. W., Miller, L. K., & Hale, G. A. Children's ability to guess the ages of adults. *Psychol. Reports*, 1967, **20**, 1265–1266.
56. Templin, M. C. The study of articulation and language development during the early school years. In F. Smith & G. A. Miller (Eds.), *The genesis of language*. Cambridge, Mass.: M.I.T. Press, 1966, pp. 173–186.
57. Templin, M. C. Longitudinal study of English morphology in children with varying articulation in kindergarten. Paper presented at the meeting of the Society for Research in Child Development, Santa Monica, Calif., March 27, 1969.

58. Terman, L. M., & Merrill, M. A. *Stanford–Binet intelligence scale*. Boston: Houghton Mifflin, 1960.
59. Terman, L. M., & Oden, M. H. *The gifted child grows up*, Vol. IV. Genetic studies of genius series. Stanford, Calif.: Stanford University Press, 1947.
60. Tiegs, E. W., & Clark, W. W. *California achievement tests*. Los Angeles: California Test Bureau, 1934.
61. Torrance, E. P. *Guiding creative talent*. Englewood Cliffs, N.J.: Prentice-Hall, 1962.
62. Uzgiris, I. C. Situational generality of conservation. *Child Devel.*, 1964, **35**, 831–841.
63. van Hekken, S. M. J. The influence of verbalization on observational learning in a group of mediating and a group of non-mediating children. *Human Devel.*, 1969, **12**, 204–213.
64. Vurpillot, E. The development of scanning strategies and their relation to visual differentiation. *J. Exper. Child Psychol.*, 1968, **6**, 632–650.
65. Vygotsky, L. S. *Thought and language*. Cambridge: M.I.T. Press, 1962.
66. Wallach, L., & Sprott, R. L. Inducing number conservation in children. *Child Devel.*, 1964, **35**, 1057–1071.
67. Wallach, M. A. & Kogan, N. *Modes of thinking in young children: A study of the creativity-intelligence distinction*. New York: Holt, Rinehart & Winston, 1965.
68. Ward, W. C. Reflection-impulsivity in kindergarten children. *Child Devel.*, 1968, **39**, 867–874.
69. Werner, E. E., & Bachtold, L. M. Personality factors of gifted boys and girls in middle childhood and adolescence. *Psychol. in Schools*, 1969, **6**, 177–182.
70. Werner, H., & Kaplan, E. Development of word meaning through verbal context: An experimental study. *J. Psychol.*, 1950, **29**, 251–257.
71. Witkin, H. A., Dyk, R. B., Faterson, H. F., Goodenough, D. R., & Karp, S. A. *Psychological differentiation*. New York: Wiley, 1962.
72. Wohlwill, J. F. Responses to class-inclusion questions for verbally and pictorially presented items. *Child Devel.*, 1968, **39**, 449–465.
73. Wolfenstein, M. *Children's humor*. Glencoe, Ill.: Free Press, 1958.
74. Wright, J. C., & Kagan, J. (Eds.), Basic cognitive processes in children. *Mono. Soc. Res. Child Devel.*, 1963, **28**:2.
75. Zigler, E., Levine, J., & Gould, L. Cognitive challenge as a factor in children's humor appreciation. *J. Personal. Soc. Psychol.*, 1967, **7**, 332–336.
76. Zimiles, H. The development of conservation and differentiation of number. *Mono. Soc. Res. Child Devel.*, 1966, **31**:6.
77. Zimiles, H., & Asch, H. A cross-cultural comparison of advantaged and disadvantaged children's ability to classify. Paper presented at the meeting of the Society for Research in Child Development, Santa Monica, Calif., March 27, 1969.

Readings in Intellectual Development

Thinking, reasoning, problem solving are obviously psychological processes. As contrasted with digestion and respiration, for instance, there are no substances or organs of which an adult is aware as the processes are going on. One of Piaget's great contributions to the understanding of human behavior is his demonstration of the fact that thinking begins with the manipulation of objects during what he calls, significantly in this connection, the sensorimotor *period of the development of intelligence. The end of the sensorimotor period occurs when the child has internalized experiences and developed images of past occurrences.*

Readers of this book are by this time probably very aware of the fact that we insist on the importance of physical and physiological structures and processes in understanding children's behavior. The first article in this chapter is a paper in which Sylvia Farnham-Diggory reports psychological experiments she did with young children as a means toward understanding the neurological systems which are used by human beings in understanding complex material. In order to explain the differences she found between boys and girls in her experiments she points out the differences that exist in the life situations of the boys and girls. Sociological, psychological, and physical facts are interwoven, supplementing and explaining each other.

The second article is part of the report of a speech given by K. Lovell in which he summarized several studies done by him and under his direction in England. This part tells about a study of gifted children between the ages of three and ten. He compares his results with the conclusions reached by Lewis Terman in a study of similarly gifted children in California in the 1920's. His main interest, however, seems to have been to find out how gifted children perform on Piagetian intellectual tasks. Terman's book about gifted children was published in 1926, the year in which the first of Piaget's books appeared in English translation.

The test used in the search reported in the third article was devised to be a relatively nonverbal test measuring the ability of young children to solve classification problems. In this paper Herbert Zimiles and Harvey Asch compare the performance of two groups of children in Mexico City with two roughly similar groups of children in New York City. They offer explanations of the rankings of the four groups on the several abilities tapped by the Matrix Test. The test was first devised in New York to investigate cognitive processes of children in that city. There is some evidence in the Mexican results that objects represented in the test were unfamiliar to those children and that this influenced the results, even though the children did not have to talk to solve the problems. Even beyond this difference, however, there were differences between the two national samples in strategy.

The Growth of Symbolic Abilities in Black and White Children*

Sylvia Farnham-Diggory
CARNEGIE-MELLON UNIVERSITY

I am reporting here only a few findings from a three-year project on the development of symbolic operational abilities in Negro and white children from 4 to 10 years of age. (More detailed information is available in Farnham-Diggory, 1970.)

I use the term "operational" in a more general sense than Piaget's (1967). In fact I worry that Piaget's compelling arguments may blind us to the fact that there's a child there—within whom those intricate, interlocking sets of Piagetian functions may or may not actually exist.

I have always been impressed by the shielded conservation experiments—which Piaget himself invented—where, for example, beakers with beads or water in them are screened from the subject so that only their tops are visible. Under these conditions, it is alleged—by Piaget among others, most notably Bruner (1964)—that when the liquid is poured from a low fat beaker into a high thin one, preoperational children are likely to say—"Well of course it's still the same. You only poured it." But when the screen is removed, the child will then look sheepish and say, "Oh, I guess I was wrong. There's more in the high one."

Aside from the arguments about whether or not they elicit true conservation, these screened experiments may be providing an important clue to the possible neurological aspects of those interlocking Piagetian functions. If, because of the screen, the child is forced to handle the liquids–conservation problem on the basis of language, remembered images, and remembered actions, then he seems better able to put that information together logically. If—when the screen is removed—he must bring immediate visual stimulation into the integration process, his logic disintegrates. It's as if the addition of the visual system—involving direct occipital stimulation—was more than he could handle at that stage of his neurological development, probably because some critical associative areas are not yet physically quite finished.

Now, if we pursue that line of reasoning, we can come up with a tentative general theory that alternative neurological systems may be available for handling complex information—even when normative systems are underdeveloped or deficient. All we have to do is find out how to engage the alternative systems. Screening out some of the information may be one way. Changing the language of the instructions may be another. Luria (1966) gives the example of changing the instruction "Reach as high as you can," to "Try to touch that spot on the

A Report to the Society for Research in Child Development Santa Monica, 1969. By permission.

* This research was supported by Public Health Service Research Grant MH-0722, from the National Institute of Mental Health.

ceiling." This literally brings different parts of the brain into operation, al-though the overt behavior may superficially appear to be the same.

Still another way of engaging alternate neurological systems would be through pretraining procedures that, in effect, enrich certain associative systems so that they are more likely to be available for later problem solving. This is what we do when we supplement a picture book of animals with a trip to the zoo. We are enriching visual and motor and speech associative potential to the picture book.

We could of course vary these enrichment or pretraining experiences in countless ways. To take the famous sentence, "See Spot run," for example, we could take a child to a playground, introduce him to a dog named Spot, and have him watch Spot running. If he didn't talk about it, we might assume that the major enrichment concerned visual or visual-memory associative systems. If he talked about it—if he said, "I see Spot running!" we would assume that something has also happened to the speech associative systems. If he just listened to others saying, "See Spot run," then presumably the enrichment would have been limited to the auditory systems. Or we might introduce a variation of this sort: we could tell the child, "pretend you're a dog named Spot. Now run!" That of course would produce motoric associations.

Although this mostly illustrates the conceptual poverty of our early reading materials, it also illustrates a method of systematically comparing the effects of different kinds of pretraining experiences on later symbolic operational capacities. Because the point of all that playground business would be to affect the child's subsequent ability to meaningfully integrate particular word-symbols, after he got back to his book in the classroom.

Now, to return to the problem of development and to introduce the problem of race, my theoretical position has been that some intersensory associative systems (which may or may not be what Piaget means by schemata) may be more available, and more trainable in young children, in boys, in girls, in black

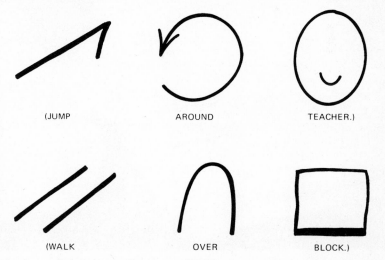

(JUMP   AROUND   TEACHER.)

(WALK   OVER   BLOCK.)

FIGURE 1.   *Sample logograph sentences. (Words were not printed on the stimulus cards.)*

children, and in lower class children—than in their counterparts. This theoretical supposition has generated a series of experiments testing the interaction of pretraining conditions with individual differences—as this interaction affects certain kinds of symbolic integrations.

Figure 1 shows a sample of the *verbal synthesis* task: the child reads simple logograph sentences—of course he learns the logographs first—and then acts out the instruction given in the sentence. If he is in fact synthesizing the information, this is clear from his behavior: he will jump around the teacher (who is the experimenter), for example. If he is not synthesizing the information, he may jump in the air, make a sign for around, and then point to the teacher. His behavior signifies mental dissociation, not mental integration, of the separate ideas represented by the logographs.

Figure 2 shows the *maplike synthesis* task: the child first learns to construct string patterns to match the card symbols, and then learns that the pattern on the left is supposed to be a bridge, the two-string pattern next to it is supposed to be a river, and the next two patterns are both roads. The child is then asked to "Make a bridge, going across a river, with a road on each side."

The correct answer would receive a score of 5, as shown in Figure 3: the bridge is going across the river, and there is a road on each side.

The most extreme incorrect answer, demonstrated in Figure 2, appears when the child lines up the string patterns, to match the cards, without relating the symbols to each other in accord with the instructions.

An additional important problem revealed by this task is illustrated by the fact that the child in Figure 2 has failed to discriminate (or to consider

FIGURE 2.   *Child performing maplike synthesis task.*

important) differences in the relative size of the strings. She made the bridge out of 3 long strings, instead of 1 long and 2 short strings—which she has actually used incorrectly to make the river. From 25 to 40 percent of the several hundred children that I have tested—in lower class or ghetto districts, both white and black—fail to make this simple discrimination. I think this is telling us something very important about the extent to which visual cues may be neurologically registered. If they are not registered, the probability that they will connect with other ideas—for example, the idea of "across" or "on each side of" —must be lower.

I have closely followed Pollack's (1969) exploration of similar perceptual deficiencies—which he thinks may be related to retinal pigmentation. The darker the retina—and of course in Negro children the retina is very dark—the lower the perceptual sensitivity (to certain kinds of illusions, for example).

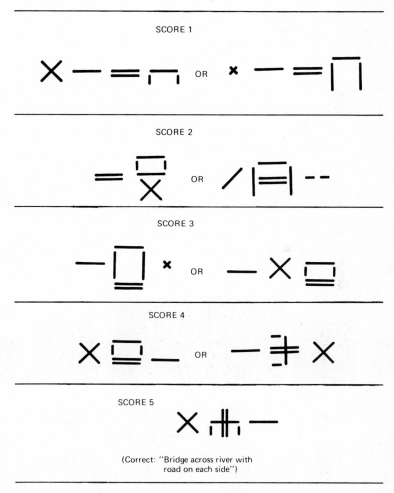

(Correct: "Bridge across river with
road on each side")

FIGURE 3.   *Score key for maplike synthesis task.*

But Pollack also concedes that social factors may intensify or compensate for a perceptual handicap of this type—just as social factors might intensify or compensate for a visual deficiency like near-sightedness. And I will be telling you shortly about some of the correlations I found which would suggest that certain aspects of lower class life may indeed produce heightened perceptual sensitivities—at least of the sort that I have been studying.

My third symbolic integration task (called *mathematical synthesis*) involves recognizing that an order in six dot-cards matches an order in six blocks—as illustrated in Figure 4. The child is shown a row of blocks which increase and then decrease in size. He is then given a scrambled pile of cards with one, two, or three inked dots on them, and instructed to "Put the dots with the blocks, the way they are supposed to go." The correct insight involves the recognition that the increasing and decreasing order in one set of materials can be coordinated with the increasing and decreasing order in the other set of materials.

Perceptual discrimination has something to do with this too. Children were tested on their ability to recognize differences between numbers of dots, and differences between sizes of blocks—and their scores on this discrimination task were significantly correlated with their scores on the final mathematical coordination task.

Now to report some of the research using these three tasks.

In the original normative study of these tasks, there were no differences between the black and white children on the verbal synthesis task. If anything the black children were better than the white ones in putting visual symbols, words, and actions together in this special way.

But there were significant racial differences on the maplike and mathematical tasks—which appear to require something more like a spatial factor. There is evidence other than Pollack's that the ability to integrate spatial or pictorial ideas may be somewhat defective in Negroes (compared to whites) whereas verbal integration abilities may not be defective (Tyler, 1956; Pettigrew, 1964). My findings would support that general view.

The second normative finding was that all three tasks improve with age, regardless of race or social class. But this could result from general growth of

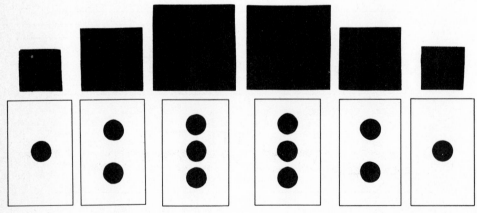

FIGURE 4.   *Correct placement of dot cards with blocks, in mathematical synthesis task.*

associative brain power. What we really need is information about specific intersensory systems that may be critical to this increased power. This is the theoretical value of attempting to accelerate symbolic integrations, by using different pretraining methods. If a verbal pretraining method does not accelerate a particular kind of synthesis, and a sensory-motor, non-verbal method does, then this may be telling us that sensory-motor networks are more involved than verbal networks, in the development of certain operational capacities. Of course arguments can be raised against this interpretation, but it is nevertheless the one I'm fondest of.

To test the acceleration potential of the verbal synthesis task, kindergarten children from a black ghetto were trained in one of the following ways: they were given practice on the reading portion of the task—actually training in visual speech coordinations. Or they were given practice on the behavior portion of the task—they practiced saying the sentences, and then acting them out, before they even saw the logographs. Or they were pretrained on both of the task components—they practiced the actions, and then they also practiced the reading.

The results were that the reading practice alone did not produce much sentence comprehension—as signalled by the child's ability to act out the synthesized sentences. A better way of producing this comprehension was letting the child practice the actions. However an even better way was to combine the pretraining procedures. Innercity kindergartners who received the combined training, produced synthesis scores which were equal to the scores of white suburban children in 4th grade. This tells us, presumably, that prior enrichment of a child's motoric associative systems may substantially assist his reading comprehension.

A similar effect was found for the mathematical task.

In a ghetto preschool, one group of children were verbally drilled in the inequalities represented by the blocks and dots. The children practiced saying "This is more than this," while pointing to different pairs of stimuli. That's a sort of visual-speech drill. Another group had a guided play experience. They had a big doll, a medium size doll, and a little doll. And each doll got a big, medium, or little truck. And each truck got a big, medium, or little elephant. And each elephant got a bubble pipe, and each pipe got some pipe cleaners— one, a few, or a lot, and so forth.

That pretraining condition enriched many sensory motor systems, but had nothing to do with the mathematical task materials, and didn't drill anything verbally. Nevertheless, the guided play pretraining produced better coordination of the block and dot materials on the final synthesis task, than did the verbal drill on inequalities.

The maplike synthesis research has not produced such straightforward acceleration functions. Actually, it's possible—among Negro children—to accelerate this ability simply by having the children memorize the maplike symbols first (which is quite easy to do), and then coordinate them without further reference to the cards—which are put out of sight. Then there is a much higher probability that the correct relations will appear.

This is similar in principle to the screened conservation task, but it doesn't solve the problem of how to get the children to do the standard maplike task rather than an altered version of it.

One aspect of the problem is that both sex and social class affect maplike synthesis capability. In lower class districts—not innercity ghettos—girls are generally better than boys on this task. In middle class districts, the black girls are also better than the black boys—but in the white group, the advantaged white boys soared above all the other groups in the sample, including the white girls.

Now this raises some interesting questions of mechanisms. We all know, of course, that advantaged white boys have fathers and tinker toys and erector sets, and various other kinds of opportunities to practice the symbolic operations of making bridges go across rivers with roads on each side.

But this comforting theoretical explanation doesn't stand us in such good stead when it comes to explaining why lower class black girls may be better than lower class black boys—not in the ghetto but in edgetown and milltown communities. I mean it's a bit silly to talk about more fathers and more tinker toys in this particular girl-boy comparison. But what about mothers and housekeeping chores? That ought to be another good way of practicing symbolic operations of this sort—you put knives and forks on each side of plates, for example, and you may have to learn to do this when the hands of the clock are lined up in a certain way. Housekeeping responsibilities generally seem to increase, for female children, as class declines—that is, lower class girls (especially older ones) presumably do more housekeeping than upper class girls. So, in one study, I separated the lower class and middle class 3rd and 4th grade girls of both races and compared them on maplike synthesis ability— and lo, the lower class girls were indeed significantly better than the middle class counterparts. But this effect was not found among the boys.

Now of course it's always interesting to find that lower class children can do anything better than middle class children, and the maplike task got even more interesting from this standpoint when I discovered that innercity boys, second graders, from a ghetto that was actually rioting during the testing period, were better than suburban black boys in 4th grade—on this maplike task. They were not better than suburban white boys, they couldn't even come close. But the ghetto boys were certainly not behaving, on this task, like the severely disadvantaged 2nd graders that they were supposed to be.

So again, casting about for ecological correlates—and father and tinker toys wouldn't do me any good here either—in fact fathers seemed to be really out of it: 40% of my boys in that experiment had fathers who were either unemployed or absent. That gave me the idea that possibly father-less, or father-weak boys, living in ghettos during these terribly dangerous periods, would have to develop perceptual acuities—in order to survive. You have to learn perceptual signals such as "soul brother" signs—which were bright orange in our city—to know which store to hide in, and which store to loot. (Many of my children were happy looters, much to the consternation of their teachers on "show-and-tell" days.) So I separated all the boys who had no fathers, or unemployed fathers, from boys whose fathers were employed and known to be in the home—and lo, the boys from the father-less or father-weak backgrounds were indeed significantly better on this maplike task, than were their strong-father counterparts. But this effect was not found among the girls.

Now, in this ghetto group, I also attempted to accelerate maplike synthesis ability in three ways: one group played with a large architects' model of bridges, rivers, and roads, for 10 minutes. A second group played with the model for 6 minutes, and spent 4 minutes being drilled, by me, in verbal statements about what they were doing—statements like, "A bridge goes across a river," and then putting the bridge across the river. A third group not only did everything the first two groups had done, but also drilled the instructions. They practiced saying, "I'm going to make a bridge, going across a river, with a road on each side," before they performed the task.

The results of this study were different for boys and girls. Among the girls, the verbalization pretraining improved their maplike synthesis capabilities. Among the boys, the verbalization training disrupted their synthesis capabilities.

So I have been formulating this kind of a conclusion about the intersensory significance of interactions between where you live, and what sex you are. Housekeeping experience may increase the verbal associative potential of girls. And this increased verbal potential may have assisted them in the performance of the maplike symbolic operations. Among boys, the factors associated with being on your own in a ghetto may sharpen non-verbal associative systems— perceptual systems, action systems—which may also help you perform maplike operations.

For the boys, the kind of pretraining that helps the girls may be disruptive. For the girls, the kind of pretraining that helps the boys may be disruptive. Presumably in both cases the disruption results from the intrusion of intersensory associative systems which the respective sexes do not normally use in performing mental operations of this type. The boys are negatively affected by verbal pretraining, and the girls are negatively affected by the ghetto life.

That, at the moment, is just a hunch. But it does suggest one way in which we could try to nail down some of the actual neurological mechanisms that may be associated with sociological differences affecting cognitive development.

References

BRUNER, J. S. The course of cognitive growth. *American Psychologist*, 1964, *19*, 1–16.

FARNHAM-DIGGORY, S. Cognitive synthesis in Negro and white children. *Monographs of the Society for Research in Child Development*, 1970, Serial No. 135.

LURIA, A. R. *Human brain and psychological processes.* New York: Harper & Row, 1966.

PETTIGREW, T. F. *A profile of the Negro American.* Princeton: D. Van Nostrand Co., 1964.

PIAGET, J. *Six psychological studies.* New York: Random House, 1967.

POLLACK, R. H. Some implications of ontogenetic changes in perception, in Elkind, D., & Flavell, J. H. (Eds.), *Studies in cognitive development.* New York: Oxford University Press, 1969. Pp. 365–408.

TYLER, L. E. *The psychology of human differences.* New York: Appleton-Century-Crofts, 1956.

Some Recent Studies in Cognitive and Language Development*

K. Lovell
UNIVERSITY OF LEEDS, ENGLAND

This paper deals with five of our more recent studies. The first concerns a study of fifty 3- to 10-year-olds, all of whom obtained a WISC Verbal Score of 140 or more. The group was in every way comparable with Terman's (1926) sample of gifted children. Five issues were studied: language, personality, mathematical attainment, logical thought, and the relationship between scores obtained on so called creativity tests and those obtained on WISC Scales and on tests of logical thinking. However, this paper does not deal with the language of these pupils, and it has little to say about their personalities; rather it concentrates on the other issues.

There are comparatively few studies of gifted children defined as those who obtain a score of 140 or more on an intelligence test, and what knowledge is available comes largely from Terman's monumental work begun more than 40 years ago. To-day, however, there are issues which did not enter into the thinking of the earlier investigators. For example, do gifted children move into Piaget's stage of formal thought much earlier than pupils of average ability as measured by I.Q. tests? . . .

In our study all the subjects were drawn from schools in two large cities. The Principals were asked to nominate pupils of outstanding intellectual ability. Over 100 pupils so nominated, were tested using WISC with the alterations suggested by the British Psychological Society. Verbal, Performance, and Full-Scale I.Q.'s were obtained. The first fifty pupils who obtained an I.Q. of 140 or more on the Verbal Scale formed the selected group; the numbers of children with I.Q.'s in the ranges of 140–144, 145–149, 150–154, and 155+ being respectively 30, 12, 4, and 4. There were thirty-five boys and fifteen girls. Twelve pupils were between 8.5 and 10.4 years, and seventeen between 10.5 and 11.7 years old. Using the British Registrar-General's Classification of Occupations it was found that nine pupils came from homes in Social Class I—major professional and managerial; twenty-two in Social Class 2—minor professional and managerial; fourteen in Social Class 3—skilled working; and four in Social Class 4—semi-skilled.

In addition to the WISC Scales the following groups of tests were used:

1. *Creativity Tests*. These comprised Hidden Shapes, Word Association, Uses for Things, Fables, and Make-up Arithmetic Problems (Getzels and Jackson, 1962).

2. *Tests of Logical Thinking*. In this group were Equilibrium in the Balance, Combinations of Colorless Liquids, Oscillation of a Pendulum

Excerpted from *Merrill-Palmer Quarterly*, 1968, *14*, 123–127. By permission.
* This is the substance of a lecture given at The Merrill-Palmer Institute in September, 1966.

(all from Inhelder and Piaget, 1958), and Concept of Volume (Lovell and Ogilvie, 1961).

3. *Mathematical Tests.* These included three tests of mathematical concepts and one of mathematical insight, all published by the National Foundation for Educational Research; Vernon's Graded Arithmetic-Mathematics Test; and a numerical series and a numerical analogies test.

All testing was performed in the pupils' schools and was on an individual basis, except that in the case of the mathematics tests up to three children were tested at the same time. In addition a Terman Personality Trait Rating Form was completed by a teacher, for each pupil, for each of the twenty-five personality traits. Thirteen grades were used for each trait.

An examination of the replies showed that only 15 out of the 150 responses to the Balance, Chemicals, and Pendulum experiments were at Piaget's stage of formal thought, while 11 of these replies were at the first stage of formal thought. Almost all the pupils understood internal volume, occupied volume, and simple displacement; but only 36 grasped that the amounts of water displaced by a single cube when immersed in a full-pint can and a full-gallon can (English gallon) were the same. Again, only 26 could understand that the amounts of water displaced by two cubes of the same size but different weights were equal. Overall, 48 per cent of the subjects answered all the questions concerning volume correctly. The proportion of younger children, 42 per cent, did not differ greatly from the proportion of older pupils, 53 per cent, passing all the tests.

Performance on the mathematics tests was as high as expected. For example, on Vernon's Graded Arithmetic-Mathematics Test the mean achievement age was 3 years 7 months in advance of the mean chronological age, with twelve pupils having attainment ages more than 4 years, and three pupils more than 5 years ahead of their chronological ages. At the same time, however, these gifted pupils had extreme difficulty with certain of the problems involving numerical series and numerical analogies, and in particular those that involved the schema of proportion. This involves the recognition of the equivalence of two ratios and depends upon the subject being able to elaborate second order relations—in the Piagetian sense. Although 48 pupils could continue the series 48, 24, 12, 6 . . . ; only 11 could continue the series 16, 24, 36, 54 . . . ; only 5 could answer the questions "3 is to 7 as 9 is to . . .," and "2 is to . . . is to 8 as 3 is to 9 is to. . . ."

It seems that while these gifted pupils do not generally attain the level of formal operational thought until 11 or 12 years of age at least, the flexibility of their first order schemas is much greater than in the case of ordinary pupils. It is as if they possess sub-schemas of much greater generality which permits transfer to new situations. Thus when gifted children reach the stage of concrete operational thought it tends to be available in a far greater variety of situations and tasks than in the case with ordinary pupils at first.

In order to look at the relationships between the responses obtained on the creativity tests and those on the other tasks, product moment intercorrelation coefficients for the cognitive measures were calculated, and a Principal Component Analysis and rotation of the principal axes by the Varimax method were carried out. Six components were extracted; the percentage variance contributed by these being respectively 39.3, 12.4, 9.7, 7.1, 6.3, and 5.6—or 80.4 per cent in all.

A large general component was found running through all these tasks even within this highly selective group; indeed it accounted for almost one-half of the identified variance. When the axes were rotated the first dimension clearly indicated an ability measured by the WISC scales, or as would be said in Britain, a general plus verbal-educational ability. The second reflected an ability to think logically in the Piagetian type situation; the summed scores of the logical tasks had a loading as high as .93 on it. The remaining dimensions suggest that divergent thinking cannot be accounted for by one dimension; rather the able pupil is "creative" in differing degrees according to the task that is set him. While the verbal creativity tests, Word Association and Uses for Things, loaded the third dimension to the extent of .76 and .82 respectively, the ability to make up numerical problems is clearly linked with the ability to work the mathematics tests as reflected in dimension 4. This study supports Burt when he wrote of divergent thinking tests (Burt, 1962, p. 295): ". . . these new tests have succeeded in eliciting supplementary activities that are rarely tapped by the usual brands of intelligence tests." On the other hand, it is clear that a great part of the identified variance of these tests is accounted for by a central intellective component which is common to a conventional test of intelligence, to tasks involving logical thinking, and to tests of mathematical attainment. Moreover, these "supplementary activities" seem to fragment in these able pupils. Wallach and Kogan (1965, p. 313) suggest that the emergence of combinatorial operations as reflected in the colorless chemicals experiment may depend on the emergence of associative (divergent) and evaluative (convergent) thinking. Our evidence does not support that if these tests of divergent thinking are regarded as adequate.

Little will be said of the findings in respect of personality. But it is of interest to note in passing that the mean scores obtained on the ratings were very close to those obtained by Terman's sample. Thus despite changes in education and life generally, both in America and in Britain between the 1920's and the 1960's, the gifted child seems to his teacher to be much the same kind of person. Further, the normalized scores on the cognitive variables were ranked and combined with twenty-one of the personality trait ratings, yielded some thirty-eight variables in all. A Principal Components Analysis of the intercorrelation matrix largely repeated the findings of our other analyses. But one point is of interest. The teachers' ratings of Originality loaded the same rotated axis (.84) as did the Logical Thinking summed scores (.63), yet Originality had a zero loading on the rotated axis which reflected the ability to answer the tests of divergent thinking on which Creativity summed scores had a loading of .82. It would seem that using Terman's personality Rating Scale, teachers think of Originality in these pupils more in terms of reasoning ability than they do in terms of inventiveness or unusual ideas. Or it may be that creativity as measured by the tests is rather too specific, or at times too trivial, to be noticed by teachers.

Gifted pupils have first order operational schemas of great flexibility, as was stated earlier. In the school situation this implies that they need suitable learning situations over a wide curriculum, with many imaginative and informative books on a wide variety of topics. But the failure of these pupils during the elementary school years to reach the level of formal operational thought, except occasionally, is a warning against the systematic provision of learning situations demanding formal thought. At the same time it is important that the pupils have access to teachers who understand their stage of cognitive development, and who can by questioning the interpretation put by these pupils on their data, persuade them to re-examine their arguments and conclusions whenever necessary in an endeavor to aid forward the onset of formal thinking. This study does not, however, give any grounds for believing that teaching procedures should be devised based upon a convergent-divergent dimension of the intellect entirely independent of I.Q.

The gifted child in Britain in the 1960's, like his counterpart in America in the 1920's, seems generally well endowed with personality traits highly regarded by Western society, and is popular with his school companions. Fears of ill-balanced personality development, and of unpopularity, are unfounded. The study confirms that the gifted child by reason of his more General Qualities and intelligence, is a most important figure in school life.

References

BURT, C. Critical notice: Creativity and intelligence, by J. W. Getzels & P. W. Jackson. *Brit. J. educ. Psychol.*, 1962, *32*, 292–98.

GETZELS, J. W., & JACKSON, P. N. *Creativity and intelligence*. London: Wiley, 1962.

INHELDER, B., & PIAGET, J. *The growth of logical thinking*. London: Routledge & Kegan Paul, 1958.

LOVELL, K., & OGILVIE, E. The growth of the concept of volume in Junior School children. *J. Child. Psychol. Psychiat.*, 1961, *2*, 118–26.

TERMAN, L. M. *Genetic Studies of Genius, Vol. 1. Mental and physical traits of a thousand gifted children*. Stanford University Press, 1926.

WALLACH, M. A., & KOGAN, N. *Modes of thinking in young children*. London: Holt, Rinehart & Winston, 1965.

A Cross-Cultural Comparison of Advantaged and Disadvantaged Children's Ability to Classify*

Herbert Zimiles and Harvey Asch
BANK STREET COLLEGE OF EDUCATION

This paper will present the results of a comparative study of classification behavior in middle-class and disadvantaged Mexican children selected from grades one to three and will examine these findings in conjunction with those

From a paper presented at Biennial Meeting of Society for Research in Child Development, Santa Monica, California, March 1969. By permission.

* This study was supported by Contract #OEO-1410 and OEO-4122 of the Office of Research and Evaluation of Project Head Start.

obtained in a previous study (Zimiles and Asch, 1967; Zimiles, 1968) which compared classification behavior of advantaged and disadvantaged of the same age range from New York. Data were gathered from Mexican children in order to extend the range of socio-cultural backgrounds of children performing the same non-verbal task and thereby to examine the impact of variation in cultural background on classification ability and related cognitive skills, and to observe whether differences in performance previously found between advantaged and disadvantaged United States children would be similarly found among Mexican children. The study also offered the opportunity to assess the usefulness of the Matrix Test as a method for studying aspects of cognition on a cross-cultural basis.

The Matrix Test was devised to measure classification ability and related skills in young children. Patterned after the work of Inhelder and Piaget (1964), each of the test's 44 items presents a matrix of 2 × 2 or 2 × 3 cells in which all but the lower right-hand cell, which is empty, contain figures which are related to each other. The subject must indicate which one of four alternative figures presented to him belongs in the empty cell by virtue of its relationship to the members of the matrix. The test is essentially non-verbal. Simple directions are given at the outset and the child need not utter a word; he needs only to point to the appropriate alternative figure.

Each item is presented individually on an 8″ × 15″ card in the form shown in Figure 1. Four classes of items have been distinguished. The first three items call for a Perceptual Matching response in that all members of the matrix are identical. To solve the problem, S must merely identify the figure among the alternatives that matches those in the matrix. These Perceptual Matching items are presented first because their simplicity makes it easy to communicate clearly to the child the basic requirements of the task, i.e., to find the member of the set of alternatives which belongs in the vacant cell of the matrix. After the first three Perceptual Matching items, 18 Class Membership items follow in which the figures in each cell of the matrix are different but are, nevertheless, members of the same class, e.g., they may all be birds or vehicles. Following the

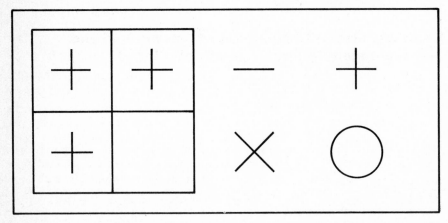

FIGURE 1.   Illustration of Matrix Test item format (example of a Perceptual Matching item).

Class Membership items are 11 One-Way Classification items in which it is the column or row membership of the vacant cell which determines the identity of the missing figure, since in these items, all members of the same column or row, as the case may be, are identical. Finally, there are 12 Two-Way Classification items in which it is the column and row membership of the vacant cell, in combination, which determines the correct response. Of the total of 44 items, 16 present geometric figures whose distinctive feature is their form or color and, in some instances, their number or order. The remaining 28 items contain representations of common objects mostly taken from illustrations in books for children.

METHOD

SUBJECTS   Subjects were selected from two schools in Mexico City. One school, located on a normal school campus, was attended by children who lived in relatively comfortable circumstances; their fathers were professionals or semi-professionals. In general, families living in the area of this school had a standard of living which corresponds approximately to that of a lower-middle-class family in the United States. The second school was located in an extremely impoverished area at the edge of the city occupied mostly by factory workers and migrant workers. In each of the two schools, the first of which we have designated as advantaged and the second as disadvantaged, slightly over 40 children were selected from each of the first three grades to serve as Ss. In those instances in which children were grouped by age or ability, the sample was determined by selecting at random from each of the strata. Approximately equal numbers of boys and girls were chosen. Unfortunately, reliable data regarding the age of the disadvantaged children were not available. However, it should be noted that the age range for this group was greater because many of the children began school later, and some were held back by the school. Therefore, portions of the samples from each of the grades were undoubtedly older than those in the advantaged school. It seemed inappropriate to exclude these children from the sample despite their older age; to do so would have introduced a clearcut bias of considerable proportion. In sum, 254 Mexican children approximately equally distributed in the first three grades from two schools, divided into a more and less privileged subgroup according to the school they attended, were studied.

The findings will be compared with those of a previous study involving groups of 40 children in each of the first three grades (kindergarten samples were also studied) selected from each of two schools in New York City.[1] One school was located in the slum of a black ghetto area; its children were for the most part from extremely deprived families. The other school was located in a very comfortable residential area made up of upper-middle-class, predominantly white families. It should be noted that the children from the New York advantage sample were living under much more privileged conditions than

[1] See Zimiles, H. "Classification and Inferential Thinking in Children of Varying Age and Social Class." Paper presented at symposium on Comparative Studies of Conceptual Functioning in Young Children, American Psychological Association meetings, San Francisco, California, September 1968.

those who constitute the advantaged group from Mexico. The pairs of groups from each country are similar in the contrast they present but not in the degree and nature of deprivation they have experienced.

PROCEDURE   All the children in both the Mexican and New York sample were administered the Matrix Test in a single session of individual testing. A single examiner, who lives in Mexico City,[2] gathered all the Mexican data. Two examiners, who tested equal numbers of children in both schools, collected the New York City data.[3] The test administration was the same in both countries, except for the identity of the examiners and the language in which the instructions were given.

RESULTS

As in the case of the findings previously obtained with the New York sample, the results from Mexico indicate consistent differences in performance between the social class groups and a steady rise as a function of age. However, the differences attributable to social class were of a smaller magnitude than those previously obtained with the New York City sample. The mean per cent of items answered correctly for each of the four item types is given in Table 1.

TABLE 1

Per Cent of Items Answered Correctly by Child Group and Grade

PERCEPTUAL MATCHING (3 ITEMS)	GRADES				ONE-WAY CLASSIFICATION (11 ITEMS)	GRADES			
	K	1	2	3		K	1	2	3
Mexican					Mexican				
Advantaged	–	82	90	92	Advantaged	–	55	65	67
Disadvantaged	–	87	72	90	Disadvantaged	–	44	45	53
New York					New York				
Advantaged	94	96	97	100	Advantaged	73	85	88	90
Disadvantaged	91	91	98	93	Disadvantaged	50	64	70	76

CLASS MEMBERSHIP (18 ITEMS)	GRADES				TWO-WAY CLASSIFICATION (12 ITEMS)	GRADES			
	K	1	2	3		K	1	2	3
Mexican					Mexican				
Advantaged	–	61	70	74	Advantaged	–	24	31	35
Disadvantaged	–	56	55	68	Disadvantaged	–	28	34	35
New York					New York				
Advantaged	73	82	84	85	Advantaged	25	41	48	48
Disadvantaged	62	73	76	80	Disadvantaged	24	24	24	27

[2] Deanne Marein gathered the data in Mexico City.
[3] Susan Lourenco and John Kaufman gathered the data in New York City.

It may be observed that almost all the children could cope effectively with the Perceptual Matching items, there was considerable success with the Class Membership, performance on the One-Way Classification items was somewhat lower, and the Two-Way Classification problems were almost consistently failed. The advantaged children almost invariably outperformed the disadvantaged, but only in the case of the One-Way Classification problems did these differences consistently achieve sizeable proportions.

When compared with the performance of the New York City sample, the Mexican children performed less well. Whereas it was the rare New York City child, even at age levels as low as five years, who failed the initial Perceptual Matching items, there were a handful of Mexican children at all age levels, from both of the schools, who failed this first item. Many of these children caught on to the demands of the test by the second item, but it remains clear that considerably more Mexican children did not understand the demands of the task upon first meeting it.

With the exception of the second-grade sample, in which the disadvantaged group performed consistently poorly, the children from the two Mexican schools performed equally well on the Perceptual Matching items and the first half of the Class Membership items—those involving categories of events of high salience to the children. As the Class Membership items became more difficult, as class membership was based on more remote characteristics of the figures, the advantaged group began to outperform the disadvantaged group by a substantial margin. The largest difference in performance between the two groups occurred in the One-Way Classification items. The groups were hardly distinguishable in their performance on the Two-Way Classification items.

Differences found between the advantaged and disadvantaged New York sample were of a somewhat greater magnitude but followed much of the same pattern except that group differences in performance on the Two-Way Classification items were as great and sometimes greater than those obtained with other item types, whereas differences between the Mexican groups on the Two-Way Classification items, because of the extreme difficulty of the items, were negligible.

Differences between the New York and Mexican groups, irrespective of social class background, were much larger and more pervasive than those differences between Mexican advantaged and disadvantaged groups. Both the advantaged and disadvantaged New York groups outperformed their Mexican counterparts at each age level by a large margin on virtually all the Class Membership and One-Way Classification items. But the most striking characteristic of these data is the wide margin by which the means of the advantaged New York group exceeded those of the other groups. A relatively consistent rank order of the four groups may be found at each of the three grade levels studied: the New York City advantaged, New York City disadvantaged, Mexican advantaged, Mexican disadvantaged. Whereas the means of the New York advantaged groups are consistently highest on all item types, the New York disadvantaged groups did not outperform either of the Mexican groups on the Two-Way Classification items.

The performance which most markedly distinguished the New York from the Mexico City groups involved items which required a change in strategy, a shift to a new basis for classification, in order to achieve solution. For example, the greatest difference between the groups was usually found on the initial item of the series of One-Way Classification problems. Apparently, the transition from Class Membership to One-Way Classification problems was particularly difficult for the disadvantaged groups. Another item which differentiated the New York and the Mexican groups presented a matrix of varying geometric figures all of which were the same color. Since the four preceding items called for a response in terms of form, relatively few children answered this item correctly.

Several kinds of items were too difficult for virtually all the children. Only substantial numbers of children from the New York advantaged group were able to solve those Class Membership problems which called for more remote categories of classification and One-Way Classification items which entailed categorization according to row membership, following a series of items which involved column membership. It was only in the New York advantaged group, too, that there were appreciable numbers of children who were able to solve the Two-Way Classification problems.

Another way of examining these data is to study the frequency distributions of scores on each of the item sets. This reveals something more about the nature of the distribution of scores than that indicated by indices of central tendency and variability. The distributions of the two Mexican school groups were often virtually identical, especially in their patterns of widespread failure on the Two-Way Classification problems. While there was very considerable overlap between these two school groups at each age level in Class Membership scores in the modal or central regions of the distribution, there were more advantaged than disadvantaged Mexican children who achieved the higher scores, and many more disadvantaged children in the lower tails of these distributions. The differences between these groups are most marked in the distribution of One-Way Classification scores. While there is considerable overlap among the higher scorers, there were many more disadvantaged children who simply were unable to solve these One-Way Classification problems.

The frequency distributions of the advantaged Mexican group bear a striking resemblance to the frequency distributions of the disadvantaged New York group. The major differences are: (1) there are more stragglers at the lower end of the distribution of Class Membership items among the Mexican advantaged group, (2) there are more perfect scores in One-Way Classification among the New York disadvantaged group, and (3) there were a few more children in the older age groups of the Mexican advantaged group who showed some signs of mastering the Two-Way Classification problem. In most respects, however, the distributions from these groups are dramatically alike.

The most striking characteristics of the frequency distributions of the New York advantaged group were the solidity of performance on the One-Way Classification problems by even the younger groups—virtually every first-grader and most kindergartners could handle most of these problems, and the appearance of small numbers of children at even the youngest age levels who could solve the Two-Way Classification problems.

SOME QUALITATIVE FEATURES OF PERFORMANCE   Response latencies to each item were recorded. They indicate that the Mexican children consistently took more time to respond to each item than did the New York children. No substantial differences between the two Mexican school groups were found. Whereas the advantaged New York children were found to take more time to respond to the more difficult than to the easier items, no such relationship between response latency and item difficulty was found among the New York disadvantaged children or either of the two groups of Mexican children.

The tendency for positional response preferences to affect performance on multiple-choice problems is not uncommon. Examination of the position of incorrect alternatives chosen indicates that there was a slight preference for responding in terms of the alternative adjacent to the empty matrix cell. This pattern was found among young disadvantaged New York children, and observed to decline with increasing age. A similar preference of approximately the same magnitude was found among the Mexican children in both school groups. In the case of the Mexican children, however, this pattern was sustained among the older groups as well.

Perseveration in the face of failure or confusion frequently occurs in the response of young children to test situations. Employing a relatively harsh criterion of perseveration, i.e., five or more consecutive identical positional responses only one of which is correct, virtually none of the New York children were found to perseverate. There was one in all of the 120 New York advantaged group and two among the disadvantaged that responded in this fashion. Among the Mexican groups of comparable age, however, there were 11 children from the advantaged group and 21 from the disadvantaged group who showed this form of perseveration.

While the 12 Two-Way Classification problems were too difficult for virtually all the children to solve, it is possible, by studying the nature of the wrong alternatives selected, to observe whether a systematic approach, a strategy, though incorrect, was nevertheless applied in dealing with these problems. One such strategy was to choose an alternative identical to the cell member in the same row as the empty cell; in short, to impose, inappropriately, a One-Way Classification scheme upon the problem. This way of responding occurred to a substantial degree among the youngest children (even at kindergarten level) in the New York advantaged children but disappeared at the older levels when they began to solve the problem. A similar pattern of One-Way Classification is barely observable among the youngest groups of the New York disadvantaged groups and the two Mexican school groups, but occurred increasingly among their older children. This trend of using a One-Way Classification strategy with increasing age was stronger among the New York disadvantaged and weakest among the Mexican disadvantaged group. Thus, for these groups, the use of an inappropriate strategy on the Two-Way Classification problems mirrored the pattern of use of appropriate strategy on other, easier to solve items.

Finally, a flexibility index was devised by recording performance on those items that marked a transition from one set of items to another, and therefore required a shift in problem-solving strategy. The per cent of these problems answered correctly for each school group is given in Table 2.

TABLE 2
Flexibility Index: Per Cent of Transitional Items Answered Correctly

| | GRADES | | | | | GRADES | | |
	K	1	2	3		K	1	2	3
Mexican					New York				
Advantaged	–	37	44	49	Advantaged	58	68	78	77
Disadvantaged	–	34	40	42	Disadvantaged	39	50	52	55

The data indicate that in each of the school groups, performance improved with age. The New York advantaged children were by far the most effective on these items, and the New York disadvantaged group substantially more effective than both of the Mexican groups. The Mexican disadvantaged group performed poorest on these transitional items.

DISCUSSION

This comparative study of advantaged and disadvantaged Mexican children revealed substantial differences between the two groups. More of the disadvantaged children floundered during the test, as evidenced by their greater tendency to perseverate and by their greater numbers at the bottom of distributions of scores.

Performance differences between the New York advantaged and disadvantaged groups were greater and extended over a wider range of item content, reflecting, perhaps, the greater difference in social-cultural background of the groups that were compared. It is of interest that the performance of the New York disadvantaged group surpassed that of the advantaged as well as the disadvantaged groups from Mexico. These differences were found in both the Class Membership and One-Way Classification series of items—those items on the test that were neither too easy nor too difficult for the age level studied.

The Mexican children took much longer to respond, but their more deliberate pace did not appear to enhance their performance. There was evidence of more confusion among them when first introduced to the task, more perseveration of response, their responses seemed more often to be affected by position preferences than by the inherent logic of the problem. These maladaptive response characteristics occurred more often and lasted longer, that is, they appeared in the older as well as the younger age groups. Even when responding incorrectly, as the New York disadvantaged usually did when presented with the Two-Way Classification problems, their incorrect response was based on a strategy. The Mexican children showed less systematic response patterns to these same items. In general, the performance of the Mexican children was like that of a slightly younger New York disadvantaged child and like a much younger advantaged child from New York.

In a previous analysis of the performance differences between the advantaged and disadvantaged children from New York, it was concluded that a major distinguishing characteristic between the groups was the ability of the advantaged children to respond to Class Membership problems in terms of attributes that were less immediately visible, or less salient among the criteria used when they typically order events. Their much greater success relative to the New York disadvantaged on the One-Way Classification problems was interpreted as further demonstration of their ability to recognize and deal effectively with a form of order that involves spatial organization, and that is not necessarily based on the high frequency with which the objects to be classified have occurred together in the past nor in their individual visually compelling quality. Among the older age groups, the performance of these children on the Two-Way Classification problems increasingly showed signs of the ability to order subjects according to two criteria of classification conjointly, that is, to engage in multi-dimensional thinking. These findings suggested further that the concept of a class or set was much more firmly rooted in the advantaged children.

In contrast, the New York disadvantaged children tended to perform effectively when the item called for an associative response. Success in classification appeared to depend much more on the degree to which the objects to be classified evoked common associations.

The data from Mexico help to identify still more primitive modes of dealing with the Matrix Test—from an inability to understand the demands of the test to a pattern of perseveration of response and positional responding. The New York disadvantaged group, while able to respond less abstractly and flexibly than their advantaged peers, were much more able to understand the task, to respond to it consistently on an associative basis, and also were more flexible in their response than either of the Mexican groups. These findings permit us to view the cognitive functioning of urban disadvantaged children in the United States from a perspective other than one which compares them with their advantaged counterparts.

Finally, it should be noted that the data of this study are clearly insufficient to make a definitive comparison of Mexican and United States children. In addition to the gross inadequacies of sampling it may well be that the Matrix Test, by virtue of the familiarity of its content, evokes a more attentive and receptive response from United States children. While there is no evidence from the present study that Mexican children performed less well on the items which involved representational as opposed to more culturally neutral geometric figures, it is possible that their general level of functioning was inhibited by the comparative strangeness of the materials.

A final note relates to the changes in performance that have been observed with age among these cross-sectional data. While the rise is consistent and unmistakable, it is extremely gradual. There is very considerable overlap in performance between distributions of five-year-olds in the kindergarten groups studied and those of eight-year-olds; there were many five-year-olds, especially from the advantaged New York group, whose scores exceeded those of large numbers of eight-year-olds. This was particularly true of performance on the One-Way Classification items, the task which produced the greatest variability in performance in the age range that was studied. Eight-year-olds are so profoundly different from five-year-olds in so many basic psychological and physical parameters that the overlap in performance among the range of age groups found in this study is noteworthy. It suggests that more refined study of age changes in performance as a function of their cognitive content is needed, that longitudinal studies of cognitive functioning may be better suited to identify significant developmental patterns, and that expectations of children's cognitive functioning based upon their chronological age are likely to be unrealistic. Age appears to be a much less decisive determinant of Matrix Test performance than was anticipated.

Bibliography

INHELDER, B., and PIAGET, J. *The Early Growth of Logic in the Child*. New York: Harper & Row, 1964.

ZIMILES, H. "Classification and Inferential Thinking in Children of Varying Age and Social Class." Paper presented at symposium on Comparative Studies of Conceptual Functioning in Young Children, American Psychological Association meetings, San Francisco, California, September 1968.

————, and ASCH, H. "Development of the Matrix Test." Document 1 of Head Start Evaluation and Research Center Progress Report of Research Studies, 1966 to 1967, December 1967.

Chapter 3

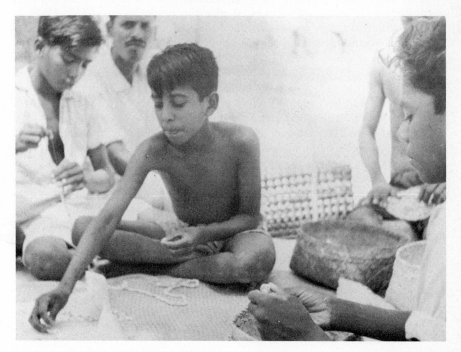

Mollie Smart

Increasing Competence As a Learner and Doer

Ever since birth, or even earlier, the child has been bringing more and more of his environment under control, through his exploration, manipulation, thinking, talking, imagining, and producing changes. Much of the satisfaction he has experienced has been the product of these activities. He has indeed been competent in many ways, including sucking milk, shaking a rattle, creeping, filling a basket with toys, riding a kiddy car, climbing the jungle gym, and playing store. All of these achievements brought joy in the process of mastery. For the most part, these activities were undertaken for themselves because they were intrinsically interesting, not because anyone urged or rewarded the child to explore, learn, and perform [96]. As the child becomes concerned with developing a sense of industry, new dimensions are added to his efforts to explore and control the environment.

127

Development of the Sense of Industry

The school-age child becomes interested in doing well and in operating in socially accepted ways. In order to behave thus, it is necessary to learn just what those patterns of thought and action are, to learn the rules of the game. As the previous chapter showed, increasing intellectual maturity results in socialized thinking, whereby the child delays responses while he checks his conclusions and decisions with those of other people, instead of jumping quickly to his own. Some of his satisfaction now comes from measuring up to standards outside himself, from fitting into a bigger and broader world. He is willing to work to learn the basic skills of his culture, the patterns of thinking and doing which mark the difference between being a little child and being a big child on the way to adulthood. He is getting ready to be a producer [28, p. 259].

The child goes about the business of learning his society's skills and rules in style which grows out of his own personality. His performance depends, for example, on how strongly he wants achievement and recognition, how anxious he feels over succeeding, and upon his tendency to reflect before responding. The cultural and social settings within which he interacts will be discussed in the next chapter. In this chapter, the child's development as a learner and producer will be considered in relation to the school, the institution designed especially for teaching him the fundamentals of knowledge.

Relation of Previous Stages to the Sense of Industry

Each stage of personality development has its roots in the past, being built out of what has gone before. The earlier sense of trust, autonomy, and initiative contribute now to the development of the sense of industry. Time orientation, locus of control, and curiosity can be understood as outcomes of previous stages and as determinants of success in establishing a healthy sense of industry.

Time Orientation. In infancy, the sense of trust is derived partly from experiences with time which come from cycles of tension, delay of satisfaction, and satiation [29, p. 181]. As tension builds up during delay, the baby anticipates fulfillment. Signs of approaching satisfaction give hope, and extended delays cause rage. Excess tension, waiting, and rage lead to lack of hope and trust, and in later childhood and adolescence, a disturbed sense of time. The ability to judge intervals of time and the ability to order events in time are related to moral development, as will be seen in a later section of this chapter. Future time orientation is related to achievement behavior which is an important aspect of the sense of industry.

Locus of Control. The toddler develops a sense of autonomy through repeated successes in purposefully controlling his environment. As he realizes that he can choose between real alternatives, as he experiences positive outcomes of choices he knows to be his own, he has a sense of autonomy. He feels that he is in charge. Reality includes places where he cannot choose and where he is not in charge. A healthy sense of autonomy grows upon a balance of freedom to choose successfully and limits on choosing. By the time the child reaches the industry stage, he has established convictions about to what extent he is in charge. He believes that he can choose and determine much of what happens to him or he feels that outside forces are largely responsible. Those who locate control outside themselves may believe that fate or luck or other people cause events. The individual with an internal locus of control believes that *he* himself causes events. A child's locus of control may vary from one area of life to another [48].

An internal locus of control is related to achievement behavior [13]. It makes sense to try harder if you believe that your efforts will have the intended results. Success and excellence, so important for development of the sense of industry, are thus dependent on belief in internal locus of control, which is an aspect of the sense of autonomy. The locus of control is established during childhood and changes little during the time between third and twelfth grades [13]. Middle-class children believe more in internal control than do lower-class children, and white children more than black [11]. This finding is logical when one considers the greater power possessed by middle-class people and whites. They really can control their environments more than can people lower on the socioeconomic ladder, and more than blacks. We would expect their children to reflect this bit of reality.

Curiosity. The preschool child involves himself with development of the sense of initiative through exploring his environment, the objects and the people in it, the actions of which he is capable. Through play, he tries on different roles and investigates different media as ways of creating and discovering. Among the treasures he gains from successful development of the sense of initiative is curiosity. There are two main forms of curiosity: seeking new experiences, and looking for answers to problems. Seeking new experience includes exploring places, objects, and people, looking for new sensory stimulation, new ideas, and new ways of moving. New experience is rewarding in itself. The second form of curiosity involves reducing uncertainty or dissonance to restore equilibrium. Seeing some differences between what he experiences and what he expects, the child seeks further information in order to resolve the conflict [71]. Insufficient new experience leads to boredom and restlessness; too great an environmental change is either shocking or frightening or both. Curiosity is aroused by appropriate degrees of unusualness and incongruity. Children vary in how much new experience they seek, how many new answers they try to find, and how great an environmental change is satisfying rather than frightening [60]. For boys, but not for girls, early (before 6 months) fear of novelty is associated with shyness and fear of strangeness in childhood [7].

During the preschool years, when the sense of initiative is developing fast, satisfying experiences with exploration lead to a lasting interest in reaching out and discovering. The richer the environment, the more curious the child can become; the more curious he is, the more he can discover in his environment. Curiosity can be both a help and a hindrance in the tasks of middle childhood. In situations where adults demand high conformity, as in schools where routines are sacred, or in homes where privacy, quiet, and order are greatly cherished, a very curious child will be too disruptive. The advantages of curiosity outweigh these small liabilities, however, since it stimulates learning and the development of the sense of industry.

Healthy psychological adjustment is associated with high curiosity in children [68]. Teachers' ratings of overall psychological health correlated positively with scores on tests in which children manipulated objects, examined them freely, and commented on them. Low-anxious children preferred more novelty than high-anxious children [70]. A sex difference was demonstrated in first grade children's and younger children's curiosity and seeking of information and experience. Boys were more curious than girls [70, 88]. Desire for novelty seems to increase with age, at least during the early years [70].

Robert J. Izzo

Intellectual competence is related to curiosity, as might be expected. One piece of evidence comes from a comparison of children whose IQs rose with those whose IQs fell during the years between the ages of 6 and 10 [51]. Responses to a projective test indicated that children with rising IQs were more curious and less passive than those with falling IQs. Another type of evidence is furnished by fifth grade children whose curiosity was judged by ratings of teachers, peers, and selves. A child was called curious to the extent that he moved toward, explored, or manipulated new, strange, or mysterious elements of his environments; showed a need or desire to know about himself and his environment; scanned his surroundings, seeking new experiences; persisted in examining and exploring. A week after hearing a story read, the children were tested for memories of it. The children with high curiosity remembered significantly more than did those with low curiosity [65, 66]. In a third study, tasks were arranged in such a way that some children experienced more curiosity than others during the problem-solving process [72]. The high-curiosity group learned more efficiently (made fewer errors) than the low-curiosity group. Children high in curiosity were found to be more flexible and consistent in thinking and also more creative than children low in curiosity [68].

Achievement Aspiration

There are two standpoints from which to consider achievement—the strength of the need or desire for it, and the behavior oriented toward it. Basic to achievement motivation, or the need for achievement, is the child's application of a standard of excellence to the performance he is judging and a feeling tone which goes along with that judgment [59]. In other words, he says, "I did well" or "He did a good job" or "He did a poor job," while having a pleasant or unpleasant feeling about the situation. The goal of achievement behavior is the attainment of approval and avoidance of disapproval, either one's own or somebody else's [15]. Achievement, then, is of the essence of the period of the development of a sense of industry. In order to become a successful learner of the ways of the culture and to become a productive member of society, thus assuring a sense of adequacy, the child must want to achieve and must, in fact, achieve.

Stability of Achievement Over Time. Both need for achievement and achievement behavior were studied over a period of 18 years at the Fels foundation. Both types of measurements showed some consistency from one age level to another. Need for achievement was tested at 8 years, by asking children to tell stories in response to pictures (Thematic Apperception Test) and analyzing for achievement themes. Retesting the children at 11 and 14, moderate correlations were found with the need for achievement at 8 years [50]. A similar study on 8 to 10-year-old boys, retested after six years, showed similar results [32]. Achievement behavior, as shown by ratings and interviews at the Fels foundation, showed some consistency from nursery school age to young adulthood. Low but significant correlations were found between ratings during preschool and elementary school years and between elementary school age and early adolescence. Girls' preschool achievement behavior was related to their adult achievement behavior, but boys' was not. By middle childhood, however, achievement striving was related to adult achievement behavior. During early adolescence, intellectual achievement behavior was predictive of adult behavior, but athletic and mechanical achievement efforts were not related to adult behavior.

Stability of Achievement Across Situations. During the early elementary school years, a child's expectations of himself tend to be consistent between intellectual, artistic, mechanical, and athletic areas [14]. If he did well in one area, he expected to do well in the others. If he held high standards in one, he was likely to hold high standards in all. However, actual achievement behavior did not show so much consistency across situations. With slightly older children, a relationship was shown between intellectual and mechanical achievement behaviors, but not between intellectual and athletic [73]. A factor analytic study on fifth grade black children, sampling a variety of achievement behaviors, shows that there is a general academic achievement dimension [89]. Achievement showed little or no consistency across situations that were different. The more similar the situations, the more similar the achievement behavior shown by boys, but not by girls. For example, tasks differ in *behavioral* requirements such as that of speaking, writing, listening, manipulating, and observing. *Social* requirements differ as to group versus individual situations, presence of audience, rigidity, and competition. *Cognitive* requirements vary as to convergence or divergence (whether there is only one answer or many), flexibility versus rigidity of thinking, level of abstraction, and receiving or synthesizing information. In addition to the general factor in academic achievement, there were five other factors: behavior in individual work situations, behavior with divergent tasks, recitation, perseverance, and behavior on convergent tasks.

Sex Differences. Achievement motivation is not the same for girls as it is for boys. Boys' achievement need and behavior have been studied much more extensively than have girls', perhaps reflecting the general attitude that it is more important for boys to achieve than it is for girls to do so. The difference is, of course, closely related to sex role. Achievement for the sake of achievement seems to motivate boys more than girls, while the seeking of approval and affection is often bound up with the achievement efforts of girls [52]. The boys' achievement behavior was more autonomously motivated, in a sample of early grade schoolboys and girls who were tested for achievement and whose parents were interviewed. For boys, but not for girls, belief in self-responsibility was correlated with scores on academic achievement tests. When academic achievement test scores were correlated with tests of achievement need, a significant relationship was found for boys but not for girls [84]. The girls' achievement was found to relate instead to their desire for affection and approval. In an experimental situation, however, boys and girls responded equally to praise by improving performance on a coding task [90].

The standards of excellence which boys set for themselves tend to be more realistic than those of girls, or at least such was true for 40 day camp children from the first three grades [16]. The boys held standards which corresponded with their performances on intelligence and achievement tests. The opposite was true of girls, whose expectations of success were negatively correlated with their intelligence scores. The sexes also differed in their beliefs about personal responsibility for success. Among the boys but not girls, the more capable ones were strongly convinced that they themselves were responsible for their own achievements. Thus the boys were practical and realistic in their attitudes toward achievement, whereas the girls were more influenced by their wishes and values. Sex role expectations probably account for the differences. Perhaps boys are criticized more than girls when their stated expectations do not fit their performances. It may be that incompetent girls are praised for saying, "I'll try," while very able girls are scolded for being boastful when they predict high success for themselves. At any rate, sex is an important determiner of achievement orientation.

Some Correlates of Achievement. High-achieving children are distinguished from average and low achievers by certain characteristics which suggest that in the early years of life, high achievers accept and internalize adult middle-class values. A group of gifted third grade children, studied through tests, observations, and parent-and-teacher interviews, indicated that superior academic achievers are likely to be independent, asking for little help from adults. These children persisted longer at problems, competed more with their peers, expressed less warmth toward their siblings, and had more guilt feelings than average children [20]. Information obtained about the same children, four years later, showed them as persistent, competitive, still mastering and striving, but sometimes aggressive and destructive in order to win, often antagonistic and belittling to adults, more anxious than formerly, and less creative than they used to be [39]. High academic achievement, then, is likely to exact a price, even during middle childhood.

Competition and Cooperation

The sense of industry is nurtured by experiences of doing well with the tasks required or encountered. The child finds out whether he has performed adequately

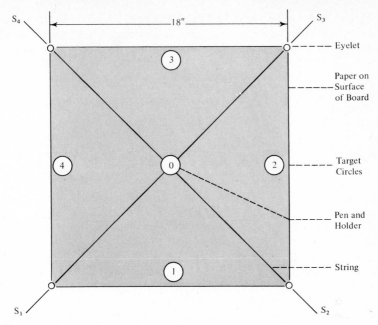

Figure 3–1. Cooperation board.

SOURCE: Reprinted with permission of author and publisher: Madsen, M. C. Cooperative and competitive motivation of children in three Mexican subcultures. *Psychological Reports*, 1967, 20, 1307–1320.

by measuring himself on the standards provided for him. Middle-class urban society tends to define success and adequacy largely in terms of competition, of doing better than other people. Some children are convinced that they have to be *best* in order to succeed. If only one in a group, or a few in a group, can succeed, then many are doomed to failure, with a resulting sense of inferiority and inadequacy. While highly competitive behavior has served important functions in our society, we are now faced with the need for more cooperative behavior for solving community problems and world problems. Other cultures, some planned and some unplanned, demonstrate different ways of institutionalizing competition and cooperation. We can get insight from research which compares our children with theirs.

Madsen and associates have used a "cooperation board" to elicit cooperative and competitive behavior from children in rural and urban Mexico [62], urban and rural communal Israel [87], and three ethnic urban United States groups [63]. Figure 3–1 is a sketch of the apparatus, a board 18 inches square. A string, fastened to a device holding a pen in the center, is strung through an eyelet fastened to each corner. A sheet of paper is placed on the board. A child sits at each corner and pulls his string. He can pull it only toward himself. If the pen is to be pulled anywhere other than in a straight line from center to corner, children have to cooperate. Circles were placed as shown in the drawing. Children were shown how they could draw lines through the circles. In the cooperative condition, children were told that each would receive a prize if they drew lines through all four circles. All children thus learned how to perform cooperatively. Then the reward conditions were changed, but the task remained the same. Each child was assigned one circle and told that he would receive a prize only if a line was drawn through his circle. Cooperation would pay off, and the children knew how to work the pen cooperatively. However, urban, middle-class children in Mexico were much more competitive in the second condition [62]. When Mexican village children were compared with three urban United States groups, results were dramatic [87]. The Afro-America and Anglo-American groups were aggressively, even wildly, competitive, and the urban Mexican Americans were competitive but less vigorous. In the three United States groups, there was no instance of group cooperation, while the Mexican village group showed no instance of competitive behavior. The experiment in Israel revealed competition in the urban group and complete cooperation in the kibbutzim. The kibbutz children discussed the problem thoroughly and planned procedures, including equal sharing of prizes.

Children compete as groups rather than as individuals in both the Soviet Union and in the kibbutzim of Israel. This arrangement reflects conscious planning on the part of educators, in order to prepare children for cooperative societies. An American psychiatrist observing in Israel found kibbutz life ideally suited to the needs of the school-age child [4, p. 202]. He has easy access to tasks which need doing, which he can do well, and which bring rewards to his age group and to the whole kibbutz. He develops little or no sense of inferiority. Bettelheim found this stage the happiest: ". . . one is impressed with the joy of living in them, how the day bubbles with interest, stimulation, excitement and satisfaction" [p. 202].

The Sense of Inferiority

An unfavorable outcome of the development of the sense of industry is too great a sense of inferiority and inadequacy. The child may have too few opportunities to succeed, too great a discrepancy between his opportunities and his resources. His cognitive limitations offer some protection against overwhelming feelings of inferiority. Cognitive conceit (see page 87), the belief that children know more than adults because adults do not know everything, serves a useful function in maintaining feelings of adequacy in the face of actual adult superiority. Damage can result from excessive unsuccessful competition with peers and siblings and from failure in school.

Anxiety. Anxiety is a stirred-up, unpleasant, tense feeling, focused only vaguely or generally. Fear indicates the same type of feeling state but with accompanying attention focused on a specific situation or problem. In childhood, according to Erikson [28, p. 408], it is difficult or impossible to distinguish fear from anxiety. Whether fear or anxiety, this unpleasant tension affects the ways in which the child approaches and deals with his job of learning and producing. Some of the tests devised to measure anxiety deal with general situations and others with particular situations, especially school. The type of statements used to test general anxiety are illustrated by the following: "I feel I have to be best in everything." "I notice my heart beats very fast sometimes." "I worry about doing the right things." "It is hard for me to go to sleep at night" [9]. Anxiety over tests is examined by means of questions such as these: "When the teacher wants to find out how much you have learned, do you get a funny feeling in your stomach?" "Do you worry a lot before you take a test?" "While you are taking a test, do you usually think you are not doing well?" [80].

White girls have been found to be higher than white boys in both types of anxiety, general and test anxiety [81]. Since this finding fits in with cultural expectations of boys and girls, it may be that the difference is partly due to youngsters trying to live up to ideal sex roles. Another contributing factor may be girls' tendency to care a great deal about approval and affection and to try to win these prizes through their achievement efforts. Boys, with their more internalized standards of excellence, would understandably worry less about what people thought of them. Black children showed higher levels of anxiety than white children, throughout the second grade population of a large eastern school system [33]. Unlike the white children, black boys were no less anxious than black girls. Their anxiety was strongly related to the mother's educational level. This finding fits with the finding that poor, lower-class parents give few rewards and little encouragement for desirable behavior, especially verbal efforts, that they require obedience and discourage exploration, curiosity, and independent thinking.

Scores on anxiety tests correlate negatively with IQ [82]. These correlations tend to increase with grade level. Probably interaction is reciprocal. Suffering more and more defeats as he goes through school, a child of low intelligence would feel increasingly inferior, anxious, and reluctant to get into the situation of being tested. Learning and achievement show complicated relationships to anxiety. Both the level of anxiety and the difficulty and type of task must be taken into account. While moderate anxiety may help the child in performing fairly easy tasks, anxiety, especially high anxiety, is likely to interfere with success on difficult tasks. To show the significance of type of task, high-anxious and low-anxious children were tested for achievement in reading and arithmetic [12]. The low-anxious group was definitely superior in arithmetic. For reading, there was a slight but insignificant difference in favor of the high-anxious group. Another study, however, a longitudinal one, found anxiety related earlier and more strongly to reading than to arithmetic [82].

The definition of success and failure will vary from one child to another, depending upon what he and others expect of him. To one person a grade of C means success, while to another, anything short of A is a failure. The aspirations of children who achieve on a low level in the class are, on the average, above the level at which they achieve. Therefore, they usually experience failure. In contrast, children who achieve on the highest level tend to pitch their aspirations lower than their achievement level. Therefore, they usually experience success. Success and failure in school are so very public, as compared with success on the job. It is impossible to hide from teachers, classmates, or parents, and even neighbors and grandparents, the exact marks or grades obtained, and just how those grades compare with Betty's, Tommy's, and Jonathan's grades. Contrasting the aspiration level of children who had chronic failure in reading and arithmetic with children who had a history of success, the successful children were seen as aspiring to levels where they succeeded, while the chronically unsuccessful ones set their aspirations with little regard for achievement [3]. Some set extremely high goals which they could never reach, as though a mere gesture would substitute for realistic action.

It seems reasonable that a very mild degree of fear or anxiety would help a child in problem solving, as long as the resulting tense feeling served to focus his attention squarely on the task at hand. A greater degree of fear would immobilize his resources, freezing them instead of energizing them. Repeated experiences with failure would lead to expectation of more failure, a feeling of worthlessness, inferiority, and inadequacy, all of which constitute the negative of a sense of industry.

Fears. Specific fears of predominantly white children were studied in Grades 3 through 6 [18]. Girls had more fears than boys, and lower socioeconomic-level children more than higher. The children were asked what they feared now, what fears they had held in the past, and what they expected to fear in the future. The children saw themselves as having been more fearful in the past than at present. They expected to have fewer fears in the future. With the exception of third grade present fears, the present and future fears of all were most often political. In former years, children were more likely to fear supernatural phenomena and animals. Probably modern communications make children aware of world problems at increasingly early ages.

Areas of Competency

Academic skills figure largely in this picture. Competencies include motor coordinations, skills as a worker at home, knowledge of games and various areas of interest, and knowledge of a religion and of a system of morals and values. In all such areas the child takes over the patterns of his culture, and while making them his own makes himself a functioning member of his society. A positive self concept, as shown by high self-esteem, is related to school achievement, as shown by correlating between self concept and achievement scores in arithmetic and reading [84]. The child benefits greatly from having a wide choice of opportunities for adequacy in order that there will be a goodly number of places in which he really does succeed. A healthy environment therefore includes broad academic areas, a variety of play activities, and chances to work at different jobs and to know many people, places, and objects.

Reading. The roots of the skill of reading lie in speech and graphic representation. In Smart and Smart, *Preschool Children* (Macmillan, 1973), we showed that speech emerges without direct teaching. So does graphic representation. All toddlers spontaneously make marks, using paper and crayon, if available, and if not, a stick in the sand or charcoal on a rock. Preschool children can separate scribbles from script [35]. A very few children learn to read on their own. A few children learn with minimal help from an older sibling or a parent. Most children learn from teachers, who guide them through the perceptual, conceptual, verbal, and motor performances necessary for success. There are many different methods of teaching reading, and these have been the subject of much research and sometimes heated opinion. There is also controversy as to *when* reading should be taught. Since success in school depends so heavily on reading, naive parents, and sometimes teachers, assume that the earlier formal instruction is begun, the better. A sound foundation for reading is built in the preschool years through development in language, graphic arts, visual and auditory perception, attention, curiosity, motor skills, and esthetic appreciation of books and stories. This vital preparation for reading is much more available to the middle-class child than to the poor child. Compensatory programs attempt to "make it up" to the child. Day-care programs, especially those which take infants and toddlers, are designed to offer opportunities for optimal growth, so as to make compensation unnecessary.

Even with good preparation for learning to read, some children learn faster and more easily than others. The lock-step of the traditional school does disservice to both fast and slow learners. The overwhelming sense of inferiority resulting from reading failure can seriously block a child in his efforts toward competency. The problem, therefore, is threefold: to arrange for each child to learn to read at the time most appropriate for him; to let him proceed at full speed for him; and to have him feel right about himself, whether he learned early or late, quickly or slowly.

The study of reading disorders is a specialized field. Causes of disorders reach into almost every facet of the child's development and relationships, to include basic physical disorders, such as perinatal brain injury, social deprivation in the form of impoverished family background and lack of early stimulation, emotional disruptions, lack of establishment of lateral dominance and preference, motor disturbances, and upsetting educational experiences.

Writing. The development of skill in writing involves eye–hand coordination of perceptual and conceptual activity. Aims, values, and practices in teaching handwriting are often rather confused [44]. For instance, if it is important for the child to learn to write in a standard style, then precise coordination is at a premium, and the child who lacks such control must work very hard, with much frustration. When handwriting style is considered an expression of individual personality rather than a standard product, the teacher will help the child to develop his own style within certain limits of legibility. If the main purpose of writing is conceived of as communication, then a high standard of legibility is in order. If writing is done mainly for the individual himself, in order to express his thoughts or take notes for himself, then speed, not legibility, is the prime essential.

Since motor control plays such a large part in learning to write neatly, according to a standard form, and since motor control is not highly correlated with IQ, reading, and other academic achievement, high skill in handwriting may be possible for many children who do not have widespread academic success. This is not to say that a very adequate student might not also write well, but only that chances to be good writers are distributed on a different basis from chances to excel in other subject matter areas. Handwriting, then, might serve some children as a much-needed source of feelings of adequacy and thus aid in development of a sense of industry.

Rarely, if ever, does handwriting express thoughts quickly enough to be efficient and satisfying. The first grader, just learning to write, would be completely frustrated if he wanted to record his thoughts. If an adult will occasionally take dictation from him, he can thus "write" stories and letters which will give him satisfaction and adequacy and which will also develop his ability to communicate through writing. Another effective aid to written expression is the typewriter. After the initial stages of learning to type, which can be done early in this stage of life, or even before, the individual can communicate and record his thoughts ever so much more quickly, efficiently, and legibly by typewriter than by hand.

Writing can be considered in a context quite different from that of making representational marks. Writing is also linguistic expression. In this sense, it shares some characteristics with thought or inner speech and some with socialized speech. A comparison of oral and written language reveals some similarities and differences [40]. The subjects were 320 children, ages 9, 11, 13, and 15, who told and wrote stories. The stories were analyzed for length, type of clauses, and unrelated words used. The findings included these: no tendency for girls to excel boys, except in length of written compositions; more subordinate clauses used in writing than in speaking, increasingly so with advance in age; more adjective and adverb clauses in writing, more noun clauses in speaking; positive correlations between subordinate clauses in writing and age, mental age, IQ, and occupational status of father; no indication that a mature level had been reached in either oral or written stories by age 15. Writing in this sense, then, is an academic skill with its own distinctive characteristics, a skill which shows continuous development throughout the school years.

Mathematics. Based on the cognitive activities of classifying, abstracting, ordering, and relating, the learning of number concepts is influenced by the experiences the child has had at home, at nursery school, and at kindergarten. His cognitive style makes a difference, too. The tendency to analyze visual arrays is helpful in abstracting numbers out of groups of objects. Spatial imagery and discrimination are probably quite important to success. Reflectivity, rather than impulsivity, is understandably an aid in problem solving. Thus the intellectual and personality development of the child have a direct bearing on the ease or difficulty he experiences in his first encounters with arithmetic in school. He soon feels adequate or inadequate in regard to mathematics, often reinforced by family or friends. Since mathematical ability is often considered appropriate for men and not for women, many girls inhibit their growth along these lines in order to fit into the sex role which they feel required to assume.

Like the teaching of reading, instruction in mathematics has undergone a revolution since mid-century. The old methods relied heavily upon rote memory and drill. In former times teachers tried to build mathematical concepts by having the child manipulate spoken and written symbols. Most likely, the children who made good progress with these methods were the ones blessed with stimulating environments, in which they had and continued to have rich opportunities for arranging, ordering, grouping, and discriminating. The "new math" incorporates knowledge about concept formation. Number concepts are built with the aid of visual perception and imagery and often other sensory experiences as well. Books and pictures are planned and arranged so as to use visual perception and imagery. Objects such as blocks, rods, beads, and cards are employed not only to provide tactile perception, but to permit the child to arrange, group, and order objects. This type of apparatus has been designed in such a way as to give insight into counting, grouping, addition, subtraction, multiplication, division, measurement, fractions, ratio, decimals, percentage, square measure, and cubic measure. Eventually, of course, the child must free himself of dependence on concrete objects if he is to go very far in mathematics.

The "new math" holds a promise of success for more children. Under the old methods, many children, especially those with limited backgrounds, experienced early failure and discouragement. Now, if a child is allowed to progress at his own rate, the school can offer him materials and experiences with which to build useful concepts. It is theoretically possible for all children (except the severely brain-damaged and ill) to be successful with mathematics in the elementary school. As a child sees himself mastering this important cultural tool, his sense of industry is enhanced, and he enjoys healthy personality growth.

Maturity As a Predictor of Academic Success. Physical maturity has been mentioned in the previous chapter as a predictor of success in first grade. A rating scale used by teachers on fifth grade children has shown that social and intellectual ratings, as well as physical, are related to achievement [69]. Significant social items included considerateness of others, cooperativeness in group activities and relationships with peers. Emotional maturity items were attentiveness, self-control, self-confidence, and anxiety. The physical considerations were size and coordination. Intellectual maturity included memory for procedures, eagerness to learn, speed of comprehension, language development.

Correlates of Academic Incompetence. A special remedial program for "educationally handicapped" children offered opportunities to find out how non-achieving children differed from children who were doing satisfactory work in school [74]. The subjects, about 2 percent of the school population, had one and a half to two years discrepancy between ability and achievement. The siblings and parents were studied, also, and compared with siblings and parents of matched controls (children of the same sex who were successful at school). Neurological and familial factors indicate some physical basis for the educational handicaps.

Compared with normal controls, the educationally handicapped children were poorer in several tests of hand and finger movements and in right–left discrimination. Medical histories showed the handicapped to have had more colic and irritability in infancy, decreased sound production, poor listening skills, difficulty in communicating with the mother, and more temper tantrums.

The educationally handicapped and their siblings shared impairments in numerical computation, sequencing, fine-perceptual-motor hand–eye coordination, memory, reading, and spelling. Parents had done less well in high school English than had parents of successful children. Fathers were poorer readers. Mothers were poorer mathematicians. The handicapped children, then, may have been influenced by both heredity and environment in their development of unsuccessful academic patterns.

Performance as a Worker

Development of the sense of industry hinges largely on feeling and being successful as a worker. Some of such feeling and being comes when the child does well in reading, writing, arithmetic, and all the other academic skills. Although school is indeed his job, he knows too that school is not identical with the work world, in which his parents and other adults earn their living. The child needs some success in that world too. Significant work experience adds greatly to his sense of adequacy, contributes to his understanding of adults, his family and society, and gives him experience which can help him in later choice of a vocation. When he does a good job, he wins recognition and respect, giving him a toehold in the work world. Boys and men, in contrast to girls and women, have been found more task-oriented, more concerned about getting the job done and done well [23]. Girls and women showed more interest than boys and men in the social-interaction aspects of the job, the maintaining of happy relations with co-workers.

Whereas simple agricultural or hunting societies offer children easy access to important work, a complex technological society provides severely limited work opportunities. Many of the jobs available both at home and otherwise are in the realm of cleaning and tidying. While necessary and useful, this type of work does not give the child the feeling of being a producer, nor even of being necessary in earning the family living. For instance, after milking the cow, collecting the eggs, and picking the strawberries, the youngster joins with his family in eating the fruits of his labor plus the contributions of other family members. There is no comparable integrating and satisfying experience for the child who straightens up his room, empties the wastebaskets, and carries the empty pop bottles out to the car. Kitchen, basement, garage, and garden do, of course, offer some opportunities for children to contribute constructively to the home. Job possibilities outside the home are probably more curtailed, as compared with those in a simpler society or in a planned society, such as the kibbutz. The young kibbutniks spend part of their time doing exactly the same work that adults do. They raise animals and chickens, cultivate vegetables, clean the house, and may even help with earning the cash income of the kibbutz [4, pp. 161–164].

Even though American children can find few real jobs in the market place (newspaper delivery is almost the only steady one), many children do real work in the organizations for children, such as Boy Scouts, Girl Scouts, 4H, Rainbow, Demolay, Future Farmers of America, Future Homemakers of America, and church clubs. In cooperation with adult leaders and his own peers, the child takes part in service projects and money-making projects, joins in consuming the profits made by the group and thereby enjoys many of the benefits of being a real producer. When leaders and peers judge his performance good, especially when they give unmistakable signs of approval and recognition (badges and pins), the youngster's feelings of adequacy are enhanced and he makes progress in the development of a sense of industry.

Recreational Activities and Interests

Children's play activities are the means by which they develop competency on many different levels and in several senses. Already discussed in Chapter 1, motor skills contribute greatly to effectiveness and adequacy. During the school age, many basic motor coordinations are integrated into games which have social meaning as well. Such games—for example, baseball—involve not only the coordinations of hitting, throwing, and running but also knowing a set of rules which tell exactly how to play and also how to feel about the game (being a good sport, competing, team spirit, and such). Performing well in such situations brings recognition, approval, and a sense of mastery over some of the complexities of the social and physical environment. Similarly, intellectual games integrate recently learned skills with social behavior, in a framework of rules. Checkers, Monopoly, and other table games are examples, along with thinking games, such as Twenty Questions and Coffee Pot.

Self-mastery, with little or no reference to other people, is the objective of certain types of games. This type includes the ancient, widespread games which appear spontaneously in the early school years and then disappear just as spontaneously. For example, the game of not stepping on cracks, in which the rule is self-set and is thought to work magic. Through this game, the child controls his own actions and controls the world. In the same way, a child sets himself an obstacle to overcome, such as hopping a certain distance on one foot or holding his breath for a given length of time. Or he seeks a certain form of anxiety in order to master it, as he does in walking on a high place or riding on a roller coaster. Imaginative play is also used in the service of self-mastery. Expressing fears, hostility, or fantasies of grandeur through dramatic play, he gains control through expressing these disturbing feelings and through distinguishing between imagination and reality.

A variety of purposes are served by the individual activities of making collections, reading, watching TV, and creating in art media, all of which the child does for pleasure and recreation. Through these means, he extends his concepts and knowledge. Reading, of course, contributes to competency in almost everything a child does, in addition to giving him enjoyment. Children read a wide range of materials, if they have chances to do so. They especially like stories which get off to a fast start, probably because of the influence of TV and the generally fast pace of modern life [56]. Books of wide appeal include historical stories (because they are full of action), plots with well-sustained suspense, animal stories, humorous tales, informational books, and books in series (because they are collections, as well as books). Although most children enjoy fantasy stories, some children are very particular about the type of fantasy they will accept [56]. Most children read comic books. In a recent year, 30 million of them were sold in this country [56]. It is estimated that each comic is read by three children. The satisfactions from comic books include quick action and adventure, short episodes, very easy reading, availability everywhere, and being an activity which other children share. Many children have nothing else to read. When the reading behavior of 323 seventh grade children was related to other aspects of their behavior, several interesting findings resulted [5]. There was no relationship between reading ability and amount or type of comic books read. Neither school adjustment nor achievement nor intelligence was related to amount and type of comic books read. The children who read comic books read more library books than did children who did not read comics.

Watching television is an important childhood activity (or perhaps it should be called passivity). The average second grade child was found to spend 17 hours a week in front of the TV while by sixth grade, the hours of viewing had increased to 28 [98]. One of the dangers of television is that it crowds out other kinds of activities. The sitting child is not practicing motor skills, which he needs in order to be physically competent; he is not playing games with other children; he is not creating. Some of the effects of television on children have been studied in both England and the United States [46, 83]. In both countries, television had a leveling effect intellectually, stepping up the information obtained by duller children and younger children and reducing the amount of information which older, bright children could have been expected to obtain without television. Comparing children's behavior before and after the families own TV sets, the English investigators found that children went to bed about 20 minutes later on the average when they owned a set. They saw no evidence of harmful physical effects, nor was there any indication that television caused fears or aggression. However, American and Canadian experimental studies have shown children to be more aggressive immediately after viewing films of aggressive models [2, 95]. Effects of viewing aggression have been shown to last for at least six months [45]. Further evidence comes from a study of over 600 third grade children [30]. Classmates' ratings on aggression were correlated with watching television programs that showed a great deal of violence. The evidence presented by these varied studies seems quite conclusive. Television constitutes a threat to children, first of all in stimulating antisocial behavior but also in restricting healthy activity.

Television also extends the child's view of real life through news reports and educational features. The great potential of "Sesame Street," the program designed for preschool children, comes to mind immediately. The success of "Sesame Street" led to the creation of another program by Children's Television Workshop.

Using new techniques, the program is designed to teach children to read and to help slow readers and those with problems in learning to read.

News reports, especially war scenes, could be expected to have disturbing effects, just as fictional violence does. Or perhaps more. Children know what is going on in the world more than any previous generation of children has known. The dangers of such overexposure are sobering.

Moral Knowledge and Judgment

The rules governing right and wrong behavior are among the important guides to thought and action which a child seeks to master in his efforts to become a functioning member of his society. He realizes that rules and laws extend beyond his family and that he has obligations and privileges outside the family. In fact, many of the basic rules about how one ought to behave can be stated fairly early in this stage of life, although reasons behind them are not understood. For example, the average 7-year-old can give appropriate answers to these questions: "What's the thing for you to do when you have broken something that belongs to someone else?" and "What's the thing for you to do if another boy hits you without meaning to do it?" [94]. Although they show some relation to conduct, moral knowledge scores are also related to intelligence [97], cultural background, and the desire to make a good impression [55].

Learning the Rules. Being able to state the rule governing behavior is only an early stage in a long process of development which continues throughout the age span under discussion. At first, rules are by definition. They cover limited situations, without reasons or explanations. Gradually the child comes to understand the involvement of more and more people and viewpoints. This process was illustrated in a study of children's concepts of money and of the relations between storekeepers, customers, clerks, and manufacturers [92]. The rules which govern buying and selling are based on complicated relationships involving arithmetic, monetary value, profit, ownership, distribution, and the roles which people play. The ways in which children grasped this network of rules and relationships are organized into a sequence of stages of broader and broader understanding. Some of the stages given with the median ages are as follows:

> *Five years eight months:* Rules exist by definition. You need money to buy with. You just can't take goods without paying. In the first of this period, any coins buy any goods. The storekeeper also gives coins. Later, a coin buys objects of certain value, coin and object being matched exactly.
>
> *Six years four months:* Rules cover indirect but imprecise relations. The child knows that a certain amount of money is necessary for a certain purchase and that the amount of change is systematically related to price and amount paid, but he cannot figure out the amounts. He understands that work is worth paying for. He begins to understand that goods cost the storekeeper something and that he pays his helper.
>
> *Seven years ten months:* The value and relations of coins are understood precisely. The children make change exactly.
>
> *Eight years seven months:* He realizes that it does not matter whether the storekeeper gives the goods first or whether the customer pays first.
>
> *Eight years nine months:* He understands more of the impersonal rules which govern buying and selling, that retailers properly charge more than wholesalers, who are too far away to be able to sell directly to the consumer.

Nine years nine months: He has impersonal, interconnected concepts of profit, credit, storekeeper, worker, customer, factory owner, and helper.

Eleven years two months: He knows that in spite of the impersonal system of profit making, personal, immoral motives sometimes prevail. The existence of a rule does not assure its being obeyed.

Moral Judgment. Moral thought and judgment, in contrast to knowledge of the rules, continue to develop throughout the school years. Although the first or second grader knows fairly well what he is supposed to do, his reasons for doing it or not doing it change as he matures. Cognitive growth is basic to the growth of moral thought and judgment. Interaction between people is a fundamental factor in both cognitive and moral development, since the child checks his ideas, beliefs, and interpretations against those of other people, modifies them in accordance with discrepancies he finds, and attempts to justify his thinking to people who disagree with him. In this give and take of social relationships, he shapes his own beliefs within the social and cultural context in which he is growing up. Six aspects of moral judgment have been demonstrated as defining moral development during the elementary school years [55]. Evidence from many different studies is in essential agreement on the development of the following attitudes and viewpoints.

Intentionality in Judgment. Young children usually judge an act by its consequences, older children by the intentions which prompted it. This tendency has been tested by Piaget's [76] story of the boy who broke 15 cups while trying to help his mother, in contrast to the boy who broke 1 cup while trying to steal jam. Almost all 4-year-olds say that the boy who broke the large number of cups was worse. About 60 percent of 6-year-olds agree. The majority of 9-year-olds say that the other boy was worse. Although by age 9, most children can apply the principle of intentionality, further cognitive growth and experience contribute to understanding of the principle. The adolescent years see a refinement in understanding and expressing the principle.

Relativism in Judgment. There is only one way in which to judge an act, according to the thinking of young children, either right or wrong. If a child and an adult conflict in judging an act, then the adult is right. To illustrate this way of thinking, children were told a story in which a friendly classmate helped a lazy pupil to do his homework, even though the teacher had forbidden the pupil to receive help. The children were asked whether the teacher thought the friendly classmate's behavior right, whether the lazy pupil thought it right, and whether the friendly classmate thought himself right. Most 6-year-olds gave only one judgment, on which all three characters were supposed to agree; most 9-year-olds realized that there were different points of view from which to make this judgment.

Independence of Sanctions. An act is bad if it elicits punishment, according to many children of 4 or 5. Between 5 and 7, most children change this point of view to believe that an act is bad because it does harm or breaks a rule. The test story was about a child who obediently watched a young sibling while the mother was away, only to have the mother spank him when she returned. The younger children said that the baby-sitting child must have been bad, because his mother spanked him; most 7-year-olds said that the child was good, because he had done good [54].

Use of Reciprocity. Several steps can be distinguished in the process of accepting the idea of doing as you would be done by. Four-year-olds rarely use the concept at all. Between 7 and 10, children usually employ it in a concrete, utilitarian way, avoiding retaliation and courting return of favors. After 10 or 11, children show more feeling about how it would be in someone else's place.

Use of Punishment As Restitution and Reform. Younger children believe that retribution should be the main basis for punishment and that severe punishment will reform the wrongdoer. Older children advocate milder punishment, with restitution rather than retribution as the aim [76].

Naturalistic Views of Misfortune. At 6 or 7, children are likely to see accidents and misfortunes as punishment for their misdeeds. This confusion diminishes with age, as the child builds more mature concepts of causality.

Further discussion of stages and types of moral judgments occurs in Chapter 5, where some growth trends are traced through childhood and adolescence.

Moral Behavior

Since the elementary school child is quite limited in his understanding and application of moral principles, he can hardly be expected to be extensively guided by them in his behavior. Rather, he is guided more by the rules of his family, peers, school, and community. He perceives rules as located outside himself, coming largely from adults. His egocentrism and resulting cognitive conceit (see page 87) makes rule-breaking not so much a moral matter but more a way of proving his cleverness by outwitting adults [27]. Although he has made some beginnings in internalizing rules, a large part of his conscience is still external.

While there seems to be a general factor resulting in individual difference in honesty, a large determiner of whether a child cheats or not is the situation in which he is tempted [8]. When a child cheats in one situation, it does not mean that he will do so in another, since cheating in one context has only a low correlation with cheating in another [41, 85]. In experimental testing of cheating, most children do some, a few a great deal, and a few only a little [41]. In other words, cheating scores were distributed normally. Cheating was also found to depend upon the ease of doing so and upon the risk of detection. No age changes in cheating and stealing have been found experimentally during the school years, although according to parents' reports, stealing and lying decreased after age 6 to 8 [37, 85].

How great a relationship is there between moral knowledge or judgment and moral conduct? Kohlberg has considered this question with the boys whose moral judgment he traced from ages 7 to 16. An experimental measure of cheating showed that those high in moral judgment cheated significantly less than those who were lower. (Also, delinquents scored lower in moral judgment than did normal working-class boys.) When teachers were asked to rate children on conscience and on fairness with peers, the boys' moral judgment correlated .31 with conscience and .51 with fairness [55]. An older study [41] showed a correlation of .43 between moral knowledge and character ratings by teachers and peers, and a correlation of .46 between moral knowledge and tests of honesty. Correlations around .40 between moral judgment and moral behavior were found for lower-class black boys and girls in kindergarten, fourth, and sixth grades [86]. These studies agree, then, that while moral conduct is related to judgment, conduct is not entirely dependent upon judgment.

Several other aspects of behavior have been found related to moral behavior. General intelligence has been shown to contribute to moral conduct [41, 75].

The ability to maintain stable, focused attention also contributes to moral conduct [55]. Probably related to this factor is the ability to control aggressive fantasy [75].

Concepts of time and perception of the passage of time are also related to moral development [86]. Lower-class black children between 5 and 12 were rated by teachers on moral conduct and were given tests of moral judgment, time concepts, and perception of time. The moral judgment tests were based on Piaget's stories. Time concepts were assessed by questions such as "Which meal do you have first, lunch, dinner, or breakfast?" and "What time is it now? What time is it in California?" Time perception was measured by asking the child to reproduce time intervals of 10, 20, and 30 seconds. Similar age-related trends were found for moral judgment, time concepts, and time perception. All three improved steadily from kindergarten to fourth grade and then leveled off. *Concepts* of time and moral *judgment* were highly correlated at all ages. *Perceptions* of time and moral *conduct* were significantly correlated at all ages. *Concepts* of time and moral *conduct* were highly correlated at all ages. Thus time concepts are related to both judgment and conduct, while perception of time is related to conduct only. Another interesting finding is that younger children with the poorest conduct scores tended to over-estimate time intervals. Results suggest that regulation of impulse and need gratification, which is essential for moral judgment and conduct, is influenced by the child's ability to order events in time. Moral development, then, is an extremely complex process which can be viewed in different ways and which is inextricably bound up with the child's psychological development and with the various relationships through which he grows.

Religious Concepts

Children search for meaning in life, for explanations of the great mysteries which puzzle all human beings, for unifying concepts. A sense of adequacy is enhanced by some success in asking questions, being able to discuss them, and finding answers which give some satisfaction. Although religion and philosophy do not occupy the school-age child as much as they do the adolescent, yet the child lays a foundation for his adolescent enquiries.

Religious concepts, like other concepts, are the products of cognitive development and social interaction. Some children receive direct teaching in the form of religious instruction carried on by their church or temple. A series of studies on denominational concepts shows age-related steps in the child's progress toward an adult understanding of his religion [24, 25, 26]. Each child was asked a series of questions about his own denomination: Is your family Protestant (Catholic, Jewish)? Are you a Protestant? Are all boys and girls in the world Protestants? Can a dog or a cat be a Protestant? How can you tell a person is a Protestant? How do you become a Protestant? What is a Protestant? Can you be a Protestant and an American at the same time? After answering *yes* or *no*, the children were asked to explain their answers.

Four aspects of denominational conception could be distinguished: knowledge of characteristics common to all members of the denomination, knowledge of class membership compatible or incompatible with membership in the denomination, knowledge of how membership in the denomination is gained or lost, and knowledge of the signs by which a member of a denomination can be recognized. With Jewish and Catholic children, each of these types of knowledge could be seen developing in three stages. With Protestant children, only the first two types of knowledge developed in three stages. The stages were

1. At about 6 years, the child had a *global, undifferentiated concept.* "What is a Catholic?" JAY: "A person." How is he different from a Protestant? "I don't know." "What is a Jew?" SID: "A person." How is he different from a Catholic? "'Cause some people have black hair and some people have blonde."
2. From 7 to 9, concepts were *differentiated* but *concrete.* "He goes to Mass every Sunday and goes to Catholic School." "He belongs to a Protestant family." Jewishness was understood both as a group of actions and as a family quality, leading to some contradictory answers. Can a dog or a cat be a Jew? STAN: "No." Why not? "They are not human." What difference does that make? "They can't go to the Synagogue or say the prayers . . . but I guess if it belonged to a Jewish family, it could be Jewish."
3. Children between 11 and 14 had a *differentiated* and *abstract* concept of their denomination. The child realizes that his religion is one religion among others. What is a Catholic? BILL: "A person who believes in the truths of the Roman Catholic Church." What is a Protestant? FAITH: "A faithful believer in God and doesn't believe in the Pope." Can a dog or a cat be Jewish? SID: "No . . . because they are not human and would not understand a religion." Gaining membership involves learning and believing. Religion is recognized as a way of categorizing people which is different from other ways, such as by nationality. Can you be an American and a Jew at the same time? "Yes . . . because Jewish is a religion and American is a nationality."

This demonstration of the growth of religious concepts with increasing age is one more illustration of how development is the result of interaction between the child and his environment. In the first stage, cognitive maturity is such that the 5- or 6-year-old can form only a global concept of being a Catholic, Protestant, or Jew. The global concept he forms, however, depends on the religion which is offered to him. Without the religious environment with which to interact, religious concepts would not come into being.

Another aspect of the exploration of the religious institution's impact on children's concepts was concerned with the understanding of causality [31]. The subjects were 153 Protestant, Jewish, and Roman Catholic boys, between 6 and 8 years of age. A rating as to the degree of religious devoutness was obtained through a questionnaire sent to the families and by rating the type of school attended. The solutions given by the subjects to problem situations were classified as animistic, anthropomorphic, and scientific. While there were no differences between the three religions, differences were significant in terms of devoutness. Children from very devout homes gave more animistic and anthropomorphic responses and fewer scientific responses than did children from less devout homes. Similarly, children attending religious schools gave more animistic and anthropomorphic responses and fewer scientific responses than did children attending public schools. Thus it could be concluded that the religious institution tended to retard the development of scientific thinking in 6- to 8-year-old boys. *Some* of the subjects from devout homes and religious schools did give scientific answers. The author pointed out that this could mean that religion and science are not inevitably incompatible. It could also mean that these youngsters, although from devout homes, were not themselves devout, and had, in opposition to their environment, developed modes of scientific thinking.

A philosophical question, fourth graders' interest in living a good life, was examined by having children write about their interests [1]. The 10 schools used were all private ones, probably Catholic. Among nine interest categories, the good life, or living a good life, ranked second. One eighth of all interests listed pertained to it. The order of interests was thus: possession of objects, good life, pets, vocation, travel, relatives, money, school and education. Under interest in good life were items pertaining to living a good life, but an even larger number of items concerned the ultimate purpose of life.

Both research and common sense indicate the importance of curiosity in stimulating intellectual functioning and development. Can curiosity, then, be encouraged and nurtured in grade school children? Experiments using a method called *Inquiry Training* show that children can learn to use curiosity for solving problems [93]. After viewing films of simple physics experiments, fifth and sixth grade children asked questions which could be answered by *yes* or *no*. The children learned to formulate, use, and test hypotheses. The process of discovery through questioning was made more real and functional by a discussion of each session, based on a tape recording of the session.

The Role of the School

Schools and the sense of industry are made for each other. It is no accident that children are sent to a special institution which imparts the wisdom of the culture at just the age when they become interested in learning it and in becoming producing members of society. What happens to the beginning pupil depends upon the personal resources he brings to school, the values of the culture as transmitted by the school, the makeup of his class, and the behavior of his teacher.

School Influences

Values Held by the School. Since the educational system is a product of the culture, the school prepares the child for the role he is expected to play. In England, the emphasis is on the child as an individual; in India, the child as a family member; in the Israeli kibbutz, the child as a community member; in the USSR, the child as a citizen. The "Open Classroom" [38] epitomizes English efforts to promote the full development of each individual as an autonomous, responsible, thinking, creative person. The child is free to choose what to do from a wealth of opportunities, although if he neglects certain basic parts of work, the teacher will direct him. Research shows that consistent use of the democratic, open style of teaching does indeed promote creativity and flexibility in problem solving [64]. The Russian first grade illustrates successful methods of creating members of collectives: cooperative children who help one another, accept criticism from one another, and put the group ahead of the individual [6]. When the pupil arrives, for example, he is to wipe his feet, greet the teachers and his seat mate by name, obey the teacher, learn all rules and duties of the classroom.

Conflicting values in the United States make the role of the school confused. Should excellence prevail over mediocrity, happiness over duty, or creativity over conformity? These are matters of philosophy or even opinion. And while the

United States Constitution guarantees separation of church and state, many people want character education as part of the curriculum. But what religion or philosophy should guide moral education? What concensus is there on the definition of a good child? Should he be competitive or cooperative, original or obedient? Some school administrators decide that the safest way is to teach academics and leave character education to the home and church. Such a reduction to the lowest common denominator stands in sharp contrast to the Soviets, who seem to know exactly what they want to teach and who do so effectively [6].

One way of getting an overall view of a nation's values is to look at the textbooks prescribed for its schoolchildren. Books and other teaching materials are instruments through which the school affects the competence of its pupils. Textbooks, however, are more than this, since they reflect the values of the whole culture, chosen by the community or even by the state, as compulsory reading for its children. Textbooks hold up the virtues and behavior which adults want children to attain. Because they are chosen by committees and the choice is influenced by additional people, the behavior exalted tends to be conventional and stereotyped. Bronfenbrenner has analyzed values upheld by the Soviets and presents a summary in pictures illustrating "Laws of the Pioneers" [6, pp. 39–48]. An analysis of American textbooks over 60 years is illustrated in Figure 3–2. The themes in stories were classified as to whether they dealt with affiliation (love and friendship), moral teaching, or achievement [19]. Achievement themes decreased steadily, moral teaching decreased from the turn of the century, and affiliation followed an uncertain course.

When Americans began to face the problems of civil rights, poverty, and deprivation, they criticized the textbooks and teaching materials in use at that time. The picture of life presented in readers was often unrealistic. Friendly and helpful behavior was almost always rewarded, for instance, while problems of aggression and greed were handled by pretending that children did not have such problems. Autonomy and initiative were usually discouraged, while skills, enjoyment, optimism, and cooperation were approved. Very conventional sex roles were upheld. Stories showed only white, middle-class children, families, and teachers. A demand for change resulted in books showing children from all ethnic groups, living in a variety of styles. The use of multiethnic readers has led to marked positive changes in the attitudes of white second grade children toward black people, according to the results of a carefully controlled experiment [58]. For older pupils, the way in which history textbooks treat slavery is significant for attitudes toward race relations [43]. Since older textbooks have been criticized as incomplete and distorted, some modern authors are trying to be more realistic and honest [10].

Children may be economically disadvantaged or disadvantaged because they come from a culturally different group. Very often membership in a minority group coexists with low income. The American public schools have been dominated by white, English, Protestant culture. Instead of building upon the knowledge and value system that the child brought with him, educators often assumed that the different child had *no* culture and must be forced into the Anglo-American mold [34]. Recent studies show how wrong such an assumption is. For example, bilingual children in several different situations have been found to do better than monolinguals in several different measures [49]. Bilingual French-Canadian 10-year-olds scored higher than monolinguals in intelligence, concept formation, and flexible thinking. Spanish-speaking first grade children who were taught in both Spanish

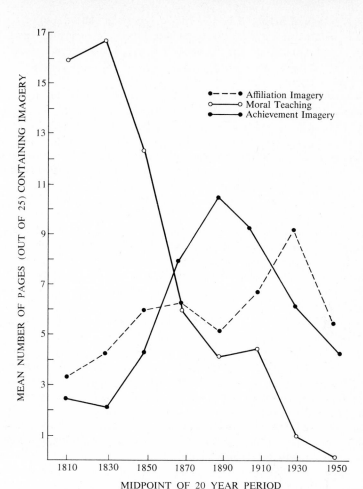

Figure 3–2. Values extolled by children's textbooks over a period of a century and a half.

SOURCE: Adapted from R. deCharms and G. H. Moeller, "Content Analysis of Children's Readers," *Journal of Abnormal and Social Psychology*, 1962, **64**, 136–162. Used by permission of the American Psychological Association and Richard deCharms.

and English did better in cognitive growth, communication skills, and social and emotional adjustment than did their peers who were taught only in English. Similar studies have yielded similar results in Mexico and the Philippines. Therefore, instead of ignoring or trying to replace what the child already knows when he enters school, the school system might better accept the child's culture as valuable and then build upon it. Not only would the child retain the cognitive advantages of his own culture but his self-esteem would be enhanced and he would be encouraged to believe that he could control what happened to him. Recent studies on American Indians make these points especially well, when they document the emptiness and despair felt by children (and adults) whose rich culture is ignored or denigrated by the monoethnic system [34, 91].

Reward System of School. The diversity in American culture results in children who differ widely in values. That is, what is rewarding to one child may not be to another. In order to learn in school, the child must get satisfaction from his efforts. Concern with disadvantaged children has led to a search for ways in which to motivate their learning.

Havighurst has analyzed the evolution of human reward-punishment system with special reference to the education of disadvantaged children. He distinguishes four main types of reward-punishments. The first, which operates during approximately the first 4 years of life, is the satisfaction or deprivation of physical-physiological appetites. Pleasure comes from food, toys, motor activity, sensory perception, and so on. A new type of satisfaction is added to the first type at about 5 years, praise-disapproval, first from parents, teachers, and age-mates. Then comes approval-disapproval, through the action of conscience or superego. Last is approval-disapproval from the ego or self which is felt to have considerable control over events. Different subcultures develop this system in children at different rates. Some investigators have found lower-class children solving problems just as well as middle-class children when rewards were tangible but not when they were verbal. For instance, one second grade boy did not count beyond 3 when asked to do so, but counted 14 candy hearts, when told that he could have as many as he could count [42].

Different subcultures teach different values and reward systems. For example, many American Indians value cooperation very highly. Their children insist upon helping one another in the classroom, even though the teacher tries to promote competition and individual performance. If such children could be encouraged to teach each other, their learning would probably be more efficient. In general, the school would probably succeed better with culturally different children if teachers could use the children's abilities instead of trying to make them over.

Relationship Between Individual Child and Type of School Program. Different programs and styles of teaching suit different children, according to the children's various cognitive and personality characteristics. For example, one child works well by himself, pursuing a topic for a long time, concentrating on it, and resenting interruptions. Another child accomplishes more when small tasks are set for him and when he can change often from one activity to another. Visual aids, teaching machines, and role playing are especially appropriate for children from low socioeconomic backgrounds, since they are likely to do better with visual than with verbal materials [78].

Different methods of teaching reading have been demonstrated to be differentially suited to children according to certain personality characteristics [36]. One system used the phonics method, which provided a maximum of structure, rules, systematic arrangements, and definiteness of directions and expectations. The other used the whole-word method, which gave a minimum of structure, because of its encouragement of intelligent guessing and its lack of rules. The children, all third graders, were rated as to compulsivity (wanting neatness, order and certainty, conforming, perfectionist, rigid, not spontaneous) and anxiety (response to a perceived threat). Compulsive children achieved at a higher level than less compulsive children in the structured classroom, but in the unstructured classroom, there was no significant difference between compulsive and noncompulsive children. The highly anxious children were at a real disadvantage in the unstructured school, where they were excelled by nonanxious children. In the structured school, there was no significant difference between anxious and nonanxious children. Therefore, unless children were assigned to a reading program on the basis of personality tests, some children would be at a disadvantage in either type of program.

Teachers and Classmates

The child interacts with a specific teacher and a class which constitutes a little social world.

The Teacher's Role. Nothing idealizes the teacher's role more beautifully than Erikson's concept of generativity, the seventh stage in personality development. In his words, "Generativity is primarily the interest in establishing and guiding the next generation or whatever in a given case may become the absorbing object of a parental kind of responsibility" [28, p. 231].

The teacher's work is one way of achieving normal adult personality development since everyone who is not to stagnate must have a stake in the next generation. The teacher chooses to nurture intellectual development in growing human beings. Thus she grows at this level while her students grow at theirs.

When the child enters school, his teacher is largely a mother substitute. He may even call her "Mother" by mistake and may do the reverse at home, calling his mother "Mrs. Jones." The attitudes toward authority he learned at home will probably carry over to school. Since nearly all first grade teachers are women, the child will most likely expect his teacher to be like his mother. His trust or mistrust, his hostility or acceptance, his dependency or autonomy will largely reflect what has gone on at home with mother. Gradually he learns the differences between

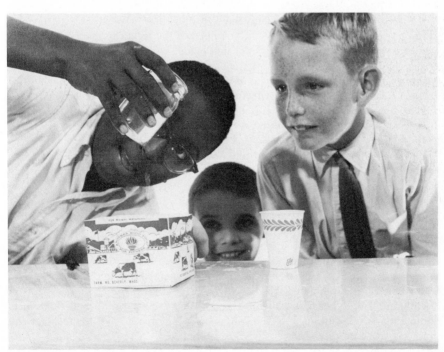

Courtesy Education Development Center

teacher and mother, both role differences and personality differences. Gradually the teacher differentiates herself more and more from mother. Moving up the grades, teachers become more subject matter-oriented and less concerned with the "whole child" and his adjustment in general. The child comes to see his teacher as the key person in his development of essential competencies.

The teacher's role varies with the sex of the teacher and sex of the child, as well as with age. There is widespread agreement that boys present more problem behavior in school than girls do. Men and women teachers differ somewhat in their interpretations of what is problem behavior and how serious it is.

Not only does the teacher present material to be learned and problems to be solved; she rewards some behavior and punishes other. Through words, smiles, frowns, attention, and ignoring, even more than through marks, displays, or gold stars, the teacher makes it plain, over and over and over again, what kind of behavior she wants from children and what she does not want. She also serves as a model of behavior, especially to those children whose needs she satisfies and who like and love her.

The Influence of Teachers' Expectations. Children are known to try to live up to the expectations that salient people hold for them. The power of expectations was found to be even greater than commonly thought, in a series of experiments by Rosenthal and associates [79]. All the children in one school were given an intelligence test. The teachers were told that the test predicted intellectual blooming and were given the names of their pupils (about 20 percent) who could be expected to spurt in academic achievement during the coming year. Each grade consisted of three classrooms, one for above average, one for average, and one for below average achievers. In each classroom, the experimental children had been picked by a table of random numbers. Thus the only difference between the experimental group and the other children was in the minds of the teachers. At the end of the year, the youngest experimental groups had made significant gains in IQ. The first graders had gained 15.4 points more than the other children in their grade. Grades 3 through 6 did not show differences in IQ gains between experimental and control groups. Reasons for the greater effect on younger children are speculative. It may be that they are more malleable. It is also possible that teachers of younger children are special, in being more interested in the whole child and more communicative of feelings, beliefs, and expectations.

Classroom Influences. The racial and socioeconomic composition of the class has important effects on the children. The type of education offered to black children has been generally inferior to that available to white children. One example from the South and one from the North will suffice. In Tennessee, black students were found to be a year and a half to two years retarded in grade level when they were transferred to white schools [99]. The same report revealed that only 49 percent of qualified black teachers passed the National Teacher's Examination, while 97 percent of qualified white teachers passed it. In New York City, time sampling of activities in the elementary schools indicated that in classrooms where black children predominated, 50 percent to 80 percent of the time was spent on disciplining and other nonacademic tasks. Where class membership was predominantly white, although of the same socioeconomic level, 30 percent of the time was spent on disciplining and nonacademic tasks [21]. The Coleman report on the nation's schools, based on over 600,000 children, concluded that the characteristics of their classmates constituted the most important influences on children [11]. Disadvantaged children achieved much more in classrooms where most of the children were middle-class. The more middle-class children, the more academic benefit accrued to the poor child in their midst. A subsequent study showed that when white children were in classes with mostly black classmates, they achieved less than when they were in mainly white classes [77]. White children in black schools with close black friends did even more poorly than white children without close black friends. Both segregation and desegregation hold problems for the black child. When the Test Anxiety Scale for Children was given to all second graders in a large eastern school system, black children were found to have significantly higher anxiety scores than white children [33]. In black de facto segregated schools, children had higher anxiety scores than did black children in integrated schools. This result may have been due to the integrated children's having higher socioeconomic status than the segregated blacks. Black children, too, can have problems in an integrated school.

The social threat of hostile, powerful white children can provoke great anxiety, impairing the child's problem solving and learning and even causing him to lower his achievement efforts so as not to compete with the whites [53]. If, however, the black child encounters friendly, acceptant white children and teachers, he is likely to feel encouraged and to raise his achievement efforts. If the academic standards are so high that he sees little chance of success, though, he is likely to become too discouraged to try hard. As probability of failure increases, likelihood of disapproval from parents and teachers also increases. As the child realizes the increasing danger of adult disapproval, he grows more fearful and hostile. Unable and/or afraid to express his hostility against adults, he turns it against himself as self-derogatory attitudes, increased expectation of failure, and desire to escape. These attitudes can be expected to weaken his performance in school [53]. Competence and the sense of industry, then, are likely to be severely handicapped by membership in a subordinate minority group. The combination of participants in every classroom is, of course, unique. Every teacher knows that each class is different and will probably admit that she behaves differently with each. A class develops certain behavior norms, some of which are in line with adult requirements, others of which are deviant. Some classes have a strong group spirit, others have many hostilities and tensions.

The teacher exerts an influence on her pupils' choice of moral standards. A series of Cornell University investigations used a moral dilemmas test to classify children as adult-conforming, peer-conforming, or autonomous, and also to find out whether children would be influenced more by parents or peers or whether they would stick largely to their own convictions [22]. When the moral questions were first presented, children were told that only researchers and computers would see their answers. Later an equivalent set of questions was given and children were told that their answers would be displayed to parents and teachers, at a PTA meeting. A third equivalent set was given and the children told that their classmates, but not teachers and parents, would see their answers. Thus the investigators could measure the amount of shift from the base condition in response to parent or peer pressure. Of special interest here is the difference between classrooms. In predominantly adult-oriented classrooms, teachers were described by their pupils as more supportive and less punitive than were those in peer-oriented classes. Principals described these teachers as less concerned with discipline and book learning than with individuality and creativity.

In peer-oriented classrooms, children reported more time spent with gangs of peers, and more misconduct. These children saw adult standards as being very different from peer standards. Peer-oriented classrooms contained the largest proportion of children who shifted under pressures from either peers or adults. There was little shifting from adult-conformity in adult-oriented classrooms. Autonomous children were somewhat more likely to come from peer-oriented classrooms. Results indicated that the children who achieved autonomy in making moral decisions did so through dealing with cross-pressures from both peers and adults. While autonomy did not result in all children who had these experiences, it is possible that the experience is necessary for development of autonomy. Other contributors to autonomy include, of course, family relationships. The autonomous children were likely to come from homes which gave them high support and moderate discipline and control, whereas the gang-oriented, peer-conformists tended to come from homes of either high punitiveness or high permissiveness. A subsequent study [47] shows that peer-oriented children are likely to have peer-oriented parents. Such parents are, for example, impressed by the argument "All the other kids are doing it."

The Child's Position in the Classroom. The child has his own social position, as a member of his school class, a position which is not necessarily the same as the social position held by his family in the community. His own position is both product and cause of his behavior and of how children and teachers feel and behave toward him. Many sociometric studies have shown that each classroom has its own social structure and that each child in it has his own place and relationships. Children in the lower positions have more difficulties than higher-status children. They are less able to cope with frustration; their teachers see them as showing more behavior problems, poorer social adjustment, and more emotional instability; they feel more disliking for other children and this increases as the year goes on; they show more aggressive–assertive or passive–hostile activity, as observed and measured on behavior schedules [57]. The interactions of children and teachers were recorded by observers who did not know the children's sociometric positions. Results yielded these insights into child–teacher interaction: teachers noticed the social behavior of low-status children more than they noticed that of high-status children; low-status boys received more criticism than high-status boys; low-status girls received more affectionate support than did other girls. The teachers were responding to the girls' seeking of affection from them, while being relatively passive in the classroom; they were responding to the boys' typical aggressive, disruptive behavior.

Summary

The child now feels a need to learn the rules of the game, as they pertain to many aspects of life, as he looks forward to taking his place as a producing member of society. His approaches to learning skills, rules, and various competencies grow out of his motivations and out of the social and cultural settings in which he grows up.

A wide choice of activities assures each child a good chance for success in one or more areas of competency. While academic excellence is out of reach for most children with limited background experience, motor skills and play activities offer them chances to excel. Reading, the key to success in school, is influenced by a multitude of physical, emotional, and experimental factors. Writing, a psycho-motor skill, serves the purpose of communication and self-expression. Mathematics, an area in which many children have experienced inferiority, can be taught on a broad base of experiences with manipulating, grouping, arranging, and ordering.

The sense of industry grows upon success as a worker at home, as well as at school and in the community. Since meaningful jobs are not always easy to find, group leaders and recreation workers often supplement the home in this important area. Play activities also contribute competencies in physical, intellectual, social, and emotional fields.

The learning of society's rules is a long process which begins by being able to state what people are supposed to do and which progresses by grasping more and more of the abstractions involved and by understanding the complicated inter-weaving of social roles. Moral judgment, involving evaluation of actions, matures along with cognitive and social growth. Moral behavior depends upon will and control, in conjunction with moral knowledge and judgment. Religious and philosophical concepts also develop through cognitive and social growth, guided by the type of concepts to which the child is exposed.

Success in development of the sense of industry is strongly influenced by the child's desire for achievement and recognition. Applying standards of excellence to himself, he and others judge his performance. A feeling tone results from that judgment, a happy feeling from approval, or an unpleasant feeling from disapproval. Both the need for achievement and achievement behavior show some consistency over time across situations and in sex differences. Boys apparently have more internalized standards and more realistic goals, whereas girls are more likely to seek approval and affection through their achievement efforts. Characteristics of high-achieving children include independence from adults, persistence, and com-petitiveness.

Anxiety has been studied as general anxiety and as anxiety in the situation of taking tests or examinations. Learning and achievement show complicated relations to level of anxiety. In general, low or moderate anxiety may aid or not deter a child in performing fairly easy tasks, and high anxiety is likely to reduce his competency. Fear of failure is a common type of anxiety of schoolchildren. Failure itself depends upon the relationship of achievement level and aspiration level. Schools often provoke anxiety in children of minority groups.

Curiosity determines the vigor with which a child seeks new experiences. New experiences contribute to further curiosity and to cognitive development. Curiosity can be stimulated by educational techniques.

The American educational system is dedicated to a number of values, some of which conflict with each other. The complexity of the culture requires that the school perform many functions, including the promotion of health and personality development, along with the teaching of traditional academic skills and knowledge. The child's success at school is influenced by his cultural level, which strongly determines his preparation for school, his social position in the classroom, and the fit between his personality and the style and philosophy of his school. Educational materials, especially textbooks, strongly reflect cultural values and concerns.

References

1. Amatora, M. Expressed interests in later childhood. *J. Genet. Psychol.*, 1960, **96**, 327–342.

2. Bandura, A., Ross, D., & Ross, S. A. Transmission of aggression through imitation of aggressive models. *J. Abn. Soc. Psychol.*, 1961, **63**, 575–582.

3. Barker, R. G. Success and failure in the classroom. *Progressive Educ.*, 1942, **19**, 221–224.

4. Bettelheim, B. The children of the dream. New York: Macmillan, 1969.

5. Blakely, W. P. Study of seventh-grade children's reading of comic books as related to certain other variables. *J. Genet. Psychol.*, 1958, **93**, 291–301.

6. Bronfenbrenner, U. Two worlds of childhood. New York: Russell Sage Foundation, 1970.

7. Bronson, G. W. Fear of visual novelty. *Devel. Psychol.*, 1970, **2**, 33–40.

8. Burton, R. V. The generality of honesty reconsidered. *Psychol. Rev.*, 1963, **70**, 481–500.

9. Castaneda, A., McCandless, B. R., & Palermo, D. S. The children's form of the manifest anxiety scale. *Child Devel.*, 1956, **27**, 315–326.

10. Child, I. L., Potter, E. H., & Levine, E. M. Children's textbooks and personality development: An exploration in the social psychology of education. *Psychol. Mono.*, 1946, **60**, 1–7, 43–53.

11. Coleman, J. S., et al. *Equality of educational opportunity.* Washington, D.C.: U.S. Govt. Printing Office, 1966.

12. Cox, F. N. Test anxiety and achievement behavior systems related to examination performance in children. *Child Devel.*, 1964, **35**, 909–915.

13. Crandall, V. C., Katkovsky, W., & Crandall, V. J. Children's beliefs in their own control of reinforcements in intellectual-academic achievement situations. *Child Devel.*, 1965, **36**, 91–109.

14. Crandall, V. J. Parents' influences on children's achievement behavior. Progress report, NIMH Grant M-2238. Yellow Springs, Ohio: Fels Institute, 1965.

15. Crandall, V. J., Katkovsky, W., & Preston, A. A conceptual formulation for some research on children's achievement development. *Child Devel.*, 1960, **31**, 787–797.

16. Crandall, V. J., Katkovsky, W., & Preston, A. Motivational and ability determinants of young children's intellectual achievement behaviors. *Child Devel.*, 1962, **33**, 643–661.

17. Crandall, V. J. Achievement. In H. W. Stevenson (Ed.), *Child psychology.* The sixty-second yearbook of the National Society for the Study of Education, Part I. Chicago: University of Chicago Press, 1963, pp. 416–459.

18. Croake, J. W. Fears of children. *Human Devel.*, 1969, **12**, 239–247.

19. deCharms, R., & Moeller, G. H. Content analysis of children's readers. *J. Abn. Soc. Psychol.*, 1962, **4**, 136–162.

20. D'Heurle, A., Mellinger, J., & Haggard, E. Personality, intellectual and achievement patterns in gifted children. *Psychol. Mono.*, 1959, Whole No. 483.

21. Deutsch, M. Minority groups and class status as related to social and personality factors in scholastic achievement. *Soc. Appl. Anthropol. Mono. No. 2.* St. Louis, Mo.: Washington University, 1960.

22. Devereux, E. C. The role of peer group experience in moral development: A research progress report. Paper presented at the Fourth Minnesota Symposium on Child Psychology, May, 1969.

23. Distefano, M. K., Jr. Changes in work-related attitudes with age. *J. Genet. Psychol.*, 1969, **114**, 127–134.

24. Elkind, D. The child's conception of his religious denomination. I: The Jewish child, *J. Genet. Psychol.*, 1961, **99**, 209–225.

25. Elkind, D. The child's conception of his religious denomination. II: The Catholic child. *J. Genet. Psychol.*, 1962, **101**, 185–194.

26. Elkind, D. The child's conception of his religious denomination. III: The Protestant child, *J. Genet. Psychol.*, 1963, **103**, 291–304.

27. Elkind, D. Cognitive structure in latency behavior. Paper presented at the conference on "Origins of Individuality." Madison: University of Wisconsin, Sept. 26–27, 1969.

28. Erikson, E. H. *Childhood and society*. New York: Norton, 1963.

29. Erikson, E. H. *Identity, youth and crisis*. New York: Norton, 1968.

30. Eron, L. D. Relationship of TV viewing habits and aggressive behavior in children. *J. Abn. Soc. Psychol.*, 1963, **67**, 193–196.

31. Ezer, M. The effect of religion upon children's responses to questions involving physical causality. In J. Rosenblith & W. Allinsmith (Eds.), *The causes of behavior*. Boston: Allyn and Bacon, 1962, pp. 481–487.

32. Feld, S. C. Longitudinal study of the origins of achievement strivings. *J. Pers. Soc. Psychol.*, 1967, **7**, 408–414.

33. Feld, S. C., & Lewis, J. *The assessment of achievement anxieties in children*. Bethesda, Md.: Mental Health Study Center, National Institute for Mental Health, 1967.

34. Forbes, J. D. *The education of the culturally different*. Washington, D.C.: U.S. Govt. Printing Office, 1969.

35. Gibson, E. J. The ontogeny of reading. *Am. Psychol.*, 1970, **25**, 136–143.

36. Grimes, J. W., & Allinsmith, W. Compulsivity, anxiety and school achievement. *Merrill-Palmer Quart.*, 1961, **7**, 247–271.

37. Grinder, R. E. Relations between behavioral and cognitive dimensions of conscience in middle childhood. *Child Devel.*, 1964, **35**, 881–891.

38. Gross, B., & Gross, R. A little bit of chaos. *Sat. Rev.*, May 16, 1970, 71 ff.

39. Haggard, E. Socialization personality and academic achievement in gifted children. *School Rev.*, 1957, 388–414.

40. Harrell, L. E. A comparison of the development of oral and written language in school-age children. *Mono. Soc. Res. Child Devel.*, 1957, **22**:3.

41. Hartshorne, H., & May, M. A. *Studies in the nature of character*. Vol. I: *Studies in deceit;* Vol. II: *Studies in self-control;* Vol. III: *Studies in the organization of character*. New York: Macmillan, 1928–1930.

42. Havighurst, R. J. Minority subcultures and the law of effect. *Am. Psychol.*, 1970, **25**, 313–322.

43. Hechinger, F. M. History texts take a new look at slavery. *New York Times*, June 14, 1970.

44. Herrick, V. E., & Okada, N. The present scene: Practices in the teaching of handwriting in the United States—1960. In V. E. Herrick (Ed.), *New horizons for research in handwriting*. Madison: University of Wisconsin, 1963.

45. Hicks, D. J. Imitation and retention of film-mediated aggressive peer and adult models. *J. Pers. Soc. Psychol.*, 1965, **2**, 97–100.

46. Himmelweit, H. T., Oppenheim, A. N., & Vince, P. *Television and the child*. London: Oxford, 1958.

47. Hollander, E. P., & Marcia, J. E. Parental determinants of peer-orientation and self-orientation among preadolescents. *Devel. Psychol.*, 1970, **2**, 292–302.

48. Jessor, R., & Richardson, S. Psychosocial deprivation and personality development. In *Perspectives on Human Deprivation*. Washington, D.C. U.S. Dept. of Health, Education, and Welfare, 1968.

49. John, V., Horner, V., & Socolov, J. American voices, *Center Forum*, 1969, **4**:1, 1–3.

50. Kagan, J., & Moss, H. Stability and validity of achievement fantasy. *J. Abn. Soc. Psychol.*, 1959, **58**, 357–364.

51. Kagan, J., Sontag, L. W., Baker, C. T., & Nelson, V. L. Personality and I.Q. change. *J. Abn. Soc. Psychol.*, 1958, **56**, 261–266.

52. Katkovsky, W., Preston, A., & Crandall, V. J. Parents' attitudes toward their personal achievements and toward the achievement behaviors of their children. *J. Genet. Psychol.*, 1964, **104**, 67–82.

53. Katz, I. Review of evidence relating to effects of desegregation on the intellectual performance of Negroes. *Am. Psychol.*, 1964, **19**, 381–399.

54. Kohlberg, L. The development of children's orientations toward a moral order. I: Sequence in the development of moral thought. *Vita Humana*, 1963, **6**, 11–33.

55. Kohlberg, L. Development of moral character and moral ideology. In M. L. Hoffman & L. W. Hoffman (Eds.), *Review of child development research*. Vol. 1. New York: Russell Sage Foundation, 1964, pp. 383–431.

56. Larrick, N. *A parent's guide to children's reading*. New York: Doubleday, 1969.

57. Lippitt, R., & Gold, M. Classroom social structure as a mental health problem. *J. Soc. Issues*, 1959, **15**, 40–49.

58. Litcher, J. H., & Johnson, D. W. Changes in attitudes toward Negroes of white elementary school students after use of multiethnic readers. *J. Educ. Psychol.*, 1969, **60**, 148–152.

59. McClelland, D. C., Atkinson, J. W., Clark, R. A., & Lowell, E. L. *The achievement motive*. New York: Appleton-Century-Crofts, 1953.

60. McReynolds, P., Acker, M., & Pietila, C. Relations of object curiosity to psychological adjustment in children. *Child Devel.*, 1961, **32**, 393–400.

61. Maccoby, E. E. Why do children watch television? *Pub. Opinion Quart.*, 1954, **18**, 239–244.

62. Madsen, M. C. Cooperative and competitive motivation of children in three Mexican subcultures. *Psychol. Rep.*, 1967, **20**, 1307–1320.

63. Madsen, M. C., & Shapira, A. Cooperative and competitive behavior of urban Afro-American, Anglo-American, Mexican-American and Mexican village children. *Devel. Psychol.*, 1970, **3**, 16–20.

64. Malone, P., & Beller, E. K. Effects of different learning environments on creativity of children. Paper presented at the meeting of the Society for Research in Child Development, Santa Monica, Calif., March 27, 1969.

65. Maw, W. H., & Maw, E. W. Establishing criterion groups for evaluating measures of curiosity. *J. Exper. Educ.*, 1961, **29**, 299–306.

66. Maw, W. H., & Maw, E. W. Information recognition by children with high and low curiosity, *Educ. Res. Bull.*, 1961, **40**, 197–201, 223–224.

67. Maw, W. H., & Maw, E. W. Selection of unbalanced and unusual designs by children high in curiosity, *Child Devel.*, 1962, **33**, 917–922.

68. Maw, W. H., & Maw, E. W. Personal and social variables differentiating children with high and low curiosity. Cooperative Research Project No. 1511, Newark, Delaware; University of Delaware, 1965.

69. Medinnus, G. R., & Robinson, R. Maturity as a predictor of school achievement. Paper presented at the meeting of the Society for Research in Child Development, Santa Monica, Calif., March 29, 1969.

70. Mendel, G. Children's preferences for differing degrees of novelty. *Child Devel.*, 1965, **36**, 453–464.

71. Minuchin, P. Correlates of curiosity and exploratory behavior. Paper presented at the meeting of the Society for Research in Child Development, Santa Monica, Calif., March 27, 1969.

72. Mittman, L. R., & Terrell, G. An experimental study of curiosity in children. *Child Devel.*, 1964, **35**, 851–855.

73. Moss, H., & Kagan, J. Stability of achievement and recognition-seeking behaviors from early childhood through adulthood. *J. Abn. Soc. Psychol.*, 1961, **62**, 504–513.

74. Owen, F. W. The Palo Alto study of educationally handicapped children. Paper presented at the meeting of the Society for Research in Child Development, Santa Monica, Calif., March 28, 1969.

75. Peck, R. F., & Havighurst, R. J. *The psychology of character development.* New York: Wiley, 1960.

76. Piaget, J. *The moral judgment of the child.* Glencoe, Ill.: Free Press, 1948.

77. Pettigrew, T. F. Race and equal educational opportunity. Paper presented at the 75th annual convention of the American Psychological Association, 1967.

78. Riessman, F. Low-income culture: The strengths of the poor. *J. Marr. Fam.*, 1964, **26**, 417–429.

79. Rosenthal, R., & Jacobson, L. Self-fulfilling prophecies in the classroom: Teachers' expectations as unintended determinants of pupils' intellectual competence. In M. Deutsch, I. Katz, & A. R. Jensen (Eds.), *Social class, race and psychological development.* New York: Holt, Rinehart and Winston, 1968, pp. 219–253.

80. Sarason, S. B., Davidson, K. S., Lighthall, F. F., & Waite, R. R. A test anxiety scale for children. *Child Devel.*, 1958, **29**, 105–113.

81. Sarason, S. B., Davidson, K. S., Lighthall, F. F., Waite, R. R., & Ruebush, B. K. *Anxiety in elementary school children.* New York: Wiley, 1960.

82. Sarason, S. B., Hill, K. T., & Zimbardo, P. G. A longitudinal study of the relation of test anxiety to performance on intelligence and achievement tests. *Mono. Soc. Res. Child Devel.*, 1964, **29**:7.

83. Schramm, W., Lyle, J., & Parker, E. B. *Television in the lives of our children.* Stanford, Calif.: Stanford University Press, 1961.

84. Sears, P. S. Correlates of need achievement and need affiliation and classroom management, self-concept, achievement and creativity. Unpublished manuscript, Laboratory of Human Development, Stanford University, 1962. Cited in Crandall [17].

85. Sears, R. R., Rau, L., & Alpert, R. *Identification and child-rearing.* Stanford, Calif.: Stanford University Press, 1965.

86. Seltzer, A. R., & Beller, E. K. Judgments of time and moral development in lower class children. Paper presented at the meeting of the Society for Research in Child Development, Santa Monica, Calif., March 27, 1969.

87. Shapira, A., & Madsen, M. C. Cooperative and competitive behavior of kibbutz and urban children in Israel. *Child Devel.*, 1969, **40**, 609–617.

88. Smock, C. D., & Holt, B. G. Children's reactions to novelty: An experimental study of curiosity motivation. *Child Devel.*, 1962, **33**, 631–642.

89. Solomon, D. The generality of children's achievement-related behavior. *J. Genet. Psychol.*, 1969, **114**, 109–125.

90. Stein, A. H. The influence of social reinforcement on the achievement behavior of fourth-grade boys and girls. *Child Devel.*, 1969, **40**, 727–736.

91. Steiner, S. LaRaza: The Mexican-Americans. *Center Forum*, 1969, **4**:1, 4–7.

92. Strauss, A. L. The development of conceptions of rules in children. *Child Devel.*, 1954, **25**, 193–208.

93. Suchman, J. R. Inquiry training: Building skills for autonomous discovery. *Merrill-Palmer Quart.*, 1961, **7**, 147–170.

94. Terman, L. M., & Merrill, M. A. *Stanford–Binet Intelligence Scale.* Boston: Houghton Mifflin, 1960.

95. Walters, R. H., & Willows, D. C. Imitative behavior of disturbed and non-disturbed children following exposure to aggressive and nonaggressive models. *Child Devel.*, 1968, **39**, 79–89.

96. White, R. W. Motivation reconsidered: The concept of competence. *Psychol. Rev.*, 1959, **66**, 297–333.

97. Whiteman, P. H., & Kosier, K. P. Development of children's moralistic judgments: Age, sex, IQ and certain personal-experiential variables. *Child Devel.*, 1964, **35**, 843–850.

98. Witty, P. A., Kinsella, P., & Coomer, A. A summary of yearly studies of televiewing—1949–1963. *Elementary English*, 1963, **40**, 590–597.

99. Wyatt, E. Tennessee. In U.S. Commission on Civil Rights, *Civil rights, U.S.A.—Public schools, southern states.* Washington, D.C.: U.S. Govt. Printing Office, 1962, pp. 105–130.

Readings in
Increasing Competence As a
Learner and Doer

The important aspects of development during the period from six to twelve have to do with the skills that are considered important by the groups of which children are members. Some of the skills are important to the child because of their meaning for him in the present; some are important for both the present and the future. Physical skills like playing baseball or playing a violin, and the coordinations necessary to such feats, mental skills like reading or memorizing, and social skills like cooperating or leading are among the ways in which children can become competent in all the skills of which human beings are capable.

Because learning plays a part in the acquisition of all skills, factors which make learning easy or difficult have been studied. In the first reading Robert Havighurst singles out one of Thorndike's laws of learning and shows how children of some minority groups have different sources of approval and disapproval than children of middle-class Americans. Freya Owen, in the next article, summarizes a study of the characteristics of educationally handicapped children and their siblings when compared with a matched group of academically successful children and their siblings.

For at least some aspects of living, Americans try to foster cooperation in children. Millard Madsen has engaged in a series of studies of cooperative and competitive behavior, using an ingenious game in which the players can behave in either way. The article by Madsen and Ariella Shapira summarizes the results of several of these studies.

The author of the final paper in this chapter, J. W. Croake, brings up to date the study of children's fears, a subject studied extensively in the 1930's but very little since then.

Minority Subcultures and the Law of Effect

Robert J. Havighurst*
UNIVERSITY OF CHICAGO

Since the 1950s we in the United States have become more and more acutely aware of and concerned about the socially disadvantaged segment of our

Reprinted from *American Psychologist, 25*, 313–322., by permission of the American Psychological Association.

* The Annual Edward L. Thorndike Award Lecture, presented to Division 15, at the meeting of the American Psychological Association, Washington, D.C., August 31, 1969.

society. We have joined a "war on poverty." We have declared racial segregation in the public schools to be illegal. We have passed a Civil Rights Act.
These things we have done out of our conviction that democracy is morally
right and can be made to work better in our society than it has in the past.

We have also defined rather accurately the "socially disadvantaged"
group as consisting of the bottom 15% of our population in terms of income and
educational achievement. Some people would argue that this is too small a
proportion. They would add another 10% to make it a quarter of the population. Others would go as far as to define all manual workers and their families
(about 60% of the population) as socially disadvantaged, but this kind of
proposition could not be supported with data on inadequacy of income,
educational achievement, stability of family, law observance, or any other
major index of standard of living. While the stable working class (or upper
working class), consisting of 40% of the population, is slightly below the white
collar group in average income, educational level, and other socioeconomic
indices, this group is not disadvantaged in an absolute sense, does not feel
disadvantaged, and has an active interchange of membership with the white
collar group between successive generations.

As for the truly disadvantaged group of 15–20% of the population, there is
disturbing evidence that this group is in danger of becoming a permanent
"underclass" characterized by absence of steady employment, low level of
education and work skills, living on welfare payments, and social isolation from
the remainder of society.

The presence of this social and human problem cannot be passed off in
any of the ways that might have been possible a century ago, or might be
possible today in the poor countries. It cannot be ascribed to inherited inferiority
of the disadvantaged. It cannot be blamed on the country's poverty, since we
are an affluent society. It cannot be passed off with the optimistic prediction
that the current group of disadvantaged will soon become assimilated into the
general society as most ethnic groups have done in the past—the Irish, Germans,
Swedes, Poles, Italians, etc.

The problem is brought to a head by the clearly established fact that the
children of this group are *not* doing as well in school or in the world of juvenile
work as did the children of poor people 50 and 100 years ago.

Furthermore, most Americans believe that true democracy means equality
of economic and educational opportunity. There is a growing conviction that
the proof of the existence of equality of economic and educational *opportunity*
is the achievement of economic and educational *equality* by the previously
disadvantaged groups within a reasonable period of time, measured by decades
and not by centuries or even by generations.

THE WAR ON POVERTY?

For the past 10 years our principal attack on the problem of social disadvantage has been through the "war on poverty." We have spent much talent
and energy and a good deal of money without raising the educational or
occupational achievement level of this group appreciably, except in a few
unusual situations. These unusual situations, in which disadvantaged children

and youth have made normal or even superior progress, do not provide us with any broad program ideas that can be applied widely. They seem to tell us that:

1. No mere quantitative changes in the school program are likely to work. It does not bring a widespread improvement to extend the school day by an hour, or the school year by a month, or to reduce class size, or to revise school attendance boundaries.

2. Close and minute attention to the process of teaching a particular subject at a particular age may be useful.

3. We should look closely at children and their particular learning behavior for clues to action.

A LOOK AT WHAT WE KNOW

Examination of known facts about school achievement of definable social groups in the United States shows that poor school achievement is not primarily a problem of ethnic subcultures, but rather is primarily a problem of the lowest socioeconomic group interacting to a limited degree with minority subcultures.

There are certain ethnic minorities that do very well—as well or better than the national average in school achievement. Outstanding among these are the Japanese, Chinese, and Jews. The adults of these groups have an average occupational status above the national average, and the children of these groups do better than the national average on tests of school achievement.

Other ethnic groups do poorly in these respects, but these groups also have substantial numbers who equal or exceed the national average. There is no single ethnic group of any size that can be said to be disadvantaged educationally and economically *as a whole group*. Negroes might be thought of as a disadvantaged group, and this would be true, historically. But at present there is a large and growing Negro middle class and a large and growing Negro upper working class whose occupational status is average or above and whose children do average or better work in school.

The same statement applies to Puerto Ricans, Mexican Americans, and American Indians. It is the least educated and the least work-trained members of these groups who do least well in American society. These groups all have substantial and growing numbers of people who perform at average or higher levels of occupational status and whose children do well in school.

Thus, when we speak of the group of socially disadvantaged people in America, we are speaking of some 15–20% of the population who are like each other in their poverty, their lack of education and work skills, but unlike each other in ethnic subculture. Crude estimates indicate that this group contains about 20 million English-speaking Caucasians, 8 million Negroes, 2 million Spanish-Americans, 700,000 Puerto Ricans, and 500,000 American Indians.

These people have poverty in common. Insofar as there is a definable "culture of poverty," they share that culture. Still, a small fraction of them, though poor, do not have the characteristics of the "culture of poverty."

It may be that their various ethnic subcultures have something to do with success or failure in school and in the labor market. If so, it must be the combination of poverty with the ethnic subculture that produces these effects. It may also be true that other ethnic subcultures, such as the Japanese and Chinese, serve to prevent poverty.

THE IMPLICIT CONTRACT

It may be useful to examine the educational problem of the socially disadvantaged in terms of the *implicit contract* that a family and a school accept when a child is entrusted by his family to a school. The parents contract to prepare their child for school entrance, both cognitively and affectively. They further contract to keep him in school and to make home conditions appropriate for his success in school. The school contracts to receive the child, teach him as well as it can, taking account of his strengths and weaknesses and the ways in which he can learn most effectively.

Very little of this contract is put into legal codes, but the education of the child is successful only when both parties carry out their obligations fully. Sometimes one or both parties fail to understand the nature of these obligations.

In the case of the socially disadvantaged parents of this country, nearly all of them fail to meet the terms of the contract. But the schools generally fail also by failing to understand how the children of these families can learn most successfully.

THE HUMAN REWARD–PUNISHMENT SYSTEM

The principal proposition of this article is that the job of educating socially disadvantaged children would be done much better if educators understood the nature of rewards and how they function in human learning, and applied this knowledge to their work with children and with parents of socially disadvantaged children.

Leads to this proposition exist in the literature of research on education, but do not force themselves on the educator. For example, Davis (1965) offered one of these clues in his paper "Cultural Factors in Remediation." He noted that his wife, then working as a substitute teacher in the Chicago public schools, made a discovery about the way disadvantaged children may learn arithmetic. In a second grade in a ghetto school she found several children, including one nine-year-old boy, who could not count beyond two or three. The following day was Valentine's Day, and she brought some candy hearts to school. She told the children they could have as many candy hearts as they could count. The *nine-year-old boy thereupon counted 14 candy hearts.* Davis goes on to say that teachers of "culturally low-status children" should learn how their children live, and then work out new materials and ways of teaching in order to *encourage* and *approve* those students who have experienced little except disapproval, stigma, and failure in the conventional school program.

In the years since 1960 a number of psychologists have studied the nature of rewards in human learning. Among others, the work of Zigler, Rotter, Katz, and Crandall has widened the field of research and has stimulated others to work in this field.

What these people have in common is the following proposition: Human learning is influenced by a variety of rewards, which are themselves arranged in a culturally based *reward-punishment system* which is learned.

This requires us to examine the nature of rewards. We cannot simply assume that "a reward is a reward and that is it," as we might be tempted to do if we were studying the learning behavior of cats, or pigeons, or rats. It was more or less obvious to researchers that reward systems might vary with social class, or with ethnic subculture. It seemed likely that a child learns his reward system mainly in the family, but also in the school, and the peer group, and the wider community.

ANALYSIS OF THE REWARD–PUNISHMENT CONCEPT

The reward-punishment concept, and its related reinforcement theory, has been developed rather differently by each of three groups of psychologists.

Learning theorists, starting with E. L. Thorndike, have tended to use the concept to refer to something done *to* the learner by an experimenter or observer that influences the behavior of the learner. On the other hand, social psychologists and personality theorists have included the subjective experience of the learner as a source of reward-punishment. Thus, a person may be rewarded or punished by his own feelings or by the attitudes of other people toward him.

Thorndike (1905) stated the law of effect as follows: "Any act which in a given situation produces satisfaction becomes associated with that situation, so that when the situation recurs the act is more likely to recur also [p. 203]."

Skinner's (1953) definition is, "We first define a positive reinforcer as any stimulus the presentation of which strengthens the behavior upon which it is made contingent [p. 84]."

These are broad enough to cover the other usages, though the social psychologists and personality theorists have stated them more fully. Thus, Hartley and Hartley (1952) say,

> Reward . . . must be very broadly defined when we consider human learning. Because human beings are capable of retaining the effects of their experiences for long periods of time and because they are capable of generalization and transfer, functional rewards . . . may be far removed from physical rewards. When we speak of rewards we mean anything that operates as a source of satisfaction for the individual . . . the attitudes other people display and the individual's own feelings may come to serve as rewards [p. 275].

Personality theorists make much of the distinction between external and internal sources of reward–punishment. Fenichel (1945) writes,

> The superego is the heir of the parents not only as a source of threats and punishments but also as a source of protection and a provider of reassuring love. . . . Complying with the superego's demands brings not only relief but also definite feelings of pleasure and security of the same type that children experience from external supplies of love [p. 105].

THEORY OF THE EVOLUTION OF REWARD–PUNISHMENT

It appears, then, that we can distinguish four major types of reward–punishments. The earliest, in terms of operation in human learning, is satisfaction or deprivation of physiological appetites—the physiological needs for food and pain avoidance. In this same category belong other material rewards that arise later in physiological development, either through the maturation of the organism or through experience—such rewards as release of sexual tensions, toys and play materials, money, and, perhaps, power over other people.

Next in order of appearance comes approval–disapproval from other persons, beginning with praise and reproof and expressions of affection and esteem from parents, and extending to approval–disapproval from others in the family and adults such as teachers, and from age-mates.

Next comes the self-rewarding and self-punishing action of the child's superego, or conscience. This is extremely important from the point of view of educational development, because it means that the child who has reached this level can become capable of pushing ahead with his own education without being stimulated and directed by his parents or his teachers or his peers.

Finally comes the rewarding and punishing action of the ego, the executive functions of the personality. This is more difficult to conceptualize as a source of reward or punishment, but it is essential for an adequate theory. It is essential as a means of *anticipation* of future reward or punishment, success or failure, which will result as a consequence of an action performed now, in the present.

Table 1 presents the theory of evolution of the human reward–punishment system, with additional considerations to be discussed in the following section of this paper.

There are six major propositions of educational significance that have received some research testing.

1. *Different subcultures carry their children along this evolutionary path at different rates and in different ways.*

Several researchers have tested this proposition using social class as the subcultural variable. Zigler and de Labry (1962) compared the performance of middle-class and lower-class six-year-old children on a task of classifying cards on the basis of color and shape, and using intangible reinforcement ("right" and "wrong") and tangible reinforcement (tokens to be cashed in for toys). They found middle-class children to be superior with intangible reinforcement, but this superiority vanished when lower-class children were given tangible rewards.

Lighthall and Cernius (1967) compared Caucasian middle-class and working-class five- and six-year-old boys on a concept-switching task using intangible and tangible reinforcers. The tangible reinforcers were metal washers that could be traded in for a toy, a ball-point pen, a piece of candy, or a dime. They did *not* find a social class difference.

Zigler and Kanzer (1962) compared white middle-class and working-class eight-year-old boys on a simple gamelike task, using two types of verbal reinforcers—praise, and knowledge of how they were succeeding. They found that middle-class boys did better when reinforced with "right" or "correct" than when reinforced with "good" or "fine," but lower-class boys were more responsive to the praise reinforcement than to the level of performance reinforcement. The conclusion from this experiment is that middle-class boys are more able to reward themselves by simple knowledge of how well they are doing than

TABLE 1

Evolution of the Human Reward-Punishment System

Age Level in Years	Nature of the Reward-Punishment	Giver of the Reward-Punishment	Action Area
0–4	Satisfaction or deprivation of physical-physiological appetites (food, sex, pain, toys, money, power)	Parents	Basic motor skills Basic mental skills
5–10	Praise-disapproval from outside persons	Teachers and other adults in a teaching role	Social skills—social personality
		Self	Special motor skills (games)
	Approval-disapproval from superego	Peers and peer groups	Special mental skills (reading, arithmetic, etc.)
10–15	Approval-disapproval from ego	Wider community	Excitement Danger, uncertain outcome, sex Knowledge
15–25			Beauty Experience and expression
Adult years			Work roles Family roles

lower-class boys, who are still at the stage where they depend mainly on external approval. However, a replication of this experiment by Rosenhan and Greenwald (1965) did not bear out these findings. McGrade (1966) made a similar study, using an administrator of the test game who was naive with respect to the purpose and hypotheses of the experiment. She failed to confirm the Zigler and Kanzer findings.

We know that this kind of experiment is complicated by side effects of the experimenter's sex in relation to the sex and age of the children, as was demonstrated by Stevenson (1961). It also seems likely that the social class variable was not sufficiently differentiated in some of these experiments. Probably there is very little difference between middle-class and stable or upper-working-class families in the ways they teach their children to move up the evolutionary reward scale. Probably the big difference is between the stable upper-working-class and the "underclass" or lower-working-class. But it appears that most of the experiments reporting on social class differences used working-class samples of the upper-working-class level.

Two studies have clearly differentiated between these working-class levels. Hess and Shipman (1965) differentiated Negro lower-class children into a group with stable upper-working-class characteristics and another group whose mothers were receiving Aid for Dependent Children. There was a substantial difference between the two groups in the mother–child relationship in a learning situation. Also, Davidson and Greenberg (1967) studied high achievers and underachievers among Harlem Negro lower-class children, and found large differences in the orderliness of the home life between the two working-class groups.

2. *There are differences between ethnic subcultures among disadvantaged groups in the reward system they teach their children.*

Although all of the severely disadvantaged families share some common characteristics of the "culture of poverty," they may also have different ethnic cultural traits which lead to different reward systems. There is evidence of such differences between Negro, Appalachian white, and some American Indian groups.

American Indians have a wide variety of tribal cultures, and therefore it is dangerous to generalize about "Indians." However, among contemporary Indian groups there appears to be a general virtue of cooperation and mutual support within an extended family and to a lesser degree within a tribal community. It might be inferred that praise–blame from family and from peer group is the most effective form of reward–punishment for Indian children living in Indian communities.

The hypothesis of peer-group rewarding power is supported by observations of school behavior in several different places. Wax (1969) reports that in both the Cherokee group in Eastern Oklahoma and the Sioux of South Dakota the children tend to form a close-knit group with its own system of control that baffles the teacher. An observer in an Oklahoma Cherokee school writes,

> Observing the upper-grade classroom, I concluded that the students regard it as their own place, the locus of their own society, in which the teacher is an unwelcome intruder, introducing irrelevant demands. It is rather as though a group of mutinous sailors had agreed to the efficient manning of "their" ship while ignoring the captain and the captain's navigational goals [p. 101].

The children do not tolerate an individual show of superior knowledge. Often a teacher cannot find any pupil who will volunteer an answer to a question that several of them know. In oral reading, the whole class tends to read together in audible whispers, so that the child who is supposed to be reciting can simply wait when he comes to a difficult word until he hears it said by his classmates. Generally, pupils like to work together, and to help each other. Consequently, the weak students are carried along by the stronger ones, and the stronger ones do not exert themselves to excel the weaker ones. This same kind of behavior was noted by Wolcott (1967) in his study of Kwakiutl children in British Columbia.

The peer group may be less effective as a source of reward–punishment for Appalachian disadvantaged children. They seem to get their rewards mainly within the family circle. Conceivably, the teacher may be a more potent source of reward for Appalachian than for Indian children, if the teacher develops a motherly or fatherly relation with them.

The Negro lower-class children may operate much more at the level of approval–disapproval from the teacher than the Indian or Appalachian children. They are less likely to have both parents in the home, and they probably get less parental approval–disapproval. They do not generally fall into the mutual help pattern of the Indian children. The peer group becomes a powerful influence on the Negro children probably after the age of 9 or 10, but its influence operates mainly in out-of-school contexts—on the playground or the street corner.

This proposition needs much more research before it can be pushed very far. But the contrasting school behavior and school success of the various minority groups argue for the existence of different systems of rewards and punishments, as well as different achievement goals to which these systems are directed.

3. *In general, external rewards (material or intangible) have positive values for disadvantaged or failing children.*

This proposition differs from the first in being valid for all social classes, leaving open the question of the relative effectiveness of these kinds of rewards in different social classes. There is a growing amount of solid, practical evidence for this proposition, growing out mainly from the *operant-conditioning* programs and experiments stimulated by Skinner. They all have in common the giving of a reward for every small step in the direction of the desired learning. Work with preschool children, such as that done by Bereiter and Engelmann (1966), is being studied widely and their practices repeated at primary grade levels.

It is not established whether material rewards, such as pieces of candy, are more effective than verbal praise. Intermediate between them is some kind of point system, whereby a child gets a point for every correct answer (sometimes a point is subtracted for errors), and the points may be "cashed in" later for material objects, or special favors such as a trip to the zoo.

Several school systems have established a "reinforcement technique" for working with children who have various kinds of school adjustment problems, academic and behavioral. This method seems to work equally well with middle-class and lower-working-class children, as long as the child is having a school problem. The procedure is to diagnose the child's problem carefully, to work out a series of small steps from where he is to where he should be, and to reward him for each step. For example, an 11-year-old boy with a third-grade reading level but otherwise average intelligence may refuse to read with his sixth-grade class, and thus make no progress. Rewarding him for reading with his class does no good, because he makes himself ridiculous in the eyes of his classmates. (The punishment is greater than the reward.) But if a counselor studies the boy, discovers his third-grade reading level, and then arranges for individual remedial work with rewards for each advance above the third-grade level, the boy may catch up with his age-mates within a few months.

Validity of a symbolic reinforcement program with underachieving children was indicated with a junior high school group in Chicago, in a situation in which one might expect social reinforcement to have relatively little value. Clark and Walberg (1968) experimented with a system of massive symbolic rewards in classes of sixth- and seventh-grade Negro children in a Chicago ghetto—all the children being in classes for after-school remedial reading, because they were from one to four years below grade level in their school work. The reward system consisted of tallies made by each child on a card containing numbered squares. Whenever a child made a correct response or showed some other sign of learning, the teacher praised him and asked him to circle the next number on his card with a special colored pencil that he was to use only for this purpose. The cards were collected at the end of the class period. No other rewards were given for the points gained.

Teachers of nine remedial classes were instructed to give praise rewards so that even the very slow ones would get several in a session. After six sessions of this sort, five of the nine teachers were selected at random, and confidentially asked to double or triple the number of rewards they gave, while the four control group teachers were told to "keep up the good work."

As a result, the experimental groups got many more tally numbers, while the control groups remained at the early levels. After five weeks a reading test was given, and the experimental groups exceeded the controls by a substantially and statistically significant amount.

4. *An effective reward system in a complex, changing society must be based on a strong ego.*

This crucial step in the reward–punishment theory being developed here conceives the ego as a source of reward–punishment, as well as the executive and planning function of the personality. To develop this set of ideas we may turn to a recent article by Bettelheim (1969) entitled "Psychoanalysis and Education." Bettelheim starts with the conventional dynamic personality theory of learning by young children through rewards given first by the id (the physiological appetites) and then by the superego (the internalized praising and blaming voice of the parents). Therefore, learning based on the pleasure principle is supplemented by learning based on the superego, which carries a child from learning for fun to learning even if it is hard work because his superego rewards him for this kind of learning and punishes him for failing to learn. We all recognize that much necessary learning is hard work, and will not take place under the pressure of the id.

Perhaps this last sentence is not quite accurate. There are a number of creative teachers and writers about teaching who in effect take the position that the way to teach children successfully (whether they are socially disadvantaged or socially advantaged) is to get the id behind their learning experience, that is, to give their "natural drive to learn," their "native curiosity," free play, and to count on their learning "creatively" in this way throughout their school experience.

For example, Kohl (1967), in his book *36 Children*, describes how he worked for a year with a class of 36 Negro slum children who were below average in academic skills. He did get results. There is no reason to doubt this. His method of encouraging them to write about their fears, their hates, and their likes, about the bad and good things they experience in their homes and streets, loosened their pens and their tongues, added to their vocabulary, and got them interested in school. It seems that Kohl was helping them marshal the forces of the id on behalf of learning. But how far can this go? How far can a slum child (or a middle-class child) go toward mastery of arithmetic, of English sentence style, of knowledge of science and history, if he is motivated only by his drive to express his feelings, or possibly also by his desire to please his friendly and permissive teacher?

We do not know how far this kind of reward will carry a child's learning. We might guess that it would carry children up to about the seventh-grade level. Therefore, we should ask Kohl and others of this school of thought to prove that their methods will carry children to the eighth-grade level. No such claims appear to have been substantiated, except in the case of socially advantaged children, such as those attending A. S. Neill's school at Summerhill, England. And some observers of this school argue that it can only work with children who have a strong British middle-class superego, and can profit from teaming their somewhat starved id with the superego in the pursuit of learning.

Bettelheim (1969) argues that the main function of education is to help the ego develop so that with the aid of the superego it controls the id, but at the same time it balances the superego by allowing reasonable satisfaction of the id. "The goal of education ought to be a well-balanced personality where both id and superego are subordinated to reality, to the ego [p. 83]." "Nothing automatically assures ego growth, neither punishment nor reward. The only thing that assures it is having the right experiences to stimulate and foster growth at the right time, in the right sequence, and in the right amount [p. 84]."

Thus, the ego becomes a source of reward and punishment through enabling the child to promise himself realistically a future reward for doing something unpleasant at the moment and through making the child take the blame for the future consequences of his mistakes of judgment or his mistakes of self-indulgence.

5. *A strongly developed ego gives a sense of personal control and personal responsibility for important events in one's life.*

The ego can only become an effective reward and punishment giver if the social environment is orderly enough to permit the ego to operate on the basis of a rational study of reality. This is substantially the case with the family and the community environment of the middle class and the stable working class in America. But the disadvantaged groups we have been considering do not experience this kind of orderliness in their environment, and do not transmit to their children a sense of confidence in an orderly environment.

Consider, for example, a child of a stable working-class home in which the family has supper at a regular time, the children have a time to play after supper, and a time to go to bed. A four-year-old child in this family has learned a routine for the evening. He finishes his supper and carries his dishes to the place where they will be washed. He then plays with toys for a while, and then goes to his bedroom, puts on his pajamas, and goes to his mother who has finished the supper dishes. He says, "I'm ready for bed. Now let's read." His mother gets out a picture book, and they "read" together for a while, he nestled against his mother's body. Then she says, "Bedtime," and they go to his bed, where she kisses him goodnight. This is an orderly environment, in which the child's ego is developing so that it can promise him satisfaction if he does his share to bring it about.

Now consider a child of a mother with six children receiving welfare payments to care for them, because she has no husband at home. Rarely is there much order in this home. Hardly can this child count on starting a train of events by doing some household chore which eventually brings him into his mother's lap to read with her. She is just too busy, too preoccupied with a hundred worries and a few desires: she may not be able to read beyond the third-grade level, and she may dislike reading. She is not likely to have learned about the necessity of her children having regular rewards and punishments given consistently by her as a means of teaching them.

A good deal of research has been done on the acquisition by children of a sense of control of rewards. Rotter (Rotter, Seeman, & Liverant, 1962) has studied the "sense of personal control of the environment." Crandall (Crandall, Katkovsky, & Crandall, 1965) studied a child's feelings about whether his own efforts determine the rewards he gets from school and from important people or whether this is a matter of luck or the whims of important people. Battle and Rotter (1963) found that middle class and white skin color tended to be associated with a sense of self-responsibility and control of the outer world's rewards and punishments. Coleman (1966) in the National Survey of Educational Opportunity asked students to agree or disagree with three statements such as "Good luck is more important than hard work for success." Negro students had a greater belief in luck as the disposer. Coleman says, "It appears that children from advantaged groups assume the environment will respond if they are able to affect it; children from disadvantaged groups do not make this assumption, but in many cases assume that nothing they will do can affect the environment—it will give benefits or withhold them but not as a consequence of their own action [p. 321]." Negro children who answered "hard work" scored higher on a test of verbal performance than did white pupils who chose the "good luck" response.

Hall (1968) studied a group of young Caucasian and Negro men aged 18–20, all from working-class families in a big city. He divided these young men into three categories according to their work adjustment—one group who had a record of stable employment or went back to school and succeeded there; one group called "rolling stones" who had a recent history of frequent job changes or of going back to school and dropping out again; and a third group whom he called "lookers" who just loafed around, neither working nor going to school. He used with them a questionnaire aimed to measure their sense of control of the environment through their efforts. There was a clear difference in scores between the three groups, the "stable performers" having the most belief in their ability to control their environment.

From these studies it can be inferred that the ego is a less powerful source of reward, and the ego is itself weaker, in the socially disadvantaged groups. The child who can predict the consequences of his behavior can maximize his rewards.

6. *People learn to operate at all of the several levels of reward by the time they reach adolescence, and the level at which they operate varies with the action area.*

This proposition directs our attention to an important set of facts that are indicated in the right-hand column of Table 1. It is possible for a person at adolescence and later to operate in terms of physiological appetite rewards in one area of action, in terms of praise–blame from peers in another area, in terms of ego reward or punishment in yet another action area.

For example, a 17-year-old boy may seek id rewards or satisfaction of physiological appetite in his relations with the opposite sex. He also may seek the id rewards of excitement in doing perilous things such as driving a fast car, diving from a high diving board, rock climbing in the mountains, gang fighting, stealing cars. Some of these things he may do alone, thus cutting off rewards from others, and it is hard to see how one can get ego rewards from doing dangerous things for no purpose other than the thrill or from matching one's wits against nature.

This same boy may play a good game of tennis or basketball partly to get the reward of approval from his peers. He may work long hours at night on a high school course in calculus for advanced standing in college, primarily because his ego tells him he will be rewarded in the future by a successful occupational career.

Probably a social class and an ethnic subculture teaches a person to choose certain areas for certain kinds of rewards. For instance, some American Indian cultures may teach their children to rely on praise–blame from peers for much of their school behavior. A big-city, Negro, lower-working-class culture may teach boys to learn to fight, to play basketball, to throw rocks at school windows, and to smoke "pot" through id rewards and peer group rewards, while it teaches them to expect punishment from teachers for their behavior and lack of achievement in school.

But a particular Negro boy may become so accurate at "shooting baskets" on the park playground that he no longer gets much feeling of reward from being the best in his neighborhood. He may happen on an older high school athlete who rewards him by playing with him, or a man in the neighborhood who tells him that he might become a second Cazzie Russell, if he keeps on. At this point his ego may become effective as a promiser of future reward if he stays in school and makes his grades and then makes the school basketball team.

The study by Gross (1967) of "Learning Readiness in Two Jewish Groups" provides a striking illustration of action areas apparently selected by the minority group subculture for differential rewards. Ninety Brooklyn Jewish boys aged about six years and all middle-class were given a set of tests of cognitive development. About half of the boys came from Sephardic families (immigrants from Arabic or Oriental countries) and half came from Ashkenazic families (immigrants from Europe). The mothers were all native-born, and English was the household language. The boys with European family background were decidedly superior in the cognitive measures to the boys with Arabic-Oriental family backgrounds. There was a 17-point IQ difference on the Peabody Picture Vocabulary Test. Yet the parents were all middle-class Jews living in the same big city. Intensive study of the family training and background experience of the two groups of boys revealed little difference except in the mothers' attitudes toward wealth. Twice as many Ashkenazic (European) mothers said that earnings were "unimportant" in their desires for their children, and three times as many Sephardic mothers said they wanted their sons to be "wealthy."

One may infer from this study that the reward systems in the two groups of families (which were very similar according to the sophisticated methods used to study them) were directed toward different areas of action.

EDUCATION OF DISADVANTAGED MINORITY GROUPS

What can we say from this partially confirmed theory about the education of disadvantaged minority groups?

First, we can say that teachers would teach better if they had a systematic theory of the working of reward and punishment in the learning of children, and if they put this theory into practice. Their theory should include the concept of a hierarchy of reward levels, and they should understand what levels of reward are operating in their classes.

Second, we can assume that most socially disadvantaged children are lower on the evolutionary reward scale, at a given age, than are the advantaged children. Therefore, the teachers of these children should reward them with a great deal of praise, and perhaps with a point system that produces material rewards.

Third, a major goal of all teachers at all levels should be to help the child strengthen his ego as a controller and rewarder of his behavior. This means that the teacher cannot be content with using praise and other forms of external reward, although these should be used when they are needed. The teacher should help the child move up the reward scale.

Progress toward strengthening the ego can only be made in school by putting order and consistency into the school situation, so that the child can learn how to control his environment on the basis of the reality principle. This can be done for individual children partly by individualized instruction which enables them to learn and to predict their own learning in relation to their effort to learn. This can be done for a school class by an orderly program in which students know what their responsibilities are, participate in making decisions about their work, and get accurate information on their progress.

Since the family of the disadvantaged child so often fails to perform its part of the implicit contract, there is bound to be dissatisfaction by school teachers and administrators with the situation, and critics will sometimes blame the school and other times the family subculture. Probably the educator will have to spend much of his energy working with parents and leaders in the local subculture, helping them and receiving help from them to create an environment in the home and neighborhood that supports the learning experience of the child and directs it along socially desirable lines.

References

BATTLE, E., & ROTTER, J. Children's feelings of personal control as related to social class and ethnic group. *Journal of Personality*, 1963, **31**, 482–490.

BEREITER, C., & ENGELMANN, A. *Teaching disadvantaged children.* Englewood Cliffs, N.J.: Prentice-Hall, 1966.

BETTELHEIM, B. Psychoanalysis and education. *School Review*, 1969, **77**, 73–86.

CLARK, C. A., & WALBURG, H. J. The influence of massive rewards on reading achievement in potential urban school dropouts. *American Educational Research Journal*, 1968, 5, 305–310.

COLEMAN, J. S. *Equality of educational opportunity*. Washington, D.C.: United States Government Printing Office, 1966.

CRANDALL, V. C., KATKOVSKY, W., & CRANDALL, V. J. Children's beliefs in their own control of reinforcements in intellectual-academic achievement situations. *Child Development*, 1965, **36**, 91–109.

DAVIDSON, H. H., & GREENBERG, J. *Traits of school achievers from a deprived background*. (Cooperative Research Project No. 2805) Washington, D.C.: United States Office of Education, 1967.

DAVIS, A. Cultural factors in remediation. *Educational Horizons*, 1965, **43**, 231–251.

FENICHEL, O. *The psychoanalytic theory of neurosis*. New York: Norton, 1945.

GROSS, M. *Learning readiness in two Jewish groups*. New York: Center for Urban Education, 1967.

HALL, W. S. Levels of productive economic and educational involvement in the culture among lower class young men: A comparative study. Unpublished doctoral dissertation, Department of Education, University of Chicago, 1968.

HARTLEY, E. L., & HARTLEY, R. E. *Fundamentals of social psychology*. New York: Knopf, 1952.

HESS, R. D., & SHIPMAN, V. Early experience and the socialization of cognitive modes in children. *Child Development*, 1965, **36**, 869–886.

KATZ, I. Some motivational determinants of racial differences in intellectual achievement. *International Journal of Psychology*, 1967, **2**, 1–12.

KOHL, H. R. *36 children*. New York: New American Library, 1967.

LIGHTHALL, F. F., & CERNIUS, V. *Effects of certain rewards for task performance among lower-class boys*. (United States Office of Education & University of Chicago Cooperative Research Project No. S-283) Chicago: Department of Education, University of Chicago, 1967.

McGRADE, B. J. Effectiveness of verbal reinforcers in relation to age and social class. *Journal of Personality and Social Psychology*, 1966, **4**, 555–560.

MARSHALL, H. H. Learning as a function of task interest, reinforcement, and social class variables. *Journal of Educational Psychology*, 1969, **60**, 133–137.

ROSENHAN, D., & GREENWALD, J. A. The effects of age, sex, and socioeconomic class on responsiveness to two classes of verbal reinforcement. *Journal of Personality*, 1965, **33**, 108–121.

ROTTER, J., SEEMAN, M., & LIVERANT, S. Internal versus external control of reinforcement. A major variable in behavior theory. In N. F. Washburne (Ed.), *Decisions, values, and groups*. Vol. 2. London: Pergamon Press, 1962.

SKINNER, B. F. *Science and human behavior*. New York: Macmillan, 1953.

STEVENSON, H. W. Social reinforcement with children as a function of chronological age, sex of experimenter, and sex of subject. *Journal of Abnormal and Social Psychology*, 1961, **63**, 147–154.

THORNDIKE, E. L. *The elements of psychology*. New York: Seiler, 1905.

———. *The fundamentals of learning*. New York: Bureau of Publications, Teachers College, Columbia University, 1932.

WAX, M. L. *Indian education in eastern Oklahoma*. (Research Contract Report No. O. E. 6-10-260 and BIA No. 5-0565-2-12-1) Washington, D.C.: United States Office of Education, 1969.

WOLCOTT, H. F. *A Kwakiutl village and school*. New York: Holt, Rinehart & Winston, 1967.

ZIGLER, E., & KANZER, P. The effectiveness of two classes of verbal reinforcers on the performance of middle- and lower-class children. *Journal of Personality*, 1962, **30**, 157–163.

———, & DE LABRY, J. Concept-switching in middle-class, lower-class, and retarded children. *Journal of Abnormal and Social Psychology*, 1962, **65**, 267–273.

The Palo Alto Study of Educationally Handicapped Children

Freya W. Owen
PALO ALTO UNIFIED SCHOOL DISTRICT

INTRODUCTION

Preliminary reports of the Palo Alto research on Educationally Handicapped pupils were presented at the Society for Research in Child Development meetings in New York City in 1967 (Owen, 1968).[1] The purpose of this introductory paper is to briefly review the earlier papers; including the major goals of the research, the sample, the data collecting procedures and the significant intellectual, medical and perceptual–motor findings.[2]

The study is being made in the Palo Alto Unified School District here in California where there is a special remedial program for "educationally handicapped" pupils (hereafter referred to as EH) (Owen, 1968). The major criteria for identification as EH is a significant discrepancy between ability and school achievement (1.5 to 2 years retarded). Approximately 2% (or 300 out of 16,000) are selected for this remedial help; hence, the children represent a rather severely impaired group academically (Money, 1966).

Purpose of the Study   Our research has two major purposes:

1. To discover whether the characteristics of these academically handicapped children can be more precisely identified and described;
2. To further clarify the causes of learning disabilities.

The design consists *first* in comparing EH children (a) with their same sex siblings, and (b) with matched same sex children who are academically successful, and their siblings, and *second*, in comparing the parents of the EH children with the parents of the Successful Academic children on a number of items. This design makes it possible to explore the familial aspects of the abnormality.

SUBJECTS   The subjects are 304 elementary and junior high school children; 244 are boys and 60 are girls.

Table 1 describes the sample. There are 76 EH children, and their 76 same sex siblings (referred to as EH and EH sibs). The 76 EH children are matched on the basis of grade, sex, and intelligence (within 10 points on the WISC) with 76 children who are successful academically (referred to as SA), and who have 76 same sex siblings (referred to as SA sibs). The two sets of siblings are matched for grade and sex.

Reprinted from a paper presented at the Society for Research in Child Development Meetings, March 28, 1969, Santa Monica, California. By permission.

[1] This research has been supported by a grant (1 RO1 HD 01730-04) from the National Institute of Child Health and Development.
[2] The investigators responsible for this project are: Principal Investigator, Freya W. Owen; Co-Investigator, Pauline A. Adams; Co-Investigator, Thomas Forrest; Consultant, Lois Meek Stolz; and Research Associate, Sara Fisher.

TABLE 1
Sample

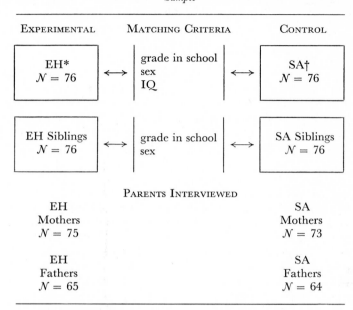

EXPERIMENTAL	MATCHING CRITERIA	CONTROL
EH* $N = 76$	⟷ grade in school sex IQ ⟷	SA† $N = 76$
EH Siblings $N = 76$	⟷ grade in school sex ⟷	SA Siblings $N = 76$

PARENTS INTERVIEWED

EH Mothers $N = 75$	SA Mothers $N = 73$
EH Fathers $N = 65$	SA Fathers $N = 64$

* Educationally Handicapped.
† Successful Academic.

We first screened the remedial population to locate EH students with same sex siblings in our school district. After obtaining written permission from the parents for their children to participate (and with the understanding that the parents, too, would be involved), the EH children were given individual mental tests to see whether they would meet the criterion of normal ability (a full scale IQ of 90 or above).

Once having selected an appropriate EH–EH sib pair, we proceeded to locate a successful academic child with an appropriate sibling to match the EH pair. A clerical assistant combed the school district rosters in order to locate several potential matches. For example, let us suppose that we were searching for a successful academic student in the sixth grade, IQ ± 10 points from 120, who also had a male sibling in the third grade. After locating five or six possibilities, we sent out a simple rating form to the appropriate classroom teachers to obtain a teacher estimate of ability and academic performance. Previous test results available from school records were also considered. We then approached the families of children who appeared to be reasonable matches and, once having obtained parent cooperation, we proceeded to test the successful academic child to see whether or not he met our requirements. We tested 184 children in order to locate the 76 matched sets of EH and SA children included in the study. Of the 76 EH subjects, 64 were located from within the population of remedial children; 12 were recommended by school principals and guidance consultants.

The mean age of the experimental and control children is ten years.

The mean age of the sibling groups is nine years, eight months. The average age difference between the EH and EH sibs is two years, nine months; between the SA and SA sibs it is two years and ten months. There are no significant differences in the distribution of older and younger siblings between the experimental and control groups. The ordinal position within the family is not significantly related to learning disability in the sample.

Data obtained from parent interviews and school records indicate that our experimental and control groups do not differ significantly in social-economic background. Palo Alto is a university and scientific community with a primarily middle- to upper-middle-class population. The educational levels of the fathers of the two groups are practically identical. Furthermore, there are no significant differences between the groups on the occupational level of the fathers (Hollingshead, 1958).

Procedures   The data-collecting procedures employed in the study involved both individual interviews and evaluations with the children and their parents. All children in the study were given psychological and educational evaluations. A research assistant contacted the various schools and set up appointments. The psychologists, Dr. Pauline Adams and Dr. Sara Fisher, saw the children without knowing whether they were experimental or control subjects. The tests administered and the order of presentation are as follows: WISC, Bender, Draw-A-Person, and Wide Range Achievement Test. In addition, a brief child interview and a rating of his behavior during the testing interviews were completed.

The research assistant also set up appointments for Dr. Thomas Forrest, the pediatric neurologist, who also examined the children without knowing whether they were experimental or control subjects. He assessed the EH, EH sibs, and the SA children medically and neurologically. Following the medical examinations, Dr. Forrest and one other physician interviewed the children's mothers to obtain family medical histories, and signed releases for the hospital birth records on the children. In 1967–1968 EEG studies were made on 25 EH's and their siblings, and 25 SA's and their siblings (total $N = 100$).

Behavior ratings of the children were obtained in the following manner. A clerical worker was given a coded list of the participating children's names and schools. She was asked to go to the schools and to type information available in the cumulative records related to school adjustment and behavior. (In California there is a particular section of the cumulative record designated for this kind of information.) Code numbers were placed on the back of the cards. Thus, it was possible for three raters to work with these cards with no knowledge about the groups to which the children were assigned in the study.

Two psychiatrists and two clinical psychologists (two men and two women) interviewed separately the mothers and fathers of the children. These interviews were recorded on tape and were transcribed. At the end of the interview, we administered reading tests (WRAT) to both the mothers and fathers of the children and obtained releases from them in order to send for their high school records (Robbins, 1963).

Information regarding the speech and language development of the children was available from the Speech and Hearing Department in the Palo Alto

Unified School District.[3] All children entering kindergarten in Palo Alto receive speech and language evaluations from qualified therapists. When difficulties are present, they are diagnosed and appropriate therapeutic measures instituted. These data were available for the EH and their siblings, as well as for the SA's and their siblings.

REVIEW OF PRELIMINARY FINDINGS

Intellectual and Achievement Functioning   In 1967 Dr. Pauline Adams reported on the intellectual and achievement functioning of the children (Adams, 1968). As indicated earlier, the EH and SA subjects were matched within 10 points on the basis of their WISC full scale IQ's. The mean Verbal and Performance Scale IQ scores of all groups except the EH's are within one IQ point of each other, while there is a significant IQ difference of 5.73 points in favor of the Performance Scale for the EH children ($p < .01$). (The EH children with a positive performance discrepancy of 15 or more IQ points were analyzed as a special sub-group to be reported later.)

An analysis of the sub-test scaled scores on the WISC demonstrated impaired ability in numerical computation, sequencing, and fine-perceptual–motor hand-eye coordination and memory. Moreover, the siblings of the EH's showed similar weaknesses.

Achievement test (WRAT) findings indicated that both EH and EH sibs were significantly ($p < .01$) behind SA and SAS in reading and spelling.

As described earlier, data were collected related to the children's behavior in school. The educationally handicapped children were rated as significantly poorer in their classroom and playground behavior. Differences between EH versus SA and EHS versus SAS were highly significant ($p < .01$). Sibling similarities are also marked.

As reported, the parents' high school transcripts and adult reading skills were evaluated. As adults, EH fathers when compared with SA were less able readers ($p < .02$). High school English grades significantly differentiate both mothers and fathers in the experimental and control groups. The successful academic children's parents were significantly better ($p < .02$). Mathematics grades did not differentiate fathers. The EH mothers, however, were significantly poorer than the SA mothers ($p < .05$).

Neurological and Medical Factors   In 1967 Dr. Thomas Forrest discussed neurological and medical measures that differentiated EH from SA children. He also explored areas where strong similarities were apparent between EH and their siblings (Forrest, 1968).

His data indicated that EH compared with SA children were impaired in the following areas:

1. The ability to reproduce a tapped pattern $p < .01$.
2. Right-left discrimination $p < .01$ (Belmont, 1965; Silver & Hagen, 1960).

---

[3] Mrs. Ruth M. Jackson, Coordinator of this program, generously contributed these data for the project.

3. Double simultaneous touch $p < .05$ (Pollack, 1957).
4. Fast alternating finger movements $p < .05$ (Hertzig & Birch, 1966).
5. Fast alternating hand movements $p < .01$.

The following medical-history factors differentiated EH from SA:

1. Irritability during infancy $p < .05$.
2. Colic $p < .05$.
3. Decreased pre-lingual sound production $p < .05$.
4. Poor listening skills after age two $p < .01$.
5. Ease of mother–child communication $p < .01$.
6. Temper tantrums $p < .05$.

Perceptual-Motor Functioning   At the earlier symposium, Dr. Sara Fisher presented data on the perceptual–motor functioning of the EH and SA children (Fisher, 1968). The two assessment instruments utilized were the Draw-A-Person (Goodenough, 1926) and the Bender-Gestalt (Bender, 1938); both differentiated significantly between EH and SA as well as between sibling groups. The Koppitz Developmental Norms (Koppitz, 1964) were used to score the Bender-Gestalt (EH versus SA, $p < .01$; EHS versus SAS, $p < .01$).

The drawings (DAP) were evaluated with the Harris Point Scale (Harris, 1963) (EH versus SAS, $p < .05$).

This is a very brief summary of previous reports of the findings of this research. Analysis has now been made of additional medical data, of hand-writing skills, of data from the parent interviews, and, in addition, a study has been made of five sub-groups within the educationally handicapped group. The complete study is being prepared for publication in 1970.

References

ADAMS, P. A. Patterns of intellectual functioning in learning disability children and their siblings compared with successful students and their siblings. *Bull. Orton Society*, 1968, 40–48.

BELMONT, L., and BIRCH, H. G. Lateral dominance, lateral awareness and reading disability. *Child Development*. March 1965, Vol. 36, #1.

BENDER, L. A visual motor Gestalt test and its clinical uses. *Research Monograph No. 3, American Ortho-psychiatric Association*, 1938.

FISHER, S. Two tests of perceptual-motor function; The Draw-A-Person and the Bender-Gestalt. *Bull. Orton Society*, 1968, 55–61.

FORREST, T. Neurological and medical factors discriminating between normal children and those with learning disability. *Bull. Orton Society*, 1968, 48–55.

GOODENOUGH, F. Measurement of intelligence by drawings. Chicago: World Book Co., 1926.

HARRIS, D. Children's drawings as measures of intellectual maturity. New York: Harcourt, Brace & World, 1963.

HOLLINGSHEAD, A. B., and F. C. REDLICH. *Social Class and Mental Illness*. New York: John Wiley and Sons, 1958.

KOPPITZ, E. *The Bender Test for Young Children*. New York: Grune and Stratton, 1964.

MONEY, J. The disabled reader. Baltimore: The Johns Hopkins Press, 1966.

OWEN, F. W. Learning disabilities: a familial study. *Bull. Orton Society*, 1968, 33–39.

Owen, F. W., and Compton, C. The learning centers in Palo Alto. *J. Learn. Dis.*, Nov. 1968, Vol. I, #11.

Pollack, M., and Goldfarb, W. The face hand test in schizophrenic children. *Arch. of Neurology and Psychiatry*. #77, 635–642, 1957.

Robbins, L. C. The accuracy of parental recall of aspects of child development and of child rearing practices. *J. Abnorm. Soc. Psychol.*, 1963, 66, 261–70.

Silver, A., and Hagen, R. Specific reading disability: delineation of the syndrome and its relationship to cerebral dominance. *Comprehensive Psychiatry*, 1960, *1* (2), 126–134.

Urban, W. *The Draw-A-Person: Catalogue for Interpretive Analysis.* Beverly Hills, Calif: Western Psychological Services, 1963.

Cooperative and Competitive Behavior of Urban Afro-American, Anglo-American, Mexican-American, and Mexican Village Children*

Millard C. Madsen and Ariella Shapira
UNIVERSITY OF CALIFORNIA

Children of three ethnic groups in Los Angeles, California, ages 7–9, performed on the cooperation board developed by Madsen. In Experiment I, Mexican-American boys were less competitive than Mexican-American girls and Afro- and Anglo-Americans of both sexes. In Experiment II, all three ethnic groups behaved in a highly competitive manner. In Experiment III, the three ethnic groups in Los Angeles behaved in a non-adaptive competitive manner while a sample of village children in Mexico behaved co-operatively.

This study is the third in a series in which subcultural differences in cooperation and competition in children have been examined. In the initial study, Madsen (1967) found highly significant differences between children from different sub-cultural settings in Mexico. Rural village children and lower-class, urban children behaved in a much more cooperative manner on an experimental task than did urban, middle-class children. The aforementioned study was motivated by anthropological observations (Lewis, 1961; Romney & Romney, 1963) of child-rearing practices in different Mexican settings.

In a second study, Shapira and Madsen (1969) found children of Israeli kibbutzim (rural communal settlements) to be more cooperative than urban, middle-class Israeli children. In this study, the magnitude of the difference in cooperative behavior was greater for boys than for girls. That children of the kibbutz would be highly cooperative in an experimental task was predictable

Reprinted from *Developmental Psychology*, 1970, *3*, 16–20. By permission.

* This research was carried out with the support of the United States Office of Economic Opportunity, Contract No. 4117. The authors are indebted to Carolyn Stern, Director of the University of California, Los Angeles, Head Start Evaluation and Research Center, for her assistance in all phases of the study.

from observations of child-rearing practices and parental values in the kibbutz as reported by Spiro (1965).

In the first two studies reported here, children of three ethnic groups in the United States, all in the city of Los Angeles, California, were examined with the use of techniques identical to those used in Mexico and Israel. The ethnic groups were Mexican-American, Afro-American, and Anglo-American.

An important difference in the selection of subjects should be noted between the present study and the two earlier studies discussed in the preceding paragraphs. In the studies in Mexico and Israel the urban and rural groups were in physical isolation from one another. In addition, the social values and educational and child-rearing practices that might lead to the differential development of tendencies toward cooperative or competitive behavior are more readily distinguishable.

In the present study, however, the subcultural groups were all residents of the same urban center, and surely subject to numerous common social and educational influences. The question being asked, then, is whether or not the more subtle influences that characterize the developmental milieu in these ethnic subcultures in an area of the United States are sufficient to produce differential tendencies to cooperate or to compete as were found between subcultural groups in Mexico and Israel.

EXPERIMENT 1

METHOD

Subjects   One hundred and forty-four children who were all enrolled in the Los Angeles public school system served as subjects. All subjects were in either the second or third grade and ranged 7–9 years of age. The three ethnic groups were equally represented by 48 subjects, 24 of each sex. Each group was selected from a single elementary school in which over 90 per cent of the students were of one ethnic group. The areas served by each of the schools were judged to be lower-middle class or below by the school authorities and by the investigators.

Apparatus   The cooperation board developed by Madsen (1967) was used (see Figure 1). The cooperation board was 18 inches square with an eyelet fastened to each corner. Strings strung through these eyelets were connected to an object which served to hold a downward pointing ball-point pen. A sheet of white paper was placed on the board prior to each trial. When the subjects, who were seated at each of the four corners of the board, pulled the strings, responses were automatically recorded by the pen. Because of the eyelets, individual subjects were only able to pull the pen toward themselves. It was therefore necessary for the subjects to cooperate in order to draw a line over designated points which were not in a direct path from the starting point in the center of the board to any of the corners. In the first experiment, four circles were drawn on the recording sheets as illustrated in Figure 1.

Procedure   Four subjects of the same sex and ethnic group were seated at the four corners of the board which was on a small table. The subjects were then told that they were going to play a game in which they could get prizes. The experimenter then demonstrated that a line could be drawn on the paper by pulling on a string.

Reward was contingent on the performance of the group on the first three

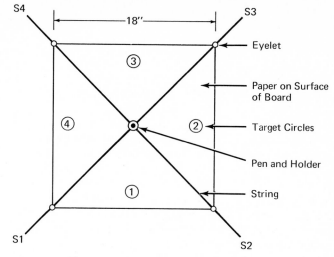

F IGURE 1.   *Cooperation board.*

trials. Prior to Trial 1, the experimenter drew numbers one through four in the circles and instructed the subjects that they were to draw a line through the circles in that order. The subjects were also told that each of them would receive a prize for each time that they crossed all four circles during a 1-minute period. On completion of a trial, the subjects were allowed to choose their prizes from an assortment of trinkets.

New instructions were given prior to Trial 4 by which reward was changed from a group to an individual basis. The experimenter wrote each subject's name in one of the circles and explained that each one now had a circle of his own, and that prizes would be given only to those whose name was in the circle that was crossed. The subjects thus received a prize for each time their designated circle was crossed. Trials 5 and 6 followed an identical procedure. It should be noted that no change was made in the task or procedure except for the change from group to individual reward.

RESULTS   The mean number of circles crossed per trial are presented in Table 1. A one-way analysis of variance of Trial 3 scores indicated that mean differences between groups did not approach significance. Thus the three ethnic groups were approximately equal in their ability to cooperate under group reward. In order to determine the relative change in the amount of cooperation with the introduction of individual reward, each group received a different score. This score was the number of circles crossed in Trial 3 minus the number of circles crossed in Trial 4.

A 2 × 3 (Sex × Ethnic Group) analysis of variance of these difference scores yielded no significant main effects. The Sex × Ethnic Group interaction approached significance ($F = 2.7$, df $= 2/30$, $p < .10$). An analysis of simple main effects of ethnic group yielded a significant effect for boys ($F = 3.88$, df $= 2/30$, $p < .05$) but not for girls. The mean decrease of 1.7 circles crossed from Trial 3 to Trial 4 by Mexican-American boys was significantly less than that of the combined Afro-American (mean drop of 6.8) and Anglo-American

TABLE 1
Mean Circles Crossed per Trial

| | TRIAL | | | | | |
| | GROUP REWARD | | | INDIVIDUAL REWARD | | |
GROUP	1	2	3	4	5	6
Anglo-American						
Boys	5.1	10.3	14.3	3.1	2.1	2.8
Girls	2.8	9.1	12.0	7.1	11.0	12.1
Mexican-American						
Boys	6.8	11.3	14.5	12.8	13.8	12.3
Girls	5.0	9.3	10.0	4.1	5.0	6.8
Afro-American						
Boys	5.5	8.0	11.5	4.7	6.0	6.1
Girls	4.5	4.8	10.7	1.5	2.5	4.1

(mean drop of 11.2) group ($F = 6.0$, df $= 1/30$, $p < .05$). The mean difference between the two latter groups did not approach significance.

The most striking result, then, was not the differential increase in competition with the introduction of individual reward, but rather the fact that all ethnic groups began to respond more competitively on Trial 4. Separate *t* tests comparing the mean number of circles crossed indicated a decrease from Trial 3 to Trial 4 that was significant at the .005 level for both Afro- and Anglo-Americans. A comparison of Trial 3 with Trial 6 scores indicated a significant difference at the .005 level for Afro-Americans, and the .05 level for Anglo-Americans, the latter being due to the boys. The mean of circles crossed by Mexican-Americans was lower on Trial 6 than on Trial 3, but fell short of the .05 level of significance. No ethnic group, therefore, improved performance over Trials 4–6 from that on Trial 3.

EXPERIMENT II

METHOD

Experiment II proceeded immediately after Experiment I with the same subjects participating in the same groups.

In Experiment I, competitive responses were nonadaptive in that they interfered with reward attainment. In Experiment II, circles were drawn on each of the four corners of the recording sheet. Competition was, therefore, somewhat more adaptive in that an individual child could pull the pen directly to his circle. The name of each child was written in the circle in front of him and they were then told that the first one to draw a line over his circle would receive a prize. The pen was placed at the center of the board at the beginning of four successive trials. A trial was terminated and no prizes were given if a circle was not crossed within 1 minute. Maximum cooperation, therefore, in terms of sharing of prizes, had to take place over trials, as opposed to within trials as in Experiment I.

R ESULTS   If the line drawn by the pen deviated more than 1 inch in either direction from the direct path from the center of the board to a circle, or reversed directions within those limits, it was scored as a competitive response. Any less deviation indicated that subjects were not pulling against each other and was, therefore, scored as noncompetitive.

The results were that the majority of subjects in all ethnic groups responded competitively. Mexican-American subjects gave more noncompetitive responses ($M = 1.7$) than did the Afro-American ($M = .7$) or Anglo-American ($M = .7$) groups. The distributions were highly skewed in that the vast majority of groups gave four competitive responses and a few groups gave four noncompetitive responses. Comparisons between groups by Mann-Whitney U tests indicated no differences that reached the .05 level of significance.

While the results of Experiments I and II indicate a tendency for the Mexican-American group to be less competitive, the differences are not very substantial. These results, therefore, are of interest only when compared to the previous studies in other cultures in which the identical techniques were used. Such a comparison indicates that the responses of children of the three ethnic groups studied in the United States were more similar than were kibbutz versus nonkibbutz children in Israel and village versus urban children in Mexico.

EXPERIMENT III

In Experiment I, the initial three group reward trials were given in order to determine whether the three samples differed in their ability to perform the cooperative tasks when motivated to do so. This is the same procedure that was followed in the previous studies in Mexico and Israel. In all three studies, all subcultural groups of the age tested were able to substantially master the task under group reward. Subsequent differences in performance between groups under individual reward could, therefore, be interpreted as due to motivation rather than to the motor or cognitive ability necessary to perform the task. Another possibility, however, is that those groups that continued to cooperate after introduction of individual reward (kibbutz, Mexican village, and Mexican-American boys) do so because the initial group reward trials amount to an instructional cooperative set. It is quite possible that some subcultural groups are more sensitive to such a set than are others. In Experiment III, therefore, subjects performed on the cooperation board for individual reward without previous training under group reward. A sample of village children in Mexico was included in order to determine if the previously found tendency to cooperate under individual reward was due to an instructional set provided by the previous reward trials.

M ETHOD

Subjects   Children of the same age range, socioeconomic level, and ethnic groups as in Experiments I and II served as subjects. The experiment was conducted during summer vacation in the United States and subjects were enrolled in day care or summer school programs. The Mexican children, also ages 7–9, were enrolled in elementary school in the village of Nuevo San Vicente, located 54 miles south of Ensenada, Mexico, in the state of Mexicali. The village has approximately 800 inhabitants, the majority of whom are supported by an agriculture-based economy. Forty children, 20 of each sex, of each United States ethnic group and 36 children, 20 girls and 16 boys, from the Mexican village served as subjects.

Procedure   Four subjects of the same sex and ethnic group were seated at the four corners of the cooperation board. Each subject was allowed to pull his string to see that his action drew a line on the paper. A sheet with four circles in positions similar to Experiment I (Figure 1) was then placed on the board and the name of each subject was written in the circle to his right. The subjects were told that each time a line was drawn over their own circle they would receive a prize. Four 1-minute trials were given with prizes distributed after each trial.

RESULTS   The mean number of circles crossed by trial and ethnic group is presented in Table 2. The result is obvious without statistical test. The three

TABLE 2
Mean Circles Crossed per Trial

	TRIAL			
GROUP	1	2	3	4
Anglo-American	1.5	.4	.8	.4
Afro-American	.9	.6	.6	.5
Mexican-American	.2	.3	.5	1.0
Mexican village	1.8	3.6	5.4	6.5

United States ethnic groups responded in a nonadaptive competitive manner over the four trials with no differences between trials, groups, or sexes approaching statistical significance. This was in marked contrast with the cooperative performance of the Mexican village subjects. The data are, in fact, nonoverlapping by the second trial. There was not a single indication of competitive behavior on the part of any of the 36 village subjects and no instances of group cooperation in the three United States ethnic groups. The few circles crossed by the latter were made during active, sometimes almost violent, competition. The performance of the Mexican-American subjects, although competitive, was consistently less vigorous than the other two United States groups. For many of the Anglo- and Afro-American groups it was necessary for the experimenter to stand and press down on the cooperation board with both hands in order to keep it from flying through the air.

DISCUSSION

The results of the three experiments indicate a high degree of nonadaptive competitiveness among children of the three United States ethnic groups. This was less true for Mexican-American boys in Experiment I in that there was not a significant drop in the number of circles crossed with the introduction of individual reward. It should also be noted, however, that the mean circles crossed by this group on Trials 4, 5, and 6 was always below that achieved on Trial 3.

The results of Experiment III indicate a dramatic difference between the United States and Mexican village children. Even though the tabled results are nonoverlapping, they do not present the vividly contrasting behavior as observed by the experimenters. The often aggressive, wild, shouting matches among the children in the United States, who were desperately but unsuccessfully trying to cross their circles, was in total contrast to the rather slow, quiet, and deliberately cooperative behavior of the Mexican village children. It should be noted, however, that urban children in Mexico (Madsen, 1967) performed on the cooperation board in much the same manner as the comppetitive groups in the United States. The cooperative behavior of the Mexican village children, therefore, represents a specific subcultural, rather than a broad national characteristic.

References

Lewis, O. *Life in a Mexican village: Tepoztlan restudied.* Urbana.: University of Illinois Press, 1961.

Madsen, M. C. Cooperative and competitive motivation of children in three Mexican subcultures. *Psychological Reports*, 1967, **20**, 1307–1320.

Romney, K., & Romney, R. The Mixtecans of Juxtlahuaca, Mexico. In B. Whiting (Ed.), *Six cultures.* New York: Wiley, 1963.

Shapira, A., & Madsen, M. C. Cooperative and competitive behavior of kibbutz and urban children in Israel. *Child Development*, 1969, **40**, 609–617.

Spiro, M. E. *Children of the kibbutz.* Cambridge: Harvard University Press, 1965.

Fears of Children

J. W. Croake

FLORIDA STATE UNIVERSITY

Previous to the thirties little had been done by way of extensive investigation into the fears of children. At this time Jersild and his associates conducted a number of studies. Since that time there have been relatively few studies reported, and there have been none in the last eleven years.

Child development and other texts, when reporting children's fears, most often refer to these studies conducted in the thirties. In recent years the world situation has altered appreciably, particularly in the political sphere. With this

Reprinted from *Human Development*, 1969, *12*, 239–247. Published by S. Karger AG Basel, New York. By permission.

alteration being transmitted through today's mass media, it is reasonable to suppose that what children of today fear may be vastly different from those fears of children 15, 20, and 30 years previous. This study was conducted to explore the nature of children's fears in a more current setting.

A comprehensive survey of the literature by the writer revealed that early studies were concerned with showing that at least some fears are innate (Kessen, 1965; Valentine, 1930). This was apparently substantiated (Watson, 1920). Later studies were more comprehensive and better controlled. These investigators disclosed that lower socioeconomic children tend to have more fears than upper socioeconomic children (Angelino, Dollins and Mech, 1956; Jersild and Holmes, 1933; Jersild, Markey and Jersild, 1933). Girls report more fears than boys and Negro children more than white children (Holmes, 1935; Jersild, Golman and Loftus, 1941; Jersild and Holmes, 1935; Lapouse and Monk, 1953; Pratt, 1943). There were inconsistent findings about the age of subjects and the number of fears. Dunlop (1951) and Lapouse and Monk (1953) found age to be an unimportant factor; whereas, Pratt (1943) and Hagman (1936) indicate that the number of fears increases with age. When working with "normal" children, there seemed to be little or no difference in the number of fears between intellectual levels (Gastwirth, 1943).

Children under four years of age were found to be most often afraid of noise and situations associated with noise (Holmes, 1936; Jersild and Holmes, 1933; Jersild and Holmes, 1935; Valentine, 1930). This was true for four-year-old girls as well, but four-year-old boys were more concerned with personal safety (Jersild, Markey and Jersild, 1933). Fear of animals was recorded as the most common fear in five and six year olds, as it was at age seven and eight, along with supernatural events and beings and safety (Dunlop, 1951; Ferguson, 1952; Holmes, 1935; Jersild, Markey and Jersild, 1933).

From age eight to adolescence, the various studies reviewed were not in unanimous agreement as to the most prevalent types of fears. Those most frequently mentioned were supernatural events and beings, school, bodily injury and punishment, and animals (Angelino and Shedd, 1953; Dunlop, 1951; Ferguson, 1952; Jersild, Markey and Jersild, 1933; Lapouse and Monk, 1953; Pintner and Levy, 1940).

METHOD

The present study which was carried out in three phases was designed to determine the number and type of fears peculiar to third and sixth grade pupils of low and high socioeconomic levels in the states of South Dakota and Nebraska. The sample was drawn from 12 schools of varying size including small town and large city systems. The subjects in all three phases were randomly selected from classroom enrolment sheets. Sex and socioeconomic level were controlled with the aim of obtaining approximately the same number of subjects in each of the categories. The socioeconomic level was determined by the Hatt-North Occupational Prestige Ratings scale.

In Phase I, 53 pupils were interviewed individually with respect to their fears. The sample in this phase included 10 upper and 16 lower socioeconomic males and 14 upper and 13 lower socioeconomic females. This was a total of 17 third, 18 sixth, and 18 ninth grade children. The responses given by these subjects were compiled to make a questionnaire which was administered to all of the Phase II population. The final questionnaire consisted of sixty-nine items including those fears which they held at present, three years previous, and those that they believed they would hold three years hence. Responses obtained from pupils in the ninth grade were used as possible stimuli for future fears and their responses appear only as a part of the questionnaire.

Illustrative items from the questionnaire and their ten categories appear below The categories were unanimously agreed upon by five professors of Educational Psychology at the University of South Dakota.[1]

Animals	*Personal Relations*
bugs	meeting new kids
wild animals	people I don't know
Future	*School*
getting married	school tests
college	getting bad grades
Supernatural Phenomena	*Home*
ghosts	afraid something will happen to mom or dad
the dark	mom or dad punishing me
Natural Phenomena	*Safety*
tornadoes	getting hurt while playing games
thunder and lightning	getting lost
Personal Appearance	*Political*
my hair style	communists taking over
my weight	war

The main purpose of Phase II was to determine the following: (1) What are the number and types of past fears? (2) What are the number and types of present fears? (3) What are the number and types of future fears?

The subjects in this phase were asked as classroom groups to respond to three administrations of the check list indicating those items which were like fears that they held at present, three years previously, and those which they believed they would hold three years hence.

Means for the various population groups are reported in table I. Also found in table I are the significance of the difference among the groups as determined by the Mann-Whitney U test. With the exception of one Catholic boarding school for lower socioeconomic Indian pupils, all but one of the 213 pupils in Phase II were white.

Phase III was concerned with interviewing a sample of children who participated in Phase II in order to gain some insight into the nature of the fears indicated in the questionnaires: (1) What sources are perceived as the genesis of fears? (2) What are the reasons for individual discrepancies between past, present, and future fears? (3) Which fears are the most intense?

The sample in this phase included: 1 upper socioeconomic third grade boy, 5 lower socioeconomic third grade boys, 2 upper socioeconomic third grade girls, 4 lower socioeconomic third grade girls, 1 upper socioeconomic sixth grade girl, 5 lower socioeconomic sixth grade girls.

RESULTS

As shown in Table 1 girls have more fears than boys, as do lower socioeconomic children in contrast to their upper socioeconomic peers. The subjects

[1] The complete list of items used in the questionnaire may be obtained by writing the author.

TABLE 1
Mean Number of Fears by Population Groups

	Past	Present	Future
GRADE THREE			
Boys ($N = 56$)	24.1†	23.1†	16.0*
Girls ($N = 51$)	30.2	28.2	22.1
Upper socioeconomic ($N = 38$)	20.4†	22.6†	16.0
Lower socioeconomic ($N = 69$)	30.7	27.2	20.5
GRADE SIX			
Boys ($N = 55$)	28.5†	23.1†	16.1†
Girls ($N = 51$)	26.2	28.6	26.8
Upper socioeconomic ($N = 32$)	28.4†	26.1†	20.7*
Lower socioeconomic ($N = 74$)	27.9	24.9	23.4
Total third ($N = 107$)	27.3	25.8	19.1
Total sixth ($N = 106$)	28.5	26.0	21.7

* $p < .05$.
† $p < .01$.

see themselves as having held more fears in the past then at present, and they see themselves as holding fewer fears in the future than at present. Statistical levels of significance are indicated between each of the population groups compared.

With the exception of third grade present tense, the most consistently held fears for all of the population group comparisons made in the present and future tenses were political. These data are presented in Tables 2 and 3. Natural phenomena were the most common past fears for all third grade subjects regardless of their sex and socioeconomic level; whereas, supernatural phenomena were the most frequently cited past fears of all sixth grade subjects with the exception of sixth grade girls who were most often fearful of natural phenomena and animals in the past.

In Phase III the twenty-four subjects were interviewed individually. When asked the genesis of each of the fears which they checked in Phase II group administration "don't know" received the majority of responses, about 75% of the total. This same order of response classes with approximately the same percentage appeared in attempting to account for fear discrepancies. A discrepancy occurred when a fear was indicated in one tense and not in another, i.e., fear of teachers was checked as being held three years previous and at present, but not anticipated as a fear three years hence.

The subjects in this phase were also given 3 × 5 cards indicating each of the fears which they had checked in Phase II. They were asked to place these cards in one of four titled piles: "I almost never worry about or am afraid of this fear," "I often worry about or am afraid of this fear," "I sometimes worry

TABLE 2

Percentage of Past, Present, and Future Fears by Reference Category for Upper and Lower Socioeconomic Levels

CATEGORIES	PAST	PRESENT	FUTURE	PAST	PRESENT	FUTURE
		GRADE THREE				
		$(N = 38)$			$(N = 69)$	
Animals	13.3	14.6	7.8	11.4	9.2	6.6
Future	2.9	3.1	7.9	5.9	6.7	8.7
Supernatural	15.9	9.3	5.6	12.9	10.3	8.7
Natural	19.3	16.3	13.2	13.9	13.8	15.2
Personal appearance	2.1	4.4	8.6	3.6	4.8	6.7
Personal relations	6.8	5.9	7.9	7.0	7.0	7.7
School	8.3	10.1	11.4	9.2	10.1	11.3
Home	8.0	8.1	7.9	10.4	10.5	10.5
Safety	12.9	13.2	9.3	12.1	12.3	11.3
Political	10.0	14.5	19.9	12.1	14.8	13.4
		GRADE SIX				
		$(N = 32)$			$(N = 74)$	
Animals	13.1	9.6	3.2	12.6	9.6	3.2
Future	4.0	6.9	13.6	4.1	5.6	8.8
Supernatural	14.5	9.4	5.3	14.6	7.8	5.0
Natural	13.9	10.4	5.8	14.3	10.5	8.8
Personal appearance	2.5	4.6	9.8	2.0	5.7	11.3
Personal relations	9.2	8.7	11.0	7.2	8.0	9.3
School	10.2	12.3	14.0	10.2	12.4	13.6
Home	9.2	8.9	6.4	11.1	10.8	10.1
Safety	13.4	10.2	8.6	12.6	10.2	8.9
Political	9.5	18.5	21.6	10.9	19.0	20.5

about or am afraid of this fear," or "I am almost always worried about or am afraid of this fear."

The most common intensity response for the majority of fear groups was "sometimes worry about." This was particularly true for the category natural phenomena and other fears with which the child actually has had some contact such as strange noises, being late for school, people laughing at me, etc. The fear category which received the highest percentage of "almost always worry about" was political.

DISCUSSION

The results of this investigation indicate that girls and lower socioeconomic children hold more fears than do boys and upper socioeconomic children. These results are consistent in general with the findings of previous studies. The

TABLE 3

Percentage of Past, Present, and Future Fears by Reference Category for Boys and Girls

	PAST	PRESENT	FUTURE	PAST	PRESENT	FUTURE
CATEGORIES		BOYS			GIRLS	
		($N = 56$)			($N = 51$)	
Animals	12.4	10.7	6.6	11.5	11.2	7.3
Future	4.7	5.1	8.1	5.3	5.9	7.7
Supernatural	13.7	10.1	8.5	13.8	9.8	7.1
Natural	14.0	14.6	13.9	16.6	14.6	15.1
Personal appearance	2.8	5.0	5.3	3.4	4.4	9.1
Personal relations	6.8	6.6	8.5	7.1	6.6	7.6
School	8.8	9.7	10.9	9.2	10.5	11.7
Home	10.3	10.0	11.0	9.2	9.5	8.7
Safety	12.8	12.3	10.4	11.9	12.9	11.0
Political	13.1	15.4	16.8	11.6	14.1	14.3
		GRADE SIX				
		($N = 55$)			($N = 51$)	
Animals	10.4	7.1	1.9	14.9	11.7	4.1
Future	4.7	7.4	11.1	13.6	4.8	9.9
Supernatural	15.1	8.3	5.6	14.1	8.2	4.8
Natural	13.3	9.6	7.3	14.9	11.2	8.1
Personal appearance	2.0	4.1	8.4	2.3	6.4	12.5
Personal relations	8.3	8.2	9.4	7.4	8.2	10.1
School	12.6	13.0	13.7	9.8	11.8	13.8
Home	9.8	10.4	8.7	11.2	10.0	9.0
Safety	12.6	10.2	9.4	13.0	10.3	9.4
Political	9.8	21.4	23.9	8.3	16.7	18.8

TABLE 4

Rank Order Correlations and Significance Levels

	CORRELATION	T*
Third Grade Past-Present	− .09	− .26
Third Grade Past-Future	.02	.05
Third Grade Future-Present	.35	1.04
Sixth Grade Past-Present	− .48	− 1.54
Sixth Grade Past-Future	.35	1.04
Sixth Grade Future-Present	.03	.09
Third Present-Sixth Past	.39	1.21
Third Future-Sixth Present	.62	2.66

* None of the T Values approached statistical significance.

apparent optimism of children is evident since all sample groups see themselves as having held more fears in the past than in the present, and they see themselves as holding fewer fears in the future than at present.

The extreme popularity and intensity of political fears was not so evident in previous research except with older adolescents (Angelino and Shedd, 1953). A comparison of the present results with those of earlier studies for comparably aged children are indicated in Table 5. Those studies which reported fears for this age group are illustrated in like categories to the present study.

Political and natural phenomena, the most common fears in this study, were not the most prominent for children of third grade age in the past. Super-natural phenomena and animals were most prevalent as found by Jersild, Markey and Jersild (1933) and Lapouse and Monk (1953).

TABLE 5

Comparison of Present Fears with Those of Previous Researchers

THIRD GRADE

	PRESENT	JERSILD, JERSILD AND MARKEY 1933	DUNLOP 1951	FERGUSON 1952	LAPOUSE AND MONK 1953
Political	1				
Animals		2		1	
Supernatural phenomena		1	*	2	
Natural phenomena	2				
Safety			1		

SIXTH GRADE

	PRESENT	JERSILD, JERSILD AND MARKEY 1933	PINTNER AND LEVY 1940	DUNLOP 1951	FERGUSON 1952	ANGELINO AND SHEDD 1953	LAPOUSE AND MONK 1953
Political	1						
Animals					2	1	
Supernatural phenomena		1					
Natural phenomena							
Safety		2		1	1		
School	2		1				1

* Where only the most frequently mentioned fear is cited, the second most common was not reported or was not classifiable in comparable categories to the present study.

Previous studies reporting fears for children of sixth grade age found school, safety, animals, and supernatural phenomena to be most prevalent. Only the most recent study, Angelino and Shedd (1953) mentioned political fears. That study found them to be the second most prominent behind fear of animals.

The Vietnam war, TV, and generally improved mass communication may account for the importance of political fears at an earlier age. TV and generally improved mass communication may also be the major reasons for the shift in fears away from animals and supernatural phenomena.

Since the attempt to account for the genesis of fears and the discrepancies in fears held from one tense to the next resulted in a majority of "don't know" responses, it was concluded that asking subjects to account for the origin and changes in fears was an inadequate source of information.

References

ANGELINO, H.; DOLLINS, J. and MECH, V.: Trends in the fears and worries of school children as related to socioeconomic status and age. J. of Genet. Psychol. *89*:263–276 (1956).
——— and SHEDD, C.: Shifts in content of fears and worries relative to chronological age. Proc. Oklahoma Acad. Sci., vol. 34, pp. 180–186 (1953).
DUNLOP, G.: Certain aspects of children's fears. Doctoral dissertation, Columbia University (New York 1951).
FERGUSON, R.: A study of children's fears; Master's thesis, University of North Carolina (Raleigh, NC 1952).
GASTWIRTH, F. and SILVERBLATT, J.: Reactions of junior high children to the war. High Points *25*:56–63 (1943).
HAGMAN, E. R.: A study of the fears of children of preschool age. J. exp. Educ. *1*:110–130 (1932).
HOLMES, F. B.: An experimental investigation of a method of overcoming children's fears. Child Develop. *7*:16–30 (1936).
———: Children's fears as observed in daily life by parents and other adults. Child. Fears *20*:1–106 (1935).
———: Fears recalled from childhood. Child. Fears *20*:107–164 (1935).
JERSILD, A.; GOLMAN, B. and LOFTUS, J.: A comparative study of the worries of children in two school situations. J. of exp. Educ. *9*:323–326 (1941).
——— and HOLMES, F.: Children's fears observed in daily life by parents and other adults. Children's Fears *20*:1–106 (1935).
——— and HOLMES, F.: A study of children's fears. J. of exp. Educ. *2*:109–118 (1933).
JERSILD, A. T. and HOLMES, F. B.: Children's fears. Child Develop. Monogr. *20*:358 (1935).
———; MARKEY, F. V. and JERSILD, C. L.: Children's fears, dreams, wishes, daydreams, likes, dislikes, pleasant, and unpleasant memories. Child Develop. Monogr. *12*:144–159 (1933).
JONES, H. E. and JONES, M. C.: A study of fear. Child. Educ. *5*:136–143 (1928).
KESSEN, W.: The child (Wiley and Sons, New York 1965).
LAPOUSE, R. and MONK, M. A.: Fears and worries in representative samples of children. Amer. J. Orthopsychiat. *24*:803–818 (1953).
MAHEN, V. B.: Some factors related to the expression of fear in a group of average and superior children; Master's thesis (Northhampton, MA, 1939).
PINTNER, R. and LEVY, J.: Worries of school children. J. genet. Psychol. *56*:67–76 (1940).
PRATT, K. C.: A study of the 'fears' of rural children. J. genet. Psychol. *67*:179–194 (1943).

VALENTINE, C.: The innate bases of fear. J. genet. Psychol. *37*:394–420 (1930).
WATSON, J.: Conditioned emotional reactions. J. of exp. Psychol. *3*:1–14 (1920).

SUMMARY

The present investigation attempted to determine the number and types of past, present, and projected future fears and the relationship among these fear tenses using a population of 290 school pupils. The subjects were also interviewed to determine the genesis and intensity of fears. The results indicate that girls have more fears than boys as do lower socioeconomic children in contrast to their upper socioeconomic peers. Children see themselves as having held more fears in the past than in the present, and they see themselves as holding fewer fears in the future than at present. Political were the most intense and most frequently mentioned present and projected fears.

Chapter 4

Louise Boyle

Social Development and Interpersonal Relationships

In his fast-expanding world, the child interacts with a greater and greater variety of teachers and influences. Relationships with peers grow more extensive and complex. While his family continues to be essential for protection, love, and teaching, the school, church, and other institutions play more and more important roles in his life. Through mass media, he contacts thoughts and events originating far from his own neighborhood.

Social and Cultural Settings

A child is born into a community, a nation, a social class, a racial group, and other such divisions of mankind to which his parents belong. Even before he is aware of these classifications of people, he is affected by his memberships in them.

As a preschool child, he is influenced largely through his family, but as a school-child, he makes many direct contacts.

Community

While community is often understood as neighborhood, or town, it can also be taken to mean the whole wide world. It can include all the people of whom one is aware. During the school years, many children do reach out beyond the confines of face-to-face contacts to relate to distant people. The newly acquired skills of reading and writing are keys to expanded relationships. A letter to Grandpa and Grandma may go right across the United States or into another country. Cousins known during vacation visits remain real throughout the year. Through pen pals, many children travel to the other side of the world to build warm friendships. The integrating experience of really helping other children is now a possibility for almost all American children at Halloween. Then they can give up their right to demand treats for themselves in order to collect for the United Nations Children's Fund. Boy Scouts and Girls Scouts spell out ways of learning about the rest of the world and facilitate the making of meaningful contacts and contributions. Schools open up vistas in time and space.

The world is indeed one level of community with which the child interacts. World concern for children is expressed through the United Nations, especially through its health and educational agencies. The federal government is another level of interaction. Here, responsibility for all children is a matter of increasing interest, with more agencies and more money being devoted to child and family welfare. Every state performs some functions for its children, dealing with such matters as health, education, and protection with more or less adequacy. Cities, towns, and sometimes townships have their special areas of responsibility too.

National

Early in the elementary school years, a child begins to have a feeling of belonging to his own country and a realization that it is different from other countries [41, pp. 30–37]. He develops attitudes toward his own country and others and forms concepts about them.

Political Attitudes. Political knowledge is, of course, related to age and cognitive development. Preschool children's political knowledge is very concrete, idiosyncratic, and irrelevant as compared with that of school-age children [74]. For example, when asked what the President does, they made comments such as he has birthdays, he talks funny, he rides horses. Schoolchildren said that he makes laws, passes bills, and makes war.

Nearly 95 percent of 17,000 schoolchildren agreed that "the American flag is the best flag in the world" and "America is the best country in the world." The young child's vague concept of his country develops rapidly during the school years. In the first stage, national symbols, such as the flag and Statue of Liberty, give support and focus for the child's feelings and concepts. The second phase sees the concept of nation acquire more cognitive substance. Ideological components increased—in terms of pride in freedom, the right to vote, and democracy. In the earlier phase, children were more likely to express pride in the President or in our beautiful parks. By fifth grade, children saw the United States and Russia as having different political systems. In the third phase, the United States is seen as a country-among-countries. From third to eighth grade, there was a steady increase in numbers of children believing that the United Nations prevents war—14 percent to 87 percent—and a decrease in those thinking that the United States prevents war—71 percent to 13 percent [41, p. 36].

Schoolchildren reflect the pertinent political issues of the day in the extent of their knowledge of specific topics [74]. When a President has just been elected, they show more knowledge of the presidency. When war is highly salient, children's responses show that they realize it.

Attitudes Toward People of Other Countries. Feelings and knowledge concerning people of other nations become elaborated during the school years. In so doing, a child also adds content to his self concept, as a person belonging to a national group. As such, he sees himself as having certain characteristics and a certain position in the world. Attitudes and ideas about foreign people and fellow countrymen were examined in 3300 children at three age levels in 11 parts of the world [57].

The children were interviewed, first with questions about themselves: "What are you? What else are you?" Then they were asked to name people from other countries who were like them and not like them and a series of questions asked about each group mentioned. Then came questions about seven particular peoples and about people of the child's own country. Finally they were asked which country they would like to belong to if they were not a member of their own. The self concepts revealed by the study showed that most 6-year-olds and 10-year-olds described themselves in terms of sex or age level (I am a boy. I am a girl. I am a child), rather than in terms of nation, religion, or role such as student. Americans, especially, were likely to describe themselves as boys or girls. In contrast, Bantu children were much more likely to describe themselves as members of a race, and Lebanese children gave a high proportion of responses using religion. Most likely the children's answers reflect the ways in which children are defined in their own cultures.

Descriptions of their own national group also reveal something of children's and adults' self concepts. The children varied in how factual and how subjective they were—the Bantu, Brazilian, and Israeli children using the largest number of factual statements, and the Turkish the smallest. Most children tended to stress the good qualities of their own nations, but Lebanese and Israelis made few references to goodness, and Bantu and Japanese hardly ever mentioned good qualities. The following list of descriptive terms shows the words most frequently used by each group for self-description:*

American: good, wealthy, free.
Bantu: mainly factual statements, similarity references.
Brazilian: good, intelligent, cultured, happy, unambitious.
English-Canadian: good, wealthy, free, cultured.
French-Canadian: good, wealthy, peaceful, patriotic.

* Knowing that children's political attitudes and concerns change with relevant political events, we might expect changes in attitudes toward national groups. This study gives information on children's thinking at one particular time. More significant, however, are the developmental trends, shown by age differences, and the differences between cultures which indicate variation in the definitions of people and hence in the self concepts of children.

French: good, intelligent, cultured, happy, bad.
German: good, ambitious, wealthy, intelligent.
Israeli: good, religious, peaceful, intelligent.
Japanese: poor, intelligent, bad.
Lebanese: similarity references and good.
Turkish: good, peaceful, ambitious, religious, patriotic, clean.

Comparisons were made between the children's descriptions of their own group and of the groups they considered desirable. The results suggest something about the children's satisfactions in being what they were. American children tended to choose British, Italian, and Canadian, whom they saw as friendly, good, and similar to themselves. French children, too, indicated satisfaction with their own nation in their choice of nations they considered good, cultured, and intelligent. Japanese, on the other hand, chose other nations whom they held to be good, wealthy, peaceful, cultured, and clean, while they described their own people as poor, intelligent, and bad. This conflict suggests dissatisfaction with their own people and consequently with themselves. Similarly, the Israeli and Brazilian children included wealth as part of their descriptions of desirable nations, but did not describe their own as wealthy.

The questions about how other groups were similar to one's own, and requests to tell about them, brought answers which showed attitudes and knowledge. American children often chose British, Canadians, French, and Italians as similar and Russians, Chinese, Africans, and Japanese as different. Many of the other groups made the same distinction, sometimes placing Americans in the "different" category. Thus a common large category seemed to be Western versus Oriental-African. Expressions of liking and affection toward other nationalities were not dependent on judgments of similarity and difference. National differences in liking of foreign people show American children to be most affectionate while Japanese, Turkish, and Israeli children show least liking of foreign peoples. The 10-year-olds, overall, showed most affection to foreign groups, but among Americans, there was a steady increase in affection from 6 to 14, while Bantu children showed no changes in affection.

Certain age trends could be seen throughout. The youngest children tended to focus on concrete details, such as physical features, clothing, language, and habits, and to give either nonevaluative replies or general responses, such as good and bad. The older children talked more about personality, politics, religion, and wealth and made more evaluative comments. The authors concluded that children come to think about foreign people in increasingly stereotyped ways during the years from 6 to 14. They attributed this trend to several factors, including more complex thinking and language, changes in their self concepts and social relationships, and changes in sources of information. Sources of information were different at different ages. Six-year-olds learned of foreign peoples mainly from their parents, films, and television: 10s and 14s got most of their information from mass media. Probably there is a relation between this increase in stereotyped thinking and the change in sources of information. Perhaps the mass media offer broad generalizations which encourage stereotypes.

Some social class differences were noticed. Middle-class children tended to express more affection toward foreign peoples than did working-class children, with a few exceptions.

Racial and Ethnic

As a member of a minority group, the school-age child directly experiences the particular attitudes and actions which other people customarily direct toward his group and which the members of his group direct toward themselves. If he is a member of a group which is easily distinguished by physical characteristics, then his experiences as a member are likely to be more intense and extensive. For many years black Americans, who are fairly distinctive in appearance, have occupied a subordinate social and economic position. Their experience is probably representative of any group so situated.

Parental teaching and expectations are known to vary with race and ethnic group. Children's attitudes toward other ethnic groups are related to their parents' attitudes. When parents were moderately punitive, children's social distance attitudes were found most closely related to the social distance attitudes which the children perceived in their parents [29]. When the child first contacts the attitudes of outsiders toward himself as a minority group member, the parents interpret those attitudes toward him and tell him how he is to think and behave. Parents are faced with the dilemma of explaining hostility, exclusion, or mere condescension while protecting their child's sense of adequacy. Even before he is touched by the world outside the family, the child of a minority group is affected by his parents' attitudes toward themselves and toward him as members of the minority. If they feel angry, resentful, and hopeless, as many poor black people do, then it is hard or perhaps impossible for their child to develop positive feelings about himself [72]. Instead of helping the child to develop competency and feelings of mastery over the environment, the disillusioned, embittered parent teaches the child what he cannot do and about the futility of trying. Although relatively little research has been done on middle- and upper-class Afro Americans, many or most of them obviously provide stable, supportive homes in which children can develop feelings of worthiness. One warm, secure, upper-class mother told of her interpretation to her 9-year-old daughter [102]. Mother and child had watched a television program about the deprivations, trials, and difficulties of being black. They had listened to a description of the unemployment crisis, ghetto living, police brutalities, and inferior schooling. Mrs. Young asked her daughter if she minded being a Negro. She answered, "No, I don't mind."

Her answer to her daughter was, "I'm glad you don't mind. There are many groups of people all over the world who have not been treated fairly. In Germany, it was the Jews; in some parts of Europe, it was the Catholics; in Vietnam, it was the Buddhists. Some people are mistreated because of color or religion and some because they are poor or blind or crippled. You should be especially proud of being Negro because, in your lifetime, you will enjoy a better America, knowing that we are the ones who helped our country to meet her commitment to all of her peoples."

Children are affected by values and hopes, as well as by tensions and hostilities. Attitudes toward achievement and occupations vary from one ethnic group to another. Mothers in six different ethnic groups were interviewed to explore their attitudes and practices in regard to their sons' achievement [79]. The boys were between 8 and 14 years of age. The ethnic groups included were French Canadian, Italian, Greek, Jewish, black and white Protestant. When the mothers were questioned about how they trained their sons for independence and what they demanded in the way of achievement, results showed that Protestants, Jews, and Greeks placed greater emphasis on independence and achievement than did Italians and French Canadians. Blacks often trained children early in independence, but tended to do little achievement training. Differences between Protestants, Jews, and Greeks were not statistically significant. Roman Catholics did significantly less achievement training than did non-Roman Catholic whites. A college education was intended for their sons by 96 percent of the Jewish, 88 percent of the Protestant, 85 percent of the Greek, 83 percent of the blacks, 64 percent of the Italian, and 56 percent of the French Canadian mothers. Vocational aspirations were explored by asking the mothers which occupations (for their sons) would satisfy them. Black mothers obtained the lowest score here, showing that they would make do with less than all the other mothers, probably a realistic reflection of the vocational opportunities which they knew existed. The order of mothers' aspirations, from high to low, was Jewish, Greek and white Protestant, Italian and French Canadian, black. This research points up the influence of ethnic group membership on a child's training in independence and achievement and the values and standards held for him in regard to education and vocation.

Social Class

Behavior and outlook on life vary considerably with the social position occupied by a family. American middle-class and lower-class behavior has been studied extensively. Less is known about the upper class, since its members are more elusive as subjects for research. Class values and behavior patterns are transmitted from parents to children through their child-rearing practices.

The cognitive behavior patterns transmitted by the lower class have been described elsewhere in this book in sections on educational deprivation. To mention it only briefly here, the lower-class child is relatively reluctant to explore and to ask questions. His mother most likely discourages assertiveness, curiosity, and imagination, encouraging him to wait to be told, to receive, to be acted upon [76].

Values. The basic values of the upper class include respect for families and lineage; a belief that money is important, but only as a means to an end; contempt for pretense, striving, status symbols, and conspicuous consumption [5]. The upper-class child enjoys the care, education, and privileges that money will buy, but he has little realization that money is involved. In contrast, the middle-class child is keenly aware of what money will buy and how striving to achieve will bring money. The upper-class child does not learn social striving, nor does he experience social anxiety, since his family is already at the top, relaxed and poised, exercising quiet good taste. The middle-class child learns that he could rise socially by behaving in certain ways.

Middle-class values are achievement and status improvement, respectability and morality, property, money, organizations, self-improvement through the church, school, and civic organizations [23]. Several obervers [20, 21] see traditional middle-class values of competition and self-improvement being tempered by an increased desire for cooperation, conformity, fitting in and popularity. Parents thus affected want their children to be fairly good at everything but not extreme in anything. Lower-class values include security and getting by rather than getting ahead; traditional, patriarchal education; traditional, clearly differentiated sex roles; pragmatism, anti-intellectualism; such excitement as news, gossip, sports, and gadgets; physical expression and power [76]. Middle-class parents value self-direction and self-control for their children more highly than do working-class parents. The latter stress obedience and conformity to external rules [55]. Since middle-class occupations permit and require more initiative and self-direction, while working-class occupations require obedience to rules and directives, it seems that parents are socializing their children for life as they know it. The very poor, also, socialize their children for what they themselves have experienced.

The very poor or the hard-core poor differ from the working class, although they resemble the working class more than they do the middle class. Some tendencies of very poor parents, as compared with parents of higher status, are the use of inconsistent, harsh, physical punishment, fatalism, magical thinking, present-orientation, authoritarianism, strict definition of sex roles, alienation, distrust of society, constricted experience, limited, concrete verbal communication, judging of behavior in terms of immediate results, passivity, low self-esteem, ignorance of sex and reproduction, distrust of opposite sex, little differentiation between children, inconsistent nurturance of children, abrupt granting of independence, marital conflict, family breakdown, little education [18].

These value systems operate not only through parental influence but also through teachers, other children, club leaders, librarians, clergymen, policemen, doctors, and everybody else who contacts children. Although a middle-class child is likely to have predominantly middle-class values held up to him, he will meet few conflicting values. A lower-class child, in contrast, faces a bewildering mixture of value systems when he enters school [53]. His teacher's values conflict with those of his family and friends; verbal achievement versus physical; self-control versus frank expression; self-improvement versus unself-conscious acceptance; equalitarianism versus patriarchy; femininity versus masculinity; tomorrow versus today. It is hard to live up to the teacher's expectations of manners, quiet, orderliness, respect for property, thinking out instead of acting out.

Interaction of Class and Family in Value Transmission. Not only do values vary from class to class, but the behavior which transmits the values also varies. Child-training practices and philosophy of the middle and lower classes have been contrasted in many studies. Table 4–1 shows some of the important areas of difference indicated in a summary of this research [20].

The transmission of values and behavior patterns is complicated. A study of boys' acquisition of achievement orientation illustrates the complex ways in which only a few variables interact [80]. Drawn from diverse social strata, 122 boys and their mothers were interviewed. Results showed middle-class mothers and sons to be more similar in values than lower-class mothers and sons. Among lower-class pairs, values were more similar if the mother was older rather than younger. Small- and medium-sized families produced more similarity in mother–son values than did large families.

Occupational Orientation. While the concepts of social class and occupational orientation overlap somewhat, certain occupations signifying higher class position than others, there are basic differences in occupation such as agricultural versus industrial or entrepreneurial versus bureaucratic. The latter was taken as the basis of a study of American contrasts in child rearing during the 1950s, when bureaucratic fathers were seen as more affectionate and less authoritarian [60]. Recently a Puerto Rican study has revealed a similar trend [61]. The subjects were boys between 9 and 12 and their parents, divided into three occupational groups:

Table 4–1 Behavior and Philosophy of Parents of Two Classes

	Working Class (Lower Class)	**Middle Class**
Behavioral requirements	Specific	Internalized standards
	Obedience, neatness, cleanliness	Honesty, self-control
	Qualities assuring respectability	Boys, curiosity; Girls, considerateness
Concept of good parent	Elicits specific behavior	Promotes development, affection, satisfaction
Response to misdeed	Focus on immediate consequences of child's actions	Takes into account child's intentions and feelings
Discipline techniques	More physical punishment	More reasoning, isolation, appeals to guilt
Role differentiation	More rigid. More paternalistic	More flexible, more equalitarian
Father as companion to child	Less	More
Permissiveness	Less to infant and young child More to older child	More to infant and young child Less to older child
Achievement demands	Less	More

Source: Data from Clausen & Williams [20].

agricultural, industrial-uneducated, and industrial-educated. Parents were interviewed as to their goals and practices. Boys were interviewed and tested. Agricultural mothers, compared with industrial mothers, stressed authority and traditional values and were more restrictive and punitive. The industrial mothers were more permissive and child-centered, sensitive to individual needs. The agricultural fathers maintained the traditional pattern of authoritarian aloofness, demanding obedience and conformity, while industrial fathers were more warm and involved. They encouraged initiative and occasional aggression, trying to strengthen their sons' achievement motivation.

Thus do parents prepare their children for coping with the world as they (the parents) experience it. Conformity, obedience, and cooperation are valuable in agricultural life; individuality, initiative, achievement, competition, and self-expression are functional in industrial life.

Relationships with Parents

The school-age stage of family life seems to be a difficult one for parents. General satisfaction over the life cycle was studied in 852 couples who were white and predominantly middle class [78]. The low point in satisfaction with family living for husbands and wives came at the time when the oldest child was between 6 and 13. Satisfaction with children was also found to be lowest in the school-age stage [13]. Beyond this rather general assessment of parental and marital satisfaction, little account has been taken of what children do to parents. Hundreds of attempts have been made to find out what parents do to children, or, more accurately, what are the results of certain parent–child interactions upon children.

The Parental Role

In a stable, unchanging society, the parental role, as well as other roles, is well-defined. Everybody understands pretty well what a good child is and what a good parent is supposed to do in order to have the child grow up correctly. While parents are not all equally successful, their differences are attributed to variations in capacities and situations, as well as to inborn differences in children. Parents behave as their parents did toward them and when in doubt, mothers turn to grandmothers to be filled in as to proper procedures. Grandmothers may not wait to be asked.

Most modern societies are changing, just as the United States is changing. The faster the changes, the less automatic are parental behaviors. Grandparents are of little help, since their ways are outmoded. Parents must think about the various aspects of their roles, and yet they are offered minimal assistance from the educational system. Using the perceptions of parents whose children were enrolled in a university nursery school, the parental role was analyzed into four main components: goal values, means-ends beliefs, means-ends capacities, and goal achievement [28].

Goal Values. What do parents want their children to become? How do they want them to act, feel, and believe? Parents choose both positive and negative goal values. Some goals are problematic in being hard to implement. As we have just seen, the broad social settings of community, nation, and class affect values. Child-rearing authorities, such as Dr. Spock and the United States Children's Bureau, also affect parents' goal values while they reflect social trends. An example of changing goals is that of "breaking the will," held to be desirable a century ago. At present, submissiveness is a negative goal, an undesirable condition.

Means-Ends Beliefs. Parents believe that certain methods will be effective in achieving their goals. Child-rearing practices are largely those believed to be means towards the ends that are valued. Five beliefs about child rearing were included in the study of parental role in highly educated fathers and mothers [28]. *Nonintervention*, in which the parent does nothing, is based on the belief that the child will outgrow undesired behavior and will perform desired behavior when he matures enough. *Behavior modification* involves positively reinforcing desirable behavior. That is, rewards and punishments are used. *Motivational modification* is persuasion or reasoning in order to change the child's desire to act or not to act in certain ways. *Situational modification* means changing the setting in the belief that a different environment will elicit desired behavior. *Modeling* is setting an example of desirable behavior in the belief that the child will imitate it.

Of all components of the parental role, means-ends beliefs are probably most responsive to child-rearing authorities. The maturational theory of Gesell (interpreted inaccurately) was very influential a generation ago in justifying nonintervention. Many parents believed that children would automatically grow out of undesirable stages into desirable ones, or that a terrible stage was imminent. Motivational modification receives much support from the popular Haim Ginott. Behavior modification is recommended by the projects of Bereiter and Engleman. Situational modification is upheld by the adherents of Montessori schools. Modeling is often supported in sermons. Bandura has analyzed the dynamics of modeling.

Means-Ends Capacities. How well can the parent carry out the child-rearing methods that he believes will implement his goals? Means-ends capacities may or may not be in harmony with means-ends beliefs. When the parent knows what he ought to do but cannot carry it out, then he feels incompetent and he probably is

Courtesy Cornell University

ineffective. For example, a father believes strongly in modeling, but he does not set the good example he wishes his child would follow. Means-ends capacities can be problem areas for parents, who may find help in parent education groups, counseling, psychotherapy, or possibly in books and articles.

Goal Achievements. How well does the child meet the parents' standards? The match between parental goal value and child behavior is a measure of success in the parent role.

Parental Attributes and Parent–Child Relationships

Parent–child interactions are strongly emotional, as well as cognitive. Children's development and behavior can be related to parents' warmth or coldness, love or hostility, restrictiveness and control versus acceptance of the child's autonomy. Researchers have studied a large number of child and parent variables in various combinations and in relation to different constructs. In the remainder of this section, we shall discuss the relation of parental behavior to children's identification, achievement, and cognitive development.

Identification with Parents

Identification is the process by which one person tries to become like another person in one or more ways. Identification with the parent of the same sex is, according to psychoanalytic theory, an important factor in the personality development of children from 6 to 12. It probably rarely if ever happens that a child identifies only with one parent to the exclusion of the other, nor is it likely to be true that identification goes on only during a limited period of time. Children also react to the expectations which salient people have of them, even though the salient people do not demonstrate the behavior. For instance, Johnny obeys Father because Father expects it, although he himself does not obey Johnny. Each has expectations of the other and each knows what the other expects of him. This sort of learning is the basis of the child's knowing how to play the father's role when he grows up, even though he has until this point played only the role of the child.

How does the child select certain parental behavior on which to model his own, and certain parental expectations with which to cooperate?

An interplay of many factors, at least some of which will not be conscious, will be involved in making such choices. Some research has been done on the influence of sex of child and sex of parent on the child's patterning of identification. For example, boys' reactions to frustration were found to resemble their fathers' reactions to frustration, while girls' were similar to mothers' [87]. The considerably different roles played by mother and father call for different behaviors and learnings in children. One way of systematizing the resulting relationships is by the concepts of *expressive* and *instrumental* roles [70]. Playing an expressive role in a group means being sensitive to the feelings, thoughts, and needs of the other people, aware of their relationships with each other, devoted to promoting their happiness and well-being, understanding them, pleasing them, and enjoying them. Within the family the person having the main responsibility for the care and emotional support of the children is therefore playing the main expressive role. To play an instrumental role is to be responsible for solving the problems facing the group and to assume authority for making decisions. The person playing the instumental role is the final court of appeals, the punisher, the family member with the primary responsibility for the discipline and training of children. The person in the instru- mental role settles disputes between members, deciding on the basis of issues involved; the person in the expressive role smooths them over, comforting and consoling the members concerned.

Parental identification of boys and girls can be explained in terms of the instru- mental and expressive roles played by parents [49]. A mother plays a family role which is largely expressive, while a father plays both roles, instrumental and expressive, with emphasis on the instrumental role. One piece of evidence for the expressive nature of mothers' roles is that they were more accurate than fathers in perceiving anxiety in their daughters [35]. (Parents were equally perceptive in estimating anxiety levels of sons.) Expressivity and instrumentality are by no means mutually exclusive. Men are both; women are both. On the average, however, men behave instrumentally more often than women, and women expressively more often than men. There are wide ranges of individual differences within each sex, so much so that one finds some men who are more expressive than the average woman and some women who are more instrumental than the average man. How- ever, let us see what happens when the mother is the expressive leader in the family and the father the instrumental.

During infancy and the early preschool years, both boys and girls are more closely attached to their mothers than to their fathers. Thus both sexes first relate to a person playing a largely expressive role. In this relationship boys and girls are exposed to love-oriented discipline and take their basic steps toward internalizing conscience. In this relationship, boys and girls learn to be expressive. The next step toward maturity for both boys and girls is to become attached to the father, outgrowing some of the infantile dependence upon the mother. The father repre- sents the reality of the outside world to his children. The father tends to react expressively with his daughters, enjoying, praising, and appreciating them as feminine creatures, while with sons he is more demanding, exerting pressure and discipline, insisting upon successful interaction with the world. The salience of the father in the family has been shown to have a vital effect on the boy's assumption of his sex role [62]. The more the son interacts with a powerful father, a man who does both punishing and rewarding, the more masculine the boy will be. Sons conformed more to fathers' expectations when fathers were warm and took part in child-rearing [42]. Girls' sex role learning has been found to be enhanced by fathers who encouraged their daughters to take part in feminine activities and by mothers who were warm and self-confident and with whom the daughters had satisfying relationships [63]. Girls' feminine responses were associated with their perceptions of their mothers as salient controllers of family resources [7].

While mothers make little difference in the demands they place on boys and girls, they tend to go along with the fathers in expecting more aggression from boys. Thus according to this theory, it is the father more than the mother who teaches boys and girls to play their sex-appropriate roles. The mother supplements his teaching, especially in defining him to the children as a worthy person, and also in choosing the children's clothing, assigning their jobs, and telling them "boys do this and girls do that." It tends to be the father, however, who has the stronger feelings and reactions about sex-inappropriate activities, especially boys engaging in feminine ones. While mothers sometimes consider it all right for boys to knit or play with dolls, fathers are usually disturbed by such activities. The mother, realizing the father's feelings, sees that the boys do behave appropriately.

Stimulation of Cognitive Development and Need for Achievement

Families promote intellectual growth in two main ways: by stimulating the child's desire for achievement, and by offering experiences through which the child can grow mentally. The desire for achievement is highlighted during these years, as being an essential in the development of the sense of industry. Normal personality development centers around becoming competent in the basic skills of the culture. Since the academic skills are a vital part of those basic skills, the encouragement of intellectual development is also the encouragement of personality development.

When a parent, especially a father, has a strong desire for intellectual competence for himself, he is likely to stimulate such achievement in his children [52]. The higher the value the father placed on intellectual achievement, the more likely he was to share intellectual activities with his children, to encourage children to engage in such pursuits, and to show great interest in the children's achievements. The mothers behaved similarly, except that they were more likely to show such reactions with daughters than with sons.

At age 10, IQs of both boys and girls were significantly correlated with IQ and education of father and of mother and with socioeconomic status and the educational stimulation and emotional support offered by the home [98]. As compared with IQs of sons, the IQs of daughters had higher correlations with parental ability, educational stimulation, and emotional support.

Need for Achievement. The aspirations which hold for their children apparently affect the ways in which parents interact with children, often producing the desired effects. Boys with high-achievement needs tend to have mothers who expected them to be self-reliant at an early age, who gave them freedom to learn, and who rewarded their independent efforts [100]. When observed working together at home, boys with high-achievement aspirations were found to have parents who held high standards for them and who gave them autonomy in working out problems. The mothers of these boys treated them warmly, freely giving both approval and criticism. The fathers showed considerable interest in and involvement with their sons [81]. Subsequent studies have confirmed and extended these findings, showing the negative effects of parental coldness, rejection, and restrictiveness and the positive effects of warmth, involvement, encouragement, and desire to help the child achieve maturity [73].

Locus of Control. Not only achievement aspiration, but also the child's belief in his own ability to control what happens, is related to parental behavior. Children between 6 and 13 were more likely to believe in internal control when parents were consistent, warm, supporting, praising, and protective, rather than dominating, rejecting, and critical [24, 51]. There was some suggestion that fathers' attitudes were more influential than mothers' in regard to children's belief in locus of control.

The child's self concept has an influence on his locus of control. Lower-class black children in grades 4 through 7 were studied in terms of self esteem and locus of control, under conditions of success and failure [30]. Failure was attributed to external causes more than success was, suggesting an adaptive mechanism by which the stigmatized child cushions his self concept. Children with higher self esteem were more likely than others to believe themselves responsible for failure and success.

General Intelligence. Rising IQs were found to be associated with certain personality characteristics in children and with certain kinds of parental behavior which most likely had been instrumental in producing the personality characteristics [88]. As might be expected from other studies already mentioned, the children whose IQs rose were, on the whole, independent children who ventured forth curiously, explored freely, competed, and showed high need for achievement. The mothers of these children took considerable interest in their children's achievements and encouraged them to master the environment [50].

Specific Measures. Several studies deal with particular parental practices and attitudes, relating them to specific aspects of children's intellectual functioning, such as distractibility, flexible thinking, curiosity, and attitudes toward mathematics. Extremes of distractible and nondistractible boys and girls were selected on the basis of a distractibility test [4]. The children were given tasks (puzzle, ring toss, anagrams, and block patterns) to do while their parents, who had been given additional information about solutions, were free to help the children as much or as little as they wished. Rather surprisingly, there was more interaction between nondistractible children and their parents than in the other group, largely due to the nondistractible children initiating it. The quality of interaction differed considerably in the two groups, however. Parents of nondistractible children gave less specific suggestions, more positive encouragement, more evaluative comments, and paid more attention to the child's contributions. Thus while these parents were highly involved, they were also teaching their children to be autonomous.

Flexible thinking in fifth grade black boys from a lower-class community was studied in relation to their fathers' and mothers' behavior [14]. The boys' flexible thinking was evaluated by means of a test designed for that purpose. Parents were observed in teaching specific tasks to their sons and were asked questions selected from the Parental Attitude Research Instrument. Results from the parents' teaching of sons showed a relationship between boys' flexible thinking and parents' manipulating the task materials a moderate amount. Thus the child was most likely to think flexibly if his parents were people who showed him something about a matches-and-squares problem and about a sorting problem, but not too much. Boys' flexible thinking was related negatively to mothers' commanding and positively to fathers' feelings of powerfulness, moderate participation with children and flexible, sympathetic standards. Studies on curiosity [59] also indicate that children are likely to develop effective methods of discovery and learning when parents encourage autonomy while maintaining mutual respect and caring.

Family Interaction and Cognitive Development. Extended, rational conversation among family members tends to happen more often at the dinner table than anywhere else [8]. This learning situation is, however, a middle-class custom. In homes of the hard-core poor, there may be no time when the family eats together. When parents and children are together, they usually talk about the most immediate concerns, not about the past and future. Discussions of concepts, causal relationships and logical consequences are almost entirely lacking [93]. Dinnertime conversation is an activity in which either educational enrichment or deprivation may occur.

Discipline

An important parental function is discipline, which, to most people, includes the regulation of children's behavior, the teaching of self control and the imparting of moral standards. Teachers are also expected to discipline children, the extent of their efforts varying with the culture. Adults often consider it virtuous to be strict disciplinarians, while simultaneously holding the goal of enjoying children and being friends with them [64].

The particular methods of discipline selected by an adult will depend upon his means-ends beliefs and his application of them, upon his means-ends capacities. Probably most people believe in and employ punishment, rewards, reasoning, and modeling. Punishment may be corporal, verbal, deprivation of objects or privileges, or withdrawal of approval and affection. Rewards, too, can be physical, verbal, object-oriented or emotional. Reasoning and explaining help the child to develop the cognitive structure basic to moral judgment. Setting a "good example" offers behavior patterns that the child imitates if he chooses to model his behavior on the adult's.

Research on Methods of Discipline. Analyses have been made of the dimensions of punishment and the interactions of punishment with other means of discipline [17, 26, 68, 69]. A typical experiment was one in which seven-year-old boys were tested in conditions of early and late punishment (the sounding of a buzzer when a forbidden toy was touched), intensity of punishment (loudness of buzzer), high and low cognitive structure (much or little explanation of why certain toys should not be touched), and high and low nurturance (much or little attention and approval from the examiner). As expected from previous experiments, response inhibition (not touching forbidden toys) was strengthened by high cognitive structure and high intensity, and somewhat increased by early punishment and nurturance. When cognitive structure was low, high intensity punishment was more effective than low, but when cognitive structure was high, intensity of punishment made no difference. Similarly, when cognitive structure was low, high nurturance strengthened response inhibition but when cognitive structure was high, nurturance made no difference. With low-intensity punishment, early timing was more effective, but when intensity was high, there was no difference between early and late timing. This experiment shows the very complex nature of discipline. While it is clear that cognitive and emotional factors interact, the experiment cannot be taken as a blueprint for parents, since it represents a highly simplified version of what happens in a home.

Studies on the more global interactions of parents and children, done by tests, interviews or observations, also give insights that can be helpful to parents but that will not tell them exactly what to do. The harmful effects of high punishment levels were suggested by the lower IQ's of children whose parents scored high in rejection and punitiveness [46]. The value of a special kind of cognitive structure is suggested by the fact that children tend to show extra concern for human well-being when parents direct their attention to the results of their actions upon the feelings and welfare of others [43]. Children go through stages of moral develop-ment as they structure and restructure their schemas underlying moral judgment [54]. As with all kinds of development, moral structures are built from many experiences, of which parent–child interactions are very influential.

Relationships with Peers

Peers are equals, or in the usual meaning, friends of about the same age. The peer group is an important socializing agent in a child's life. The type of influence exerted by the peer group varies from one culture to another. In the United States and England, the peer group is often sharply differentiated from the world of adults. Children have secrets, codes, and a common culture [67], with which they promote feelings of solidarity in the group and separation from adults. Together they explore ideas, as well as the physical world. Parents often feel that children are entitled to privacy with their friends. Adults expect a certain amount of child-hood misbehavior or resistance to adult standards. Much of our research on parent and peer influences is built on the assumption that there will be conflicts between the two. The situation is different in the Soviet Union, where the peer group is systematically manipulated to promote conformity to adult-given standards [10]. Whatever the functions of the peer group, they are related to parent–child rela-tionships, to the school system, and to the culture as a whole.

Learning of Values, Behavior, and Attitudes

Children expose one another to a variety of sets of values which stem from memberships such as those of family, class, and ethnic origin. The values of a peer group are especially compelling, since a youngster has to accept them in order to be accepted as a member. If the peer values are not too different from those of his family and teachers, a mild conflict between them only serves to differentiate him from adults and to give him a feeling of belonging to the gang. He will suffer if values differ greatly, as when his peers idealize the member who pilfers successfully, while his family requires honesty. Peers reinforce many values which adults approve sincerely but less enthusiastically. Physical bravery in boys is an example. Most parents make some effort to discourage crying and fussing over hurts and dangers, but the group may insist upon bravery, with expulsion the penalty for being a "sissy."

The peer group teaches its members how to act and how to think. Skills are learned through imitation and practice, coordinations, games, the arts, humor, language. Some of the behavior is childhood ritual, which is passed from one generation of schoolchildren to the next and almost forgotten by adults [67]. It includes the chants used with jumping rope and bouncing balls:

> One, two, three O'Leary
> I spy Miss McGary
> Sitting on a huckleberry
> Reading a dictionary.

> Down in the valley where the green grass grows
> There sat Helen as sweet as a rose
> She sang and she sang and she sang so sweet
> Along came her fellow and kissed her on the cheek.

It includes wishing on white horses and "stamping" the first robins of spring (not literally, just touching one thumb to the tongue and pushing it into the other—open—palm).

The group may require certain modes of speech, a secret language such as Pig Latin or simply modified English, tending toward toughness and crudity through dropping G's and mixing up rules about plurals and tenses. Most boys and girls learn vulgar words for sex and elimination processes. It is very exciting and status-defining to use the four-letter words and some swear words, too.

Matters of taste and fashion come strongly under peer influence. It becomes essential to wear woolen knee socks, white ankle socks, or nylon stockings according to what the other girls are wearing, regardless of the weather or of what Mother thinks. One winter everybody slides down the hill on sleds, but the following winter the only vehicle worth sliding on is a tray. The next year, trays are out, but one must buy a gadget which manufacturers have thoughtfully designed to be almost like trays. The group even has strong opinions as to the best kind of candy and gum, opinions which change rapidly.

Conformity. The extent and nature of children's conformity to group pressure has been investigated in classroom situations. In one study of lower- and middle-class boys and girls ages 7, 10, and 13, the perceptually-ambiguous task required judging how long a light remained on and how far it moved [36]. The control subjects made judgments privately, while the experimental subjects answered in groups of three, where each could hear the answer of the other two children. Results showed conformity increasing with age, with a greater increase between 7 and 10 than between 10 and 13 years. Girls conformed more than boys. Age changes in boys were greater than those in girls, the 7-year-old boys conforming considerably less than girls their age, but 13-year-old boys conforming on about the same level as girls. A similar study employing unambiguous tasks as well as ambiguous ones showed conformity *decreasing* with age when tasks were unambiguous [45]. Thus it seems that children increase with age in their desire to be correct as well as in their desire to fit in with peers. When the answer is clearly indicated, they tend to choose right, increasing in this tendency with age. When it is difficult to discern, they are influenced by peers, also increasing in this tendency as they grow older. When children were faced with choices in social situations, conformity to parents, as opposed to peers, decreased significantly between Grades 3 and 7 [96].

Table 4–2 Experiences with Parents and Peers and Responses to Parent and Peer Pressures in Preadolescence

	1 Autonomous	2 Adult- Oriented	3 Peer- Oriented	4 Adult- & Peer- Oriented
Control, punishment	moderate	low	high or low	low
Nurturance	high	high	low	high
Contact with mother	high	high	low	
Contact with peers	high	low	high	high
Peer orientation of parents			high	

Sources: E. C. Devereux [27]; also E. P. Hollander & J. E. Marcia, Parental determinants of peer-orientation and self-orientation among preadolescents. *Devel. Psychol.*, 1970, **2**, 292–302.

The Cornell study of conformity to parent and peer pressures described on pages 153–154, showed some age-level effects for moral judgment [27]. From fifth through eighth grade, children conformed less to adult pressure and more to peer pressure. Conformity to peer pressure was also related to the extent of the child's involvement in and experience with the peer group. Children, especially boys, responded more to peer pressures when they belonged to gangs in which misconduct was frequent. This study confirmed the sex difference found in other studies. Girls responded more than boys to adult pressures. The nature of the dilemmas presented bore some relation to whether children responded more to parents or peers. When issues were seen as serious, children were more likely to conform to adults. Other influences on the children included the nature of the classroom group in which they were, the type of teacher in charge of the class and, as previously described, the parents. There was evidence that autonomous children were likely to have higher IQs than the others.

From cross-culture studies, the Cornell researchers have concluded that peer interaction contributes importantly to the development of moral autonomy [27]. Autonomy seems to develop out of peer experience in the child whose home gives him moderate to high support (nurturance) and moderate levels of discipline and control. Under these circumstances, the child is likely to have the ego strength necessary for making use of adult–peer cross-pressures. Without nurturant, moderately controlling parents, peer-interaction makes for peer-conformity. Without peer-interaction, the nurturant, controlling parents make for parent-conformity. Different combinations of parent-interaction and peer-interaction and of parent–peer cross-pressures were seen in various countries where the study was carried on. Soviet children were most adult-conforming, English most peer-conforming. Americans were second in adult-conformity, Germans third. It was noted that while Soviet children have a great deal of peer-interaction, there is little or no discrepancy between adult and peer values, especially in boarding schools. Hence peer pressures and adult pressures tend to work in the same direction.

Self Concept. Every child's self concept of himself is built partly through seeing himself as others see him. As a person who belongs to a peer group, liked and accepted by them, he feels himself to be a worthy person. (And, if he is not accepted, he feels unworthy.) If his friends laugh at his jokes and call him amusing, he sees himself as a wit. If they call her "Fatso," she believes that she is *too* fat.

Measuring himself against the standards of peers is another way in which a person's self concept is built. Age-level segregation plus great emphasis on competition make American childhood a very competitive time. It is especially important for a boy to be able to measure up in motor skills. Unless others regard him as adequate in physical coordination, his self concept is likely to suffer. When needed, compensatory physical education can make an important contribution to a boy's self concept [22, p. 135].

Even though peers cooperate in their play, they owe each other nothing in the sense that family members have obligations to each other. Group loyalty is comparatively ephemeral, depending on continuing to meet competitive standards of behavior. The feeling which a youngster gets from successful competition with his age-mates is *adequacy*. Since these years are most critical for development of a sense of adequacy, this aspect of peer influence is a vital one.

Self concept is related to social class, race, and sex. While peer reactions are doubtless influenced by the child's class-related and race-related behavior and appearance, his self concept is shaped by people of all ages, including peers. Development of self concept from first to fifth grade was studied in black and white children whose mothers were on welfare [16]. Not surprisingly, the self concepts of these children from the lowest economic level decreased between first and fifth grades. Girls were more negative than boys in self concept. Black girls were much lower than black boys, and at the first grade level were much lower than white girls. This study is in agreement with other research which indicates that as the child accumulates experience and matures cognitively, he understands more fully what it means to be a member of a racial or ethnic minority [72].

Position in the Group, Acceptance and Rejection

Children vary in how much they are liked by other children and in how many other children like them. Sociometry is a way of finding out where each child in a group stands in relation to the other children in it: who likes him, who does not like him, and who is indifferent or mild in attitudes toward him. When these data are collected for each child, a picture of relationships within the group can be drawn. By means of sociometry, group relations can be measured and described [66]. Each child is asked to name one or more group members with whom he would like to engage in one or more activities (to sit beside, to go to the movies with, to work with, and so on). The choices are then represented by symbols on a diagram, using arrows to indicate the direction of each choice. Figure 4–1 is a sociogram which shows the friendships of a group of first grade children. Although the majority of choices are between children of the same sex, there are also cross-sex choices. Note the pentagon to the right of the centers which includes a boy chosen by every one of a group of four girls. See the triangle of boys to the lower left of center. One of the boys also chose a girl and one another boy.

The characteristics of children who are accepted or rejected have been assessed by many investigators, using a variety of measuring devices. Friendliness and sociability are, not surprisingly, associated with acceptance, whereas rejection or nonacceptance are associated with hostility, withdrawal, and similar negative social attitudes. Greater intelligence and creativity, if they are not too far above the level of the group, are typical of popular children. Boys are accepted by other boys if they have athletic ability, muscular strength, and are above average size. Socio-

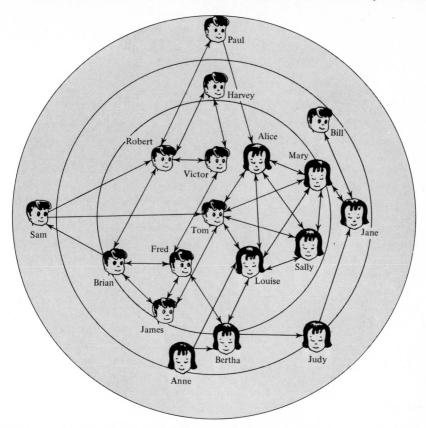

Figure 4–1. A sociogram showing friendship choices in a first grade.

SOURCE: Reprinted by permission from Mary L. Northway, *A Primer of Sociometry*, 2nd edition. Copyright © 1967, University of Toronto Press.

economic class also makes a difference, since children tend to choose friends of their own class or a higher one [15]. Older preadolescents fluctuate less than younger ones over a two-week period in their choices of friends [44]. This age trend continues on into adolescence, and is evident from the experience of adults, most of whom recognize that their friendships change slowly over a period of years.

Personal Characteristics As Seen by Other Children. An approach to the topic of peer acceptance started with the question "How do children perceive one another?" [101]. The subjects were 267 white and black children, 8 to 13, living in a summer camp. Strangers to each other at the beginning, they lived in groups of eight for two weeks. Each child was asked to choose a child whom he knew most about and to tell all about him. Adults made systematic behavior observations of the camp life. In telling about each other, children showed two strong tendencies: they made broad positive or negative judgments; the judgments were mainly in terms of actions that had direct interpersonal consequences. Individuals showed consistency in the ways in which they described others, whether they described the same child twice or a different child. Within this consistency, there were changes over the two-week period in increasing emphasis on interaction between persons and in giving more organized descriptions. There were some sex differences. Girls emphasized

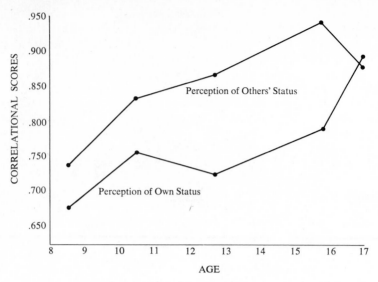

Figure 4–2. Age changes in the ability to judge one's own sociometric status and to judge the status of another person.

SOURCE: Reprinted by permission from D. P. Ausubel, H. M. Schiff, and E. B. Gasser, "A Preliminary Study of Developmental Trends in Socioempathy: Accuracy of Perception of Own and Others' Sociometric Status," *Child Development*, **23**, Figure 1. Copyright © 1952, The Society for Research in Child Development, Inc.

nurturing behavior, boys nonconforming and withdrawn behavior. Older children evidenced a slight tendency to give more complex reports. When children were divided into categories according to the adults' observations, these results were found: active and friendly children gave more complex descriptions of peers than did withdrawn or hostile children; active children were more explicit than withdrawn; friendly children made more inferential statements than hostile children; there was a consistent but nonsignificant tendency for friendly children to describe others in a more organized fashion than hostile children. These results suggest that those who take an active part in social relationships perceive other people more sharply than do these who are less active.

Socioempathic ability, the ability to perceive one's own status in a group and the statuses of others, tends to increase with age [1]. Children from Grade 3 through Grade 12 were asked to rate all of their classmates as to acceptability as friends, and to predict how each of the classmates would rate them and be rated by the group. True sociometric status was calculated for each child from the first rating. Accuracy of perception of sociometric status was calculated by correlating the mean predicted statuses with the sociometric statuses. Figure 4–2 shows the correlational scores for accuracy of perception (socioempathic ability) at each age between 8 and 17.

Personal Characteristics As Reflected by Tests. The behavior characteristics valued by low- and high-socioeconomic groups of 12-year-olds were studied by using a Guess-Who test [71]. Results showed definite socioeconomic and sex differences in the prestige value of various clusters of behavior patterns. Fighting ability was important to all boys in determining leadership position, but more important to low-socioeconomic boys. Restlessness was less acceptable to High Boys than to Low. An eminent fighter among Low Boys was likely to be also a ladies' man, but among High Boys, the friendly, conforming, "little gentleman" had success with the girls. Among High Boys, the classroom intellectual was not a leader but was not rejected. Such a person among Low Boys would be considered too effeminate and yielding to deserve any recognition. Low Girls were more sharply differentiated as to aggressiveness than were High Girls. Among Low Girls, the fighting tomboy was the one who went out with boys, while among High Girls, the "little lady" was more interested in and successful with boys. The tomboy was unpopular with High Girls, but had considerable prestige with Low Girls. High Boys and Girls value some conformity to adult standards in the classroom and at parties, while low groups did not.

Personalities of very popular, average, and unpopular children were studied with the Rorschach test among other tests [65]. The least popular children showed less emotional control, appeared to be more self-centered, moody, and impulsive, and were often unable to react to a situation even though they desired to participate. The very popular children showed great sensitivity to the social situation, conventional interpretations of social situations, little originality, strong need for affection, and a conscious striving for approval. A more recent study indicates that girls with high need for approval are likely to be popular, while boys with high need for approval are likely to be unpopular [95]. This finding fits with sex role typing which prescribes social responsiveness and pliability for feminine behavior.

Although popular children differed from one another in many ways, all of them had two characteristics in common: they put forth a great deal of energy, and they used their energy for purposes approved by the group [65]. The popular child was likely to be a conformist. He was likely to be conventional rather than creative. He tended to be sympathetic to the needs and wants of others. Some unpopular children were simply unliked, and others actively disliked. They had in common a lack of energy directed to group purposes, but the disliked child used his abounding energy in ways which conflicted with the interests of other children.

Children at both extremes of popularity showed more emotional disturbance than did the average children. Great striving for popularity may be due to feeling a lack of love. The very popular child may pay a severe price in energy expenditure and anxiety. Some children were, of course, both popular and well-adjusted.

Although a person's name is not a personality attribute, still it is a part of him. Research shows that it is an *influential* part of an elementary school child [58]. Popularity was correlated with the group's liking for the first name. Social acceptance within the group was also correlated with ratings for first names derived from outside groups, that is, from children who did not know the bearers of the names involved.

Leadership. Comparisons on a large number of physical, sociological, intellectual, and social variables were made between 6- to 11-year-old children [37]. One group of 278 subjects had been frequently chosen as leaders. The contrast group of 416 had rarely or never been chosen as leaders. Leaders, as a group, were significantly healthier, more active, more aggressive, more intelligent, higher achievers, more gifted, more likely to be Caucasian, more socially adept, and better adjusted. The individual leader excelled in at least one of the areas of physical, mental, and social development, but not necessarily in all three.

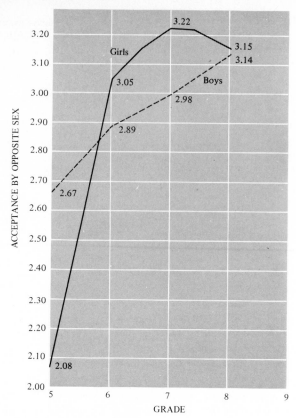

Figure 4–3. Acceptance by the opposite sex.
SOURCE: Data from Reese [75].

Boy–Girl Relationships

Acceptance of members of the opposite sex by boys and girls in Grades 5 through 8 was measured by means of a sociometric test [75]. Since ratings at each level were below neutral, and thus unfavorable, both sexes tended to reject the opposite sex. In the beginning of the year in fifth grade, girls accepted boys significantly more than boys accepted them. However, by the end of the fifth academic year and during the subsequent years through eighth grade, boys accepted girls more than the reverse. Figure 4–3 shows the scores for acceptance of the opposite sex by boys and girls at each level. A child's level of acceptance by the opposite sex was positively related to his score of acceptance by his own sex.

As Figure 4–3 suggests, both boys and girls make progress throughout the grades in becoming more acceptable to the opposite sex. This progress has been analyzed into a series of steps in heterosexual development, steps which occur in a developmental sequence [9]. That is, step A regularly occurs before step B and step C. The steps in the sequence established were wanting to marry some day; having a girl friend or boy friend now; having ever been in love; preferring the opposite sex as a companion for going to the movies; having had a date. This sequence held for suburban boys and girls, urban white boys and girls, urban

Item

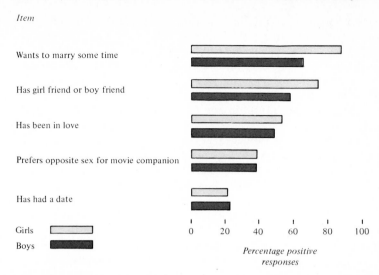

Wants to marry some time

Has girl friend or boy friend

Has been in love

Prefers opposite sex for movie companion

Has had a date

Girls

Boys

Percentage positive responses

0   20   40   60   80   100

Figure 4-4. Heterosexual development scale, showing percentage of positive responses to each item by children 10–12 years old.

SOURCE: Data from Broderick and Rowe [9].

black girls, and rural white boys. Figure 4–4 shows the percentage of positive answers on each item from boys and girls from a Kansas sample, in which rural and urban were represented. The subjects were mostly white, Protestant, and lower class. The first item represents a global concept, that marriage some day would be desirable. Next the child narrows his sights to the idea of having a girl friend or boy friend. Often this relationship is nonreciprocal and exists largely in the mind of one child. The next step, being in love, often refers to the one chosen as boy friend or girl friend, who may still be unaware of his status as love object. Then comes the specific step of appreciating the opposite sex as a companion for going to the movies. Only after this is the child likely to actually go on a date. Thus does the child differentiate dating behavior out of the general desirability of marriage, and a specific girl (or boy) of the opposite sex. In a sample of English 12-year-olds, 90 percent of girls and 57 percent of boys expressed a positive attitude toward marriage [9], figures quite similar to the American ones of 85 percent and 62 percent.

Sex Role Differentiation

Boys make progress toward thinking, feeling, and acting like men, girls like women. There are great variations in how these processes occur, however, and variations in the end results. In the section on parent–child relations, the influence of each of the parents on sex-role learning was discussed. Children also teach each other sex-appropriate attitudes and behavior. Sex role preferences have been found to be well established by 5 years of age [97]. A longitudinal study indicated that sex role preferences established between 6 and 10 years of age tend to be fairly stable into adulthood [50].

Children's evaluations of sex roles were studied in Grades 1, 2, and 3, in terms of good–bad, happy–sad, strong–weak and big–little [40]. First grade boys were more favorable toward being a boy and girls toward being a girl. The same attitudes were more pronounced in third grade, with boys lowering their evaluations of the opposite sex role more than girls. Boys regarded femininity as both bad and weak, while girls regarded masculinity as bad but not weak.

American girls are allowed greater latitude in sex-appropriate behavior than are boys. Girls incur little or no censure for being tomboys, whereas a boy is severely frowned upon for being effeminate. These statements are borne out by test findings which showed that second, third, and fourth grade girls made many choices of masculine activities, whereas boys showed a strong preference for masculine activities [11]. Girls show a wider range of play preferences than boys, girls taking in many masculine activities along with feminine ones, boys sticking largely to masculine games [82]. Certain playthings are established as appropriate for boys at an earlier age than are corresponding appropriate toys designated for girls [38]. Not only are boys' play roles defined earlier [25], but they are defined more strictly [38]. It seems likely that boys learn their roles as much by avoiding feminine behavior as by acquiring masculine patterns ("Don't be a sissy!"), even when offered a choice between old, dilapidated neutral toys and new, attractive "female" playthings [39]. The same is true of the books which girls and boys choose to read. Boys tend to read boys' books only, while girls read girls' books and boys' books. It is likely that over the years the cultural definition of the girl role has expanded, whereas that of the boy's role has not. Table 4–3 shows the activities which were attributed to girls, boys, and both sexes by children 8 to 11 years old [38]. The percentage of attribution by boys and by girls is shown with each activity listed. For instance, all boys and all girls agree that playing with a doll carriage is a female activity, while 80 percent of girls and 90 percent of boys say that climbing trees and carrying wood into the house are male activities. Concepts of the feminine role, as revealed by this study, seemed to parallel traditional adult female activities to a greater extent than did childhood concepts of the male role parallel adult male activities.

By sixth grade, sex roles begin to have a different look [47]. Girls are not so free after all. At least for the culture of one sixth grade class, there was a real difference in the way sex roles were defined, as determined by using personality and sociometric tests. Boys who were active initiators and organizers enjoyed wide acceptance by classmates, while girls with these qualities were more rejected by classmates and felt more anxious than the other girls. In generalizing about the American middle-class culture this study concludes, "Boys are expected to be somewhat aggressive, direct and analytic, while girls are taught more submissive, conforming, 'ladylike' type of behavior. The girl who identifies with this role gains acceptance and is subjectively aware of fewer discomforts. . . ." In other words, the sixth grade boys were rewarded for playing instrumental roles, and the girls were rewarded for playing expressive roles. The instrumental role requirement for boys was laid down earlier than the requirement for girls.

A study of creativity demonstrated the restriction of sex role by pressures in the classroom [94]. Boys and girls gave ideas and solutions to problems which contributed to the success of the groups for which they were working. Then they were asked to rate themselves and the others on value of contribution. The whole group ranked the boys' contributions ahead of the girls. The objective reality was that boys and girls were equal in contributions. Thus both boys and girls considered that what boys had done was better than what girls had done when both sexes actually had done the same.

Table 4–3 Percentages of Boys and Girls Seeing Various Activities as Being Either Masculine or Feminine

| | | Percentage of Attribution | |
		Female Sample	Male Sample
Item	Description of Activity		
	A. Implemented mostly by girls		
53	plays with doll carriage	100.0*	100.0*
40	plays with toy sewing machine	98.9*	97.5*
43	plays with toy dishes	96.7*	100.0*
46	plays with toy carpet sweeper	95.6*	92.5*
47	plays with toy pocketbook	94.4*	97.5*
49	plays with toy electric mixer	91.0*	87.5*
29	helps mother hang clothes	90.0*	82.5*
37	plays with little girl	88.8*	90.0*
14	cares for baby when parents away	87.8*	85.0*
35	dusts table	86.7*	72.5†
56	plays with jump rope	81.1*	90.0*
33	dries dishes	78.9*	68.4‡
23	washes dishes	77.8*	80.0*
25	clears table	73.3*	72.5†
16	takes dancing lessons	65.6†	70.0‡
51	plays with jacks	64.4†	72.5†
	B. Implemented mostly by boys		
38	plays with toy air-rifle	94.4*	95.0*
32	hitches ride on back of truck	91.1*	82.5*
52	plays with toy trucks	91.1*	90.0*
55	plays with fort and soldiers	90.0*	97.4*
21	helps man fix ceiling	86.5*	92.5*
45	plays with ball and bat	81.1*	92.3*
13	carries wood into house	80.0*	90.0*
27	climbs trees	80.0*	90.0*
54	plays with toy tool bench	80.0*	92.5*
24	plays with little boy	79.5*	77.5*
50	plays with drums	78.9*	77.5*
57	plays with jack-knife	78.7*	95.0*
39	plays with erector set	76.7*	82.5*
15	goes with man to ballgame	76.4*	70.0‡
10	plays in messy empty lot	75.6*	72.5†
8	plays in street	74.7*	77.5*
42	plays with electric train	73.3*	85.0*
17	shovels snow off walk	66.7†	75.0†
44	plays with marbles	66.7†	72.5†
2	plays on roofs	63.3‡	70.0‡
	C. Implemented by both sexes		
5	plays at beach	84.4*	94.5*
12	plays in country fields	72.2*	72.5†
1	plays on playground	69.2*	75.0†
48	owns and takes care of puppy	65.2†	56.4‡
7	plays in park	63.7†	72.5‡

* Probability is beyond the .001 level.
† Probability lies between the .01 and the .001 levels.
‡ Probability lies between the .05 and the .01 levels.

Source: Reprinted by permission from R. E. Hartley and F. P. Hardesty, "Children's Perceptions of Sex Roles in Childhood," *Journal of Genetic Psychology*, **105**, Table 2, p. 48. Copyright © 1964, The Journal Press.

A child also restricts his own achievement in accordance with sex role expectations. Sixth grade boys and girls were given tasks which were actually neutral but were presented as appropriate to boys, girls, or both [92]. Boys did their best on the "masculine" tests, worst on the "feminine," and in between on the "tests for both." Girls did equally well on the "feminine" and "tests for both" but worse on the "masculine." Thus expectations of self and others, as well as achievement behavior are affected by the child's evaluation of sex role and of behavior appropriate to it.

Development of Understanding and Caring

As the young human being grows to maturity in his relationships with other human beings, he sees more and more clearly that other people have thoughts, feelings, and perceptions which relate them to him and to others. As an infant, he treated his peers more as objects than as persons, but as a schoolchild, he realizes that peers are persons much like himself and that even older and younger individuals share many human characteristics with him. As he comes to understand what life is like from the standpoint of another person, he also comes to care about it and he tries to make good things happen to other people. Altruism, or prosocial behavior, is linked thus with the development of role-taking ability and understanding. The development of prosocial behavior has other antecedents, some of which have been identified in recent research.

Understanding, Role Taking, and Communication

The child's self concept is basic to his conceptions of other people's roles and their relation to his. As he achieves conceptual thought, he can keep his own point of view in mind while trying on the role of another. This is *empathy:* he can think himself into another person, imagine how it is to be that person and still remember that he is himself, with his own thoughts, feelings, and perceptions. Deeper friendships can thus grow. Empathy increases throughout the school years as shown by studies of children's understanding, role taking, and communication.

Children of 6, 9, and 12 years were shown films offering a rich representation of person-to-person interaction [32]. Analyses of spontaneous comments and answers to questions showed age-related trends. Children apparently infer thoughts and/or intentions before feelings and feelings before interpersonal perceptions. Three major categories were, in order: reporting-describing, explaining, and interpreting. Younger children were likely to report objective situation-action and dialogues before they tried to explain behavior. The 6-year-olds answered questions literally and often gave details that seemed irrelevant to adults. The earliest explanations were in terms of situation, later ones in psychological terms, and still later, in terms of interpersonal perceptions. Six-year-olds more often described characters as reacting with feelings, while older ones described them more as thinking, having intentions, and communicating, as well as feeling. Although the greatest increase in understanding personal interaction took place between 6 and 9, there were also increases between 9 and 12. Another study of empathy [86] showed that empathy tended to increase with age, but that there were wide individual differences within each age level. Although there were no sex differences in general, the spurts in growth of empathy came at different times for boys and girls. Empathy

Table 4–4 Related and Unrelated Contribution to Class Discussions in Elementary Grades

Contribution	Grade 2 (62 Pupils)	Grade 4 (54 Pupils)	Grade 6 (45 Pupils)
New Topic, not obviously related to what earlier speaker had said	87%	33%	23%
New Topic, but apparently suggested by something said by a previous contributor	8	24	33
Logical Continuation of a topic previously introduced	4	43	44

SOURCE: Table adapted by A. T. Jersild, *Child Psychology*, Sixth edition (Englewood Cliffs, N.J.: Prentice-Hall, 1968), p. 455, from H. V. Baker, *Children's Contributions in Elementary School General Discussion*. Child Development Monographs No. 29, pp. 32–33. Copyright Teachers College, Columbia University, 1942. Reprinted by permission.

related to general intelligence and to cognitive awareness of the social and emotional environment. Empathy varied inversely with the size of the child's family and depended somewhat on his ordinal position.

As the child grows more adept at shifting back and forth between his own position and those of others, he can sustain conversations more adequately. When a child talks egocentrically, he expresses himself, but he does not develop a topic. Now he takes on more responsibility of trying to understand what others are communicating to him and of speaking in such a way that they will understand him. This is not to say that all talking is going to be true conversation when once a child can appreciate another viewpoint. Far from it. Even adults are known to engage in egocentric speech. Table 4–4 shows how gradual is children's increase in ability to sustain a discussion. Note that even in Grade 6, 23 percent of the comments made in the discussion period were not related to the topic which had been introduced and developed [2].

Verbal communication skills have been investigated in terms of the child's ability to understand the other person's role and capacities, and the child's ability to use that understanding as a tool in communicating with other persons [33, 56]. In one of these studies [33], Adult A taught the child to play a parchesilike game. Then the child was asked to teach the game to blindfolded Adult B. As might be expected, children increased in communicating ability as they increased in age from Grade 2 through 12. Some of the youngest children were almost entirely indifferent to the blindfold, making comments such as "Pick up this and put it in there." None of the oldest group failed to take some account of the blindfold. This experiment illustrates the child's gradually increasing capacity to put himself in the place of the other person and to use his mobility of thought for improved interpersonal communication, sending messages which are meaningful to the other person. Maturity of the listener plays a complementary part in communication. When children from kindergarten through eighth grade were given a task of verbally communicating graphic designs, success was seen to hinge upon the age of the listener as well as the age of the speaker [56]. Such tasks depend upon at least two abilities in the speaker: his ability to use language and concepts which describe the object or action, and his ability to judge what would be meaningful to the other person. The latter involves role taking.

The development of role-taking ability is likely enhanced by experience with a breadth and variety of social experiences and relationships, with peers, older people, and younger children. Parents contribute by communicating to the child the effects of his actions upon them and by encouraging the child to imagine how he would feel if he were experiencing what another person is now undergoing [48]. An experiment in training second graders to focus on intentions rather than results met with some success [34]. Sociodramatic play, which is so important for the social and cognitive integration of the preschool child, is also useful in stimulating role-taking ability during the early elementary school years.

Through play with peers and its resultant social insights, children gain increasing understanding of social organization. The nature of rules and moral order is clarified gradually through playing games with peers (in addition to experiences with parents and others). The following example shows two boys experimenting with lawmaking.

During a quiet hour at camp, a counselor noticed an 8- and a 9-year-old playing checkers. After some moments of orderly play, Jake made an extremely irregular move. Steve, watching intently, said nothing. A little later, when Steve broke the rules flagrantly, Jake was silent. "Don't you know you can't do that, Steve?" the counselor broke in. "And, Jake, you made a mistake, too."

"That was no mistake," Jake explained. "We made a rule that each person can cheat once during each game. I cheated and Steve cheated. Now we have to finish without cheating."

Although Steve and Jake were in the stage of cognitive development where they generally considered rules as *given* by a vague authority, their cooperative play was the means by which they found that man, even middle-sized boys, can make rules. They learned that by coming to an agreement with each other, they could play satisfactorily within limits which they created.

Prosocial Behavior

Being kind to other people is called prosocial behavior, or altruism. It may take the form of trying to make the other person feel happy or it may be an attempt to relieve him of pain or threats. Some norms of behavior prescribe altruism as parts of certain roles, such as the parent's nurturant behavior toward the child. Prosocial behavior is expected between people who love each other (who are attached). People also do kindnesses for others whom they do not know or who are casual friends or acquaintances. Again, the giving may be normative, as when Christians contribute to the collection plate or Hindus give to beggars. Or the kindness may be autonomous, when the altruist expects neither rewards, recognition, nor punishment for his actions. Erikson holds that the sense of generativity is necessary for full human development [31, pp. 266–268]. Generativity involves true caring, primarily for the development of the next generation but also for other kinds of development and creativity. As in all of Erikson's senses, there are forerunners in earlier stages, before the stage of crisis. The altruism of the child may well be the shadow of generativity to come, when the adult cares, gives, and comforts without thought of what he will get in return or of what people will think of him.

Concepts of Kindness. Adults hold a number of generally accepted criteria of kindness. A person is considered kind when he intentionally benefits another person. The degree of kindness is judged by the strength of the actor's desire to benefit the other person. Other kinds of motivation, particularly self-interest, modify the degree of kindness.

A picture of judgments of kindness was given to samples of age levels from kindergarten through graduate school and economic levels of wide variety [3]. For example, one choice was between a nursery school child who gave another child a block he was not using and a child who gave a block that he needed. The second child was judged kinder, because he sacrificed himself. In addition to self-sacrifice, the story themes included intentionality, choice, obedience, obligation to a guest, trade, bribe, returning a favor, equalizing benefits, and the importance of the benefit. Judgments for each picture-story showed age trends and these varied between stories. By finding the age after which there was no significant increase in understanding, the authors found when each particular kindness concept was understood. By second grade, children understood intentionality and the role of self-interest in a trade. By fourth grade, they appreciated the difference between having and not having a choice, and the roles of choice, obedience, self-sacrifice, obligation, and bribe. Returning a favor was not fully understood until eighth grade and even then, equalizing benefits was not comprehended in adult style. The young child seems to understand kindness in a global way and to differentiate it as he matures. No sex differences were found. Children in Catholic parochial schools, both middle- and lower-class, developed kindness concepts somewhat earlier than children in lower-class public schools.

Experiments on Giving. Children are likely to give (to make charitable donations) after watching other people give. One demonstration of this phenomenon was done with fourth and fifth grade children, who played a bowling game with an adult model [85]. When the model won, he took two gift certificates from the large supply provided and placed one in a box labeled "Trenton Orphans' Fund." When the child won, the model looked the other way, so as to show no reaction to whether the child donated or not. Sixty-three percent of the children donated. The model then left the child alone, ostensibly in complete privacy, to play the game and to do as he pleased with the pile of gift certificates. Under these circumstances, about half of the group that had observed a donating model gave, while among a group not exposed to a model, none gave. Among those who had been exposed and who had given in the presence of the model, two thirds gave and one third did not. Among those who had not given in the model's presence, only 6 out of 44 gave. These results suggest that rehearsal of charitable behavior in the presence of a model facilitates internalized or autonomous giving. Thus normative giving is likely to facilitate autonomous giving. The child who, with his parent, contributes to the collection plate or to the beggar has an experience which disposes him toward later giving on his own. Further studies on the role of rehearsal have shown that when rehearsal is voluntary, rather than enforced, its effects last longer and generalize to more situations [83]. Children who had voluntarily rehearsed in the model's presence and who had then given to the Trenton Orphan's Fund were subsequently more likely to give to UNICEF. Excitement or pleasant emotional arousal during observation and rehearsal is likely to facilitate internalization of altruism [83].

Children hear many exhortations to be good, kind, and generous. The effect of preaching on giving has been investigated. When children were told that they should donate, more of them immediately gave than did children who had observed a model and who had observed and rehearsed [99]. When the groups were again compared, a week later, there was no difference in numbers giving, because the number giving in response to verbal exhortation had decreased, while the other groups remained more stable. Inconsistency in practice and preaching affects child behavior predictably. Children tended to imitate the model's *actions*, whether he practiced charity and preached greed, or practiced greed and preached charity [12]. What the child says, however, is affected by what the model says. The child is likely to put verbal emphasis on the norm preached by the model. Children had difficulty in recalling the model's words and deeds when they were contradictory.

Age trends and sex differences in altruism have been found [84]. Normative altruism, as shown by giving when observed, increased with age, but internalized or autonomous altruism, indicated by private giving, had little relationship to age. More girls than boys showed internalized altruism. Teachers' ratings of obedience were positively related to both types of altruism at age 8. Helpfulness was related to internalized altruism throughout the age range 6 through 10 [84].

Experiments on Helping. As the child increases in role-taking and communication skills, and consequently in empathy, he might be expected to take more care of others. Feeling their distress or pain, he would try to relieve it, and as he gains in general competence, he would be more able to offer effective help. The influence of age on attempts to help was investigated, along with the influence of a companion versus being alone [90]. Children from kindergarten through sixth grade were tested alone or in pairs. The experimenter left the room, leaving the child playing. Then the noise of a chair falling and the crying and moaning of a 7-year-old girl was played on a tape recorder in the next room, while the experimenter observed through a one-way mirror. If the child went into the adjoining room, the experimenter also went and explained that it was a tape and asked him how he felt about it. All older children were told about the tape. Younger children who went to look for the experimenter were told that the other child was all right and had gone back to her classroom. They and the children who did not attempt to help were encouraged to tell what they thought and felt when they heard the distress sounds. Of the children alone, 32 percent tried to help. Sixty-one percent of the pairs did. The smallest percentages of numbers helping were in the kindergarten and sixth grade, the youngest and oldest. The scores for helping behavior were curvilinear, increasing up to second grade and decreasing after that.

A subsequent experiment sought to explain why the older children gave less help than those in the middle of the age range. Seventh graders were tested as individuals in a situation similar to the one described [90]. To half of these subjects, the experimenter gave permission to leave the room if they wished and to the other half, nothing was said about leaving. Results showed a significant difference in attempts to help. Half of those who had permission to leave tried to help, while only a sixth of the others tried. The percentage helping was as great as the percentage of individual second graders helping in the previous experiment. Thus it seems that the older children's reluctance to help a child in distress was due not to callousness or lack of empathy but to being unwilling to risk doing wrong. In another variation on this experiment, kindergarten and first grade children were given the responsibility of helping if "anything happens" [91]. These children did indeed help more than children who heard distress sounds without having received permission or instructions. The author suggests that our society overemphasizes "thou shalt not" and does not pay enough attention to teaching prosocial behavior.

Summary

The elementary school years bring a great expansion of environment and resulting experiences for the child. His experiences are determined and limited by the different social and cultural settings into which he is born. His nation affects his values, especially in regard to the value placed upon the individual in contrast to the group and also in regard to materialism and standards of excellence. Racial and ethnic memberships determine many of the prejudices and hostilities which the child encounters, as well as the attitudes, practices, and aspirations of his parents. Social class membership is related to values, parental behavior, and resulting cognitive stimulation for children.

A modern trend in parental behavior seems to be a change away from paternalistic authoritarianism toward cooperative families where both parents are affectionate and nurturant. The parental role can be studied in terms of goal values, means-ends beliefs, means-ends capacities and goal achievements. Children learn to play adult roles by identifying with their parents. Mothers and fathers demonstrate different roles, both of which contribute to the development of boys and girls. Discipline, an important parental function, includes the regulation of behavior, the teaching of self-control, and the imparting of moral standards. Parents vary in their disciplinary methods, using various combinations of corporal and verbal punishment, withdrawal of privileges, acceptance of the child's behavior and feelings, understanding, trust, and rewards. Experimental research on methods of discipline reveals complex interactions between timing and intensity of punishment, cognitive structure, and nurturance. Studies of parent and child behavior support the idea that many dimensions of discipline are important, with cognitive structure of particular significance in moral development. Parents promote intellectual growth in their children by holding aspirations for them, by caring for them in ways which promote independence and the building of desire for achievement, and by giving them experiences which are stimulating, especially conversations.

Children gain much from friends in the way of knowledge, experience, and satisfaction. Values learned in the family are modified through peer interaction. New behavior patterns, learned from peers, promote growth in various areas, especially a conviction of competence. Children often bow to group pressures, even when exerted against their standards and beliefs. A youngster's concept of himself is strongly influenced by the ways in which his peers regard him. Popularity and social position in the group can be tested and measured. The ability to perceive one's own status and the statuses of others increases with age. While different characteristics may be appealing in different groups, in general, popular children tend to be those with abundant energy, who use their energy for group-approved purposes. The very popular child may pay a price, psychologically, for his extended efforts to adjust to the needs and wishes of others.

Boy–girl relationships, like parent–child relationships, have changed over the decades. A friendlier, more cooperative spirit seems to have arisen between boys and girls, in contrast to the extreme antipathy which used to exist during part of the elementary school years. Girls' attitudes toward the opposite sex change more during this period than boys' do.

Peers grow in understanding of each other through this period. Increased cognitive growth is both cause and result. With increased flexibility of thought, the child can take and hold the point of view of another person. Thus he can understand, accept, communicate, and cooperate increasingly. Through these interactions with peers, he deepens his understanding of the whole social group to which he belongs.

References

1. Ausubel, D. P., Schiff, H. M., & Gasser, E. B. A preliminary study of developmental trends in socioempathy: Accuracy of perception of own and others sociometric status. *Child Devel.*, 1952, **23**, 111–128.
2. Baker, H. V. Children's contributions in elementary school discussion. *Child Devel. Mono.* No. 29. New York: Teachers College, Columbia University, 1942.
3. Baldwin, C. P. & Baldwin, A. L. Children's judgments of kindness. *Child Devel.*, 1970, **41**, 29–47.
4. Bee, H. L. Parent–child interaction and distractibility in 9-year-old children. *Merrill-Palmer Quart.*, 1967, **13**, 175–190.
5. Bell, R. R. *Marriage and family interaction.* Homewood, Ill.: Dorsey, 1963.
6. Bettelheim, B. The children of the dream. New York: Macmillan, 1969.
7. Biller, H. B. Maternal salience and feminine development in young girls. *Proc. 77th Annual Convention of the American Psychological Association*, Washington, D.C., 1969, **4**, 259–260.
8. Bossard, J. H. *The sociology of child development* (3rd ed.). New York: Harper, 1960.
9. Broderick, C. B., & Rowe, G. P. A scale of preadolescent heterosexual development. *J. Marr. Fam.*, 1968, **30**, 97–101.
10. Bronfenbrenner, U. *Two worlds of childhood.* New York: Russell Sage Foundation, 1970.
11. Brown, D. G. Sex-role development in a changing culture. *Psychol. Bull.*, 1958, **55**, 232–242.
12. Bryan, J. H., & Walbek, N. H. Preaching and practicing generosity: Children's actions and reactions. *Child Devel.*, 1970, **41**, 329–364.
13. Burr, W. T. Satisfaction with various aspects of marriage over the life cycle: A random middle class sample. *J. Marr. Fam.*, 1970, **32**, 29–37.
14. Busse, T. V. Child-rearing antecedents of flexible thinking. *Devel. Psychol.*, 1969, **1**, 585–591.
15. Campbell, J. D. Peer relations in childhood. In M. L. Hoffman & L. W. Hoffman (Eds.), *Review of child development research.* Vol. 1. New York: Russell Sage Foundation, 1964.
16. Carpenter, R., & Busse, T. Development of self concept in Negro and white welfare children. *Child Devel.*, 1969, **40**, 935–939.
17. Cheyne, J., & Walters, R. H. Intensity of punishment, timing of punishment, and cognitive structure as determinants of response inhibition. *J. Exper. Child Psychol.*, 1969, **7**, 231–244.
18. Chilman, C. Poor families and their patterns of child care: Some implications for service programs. In Chandler [19], pp. 217–236.
19. Chandler, C. A. et al. (Eds.), *Early child care: The new perspectives.* New York: Atherton, 1968.
20. Clausen, J. A., & Williams, J. R. Sociological correlates of child behavior. In H. W. Stevenson (Ed.), *Child psychology.* The Sixty-second Yearbook

of the National Society for the Study of Education, Part II. Chicago: University of Chicago, 1963, pp. 62–107.

21. Coleman, J. S. *The adolescent society*. Glencoe, Ill.: Free Press, 1961.
22. Cratty, B. J. *Perceptual-motor behavior and educational processes*. Springfield, Ill.: Charles C. Thomas, 1969.
23. Davis, A. *Psychology of the child in the middle class*. Pittsburgh: University of Pittsburgh, 1960.
24. Davis, W. L., & Phares, E. J. Parental antecedents of internal-external control of reinforcement. *Psychol. Rep.*, 1969, **24**, 427–436.
25. DeLucia, L. A. The toy preference test: A measure of sex-role identification. *Child Devel.*, 1963, **34**, 99–106.
26. Deur, J. L., & Parke, R. D. The effects of inconsistent punishment on aggression in children. *Devel. Psychol.*, 1970, **1**, 403–411.
27. Devereux, E. C. The role of peer group experience in moral development: A research progress report. Paper presented at the Fourth Minnesota Symposium on Child Psychology, May, 1969.
28. Emmerich, W. The parental role: A functional-cognitive approach. *Mono. Soc. Res. Child Devel.*, 1969, **34**:8.
29. Epstein, R., & Komorita, S. S. Childhood prejudice as a function of parental ethnocentrism, punitiveness, and out-group characteristics. *J. Per. Soc. Psychol.* 1966, **3**, 259–264.
30. Epstein, R. & Komorita, S. S. Self-esteem, success-failure and locus of control in Negro children. *Devel. Psychol.*, 1971, **4**, 2–8.
31. Erikson, E. *Childhood and society* (2nd ed.). New York: Norton, 1963.
32. Flapan, D. *Children's understanding of social interaction*. New York: Teachers College Press, 1968.
33. Flavell, J. H. Role-taking and communication skills in children. *Young Children*, 1966, **21**, 164–177.
34. Glassco, J. A., Milgram, N. A., & Youniss, J. Stability of training effects on intentionality in moral judgment in children. *J. Pers. Soc. Psychol.*, 1970, **14**, 360–365.
35. Grams, A. Child anxiety: Self-estimates, parent reports and teacher ratings. *Merrill-Palmer Quart.*, 1965, **11**, 261–266.
36. Hamm, N. H., & Hoving, K. L. Conformity of children in an ambiguous perceptual situation. *Child Devel.*, 1969, **40**, 773–784.
37. Harrison, C. W., Rawls, J. R., & Rawls, D. J. Differences between leaders and non-leaders in six- to eleven-year-old children. *J. Soc. Psychol.*, 1971 (in press).
38. Hartley, R. E., & Hardesty, F. P. Children's perceptions of sex roles in childhood, *J. Genet. Psychol.*, 1964, **105**, 43–51.
39. Hartup, W. W., Moore, S. G., & Sager, G. Avoidance of inappropriate sex-typing by young children. *J. Consult. Psychol.*, 1963, **27**, 467–473.
40. Helper, M. M. Comparison of pictorial and verbal semantic scales as used by children. *J. Genet. Psychol.*, 1970 **117**, 149–156.
41. Hess, R. D. & Torney, J. V. *The development of political attitudes in children*. Chicago: Aldine, 1967.
42. Hill, J. P. Similarity and accordance between parents and sons in attitudes toward mathematics. *Child Devel.*, 1967, **38**, 777–791.
43. Hoffman, M. L. & Salzstein, H. D. Parent discipline and the child's moral development. *J. Pers. Soc. Psychol.*, 1967, **5**, 45–57.

44. Horrocks, J. E., & Buker, M. E. A study of the friendship fluctuations of preadolescents, *J. Genet Psychol.*, 1951, **78**, 131–144.
45. Hoving, K. L., Hamm, N., & Galvin, P. Social influence as a function of stimulus ambiguity at three age levels. *Devel. Psychol.*, 1969, **1**, 631–636.
46. Hurley, J. R. Parental malevolence and children's intelligence. *J. Consult. Psychol.*, 1967, **31**, 199–204.
47. Iscoe, I., & Carden, J. A. Field dependence, manifest anxiety and sociometric status in children. *J. Consult. Psychol.*, 1961, **25**:184.
48. Jessor, R., & Richardson, S. Psychosocial deprivation and personality development. In *Perspectives on Human Deprivation*. Washington, D.C.: U.S. Department of Health, Education, and Welfare, 1968.
49. Johnson, M. M. Sex-role learning in the nuclear family, *Child Devel.*, 1963, **34**, 319–333.
50. Kagan, J., & Moss, H. A. *Birth to maturity*. New York: Wiley, 1962.
51. Katkovsky, W., Crandall, V. C., & Good, S. Parental antecedents of children's beliefs in internal-external control of reinforcements in intellectual achievement situations. *Child Devel.*, 1967, **38**, 765–776.
52. Katkovsky, W., Preston, A., & Crandall, V. J. Parents' attitudes toward their personal achievements and toward the achievement behaviors of their children. *J. Genet. Psychol.*, 1964, **104**, 76–82.
53. Katz, I. Factors influencing Negro performance in the desegregated school. In M. Deutsch, I. Katz, & A. R. Jensen (Eds.), *Social class, race and psychological development*. New York: Holt, Rinehart and Winston, 1968, pp. 254–289.
54. Kohlberg, L. *Stages in the development of moral thought and action*. New York: Holt, Rinehart and Winston, 1969.
55. Kohn, M. L., & Schooler, C. Class, occupation and orientation. *Am. Soc. Rev.*, 1969, **34**, 659–678.
56. Krauss, R. M., & Glucksberg, S. Some characteristics of children's messages. Paper presented at the meeting of the Society for Research in Child Development, Santa Monica, Calif., March 27, 1969.
57. Lambert, W. E., & Klineberg, O. *Children's views of foreign people*. New York: Appleton-Century-Crofts, 1967.
58. McDavid, J. W., & Harari, H. Stereotyping of names and popularity in grade-school children. *Child Devel.*, 1966, **37**, 453–459.
59. Maw, W. H., & Maw, E. W. Children's curiosity and parental attitudes. *J. Marr. Fam.*, 1966, **28**, 343–345.
60. Miller, D. R., & Swanson, G. E. *The changing American parent*. New York: Wiley, 1958.
61. Mussen, P., & Beytagh, L. Industrialization, child-rearing practices, and children's personality. *J. Genet. Psychol.*, 1969, **115**, 195–216.
62. Mussen, P., & Distler, L. Child-rearing antecedents of masculine identification in kindergarten boys. *Child Devel.*, 1960, **31**, 89–100.
63. Mussen, P., & Rutherford, E. Parent-child relations and parental personality in relation to young children's sex-role preferences. *Child Devel.*, 1963, **34**, 589–607.
64. Newson, J., & Newson, E. *Four years old in an urban community*. Chicago: Aldine, 1968.
65. Northway, M. L. *What is popularity?* Chicago: Science Research Associates, 1955.

66. Northway, M. L. *A primer of sociometry* (2nd ed.). Toronto: University of Toronto Press, 1967.

67. Opie, I., & Opie, P. *The lore and language of school children*. Oxford: Clarendon, 1959.

68. Parke, R. D. Effectiveness of punishment as an interaction of intensity, timing, age, nurturance, and cognitive structuring. *Child Devel.*, 1969, **40**, 213–235.

69. Parke, R. D., & Walters, R. H. Some factors influencing the efficacy of punishment training for inducing response inhibition. *Mono. Soc. Res. Child Devel.*, 1967, **32**:1.

70. Parsons, R., & Bales, R. F. *Family, socialization and interaction process.* Glencoe, Ill.: Free Press, 1955.

71. Pope, B. Socioeconomic contrasts in children's peer culture prestige values. *Genet. Psychol. Mono.*, 1953, **48**, 157–220.

72. Proshansky, H., & Newton, P. The nature and meaning of Negro self-identity. In M. Deutsch, I. Katz, & A. R. Jensen (Eds.), *Social class, race and psychological development*. New York: Holt, Rinehart and Winston, 1968, pp. 178–218.

73. Rau, L., Mlodnosky, L. B., & Anastasiow, N. Child-rearing antecedents of achievement behaviors in second-grade boys. Final Report of U.S.O.E. Cooperative Research Project No. 1838. Palo Alto: Stanford University, 1964.

74. Rebelsky, F., Conover, C., & Chafetz, P. The development of political attitudes in young children. *J. Psychol.*, 1969, **73**, 141–146.

75. Reese, H. W. Attitudes toward the opposite sex in late childhood. *Merrill-Palmer Quart.*, 1966, **12**, 157–163.

76. Riessman, F. *The culturally deprived child*. New York: Harper, 1962.

77. Riessman, F. Low-income culture: The strengths of the poor. *J. Marr. Fam.*, 1964, **26**, 417–429.

78. Rollins, B. C., & Feldman, H. Marital satisfaction over the family life cycle. *J. Marr. Fam.*, 1970, **32**, 20–28.

79. Rosen, B. C. Race, ethnicity and the achievement syndrome. *Am. Soc. Rev.*, 1959, **24**, 49–60.

80. Rosen, B. C. Family structure and value transmission. *Merrill-Palmer Quart.*, 1964, **10**, 25–38.

81. Rosen, B. C., & D'Andrade, R. The psychosocial origins of achievement motivation. *Sociometry*, 1959, **22**, 185–218.

82. Rosenberg, B. G., & Sutton-Smith, B. A revised conception of masculine-feminine differences in play activities. *J. Genet. Psychol.*, 1960, **96**, 165–170.

83. Rosenhan, D. L. Some origins of concern for others. In P. Mussen, J. Langer, & M. Covington (Eds.), *Trends and issues in developmental psychology*. New York: Holt, Rinehart and Winston, 1969, pp. 134–153.

84. Rosenhan, D. L. Studies in altruistic behavior: Developmental and naturalistic variables associated with charitability. Paper presented at the meeting of the Society for Research in Child Development, Santa Monica, Calif., March 29, 1969.

85. Rosenhan, D. L., & White, G. M. Observation and rehearsal as determinants of prosocial behavior. *J. Pers. Soc. Psychol.*, 1967, **5**, 424–431.

86. Ruderman, L. An exploration of empathic ability in children and its relationship to several variables. Unpublished doctoral dissertation, Teachers College, Columbia University, 1961.

87. Sethi, R. R. The relation between parental consistency in response to frustration and children's imitation of parental responses. Unpublished Ph.D. thesis, Oregon State University, 1969.

88. Sontag, L. W., Baker, C. T., & Nelson, V. L. Mental growth and personality development: A longitudinal study. *Mono. Soc. Res. Child Devel.*, 1958, **23**:2.

89. Staub, E. Effects of variation in permissibility of movement on children helping another child in distress. Proc. 77th Annual Convention, *American Psychological Association*, 1969, **4**, 385–386.

90. Staub, E. A child in distress: The influence of age and number of witnesses on children's attempts to help. *J. Pers. Soc. Psychol.*, 1970 (in press).

91. Staub, E. A child in distress: The effect of focusing responsibility on children on their attempts to help. *Devel. Psychol.*, 1970, **2**, 152–153.

92. Stein, A. H., Pohly, S. R., & Mueller, E. The influence of masculine, feminine, and neutral tasks, on children's achievement behavior, expectancies of success and attainment values. *Child Devel.*, 1971, **32**, 195–207.

93. Taba, H. Cultural deprivation as a factor in school learning. *Merrill-Palmer Quart.*, 1964, **10**, 147–159.

94. Torrance, E. P. Changing reactions of preadolescent girls to tasks requiring creative scientific thinking. *J. Genet. Psychol.*, 1963, **102**, 217–223.

95. Tulkin, R., Muller, J. P., & Conn, L. K. Need for approval and popularity: Sex differences in elementary school students. *J. Consult. Clin. Psychol.*, 1969, **33**, 35–39.

96. Utech, D. A., & Hoving, K. L. Parents and peers as competing influences in the decisions of children of differing ages. *J. Soc. Psychol.*, 1969, **78**, 267–274.

97. Ward, W. D. Process of sex-role development. *Devel. Psychol.*, 1969, **1**, 163–168.

98. Werner, E. E. Sex differences in correlations between children's IQs and measurements of parental ability and environmental ratings. *Devel. Psychol.*, 1969, **1**, 280–285.

99. White, G. M. *The elicitation and durability of altruistic behavior in children.* Unpublished Ph.D. dissertation, Princeton University, 1967.

100. Winterbottom, M. The relation of need for achievement in learning experiences in independence and mastery. In J. Atkinson (Ed.), *Motives in fantasy, action and society.* Princeton: Van Nostrand, 1958, pp. 453–478.

101. Yarrow, M. R., & Campbell, J. D. Person perception in children. *Merrill-Palmer Quart.*, 1963, **9**, 57–72.

102. Young, M. B. A Negro mother speaks. *Parents'*, 1964, **39**:7, 50–51, 78.

Readings in
Social Development and
Interpersonal Relationships

During the school years in America children get a great deal of experience with other people. During the school hours children see principally others of their own age; outside of school they see people who may be either related to them or unrelated and who may be of all ages. The development of motor and intellectual skills increases their modes of operation with others. As they develop cognitively they become able to understand principles of interaction with other people, both children and adults.

In the first article Ross Parke reviews research on the effects of punishment on children's behavior. He points out that until recently there was very little such research and makes it clear that he is not advocating the use of punishment in helping children learn. His last sentence is "punishment is only one technique which can be used in concert with other training tools such as positive reinforcement to shape, direct, and control the behavior of developing child."

The next article, by Wade Harrison and James and Donna Rawls, is a study of some of the characteristics of a sample of leaders among six- to eleven-year-olds as contrasted with a sample of nonleaders from the same population. Robert Krauss and Sam Glucksberg report a study of the development of the ability to communicate information. The aim here to is to understand better how accurate communication is achieved.

The final paper, by Carlfred Broderick and George Rowe, shows that in two large samples of American preadolescents most of the boys and girls went through a set of stages of interest in the company of the other sex. It thus substantiates through research an epigenetic development which has been discussed for some time in child development literature.

Some Effects of Punishment on Children's Behavior*

Ross D. Parke
UNIVERSITY OF WISCONSIN

Punishment is an effective way of controlling deviant behavior in children. Yet, there are many aspects to punishment which must be considered before it is used. Some of these are

Reprinted from *Young Children*, 24, 225–240. Copyright © 1969 National Association for the Education of Young Children. By permission.

* The preparation of this paper and some of the studies that are reported here were supported in part by Research Grant GS 1847, National Science Foundation.

timing, intensity, consistency, and the undesirable effects which punishment can cause when not administered properly.

A casual review of magazines, advice to parent columns or (until recently) the psychological journals quickly reveals that there is considerable controversy concerning the usefulness of punishment as a technique for controlling the behavior of young children. For many years the study of the impact of punishment on human behavior was restricted to armchair speculation and theorizing. In part, this paucity of information was due to the belief that punishment produced only a temporary suppression of behavior and that many undesirable side-effects were associated with its use. Moreover, ethical and practical considerations prohibited the employment of high intense punishment in research with human subjects—especially children—thus contributing to this information gap.

However, through both studies of childrearing and recent laboratory investigations, some of the effects of punishment on children's social behavior are being determined. It is the main aim of this paper to review these findings and assess the current status of our knowledge concerning the effects of punishment.

TIMING OF PUNISHMENT

A number of years ago at Harvard's Laboratory of Human Development, Black, Solomon and Whiting (1960) undertook a study of the effectiveness of punishment for producing "resistance to temptation" in a group of young puppies. Two training conditions were used. In one case the dogs were swatted with a rolled-up newspaper just *before* they touched a bowl of forbidden horsemeat. The remaining pups were punished only *after* eating a small amount of the taboo food. On subsequent tests—even though deprived of food—the animals punished as they approached the food showed greater avoidance of the prohibited meat than animals punished after committing the taboo act. This study is the prototype of a number of studies recently carried out with children; and it illustrates the importance of the *timing* of the punishment for producing effective control over children's behavior.

In recent studies of the effects of timing of punishment on children's behavior, the rolled-up newspaper has been replaced by a verbal rebuke or a loud noise, and an attractive toy stands in place of the horsemeat. For example, Walters, Parke and Cane (1965) presented subjects with pairs of toys—one attractive and one unattractive—on a series of nine trials; the 6–8 year-old boys were punished by a verbal rebuke, "No, that's for the other boy," when they chose the attractive toy. As in the dog study, one group of children was punished as they approached the attractive toy, but before they actually touched it. For the remaining boys, punishment was delivered only after they had picked up the critical toy and held it for two seconds. Following the punishment training session, the subjects were seated before a display of three rows of toys similar to those used in the training period and were reminded not to touch the toys. The resistance-to-deviation test consisted of a 15-minute period during which the boy was left alone with an unattractive German-English dictionary and, of course, the prohibited toys. The extent to which the subject touched the toys in the absence of the external agent was recorded by an observer located behind a one-way vision screen. The children's data paralleled the puppy results: the early punished children touched the taboo toys less than did the boys punished late in the response sequence. This timing of punishment effect has been replicated by a number of investigators (Aronfreed & Reber, 1965; Parke & Walters, 1967; Cheyne & Walters, 1968).

Recent extensions of this experimental model indicate that this finding is merely one aspect of a general relationship: *the longer the delay between the initiation of the act and the onset of punishment, the less effective the punishment for producing response inhibition.* This proposition is based on a study in which the effects of four delay-of-punishment positions were examined (Aronfreed, 1965). Using a design similar to Walters, Parke & Cane (1965), Aronfreed punished one group of children as they reached for the attractive toy; under a second condition, the subject was permitted to pick up the attractive toy and was punished at the apex of the lifting movement. Under a third condition, six seconds elapsed after picking the toy up before punishment was delivered. In the final group, six seconds after the child picked up the toy, he was asked to describe the toy and only then was punishment administered. The time elapsing between the experimenter's departure until the child made the first deviation steadily decreased as the time between the initiation of the act and the delivery of punishment increased.

Punishment also may be less effective in facilitating learning in young children if the punishment is delayed. Using a learning task in which errors were punished by the presentation of a loud noise combined with the loss of a token, Walters (1964) found that punishment delivered immediately after the error speeded learning more than did punishment which was delayed 10 seconds or 30 seconds.

Since it is often difficult to detect and punish a response in the approach phase of a transgression sequence, the practical implications of these studies may be questioned. However, Aronfreed (1968) has noted one feature of naturalistic socialization that may dilute the importance of punishing the act in the execution phase. "Parents frequently punish a child when he is about to repeat an act which they dislike" (p. 180). In this case, punishment may be delivered in the early stages of the next execution of the act, even though it is delayed in relation to the previously completed commission of this same deviant behavior.

In addition, the importance of timing of punishment may be contingent on a variety of other features of punishment administration, such as the intensity of the punishment, the nature of the agent–child relationship, and the kind of verbal rationale accompanying the punishment. The effects of these variables will be examined in the following sections.

INTENSITY OF PUNISHMENT

It is generally assumed that as the intensity of punishment increases the amount of inhibition will similarly increase. It is difficult to study severity of punishment in the laboratory due to the obvious ethical limitations against using potentially harmful stimuli in experimentation with children. Consequently, until recently most of the evidence concerning the relative effectiveness of different intensities of punishment derived either from animal studies or from child-rearing interview studies.

The animal studies (e.g., Church, 1963), in which electric shock is used as the punishing stimulus, have supported the conclusion that more complete suppression of the punished response results as the intensity of the punishment increases. On the other hand, the child-rearing data relating to the effects of intensity on children's behavior have not yielded clear cut conclusions. It is difficult, however, to assess the operation of specific punishment variables using rating scales of parent behavior because most of these scales confound several aspects of punishment, such as frequency, intensity and consistency (Walters & Parke, 1967). Differences between scale points may, therefore, be due to the impact of any of these variables, either alone or in combination.

Recent laboratory studies have avoided some of these short-comings and have yielded less equivocal conclusions concerning the effects of punishment intensity on children's behavior. Using the resistance-to-deviation model already described, Parke and Walters (1967) punished one group of boys with a soft tone (65 decibels) when they chose an attractive but prohibited toy. A second group heard a loud one (96 decibels) when they chose the attractive toy. In the subsequent temptation test, children who were exposed to the loud punisher were less likely to touch the prohibited toys in the experimenter's absence than were boys exposed to a less intense version of the tone. This finding has been confirmed using a noxious buzzer as the punishing stimulus (Cheyne & Walters, 1967; Parke, 1969).

The Parke study has also yielded some suggestive evidence concerning the impact of intensity variations on other aspects of punishment such as timing. Under conditions of high intensity punishment, the degree of inhibition produced by early and late punishment was similar. Under low intensity conditions, however, the early punished subjects showed significantly greater inhibition than subjects punished late in the response sequence. Thus, timing of punishment may be less important under conditions of high intensity punishment. However, the generality of this conclusion is limited by the narrow range of punishment intervals that have been investigated; perhaps when punishment is delayed over a number of hours, for example, this relationship would not hold. Further research is clearly required.

Other research has indicated, however, that high intensity punishment may not always lead to better inhibition or be more effective in controlling children's behavior than low intensity punishment. A study by Aronfreed and Leff (1963), who investigated the effects of intensity of punishment on response inhibition in a temptation situation, illustrates this possibility. Six- and seven-year-old boys were given a series of choice trials involving two toys roughly comparable in attractiveness, but which differed along certain stimulus dimensions that the child could use to distinguish between punished and non-punished choices. For two groups, a simple discrimination between red and yellow toys was required; the other groups of subjects were exposed to a complex discrimination between toys which represented passive containers and toys with active internal mechanisms. The punishment consisted of verbal disapproval (no); deprivation of candy, and a noise; the intensity and quality of the noise were varied in order to control the noxiousness of the punishment. Following training, each child was left alone with a pair of toys of which the more attractive one was similar in some respects to the toys that had been associated with punishment during the training procedure. Provided that the discrimination task was relatively simple, response inhibition was more frequently observed among children who received high intensity punishment. When the discrimination task was difficult, however, "transgression" was more frequent among children under the high intensity punishment than among children who received the milder punishment. As Aronfreed and Leff noted, the complex discrimination task combined with high intensity punishment, probably created a level of anxiety too high for adaptive learning to occur. When subtle discriminations are involved, or when the child is uncertain as to the appropriate response, high intensity punishment may create emotional levels that clearly interfere with learning and therefore retard inhibition of undesirable behaviors.

NATURE OF THE RELATIONSHIP BETWEEN THE AGENT AND RECIPIENT OF PUNISHMENT

The nature of the relationship between the socializing agent and the child is a significant determinant of the effectiveness of punishment. It is generally assumed that punishment will be a more effective means of controlling behavior when this relationship is close and affectional than when it is relatively impersonal. This argument assumes that any disciplinary act may involve in varying degrees at least two operations—the presentation of a negative reinforcer and the withdrawal or witholding of a positive reinforcer (Bandura & Walters, 1963). Physical punishment, may, in fact, achieve its effect partly because it symbolizes the withdrawal of approval or affection; hence punishment should be a more potent controlling technique when used by a nurturant parent or teacher.

Sears, Maccoby and Levin (1957) provided some evidence in favor of this proposition. Mothers who were rated as warm and affectionate and who made relatively frequent use of physical punishment were more likely to report that they found spanking to be an effective means of discipline. In contrast, cold, hostile mothers who made frequent use of physical punishment were more likely to report that spanking was ineffective. Moreover, according to the mothers' reports, spanking was more effective when it was administered by the warmer of the two parents.

A study by Parke and Walters (1967) confirmed these child-rearing findings in a controlled laboratory situation. In the investigation the nature of the experimenter-child relationship was varied in two interaction sessions prior to the administration of punishment. One group of boys experienced a 10-minute period of positive interaction with a female experimenter on two successive days. Attractive constructional materials were provided for the children and, as they played with them, the female experimenter provided encouragement and help and warmly expressed approval of their efforts. A second group of boys played, in two 10-minute sessions, with relatively unattractive materials while the experimenter sat in the room without interacting with the children. Following these interaction sessions, the children underwent punishment training involving verbal rebuke and a noxious noise for choosing incorrect toys. In the subsequent test for response inhibition, children who had experienced positive interaction with the agent of punishment showed significantly greater resistance to deviation than boys who had only impersonal contact.

It is difficult to determine whether this effect is due to an increase in the perceived noxiousness of the noise when delivered by a previously friendly agent or whether the result derives from the withdrawal of affection implied in the punitive operation. Probably it was the combination of these two sources of anxiety which contributes to our findings. A recent study by Parke (1967), while not directly concerned with the relative importance of these two components, found that nurturance-withdrawal alone, unaccompanied by noxious stimulation, can effectively increase resistance to deviation in young children. Two experimental treatments were employed. In one condition—the continuous nurturance group—the subjects, six- to eight-year-old boys and girls, experienced 10 minutes of friendly and nurturant interaction with either a male or female experimenter. Subjects in the nurturance-withdrawal group experienced five minutes of nurturant interaction, followed by five minutes of nurturance-withdrawal during which the experimenter turned away from the child, appeared busy, and refused to respond to any bid for attention. Following these manipulations, all subjects were placed in a resistance-to-deviation situation, involving a display of attractive, but forbidden, toys. In the instructions to the subject, it was made clear that if the subject conformed to the prohibition, the experimenter would play with him upon returning. In this way the link between resistance-to-deviation and nurturance was established. As in previous experiments, a hidden observer recorded the child's deviant activity during the 15-minute period that the adult was absent from the room. The results provided some support for the hypothesis, with subjects in the nurturance-withdrawal group deviating significantly less often than subjects in the continuous-nurturance condition. However, it was also found that nurturance withdrawal influenced girls to a greater degree than boys, and that the effect was most marked with girls experiencing withdrawal of a female agent's nurturance.

These data are consistent with previous studies of nurturance withdrawal, which have indicated that withdrawal of affection may motivate the previously nurtured child to engage in behavior that is likely to reinstate the affectional relationship (e.g., Hartup, 1958; Rosenblith, 1959, 1961). In the present study, the greater resistance to deviation of the subjects in the inconsistent nurturance condition may thus reflect an attempt to win back the experimenter's approval through conformity to his prohibition.

REASONING AND PUNISHMENT

In all of the studies discussed, punishment was presented in a relatively barren cognitive context. Very often, however, parents and teachers provide the child with a rationale for the punishment they administer. Is punishment more effective when accompanied by a set of reasons for nondeviation? The answer is clearly positive. For example, Sears, Maccoby and Levin (1957), in their interview study of child-rearing practices, found that mothers who combine physical punishment with extensive use of reasoning reported that punishment was more effective than mothers who tended to use punishment alone. Field investigations, however, have yielded little information concerning the relative effectiveness of different aspects of reasoning. In the child training literature, reasoning may include not only descriptions of untoward consequences that the child's behavior may have for others, but also the provision of examples of incompatible socially acceptable behaviors, explicit instructions on how to behave in specific situations, and explanations of motives for placing restraints on the child's behavior. Moreover, these child training studies do not indicate the manner in which the provision of reasons in combination with punishment can alter the operation of specific punishment parameters such as those already discussed—timing, intensity, and the nature of the agent–child relationship.

It is necessary to turn again to experimental studies for answer to these questions. Aronfreed (1965) has conducted a pioneering set of studies concerning the impact of reasoning procedures on the timing of punishment effect. In the earlier timing experiments, cognitive structure was minimized and no verbal rationale was given for the constraints placed on the child's behavior. In contrast, children in a second group of experiments were provided, in the initial instructions, with a brief explanation for not handling some of the toys. In one variation, for example, the cognitive structuring focused on the child's intentions. When punished, the child was told: "No, you should not have *wanted* to pick up that thing." The important finding here was that the addition of reasoning to a *late*-timed punishment markedly increased its effectiveness. In fact, when a verbal rationale accompanied the punishment the usual timing of punishment effect was absent; early- and late-timed punishments were equally effective inhibitors of the child's behavior. Other investigators have reported a similar relation between reasoning operations and timing of punishment (Cheyne & Walters, 1968; Parke, 1969). In these latter studies, the reasoning procedures presented in conjunction with punishment did not stress intentions, but focused on the consequences of violation of the experimenter's prohibition.

The delay periods used in all of these reasoning studies were relatively short. In everyday life, detection of a deviant act is often delayed many hours or the punishment may be postponed, for example, until the father returns home. An experiment reported by Walters and Andres (1967) addressed itself directly to this issue. Their aim was to determine the conditions under which a punishment delivered four hours after the commission of a deviant act could be made an effective inhibitor. By verbally describing the earlier deviation at the time that the punishment was administered, the effectiveness of the punishment was considerably increased in comparison to a punishment that was delivered without an accompanying restatement. An equally effective procedure involved exposing the children to a videotape recording of themselves committing the deviant act just prior to the long-delayed punishment. A partially analogous situation, not studied by these investigations, involves parental demonstration of the deviant behavior just before delivering the punishing blow. In any case, symbolic reinstatement of the deviant act, according to these data, seems to be a potent way of increasing the effectiveness of delayed punishment.

A question remains. Do reasoning manipulations alter the operation of any other parameters besides the timing of the punishment? Parke (1969) examined the modifying impact of reasoning on the intensity and nurturance variables. When no rationale was provided, the expected intensity of punishment effect was present: high intensity punishment produced significantly greater inhibition than low intensity punishment. However, when rationale accompanied the punisher, the difference between high and low intensity of punishment was not present.

As noted earlier, children who had experienced nurturant interaction with the punishing agent prior to punishment training deviated less often than subjects in the low nurturance condition. However, this effect was present in the Parke (1969) study only when no rationale accompanied the noxious buzzer. When the children were provided with a rationale for not touching certain toys, the children who had experienced the friendly interaction and children who had only impersonal contact with the agent were equally inhibited during the resistance-to-deviation test period.

Taken together, these experiments constitute impressive evidence of the important role played by cognitive variables in modifying the operation of punishment.

A common yardstick employed to gauge the success of a discrepancy procedure is the permanence of the inhibition produced. It is somewhat surprising, therefore, that little attention has been paid to the stability of inhibition over time as a consequence of various punishment training operations. One approach to this issue involves calculating changes in deviant activity occurring during the resistance-to-deviation test session in experimental studies. Does the amount of deviant behavior increase at different rates, for example, in response to different training procedures? As a first step in answering this question, Parke (1969) divided the 15-minute resistance-to-deviation test session into three

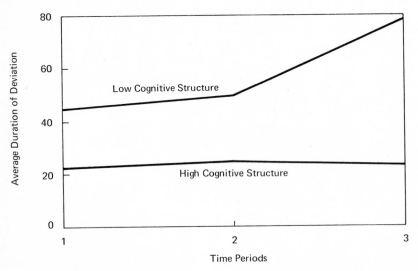

FIGURE 1.   *Stability of duration of deviation over three five-minute periods for high-cognitive and low-cognitive structure conditions.*

five-minute periods. As Figure 1 indicates, the low cognitive structure subjects (no rationale) increased their degree of illicit toy touching over the three time periods while the degree of deviation over the three intervals did not significantly change for the high cognitive structure (rationale provided) subjects. Cheyne and Walters (1968) have reported a similar finding. These data clearly indicate that the stability of inhibition over time was affected by the reasoning or cognitive structuring procedures. The interesting implication of this finding is that inhibition—or internalization—may *require* the use of cognitively-oriented training procedures. Punishment techniques that rely solely on anxiety induction, such as the noxious noises employed in many of the experiments discussed or the more extreme forms of physical punishment sometimes used by parents may be effective mainly in securing only short-term inhibition.

The type of research reviewed here does not provide us with any information concerning the relative effectiveness of reasoning procedures for producing behavioral control at different ages. It is likely that developmental trends will be discovered in light of recent Russian work (e.g., Luria, 1961) which indicates that the child's ability to use verbal behavior to control motor responses increases with age. Possibly with younger children response inhibition will be most successfully achieved by a reliance on physical punishment techniques which stress the production of anxiety. With older children, punishment techniques which diminish the role of anxiety and which stress the role of verbal control of motor behavior through the appeal to general rules, will be more effective in producing response inhibition (Parke, 1968).

CONSISTENCY OF PUNISHMENT

In naturalistic contexts, punishment is often intermittently and erratically employed; consequently, achieving an understanding of the effects of inconsistent punishment is a potentially important task. Data from field studies of delinquency have yielded a few clues concerning the consequences of inconsistency of discipline. Glueck and Glueck (1950) found that parents of delinquent boys were more "erratic" in their disciplinary practices than were parents of nondelinquent boys. Similarly, the McCords (e.g., McCord, McCord & Howard, 1961) have found that erratic disciplinary procedures were correlated with high degrees of criminality. Inconsistent patterns involving a combination of love, laxity and punitiveness, or a mixture of punitiveness and laxity alone were particularly likely to be found in the background of their delinquent sample. However, the definition of inconsistency has shifted from study to study in this delinquency research, making evaluation and meaningful conclusions difficult (Walters & Parke, 1967).

In a recently completed experiment, Deur and Parke (1968) examined the effects of inconsistent punishment on aggression in young children. Aggression was selected as the response measure in order to relate the findings to previous studies of inconsistent discipline and aggressive-delinquent behavior. An automated Bobo doll similar to that previously employed by Cowan and Walters (1963) was used to measure aggression. The child punches a large padded stomach of the clown-shaped doll and the frequency of hitting is automatically recorded. In principle, the apparatus is similar to the inflated punch toys commonly found in children's homes. To familiarize themselves with the doll, the six- to nine-year-old boys used in this study punched freely for two minutes. Following this warm-up or baseline session, the subjects underwent one of three training conditions. In one case the boys were rewarded with marbles each time they punched the Bobo doll for 18 trials. Subjects in the second training condition received marbles on nine trials, while on the remaining trials punching was neither rewarded nor punished. The final group of boys was rewarded on half of the trials, but heard a noxious buzzer on the other nine trials of the training session. The children were informed that they were playing the game "badly."

The aims of the study were to examine the effects of these training schedules on resistance to extinction—where both rewards and punishers were discontinued—and on resistance to continuous punishment—where every punch was punished. In the next part of the study, therefore, half of the children in each of the three groups were *neither* rewarded nor punished for hitting the Bobo doll. The remaining subjects heard the noxious buzzer each time they punched. The boys had been informed at the outset of the training session that they could terminate the punching game whenever they wished. The main index of persistence was the number of hitting responses before the child voluntarily ended the game. The results are shown in Figure 2. The punished subjects made fewer hitting responses than did subjects in the extinction conditions, which suggests that the punishment was effective in inhibiting the aggressive behavior. The training schedules produced particularly interesting results. The inconsistently punished subjects showed the greatest resistance to extinction. Moreover, these previously punished children tended to persist longer in the face of consistent punishment than the boys in the other training groups. The effects were most marked in comparison to the consistently rewarded sub-

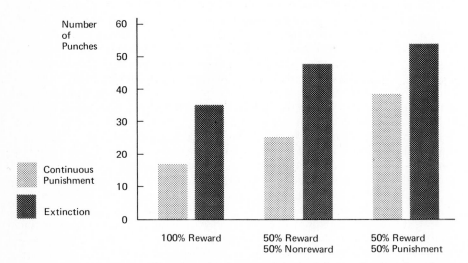

FIGURE 2.   *Mean number of punches in post-training period as a function of consistency of reward and punishment.*

jects. The implication is clear: the socializing agent using inconsistent punishment builds up resistance to future attempts to either extinguish it or suppress it by consistently administered punishment.

The particular form of inconsistency employed in this study represents only one of a variety of forms of inconsistency which occurs in naturalistic socialization. Consistency, as used in the present research, refers to the extent to which a single agent treats violations in the same manner each time such violations occur. Of equal importance would be studies of inter-agent inconsistency. For example, what effect will one parent rewarding aggressive behavior and the other parent punishing the same class of behaviors have on the persistence of aggressive response patterns? Similar inconsistencies between teacher and parental treatment of deviant behavior and the discrepancies between peer and teacher reactions to unacceptable behaviors require examination.

UNDESIRABLE CONSEQUENCES OF PUNISHMENT

The foregoing paragraphs indicate that punishment is effective in producing response suppression. Nevertheless, punishment may have undesirable side-effects which limit its usefulness as a socializing technique. In the first place, the teacher or parent who employs physical punishment to inhibit undesirable behaviors may also serve as an aggressive model. Bandura (1967) has summarized this viewpoint as follows: "When a parent punishes his child physically for having aggressed toward peers, for example, the intended outcome of this training is that the child should refrain from hitting others. The child, however, is also learning from parental demonstration how to aggress physically. And the imitative learning may provide the direction for the child's behavior when he is similarly frustrated in subsequent social interactions" (1967, p. 43).

Evidence supporting this position is, at best, indirect. There is a sizable body of data indicating a relationship between the frequent use of physical punishment by parents and aggressive behavior in their children (Becker, 1964). However, the increases in aggression could possibly be due to the *direct* encouragement that punitive parents often provide for behaving aggressively outside the home situation. Alternatively, highly aggressive children may require strong, physically punitive techniques to control them. Thus, even if it is assumed that the punitive parent acts as an aggressive model there is no evidence demonstrating that children imitate the aggressive behaviors the disciplinarian displays while punishing the child. It is recognized that exposure to aggressive models increases aggressive behavior in young children (Bandura, 1967); however, it is of questionable legitimacy to generalize from Bobo doll studies to children imitating a physically punitive adult who is often carrying out a justified spanking in line with his role as parent or teacher.

The results of a recent study by Slaby and Parke (1968) are relevant. Children were exposed to a film-mediated model who was disciplined for touching prohibited toys. In one case, the film agent "spanked" the child for touching the toys; in the second case, the adult on the film "reasoned" with the deviant model after detecting the violation of the prohibition. In addition to testing the child's resistance to deviation, the amount of aggression that a child would direct to a peer was assessed. Under the guise of helping the experimenter teach another child arithmetic problems, the subject was given the opportunity to punish the other child by "punching" him each time he made a mistake. A punch was administered by depressing a button on the subject's panel, which activated a punching machine in the adjacent room. Both the number and intensity of punches were recorded for each subject. The subjects who saw the physically punitive disciplinarian were more aggressive than the children exposed to the verbal reasoning sequence, although the differences were only of borderline statistical significance. Replication of this study is needed before a definite conclusion can clearly be drawn.

Another undesirable consequence of punishment is the effect on the agent-child relationship. As a result of punishment, the child may be motivated to avoid the punishing parent or teacher. Consequently, the socialization agent may no longer be able to direct or influence the child's behavior and encourage the development of appropriate behaviors. Conditions such as the classroom often prevent the child from physically escaping the presence of the agent. Continued use of punishment in an inescapable context, however, may lead to passivity and withdrawal (Seligman, Maier & Solomon, 1969) or adaptation to the punishing stimuli generally employed. In any case, whether escape is possible or not, the quality of the agent-child relationship may deteriorate if punishment is used with high frequency; punishment administered by such an agent will, therefore, be less effective in inhibiting the child.

The undesirable effects of punishment mentioned here may occur mainly in situations where the disciplinary agents are indiscriminatively punitive. In child-training contexts where the agent rewards and encourages a large proportion of the child's behavior, even though selectively and occasionally punishing certain kinds of behavior, these side effects are less likely to be found (Walters & Parke, 1967).

CONCLUSION

This review leaves little doubt that punishment can be an effective means of controlling children's behavior. The operation of punishment, however, is a complex process and its effects are quite varied and highly dependent on such parameters as timing, intensity, consistency, the affectional and/or status relationship between the agent and recipient of punishment, and the kind of cognitive structuring accompanying the punishing stimulus.

It is unlikely that a socialization program based solely on punishment would be very effective; the child needs to be taught new appropriate responses in addition to learning to suppress unacceptable forms of behavior. "In fact, in real-life situations the suppressive effect of punishment is usually only of value if alternative pro-social responses are elicited and strengthened while the undesirable behavior is held in check. The primary practical value of studies of parameters that influence the efficacy of punishment is . . . to determine the conditions under which suppression will most likely occur" (Walters & Parke, 1967, p. 217). From this viewpoint, punishment is only one technique which can be used in concert with other training tools such as positive reinforcement to shape, direct, and control the behavior of the developing child.

References

ARONFREED, J. Punishment learning and internationalization. Some parameters of reinforcement and cognition. Paper read at biennial meeting of Soc. for Research in Child Develm., Minneapolis, Mar., 1965.

—— *Conduct and Conscience.* New York: Academic Press, 1968.

—— & Leff, R. The effects of intensity of punishment and complexity of discrimination upon the learning of an internalized inhibition. Unpubl. mss. Univ. of Pennsylvania, 1963.

—— & Reber, A. Internalized behavioral suppression and the timing of social punishment. *J. pers. soc. Psychol.*, 1965, 1, 3–16.

BANDURA, A. The role of modeling processes in personality development. In. W. W. Hartup & Nancy L. Smothergill (eds.), *The Young Child.* Washington: Natl. Assn. for the Education of Young Children, 1967, pp. 42–58.

—— & WALTERS, R. H. *Social Learning and Personality Development.* New York: Holt, Rinehart & Winston, 1963.

BECKER, W. C. Consequences of different kinds of parental discipline. In M. L. Hoffman & Lois W. Hoffman (eds.), *Review of Child Development Research*, Vol. 1. New York: Russell Sage Foundation, 1964, pp. 169–208.

BLACK, A. H., SOLOMON, R. L., & WHITING, J. W. M. Resistance to temptation in dogs. Cited by Mowrer, O. H., *Learning Theory and the Symbolic Processes.* New York: John Wiley, 1960.

CHEYNE, J. A. & WALTERS, R. H. Timing and intensity of punishment and cognitive structuring as determinants of response inhibition. Unpubl. mss., Univ. of Waterloo, 1968.

CHURCH, R. M. The varied effects of punishment on behavior. *Psychol. Rev.*, 1963, 70, 369–402.

COWAN, P. A., & WALTERS, R. H. Studies of reinforcement of aggression: I. Effects of scheduling. *Child Develm.*, 1963, 34, 543–551.

DEUR, J. L. & PARKE, R. D. The effects of inconsistent punishment on aggression in children. Unpubl. mss., Univ. of Wisconsin, 1968.

GLUECK, S. & GLUECK, ELEANOR. *Unraveling Juvenile Delinquency.* Cambridge: Harvard Univ. Press, 1950.

HARTUP, W. W. Nurturance and nurturance-withdrawal in relation to the dependency behavior of preschool children. *Child Develm.*, 1958, 29, 191–201.

LURIA, A. R. *The Role of Speech in the Regulation of Normal and Abnormal Behavior.* New York: Liveright, 1961.

McCORD, W., McCORD, JOAN & HOWARD, A. Familial correlates of aggression in non-delinquent male children. *J. abnorm. soc. Psychol.*, 1961, 62, 79–93.

PARKE, R. D. Nurturance, nurturance withdrawal and resistance to deviation. *Child Develm.*, 1967, 38, 1101–1110.

——. The role of punishment in the socialization process. Paper read at Miami Symposium on Social Behavior, Miami, Ohio, Nov., 1968.

——. Effectiveness of punishment as an interaction of intensity, timing, agent nurturance and cognitive structuring. *Child Develm.*, 1969, in press.

—— & WALTERS, R. H. Some factors determining the efficacy of punishment for inducing response inhibition. *Monographs of the Soc. for Research in Child Develm.*, 1967, 32 (Serial No. 109).

ROSENBLITH, JUDY F. Learning by imitation in kindergarten children. *Child Develm.*, 1959, 30, 69–80.

——. Imitative color choices in kindergarten children. *Child Develm.*, 1961, 32, 211–223.

SEARS, R. R., MACCOBY, ELEANOR E. & LEVIN, H. *Patterns of Child Rearing.* Evanston, Ill.: Row, Peterson, 1957.

SELIGMAN, M. E. P., MAIER, S. F. & SOLOMON, R. L. Unpredictable and uncontrollable aversive events. In F. R. Brush (Ed.), *Aversive Conditioning and Learning.* New York: Academic Press, 1969.

SLABY, R. & PARKE, R. D. The influence of a punitive or reasoning model on resistance to deviation and aggression in children. Unpubl. mss., Univ. of Wisconsin, 1968.

WALTERS, R. H. Delay-of-reinforcement effects in children's learning. *Psychonom. Sci.,* 1964, 1, 307–308.

———— & ANDRES, D. Punishment procedures and self-control. Paper read at Annual Meeting of the Amer. Psychological Assn., Washington, D.C., Sept., 1967.

———— & PARKE, R. D. The influence of punishment and related disciplinary techniques on the social behavior of children: theory and empirical findings. In B. A. Maher (Ed.), *Progress in Experimental Personality Research,* Vol. 4, 1967, pp. 179–228.

———— PARKE, R. D., & CANE, VALERIE A. Timing of punishment and the observation of consequences to others as determinants of response inhibition. *J. exp. child Psychol.,* 1965, 2, 10–30.

Differences Between Leaders and Non-leaders in Six- to Eleven-Year-Old Children*

C. Wade Harrison
TEXAS CHRISTIAN UNIVERSITY

James R. Rawls and Donna J. Rawls
VANDERBILT UNIVERSITY

The present study was designed to investigate incidence of leadership ratings among 6 to 11 year old children as it is related to intellectual ability, academic performance, social inter-action patterns, medical history, TAT responses, and scores on a number of other psychological tests. The leader sample consisted of 278 Ss rated by their teachers as being frequently chosen as leaders (143 boys and 135 girls), while non-leaders consisted of 416 Ss who were rated as seldom or never chosen (206 boys and 210 girls) Results indicated that children who were more frequently chosen as leaders were healthier, more intelligent, higher achievers in school, more socially adept, and better adjusted than those children who were infrequently chosen as leaders.

In the extensive literature of leadership research, there is surprisingly little data that is directly related to leadership behavior in young children. The

Reprinted from a paper presented at the Southwestern Psychological Association meetings, April 18–20, 1968, New Orleans, Louisiana. By permission. See also *Journal of Social Psychology,* 1971 (in press).

* Appreciation is expressed to the National Center for Health Statistics for permission to use the data upon which this study was based.

purpose of the present study was to investigate differences between children rated as leaders and non-leaders in a large sample of six- to eleven-year-old children.

Leadership among children has been found to be highly related to social participation (Parten, 1933), social acceptance, and popularity (Bonney, 1943; Tuddenham, 1951). As suggested by Pikunas and Albrecht (1961), the child who surpasses his peers in strength or achievement in preferred activities usually has a direct opportunity to assume leadership. If this child is aware of the likes and dislikes of other children and is friendly, enthusiastic, and daring, he is even more likely to assume a leadership role among his peers.

The present study was designed to investigate incidence of leadership among children as it is related to intellectual ability, academic performance, social interaction patterns, medical history, TAT responses, and scores on a number of other psychology tests.

METHOD

SUBJECTS Ss were drawn from a national sample of 2,012 children included in the Health Examination Survey, conducted by the National Center for Health Statistics. The S population consisted of 694 children ranging in age from six to eleven years old. There were 349 boys and 345 girls.

The criterion for being considered as a leader or a non-leader was a teacher rating of the frequency with which each child was chosen a leader. Frequency of being chosen a leader was allotted three categories of response: (a) frequently chosen, (b) average incidence, (c) seldom or never chosen. Only those Ss who were frequently chosen or who were seldom or never chosen were included in the sample. The group of leaders selected included 278 Ss who were frequently chosen (143 boys and 135 girls), while the non-leaders consisted of 416 Ss who were seldom or never chosen (206 boys and 210 girls).

PROCEDURE   The communities from which the children were drawn were selected according to the field data collection locations of the National Center for Health Statistics. Ss were examined on site within each community in special examination trailers.

Data collected included medical and dental examinations, medical histories, teacher ratings, and ratings by mothers. Demographic data such as socio-economic status, income level, residential location, etc., were also gathered. Psychological tests included the WRAT reading and arithmetic subtests, the Draw-a-Man test and the WISC vocabulary and block design subtests. In addition, TAT protocols for cards 1, 2, 5, 8, and 16 were tape recorded and subsequently transcribed and scored. All psychological tests were administered and scored by psychologists holding a master's degree.

RESULTS

Results are presented in Table 1. A scale based upon S's medical history indicated that those Ss defined as leaders were significantly healthier than non-leaders ($p < .02$). A scale assessing present health also showed leaders to

TABLE 1
A Comparative Analysis of Leaders and Non-leaders

| VARIABLES | SIGNIFICANCE LEVEL | DIRECTION OF SIGNIFICANCE | |
		LEADERS	NON-LEADERS
General health	< .02	*	
Motor activity	< .001	*	
Aggression	< .01	*	
Frequency of disciplinary action	< .01	*	
Intellectual ability	< .001	*	
Academic performance	< .001	*	
Gifted	< .001	*	
Overall adjustment	< .001	*	
Chosen first	< .001	*	
Well liked	< .05	*	
Race	< .05	*	
WRAT reading	< .05	*	
WISC vocabulary	< .05	*	
WISC block design	< .05	*	
Emotionally disturbed	< .01		*
Sex	N.S.		
Residence location	N.S.		
Income level of parents	N.S.		
Incidence of childhood diseases	N.S.		
Incidence of asthma	N.S.		
Hayfever	N.S.		
Other allergies	N.S.		
Heart disease	N.S.		
Nursery school attendance	N.S.		
Kindergarten attendance	N.S.		
Tension level	N.S.		
Temper outbursts	N.S.		
WRAT arithmetic subtest	N.S.		

be healthier ($p < .01$). Teacher ratings indicated that leaders displayed significantly more motor activity ($p < .001$) and were more aggressive ($p < .01$).

With respect to school performance, Ss identified as leaders showed a significantly greater frequency of disciplinary actions ($p < .01$), but also scored significantly higher on teacher ratings of intellectual ability ($p < .001$)and academic performance ($p < .001$). In a similar vein, teachers indicated that a greater number of gifted children were among those considered as leaders ($p < .001$).

Teacher ratings indicated that non-leaders were more frequently emotionally disturbed ($p < .01$). In contrast, leaders were rated significantly higher on overall adjustment ($p < .001$).

When choosing sides for games and activities, leaders were more often chosen toward the first ($p < .001$). Leaders were also rated as being well liked and more popular than non-leaders ($p < .05$).

Race was also found to differentiate leaders and non-leaders. Leaders were Caucasian significantly more often than not ($p < .05$). In other words, a significantly greater number of non-Caucasian Ss were found in the non-leader group than were in the leader group.

With regard to the psychological test data, leaders scored significantly higher on the WRAT reading subtest ($p < .05$), the WISC vocabulary subtest ($p < .05$) and the WISC block design subtest ($p < .05$). Leaders also scored in the expected direction on the Draw-a-Man test, but this failed to reach significance at the .05 level.

Analysis of TAT protocols showed no identifiable patterns of language production or thematic expression discriminating leaders from non-leaders. However, a few isolated language and thematic variables did significantly differentiate the two groups. These differences are presently undergoing more extensive investigation.

The following variables showed no relationship with frequency of being chosen a leader: sex; residence location; income level of parents; incidence of childhood diseases; incidence of asthma, hay fever, and other allergies; heart disease or other serious illnesses; nursery school or kindergarten attendance; tension level; temper outbursts; incidence of early trauma and scores on the WRAT arithmetic subtests.

DISCUSSION

Results of the present study indicated that children who were more frequently chosen as leaders were healthier, more intelligent, higher achievers in school, more socially adept, and better adjusted than those children who were infrequently chosen as leaders. In short, leaders displayed greater potential to excel physically, mentally, and socially.

On the surface, these data are reminiscent of Terman's (1925) early findings with exceptional children, in that he found exceptionally bright children to be taller, heavier, and socially more poised than normal children. However, close scrutiny of these data disclosed that leaders taken as a group were not necessarily physically superior *and* mentally superior *and* socially superior. Instead, the data indicated that when taken individually, children who were frequently chosen as leaders excelled in at least one of these areas.

An earlier study by Chowdhry and Newcomb (1952) showed the ability to be sensitive to the needs of the group to be a necessary but not a sufficient condition for being chosen a leader. Several other investigators have shown the selection of a leader to be a function of his ability to satisfy the needs of the group. Bonney (1943) and Pikunas and Albrecht (1961) have suggested that those children who surpass their peers in strength or achievement have a direct opportunity to assume leadership. Findings of the present study lend strong support to these earlier suggestions. Because childhood leaders excelled mentally, physically, and socially, they were better equipped to assume positions of leadership in group activities.

References

BONNEY, M. E. The constancy of sociometric scores and their relationship to teacher judgments of social success, to personality self-ratings. *Sociometry*, 1943, *6*, 409–424.

CHOWDHRY, K., & NEWCOMB, T. M. The relative abilities of leaders and non-leaders to estimate opinions of their own groups. *Journal of Abnormal and Social Psychology*, 1952, *47*, 51–57.

PARTEN, M. B. Leadership among preschool children. *Journal of Abnormal and Social Psychology*, 1933, *27*, 430–440.

PIKUNAS, J., & ALBRECHT, E. J. *Psychology of human development.* New York: McGraw-Hill Book Co., 1961.

TERMAN, L. M., BALDWIN, B. T., & BRONSON, E. *Genetic studies of genius. The mental and physical traits of a thousand gifted children*, Vol. 1. Stanford, California: Stanford University Press, 1925.

Some Characteristics of Children's Messages

Robert M. Krauss

RUTGERS UNIVERSITY

Sam Glucksberg

PRINCETON UNIVERSITY

In previously reported research employing a two-person communication task, we have found that children display an increasing competence for accurate communication as a function of age. This effect has been shown to hold for matched-age pairs ranging from kindergarten to fifth grade (Krauss and Glucksberg, 1969) and below we will present some more recent data to show that the same effect is obtained when the age of speaker and listener are varied orthogonally. But today we would like to look beyond the issue of gross developmental differences in communicator accuracy and examine some of the age-differential characteristics of children's message which may underly differences in communicator accuracy.

Let us first describe the experimental communication task we have been employing and review in somewhat greater detail the results we have previously obtained. Then we will take a moment to speculate on the sorts of processes which might be responsible for these results and attempt to evaluate these speculations on some recently obtained data.

In most of our experiments, subjects are given the task of communicating about a set of novel graphic designs. The set of designs is illustrated in Figure 1. The property they have in common is their low codeability (Brown and Lenneberg, 1954). That is, they are difficult to name or characterize, each one eliciting

From a paper delivered at the meetings of the Society for Research in Child Development at Santa Monica, California, April, 1969. Reprinted by permission of the authors.

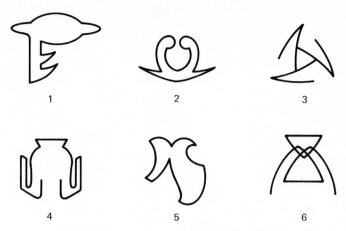

FIGURE 1.   *The graphic designs employed.*

from a group of speakers a wide variety of verbal labels. The designs are reproduced on the four vertical facets of a 2-inch wooden block, one design per
block. Each block has a hole drilled vertically through its center so that it can
be stacked on a wooden dowel. The experimental situation is illustrated in
Figure 2. There are two subjects, designated the speaker and the listener, each
of whom is given a duplicate set of blocks imprinted with the novel designs. The
speaker receives his blocks in a dispenser so constructed that the blocks must be
removed one at a time in a predetermined order. The listener receives the six
blocks spread out before her in random order. The subjects are separated by an
opaque screen placed so that they can neither see each other nor each other's
blocks.

The task is introduced to the subjects as a game called "Stack the Blocks."
The object of the game is to build two identical stacks of six blocks. The speaker
is instructed to remove the blocks from the dispenser one at a time and stack them
on his peg. At the same time, he is told, he must instruct his partner, the listener,
which block to stack on her peg. No restrictions are placed on either subject's
speech.

Before playing the game with the novel designs, subjects are given several
pretraining trials using a set of blocks imprinted with familiar objects (animals,
circus figures, etc.,). Since virtually all children can identify and name the
figures depicted on the pretraining blocks, this procedure greatly simplifies teaching the rules of the game. At the same time it ensures that defective performance
on the experimental task can be attributed to difficulties in dealing with the
novel designs and not simply to an inability to follow the rules of the game.

In our earliest study, done with nursery school age children, we observed
that the absurdly poor communicator performance of our subjects seemed to
derive from the idiosyncratic or egocentric nature of their messages. This
observation was reinforced by the finding that the same messages which communicated poorly or not at all to both young and adult listeners resulted in
extremely accurate choice behavior when they were addressed to the subjects
who initially had uttered them. Clearly the messages were in some sense

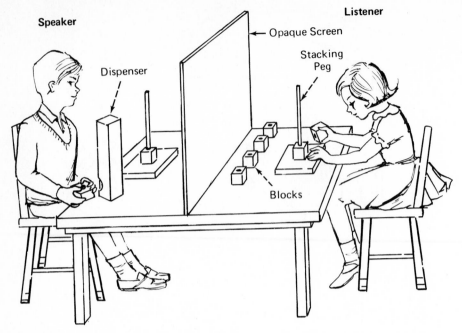

FIGURE 2.   *Experimental situation. Although a male speaker and female listener are shown, most of the studies employ same-sex pairs.*

"meaningful"; but their meaning was essentially private—which is simply another way of saying that they were not effective in an inter-personal communicative context.

But why should this be so? Let us look back for a moment at our communication task. How did our subjects go about communicating these rather exotic designs? If our stimuli had been representations of familiar objects (e.g., chairs, cups, horses) few children would have experienced difficulty; the simple strategy would have been to name the pictured objects. Indeed, this is precisely what subjects did in the pre-training phase of the experiment and all of our subjects can do it at least passably well. But our novel stimuli, by design, are not familiar. Hence, subjects have no well-formed names for them. The only viable strategy is for the subject to liken the designs to things for which he has names (a part of a figure may resemble a "snake" or a "saucer") and to use this resemblance with the necessary qualifications to guide his partner's identification. (There is, of course, another possibility—to give an exhaustive geometric description of the figure—but this is beyond our subject's capacity and, even if it were not, would probably be unproductive.)

So, at the very least, our subjects must have available in their repertoires a set of relevant concepts. They must be able to recognize elements of figures that look like snakes and saucers and, equally important, they must know the appropriate word-labels for these concepts.

But this alone is insufficient. The young subject in our early experiment who called a figure "mommy's hat" had obviously seen a resemblance between these two referents. The reason her message was uncommunicative was the small likelihood of some other person having any precise idea of what the latter referent looked like. Her message was perfectly adequate for herself, but not for anyone else.

This distinction, analogous to what Vygotsky (1962) has referred to as "inner" and "external speech," is one that is clearly reflected in adult usage. We are very much aware that the way we refer to things for our private use may communicate inadequately to another person. If I were to make up a list of "things to do" for my own use, it would be very different from the set of instructions I would provide for another person doing the same things. Indeed, competent adult communicators are careful to differentiate among the encodings appropriate for different listeners.

An experiment by Krauss, Vivekananthan and Weinheimer (1968) illustrates some of the differences between encoding for oneself and encoding for others. Subjects were asked to provide names for a set of color chips under one of two conditions. In the "Social Encoding Condition," subjects were told that the names they provided would, on some later occasion, be given to another person who would be asked to identify the color referred to. In the "Non-social Encoding Condition," subjects were told that they themselves would be called back in a few weeks and asked to make the color identifications from their own names. Actually, two weeks later all subjects were recalled and given three different types of names randomly intermixed. Some of the names were the ones the subject herself had given previously, some were names given by another subject under Social encoding instructions, and some were names given by another subject under Non-social encoding instructions. They were asked to identify for each name the color referred to. It was quite clear that subjects were best able to identify colors from names they themselves had provided, and this was independent of whether these names had been given under Social or Non-social instructions. They were somewhat less accurate in identifying colors from names provided by another person, under Social encoding instructions. For names encoded by others under Non-social instructions, identification accuracy was considerably poorer. A recent replication of this experiment, using male subjects and photographs of faces instead of color chips for stimuli, produced identical results.

In one sense, the behavior of our adult subjects in the Non-social encoding conditions was similar to that of the children in the experiment described above: they were providing messages which were privately (but not publicly) comprehensible. There was, however, an important difference: the adult behavior was task-appropriate; our subjects had no reason to believe that their messages would ever be transmitted to anyone else.

These results lead us to believe that, in addition to an adequate conceptual repertoire, a speaker must also have available some mechanism for determining which of the several possible alternative encodings present in his repertoire will communicate most effectively. The precise nature of such a mechanism we will leave open for the present. Let us, instead, turn to some relevant data.

It is fairly easy to demonstrate that the ability of children to communicate increases with age. Figure 3 indicates this, plotting the number of errors as a function of repetitive trials in our communication task for children in

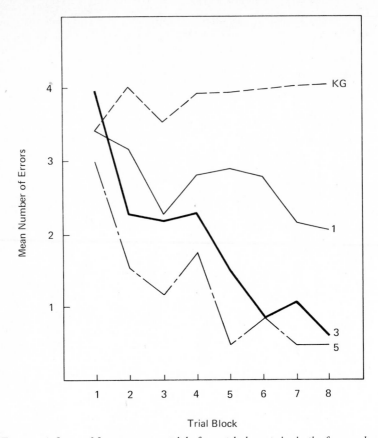

FIGURE 3. *Mean errors over trials for matched-age pairs in the four grades.*

kindergarten, first, third, and fifth grades (Krauss and Glucksberg, 1969). A similar result is obtained when one varies the grade of speaker and listener independently. Figure 4 shows the mean number of errors for first, third, and fifth grade speakers who are communicating to first, third, or fifth grade listeners. Note that there is an effect for speaker's grade and for listener's grade, both effects in the direction of increased accuracy with increasing age.

But what is it our subjects are saying that gives rise to these results? In nearly all of these experiments we have transcribed our subjects' utterances verbatim for analysis. The data I will discuss was taken from a partial replication of the experiment discussed above using subjects in kindergarten, fifth and eighth grade. We chose these transcripts for analysis because it seemed more likely that the wide age range would maximize the possibility of detecting differences.

What we did was to count the number of conceptual responses for each speaker's message on the first trial. We chose the first trial because these messages are uncontaminated by contributions from the speaker's partner in a way that later messages may not be. By a conceptual response we mean the mention of a

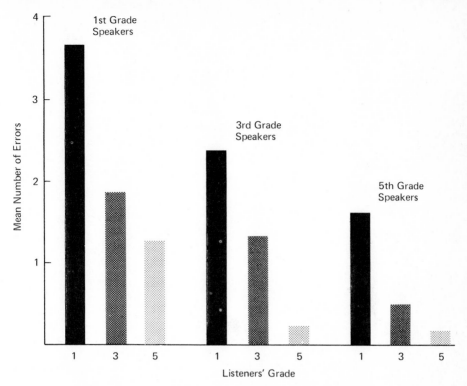

F I G U R E 4.   *Errors as a function of speaker and listener age.*

distinct descriptive element of a figure. So if a subject said that a figure looked like "snakes in a saucer" we would count two conceptual responses: snakes and saucer. A description like "a space-ship with points at either end and a wrench hanging down in back" would be coded as containing two conceptual responses, viz., space ship and wrench. The coding scheme is somewhat rough, but coders can use it with reasonably good reliability once they have some practice.

We would expect that the conceptual repertoires of our subjects would increase with age and that this would be reflected in the number of conceptual responses they gave in the communication task. The data are shown in Figure 5. The total number of conceptual responses are shown for kindergartners, fifth graders and eighth graders. Kindergartners on the average give only about two-thirds as many conceptual responses as fifth graders. And note that fifth graders and eighth graders give roughly the same number of conceptual responses—if anything the margin is trivially in favor of the younger group. We were somewhat surprised by this result but the wisdom of hindsight convinces us that it should not be too troubling. But if we look at the communication accuracy data for these same subjects, one fact is quite obvious: eighth grade speakers are more adequate communicators than fifth graders. The number of errors for fifth and eighth grade speakers communicating with their age peers are shown in Figure 6. The difference is clear. If one raises the objection that

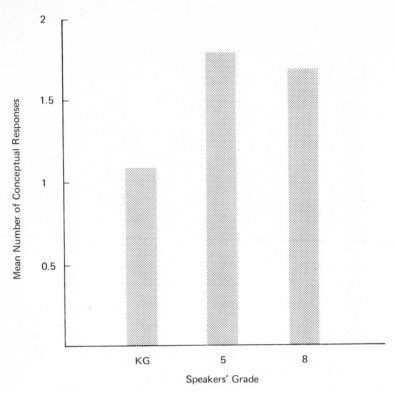

FIGURE 5.   *Mean number of conceptual responses per figure.*

this does not take into account the effect of the listener's age (and we know from previous work that the listener's age does have an effect), we can compare the performance of these two groups of subjects talking to listeners of the same age— namely kindergartners. This is shown in Figure 7. If anything, the difference is accentuated. Kindergartners are at best woefully inadequate partners but their performance when paired with eighth graders is vastly superior to what they do with fifth graders. Indeed, the performance of kindergarten listeners with fifth grade speakers shows relatively little improvement over trials.

Recall, however, that the conceptual repertoires of fifth and eighth grade speakers, to the extent that they are tapped by our measure, differ not at all. How, then, can we explain the increased effectiveness of the older subjects? Returning to our earlier argument, we hypothesized that a large repertoire was a necessary but insufficient condition for effective communication. In addition to the repertoire, it is necessary that a speaker have the ability to select out of that repertoire concepts that are at least potentially socially meaningful.

Unfortunately the communicative meaningfulness of a given conceptual response, although intuitively reasonably clear, is difficult to characterize operationally. If one who is familiar with the six stimulus figures simply reads the messages, it is obvious which are good ones (i.e., communicate effectively)

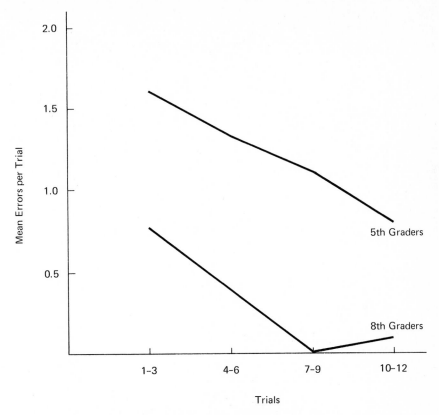

F I G U R E 6.   *Mean number of errors per trial (matched-age pairs).*

and which do not. But when one does this, he is simply taking the role of the listener in our experiment. What we need is a measure which we can apply to the messages themselves and which does not take into account the choice response of a real or role-playing listener. We know of no measure which does this precisely. But there are some which, it may be argued, are relevant to it.

The work of several sets of investigators (e.g., Brown and Lenneberg, 1954; Lantz and Stefflre, 1964; Krauss and Weinheimer, 1967; and Krauss, Vivekananthan and Weinheimer, 1968) provides some direct and indirect evidence for the proposition that the communality of names given to stimuli is a good index of how adequately the stimuli can be communicated. Brown and Lenneberg found that differences in the communality of names given to color chips was a good predictor of how accurately the colors could be identified on a delayed recognition task. Lantz and Stefflre showed that the same communality index was correlated with communication accuracy. Krauss and Weinheimer demonstrated that the communality index varied appropriately with the stimulus context in which the referent stimulus was set. And, in the experiment referred to above, Krauss, Vivekananthan and Weinheimer found that a rough analog of the communality index varied depending on whether a

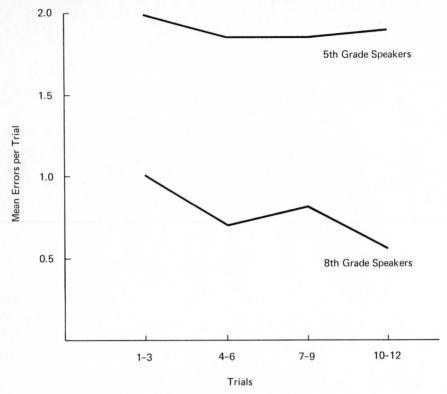

F I G U R E 7.   *Mean number of errors per trial (kindergarten listeners).*

speaker's manipulated encoding condition was public or private. We would not argue that a communality index is the best measure imaginable to be applied to our data. Rather, it is the best one we could think of and there is at least some rationale for its use.

Therefore, we calculated from our transcripts the proportion of conceptual responses that were not unique—that is, were used by more than one speaker. We did this separately by grade and figure. This proportion will serve as our communality index. The results of this analysis are presented in Figure 8. Note that for kindergartners the proportion of conceptual responses given by more than one speaker was relatively low, less than one in five. And recall that this is so despite the fact that kindergartners as a group give a relatively small number of different conceptual responses to begin with. Clearly these responses, few in number though they may be, are a remarkably heterogeneous lot.

Now let us look at the data for fifth and eighth graders; bearing in mind the fact that the total number of conceptual responses given by subjects in these two groups is roughly the same. For eighth graders, about 35 percent of the conceptual responses given are used by more than one speaker; for fifth graders this figure drops to 28 percent. Not a very large difference perhaps, but nearly as large as the difference between fifth graders and kindergartners.

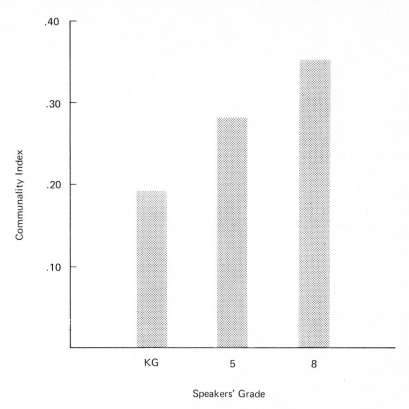

F I G U R E 8.   *Proportion of conceptual responses used by more than one speaker.*

Sometimes qualitative data is more compelling than summary statistics. When eighth graders communicate with kindergartners, 80 percent of them use the conceptual response "flying saucer" in talking about Figure 1. Only 20 percent of the fifth graders do so. We know that "flying saucer" is a pretty good name for this figure and it is the modal response for adults. Another example: 70 percent of our eighth graders use the conceptual response "triangle" as part of their message for Figure 3, contrasted with 20 percent of the fifth graders. Across all figures the modal frequency is greater in five out of six cases for eighth graders compared to fifth graders.

We have previously (Glucksberg and Krauss, 1967) presented a model of communication process which postulates an editing process intervening between a speaker's selection of a conceptual response and his use of that response in a message. In editing, the speaker presumably takes into account relevant aspects of his listener, the likelihood that the conceptual responses might be applied to stimuli other than the referent stimulus, and so forth. In many respects this model is similar to a mathematical model proposed by Rosenberg and Cohen (1966). The Rosenberg-Cohen model postulates two stages in the speaker's formulation of a message. In the first stage, called sampling, the speaker samples from his repertoire of word associations to the target stimulus—the one he is trying to communicate. In the second stage, called comparison, the speaker evaluates the probable effectiveness of his message by comparing the associative value of the sampled word-message to both the target stimulus and to the non-referent stimuli. If the associative value is greater for the former than for the latter, the speaker will (with a certain probability) emit the word-message. Otherwise, he will reject it and sample another word, subjecting it to the comparison process, and so on until finally he emits a word message. The sampling is done with replacement so that the possibility exists of the speaker actually emitting a message he has previously rejected. Rosenberg and Cohen have used words as their stimuli, enabling them to use word association norms to estimate the speakers' repertoires, but this has been a matter of convenience and not an intrinsic limitation on the model.

Cohen and Klein (1968) have employed this model to explain differences in communicative effectiveness found among third, fifth and seventh grade subjects on their word association-communication task. Briefly stated, they interpret their finding as indicating that the lack of effectiveness of young speakers derives not from a deficiency in the comparison stage (comparable to our editing process), but rather from the paucity of the repertoire from which the speaker samples.

We would suggest that both factors may be at work. Clearly, the kindergartner's repertoire of conceptual responses is meager in comparison to that of the fifth and eighth grades. But even the fifth grader, whose task-relevant repertoire appears to be every bit as extensive as that of the eighth grader, seems at times to use available conceptual responses injudiciously.

It may be, of course, that the hierarchical organization or the associative structure of repertoires for the two grades differ. If that were the case, if the responses were present, but at a lower strength, this would fit with the explanation offered by Cohen and Klein. Alternatively, it may be the case that younger and older subjects differ in the adequacy of their editing-comparison process. It is this latter explanation that we prefer, but at present we have little more than our intuitions to support it.

References

BROWN, R., and LENNEBERG, E. H. A study in language and cognition. *Journal of Abnormal and Social Psychology*, 1954, *49*, 454–462.

COHEN, B. D., and KLEIN, J. F. Referent communication in school age children. *Child Development*, 1968, *39*, 597–609.

GLUCKSBERG, S., and KRAUSS, R. M. What do people say after they have learned how to talk? Studies of the development of referential communication. *Merrill-Palmer Quarterly*, 1967, *3*, 309–316.

KRAUSS, R. M., and GLUCKSBERG, S. The development of communication: Competence as a function of age. *Child Development*, 1969, *40*, 255–266.

————, VIVEKANANTHAN, P. S., and WEINHEIMER, S. "Inner speech" and "external speech": Characteristics and communication effectiveness of socially and non-socially encoded messages. *Journal of Personality and Social Psychology*, 1968, *9*, 295–300.

————, and WEINHEIMER, S. Effect of referent similarity and communication mode on verbal encoding. *Journal of Verbal Learning and Verbal Behavior*, 1967, *6*, 359–363.

LANTZ. D., and STEFFLRE, V. Language and cognition revisited. *Journal of Abnormal and Social Psychology*, 1964, *69*, 472–481.

ROSENBERG, S., and COHEN, B. D. Referential processes of speakers and listeners. *Psychological Review*, 1966, *73*, 208–231.

A Scale of Preadolescent Heterosexual Development*

Carlfred B. Broderick
PENNSYLVANIA STATE UNIVERSITY

George P. Rowe
UNIVERSITY OF MISSOURI

A five-item scale of social heterosexuality was developed in a sample of 1,029 ten-, eleven-, and twelve-year-olds in Pennsylvania. Since the theory of a sequence of developmental stages makes the same requirements of items as does a Guttman scale, it was suggested that these items represented a series of steps in the development of normal heterosexuality at these ages. The study was replicated with a sample of 610 children of the same age in Missouri, and the results supported the same conclusion.

In previous papers data have been reported to indicate that, far from being a period of heterosexual latency, preadolescence includes a number of important steps in the process of social heterosexual development.[1] The present paper addresses itself to the question of whether there is a sequence of stages during the 10-to-12 age span which build one upon the other like a pyramid, in such a way that each ascending step is dependent upon the successful completion of each earlier step. If such a series of steps could be firmly established, we would be approaching an empirically based addition to the current theories of heterosexual development which focus primarily on preschool familial factors.[2]

Reprinted from *Journal of Marriage and the Family*, February 1968, *30*, (1), 97–101. By permission.

* The Pennsylvania study was supported in part by a grant originally designated MH-04974 from the National Institute of Mental Health, but then transferred to the National Institute of Child Health and Human Development under the designation HD-00882. The data for the Pennsylvania part of the research were collected in the spring of 1962. The Missouri data were collected in the winter and spring of 1965.

[1] Carlfred B. Broderick and Stanley E. Fowler, "New Patterns of Relationships Between the Sexes Among Preadolescents," *Marriage and Family Living*, 23 (February, 1961), pp. 27–30; Carlfred B. Broderick, "Social Heterosexual Development Among Urban Negroes and Whites," *Journal of Marriage and the Family*, 27 (May, 1965), pp. 200–203; Carlfred B. Broderick, "Socio-Sexual Development in a Suburban Community," *Journal of Sex Research*, 2 (April, 1966), pp. 1–24; and Carlfred B. Broderick, "Sexual Behavior Among Preadolescents," *Journal of Social Issues*, 22 (April, 1966), pp. 6–21.

[2] See, for example, Jerome Kagan, "Acquisition and Significance of Sex Typing and Sex Role," in *Child Development Research*, ed. by Martin L. Hoffman and Lois W. Hoffman, New York: Russell Sage Foundation, 1964, pp. 137–167; Urie Bronfenbrenner, "Freudian Theories of Identification and Their Derivatives," *Child Development*, 31 (March, 1960), pp. 15–40; Robert Winch, *Identification and Its Familial Determinants*, Indianapolis: Bobbs-Merrill, 1962; Daniel G. Brown and David B. Lynn, "Human Sexual Development: An Outline of Components and Concepts," *Journal of Marriage and the Family*, 28 (May, 1966), pp. 155–162.

SAMPLES

The research strategy involved two phases. First the presence of developmental steps was documented in a sample of ten- to twelve-year-olds in Pennsylvania. Then, independently, the same items were administered to a sample of ten- to twelve-year-olds in Missouri. The second study, coming after the analysis of the first study was completed, served as a test of the generalizability of the earlier findings.

The first sample included all of the ten- to twelve-year-olds in the fifth, sixth, and seventh grades of ten central Pennsylvania schools. The districts were chosen so as to encompass rural, suburban, and urban-industrial communities. In general, the rural and urban children came from the blue-collar class, and the suburban children came from the upper-middle class. All of the students from rural and suburban areas were white, but in the urban districts about 25 percent were Negro. In all there were 1,029 subjects in the Pennsylvania samples, 530 boys and 499 girls.

The Missouri sample consisted of 312 boys and 298 girls about equally divided among grades five, six, and seven in four localities within a radius of 75 miles from Kansas City. Subsamples included central Kansas City, an established contiguous suburb, a non-metropolitan city of about 25,000 population, and a rural county. Some general characteristics of this sample were that all subjects were white, 93 percent were Protestant, and the majority of the families were rated in the lower half on a modified McGuire-White Index of Social Status.

DATA COLLECTION AND ANALYSIS

The schedules administered to the two samples were identical in most of the items, although each included some questions omitted in the other. In addition to background items, the questions were concerned with attitudes toward marriage, kissing, dating, and romantic movies. There were, in addition, questions on experience, if any, with kissing, dating, and being in "love." Projective and sociometric items were also included. A descriptive analysis of much of this information has been reported elsewhere.[3]

In working with the data from the first study, it became apparent that, while the percentage of subjects answering positively to various items fluctuated considerably from group to group, a number of items appeared to hold their relative ranks for each age, sex, and locality group. This suggested the possibility that they were related to each other in a sequential pattern. Since the theory of a sequence of developmental stages makes the same requirements of items as does a Guttman scale, Guttman-scale analysis was employed. This procedure tested the proposition that the items were related to each other in such a way that a positive response on a given item was indicative of a positive response on all "easier" (or, in this case, "earlier") items.

Traditionally, Guttman-scale analysis provides a descriptive statistic, the

---

[3] Broderick, "Socio-Sexual Development in a Suburban Community," *op. cit.*; and George P. Rowe, *Patterns of Interpersonal Relationships Among Youth Nine to Thirteen Years of Age*, unpublished Ph.D. dissertation, The Florida State University, 1966.

coefficient of reproducibility, which indicates the extent to which the actual responses to the items correspond to the theoretical pyramidal model. A coefficient of .90 is generally considered acceptable, particularly if an examination of the individual items reveals that none of them is contributing an undue share of the error.[4]

The coefficient of reproducibility has been correctly criticized, however, in that it gives no indication at all of the probability of getting a particular level of reproducibility by chance alone. In order to meet this objection, the number of exact scale-type responses expected by chance was computed and compared with the observed number of exact scale-type responses. The data were then submitted to Chi-square analysis.[5]

The five items which emerged from preliminary analysis as being most promising on empirical and logical grounds were the following, listed here in the same order in which they might hypothetically occur in the life of an individual: (1) desiring to marry someday, (2) having a current girlfriend (boyfriend for the girls), (3) having been in love, (4) preferring a companion of the opposite sex over a member of the same sex or no companion at all when going to a movie, and (5) having begun to date. The exact wording and coding of each of these items is recorded in Table 1.

T A B L E 1
Five Items of the Social Heterosexuality Scale

---

1. "Would you like to get married someday?" *Yes* response was scored as positive, *No* and *Don't know* were scored as negative.
2. "Do you have a girlfriend now?" (or "Do you have a boyfriend now?" for the girls). *Yes* or *No.*
3. "Have you ever been in love?" *Yes* or *No.*
4. "Suppose you were in the pictures, place a number '1' by the picture which shows the situation you would like best . . ." One of the pictures showed a child, alone, at the ticket window of a moving picture theater, another showed him (her) in the same situation with a companion of the opposite sex and a third showed him (her) with a companion of the same sex. The item was scored positively if the opposite sex companion was rated first choice and negatively if it was not.
5. "Have you ever had a date?" *Yes* or *No.*

PENNSYLVANIA FINDINGS

As indicated in Table 2, these five items meet the criteria which have been established for scalability. The Guttman coefficient of reproducibility was .91 for the total group of boys and .93 for the girls. Both exceed the arbitrary .90

[4] For an excellent source on the evaluation of item error, see R. N. Ford, "A Rapid Scoring Procedure for Scaling Attitude Questions," *Public Opinion Quarterly*, 14 (1950), pp. 507–532.
[5] This technique was suggested first by Festinger but because of the complex computation involved has seldom been used. See Leon Festinger, "The Treatment of Quantitative Data by Scale Analysis," *Psychological Bulletin*, 44 (1947), pp. 149–161. Present computer technology renders the problem simple, however, and this feature has been built into a FORTRAN program for Guttman-Scale analysis written by the senior author. It is available through the Computation Center of Pennsylvania State University.

TABLE 2

Guttman-Scale Analysis of Five Items for Pennsylvania Boys and Girls
Ten to Twelve Years of Age

ITEM	TOTAL RESPONDING		PERCENT POSITIVE RESPONSE		PERCENT ERROR	
	GIRLS	BOYS	GIRLS	BOYS	GIRLS	BOYS
Want to marry	492	514	84	62	4	11
Have girlfriend/boyfriend	487	506	71	56	6	7
Have been in love	479	506	51	47	8	10
Prefer opposite sex for movies	476	483	39	39	10	11
Have had a date	495	525	22	24	5	8

	GIRLS	BOYS
Coefficient of reproducibility	.93	.91
Expected number of exact scale-type responses	234.8	176.6
Observed number of exact scale-type responses	324.0	317.0
Chi-square	64.0	167.3
p less than	.001	.001

level which most often is accepted. It can also be seen that none of the five individual items failed to fit into a perfect scale-type in more than 15 percent of the cases, thus meeting the criterion for items established by Ford.[6] Finally, the observed number of exact scale-type responses exceeded the expected number by a statistically significant margin. The Chi-square for the boys (1 degree of freedom) was 167.3 and for the girls 64.0, in each case far exceeding the criterion for significance at the .001 level.

These five items, then, meet all of the requirements for scalability, and by implication they constitute a series of pyramidally related developmental stages.

It should be noted that the items did not scale equally well in all of the subgroups. In general they scaled better with ten- and eleven-year-olds than with twelve-year-olds. When applied to a sample of older children from the same school districts (ages 13 to 17), the scale broke down altogether, indicating perhaps that in adolescence developmental factors may be overshadowed by other factors such as social pressures to date.

Of the eight residence-by-sex-and-race subgroupings, the items met all of the criteria for scaling among suburban boys and girls, urban white boys and girls, urban Negro girls, rural boys. Rural girls just failed to meet the Chi-square criterion and probably do not call for an explanation. Among Negro boys, however, the items did not scale well at all, and this probably

---

[6] Ford, *op. cit.*

reflects the general atypicality of heterosexual social development in this sub-group as discussed in a previous article.[7]

MISSOURI FINDINGS

In order to test the applicability of this scale beyond the limits of the population in which it was first observed, the same five items were included in the Missouri study and analyzed for scalability.

It can be seen from Table 3 that the replicated Missouri study gives very nearly the same results as were found earlier in Pennsylvania. The coefficient of reproducibility, the percent error on each item, and the statistically significant differences between the observed and the expected scale-type responses suggest that all of the requirements for scalability have been met.

TABLE 3

Guttman-Scale Analysis of Five Items for Missouri Boys and Girls Ten to Twelve Years of Age

ITEM	TOTAL RESPONDING		PERCENT POSITIVE RESPONSE		PERCENT ERROR	
	GIRLS	BOYS	GIRLS	BOYS	GIRLS	BOYS
Want to marry	298	311	85	62	5	12
Have girlfriend/boyfriend	298	312	72	57	6	6
Have been in love	298	312	50	47	8	10
Prefer opposite sex for movies	269	275	35	34	7	8
Have had a date	298	310	11	19	2	6

	GIRLS	BOYS
Coefficient of reproducibility	.95	.91
Expected number of exact scale-type responses	159.7	114.2
Observed number of exact scale-type responses	217.0	194.0
Chi-square	44.3	88.0
p less than	.001	.001

When each age and sex group was scaled separately, the coefficients of reproducibility ranged from .90 to .96. Only in one instance did an individual item pass the level of acceptable error (ten-year-old boys on the dating item). In each case the observed number of exact scale-type responses exceeded the number expected by chance to a statistically significant degree.

DISCUSSION

The evidence is compelling that there does exist a pyramidally structured set of stages which most preadolescent boys and girls undergo in pursuit of

[7] Broderick, "Social Heterosexual Development Among Urban Negroes and Whites," *op. cit.*

social heterosexual maturation. These steps are represented in these studies by items which meet the criteria for a stable Guttman scale among preadolescents of various ages from a wide range of social and geographic backgrounds.

Work on the sociosexual awareness of preschool children has indicated that recognition of the heterosexual nature of marriage is one of the key conceptual tasks of the early years.[8] The present findings underscore the relevance of the next logical step, coming to view marriage as an attractive element in one's own projected future. From these data it would appear that, until this fundamental step is achieved, further progress in relating socially to the opposite sex is inhibited during preadolescence.[9]

Commitment to the desirability of marriage, in turn, appears to lead, sooner or later, to singling out some member of the opposite sex as particularly attractive and placing him or her in the special category of "boyfriend" or "girlfriend." In an earlier analysis of these data,[10] it was noted that at this age the boyfriend-girlfriend relationship was quite likely to be nonreciprocal and that commonly the object of affection was unaware of his or her status. Despite the largely imaginary nature of these relationships, however, the children who feel these attachments apparently take them quite seriously. The majority described themselves as having been "in love"; and it seems probable that in most cases the reference was to the current relationships, since all but a few reported first being in love within the last year.

Having been in love, in turn, seems to be a prerequisite for appreciating the companionship of the opposite sex when going to the movies. Those who have never loved are likely, as a group, to prefer going alone or with a like-sex friend. Finally, it appears that some appreciation of the desirability of a cross-sex companion precedes the next big step, actually going out on a date.

The significant finding of these studies, of course, is not centered upon the importance of these particular items (other items could probably be found which would serve as well), but rather upon the existence of a heterosexual developmental continuum among adolescents.

The continuum itself might be speculatively described in terms of movement along two of Parsons' pattern variables. On the diffuse-specific axis it is clear that the movement is toward the specific. The rather global concept of being married someday shrinks first to the boundaries of a fantasied relationship with a real age mate and then even more as that fantasy is disciplined by experience. Finally it is focused upon a specific date with a specific girl on a specific occasion and with a quite limited range of behavior to choose from.

On the particularistic-universalistic axis, the course of development appears to move from the universalistic to the particularistic, at least for the first three steps. One moves from wanting to marry somebody, to having a particular girlfriend, to being in love with this particular girlfriend. The location of the next two steps on this continuum is less clear. It is not known whether the desire to take a girl to the movies is generic or particular. Our own tendency would be to assume that at this age wanting to go to the movies alone with a girl is

---

[8] Constance Bennifield Farrell, *Awareness and Attitudes of Preschool Children Towards Heterosexual Social Relationships*, unpublished master's thesis, The Pennsylvania State University, 1966.
[9] As noted earlier, there is some evidence that this prerequisite breaks down at later ages.
[10] Broderick, "Socio-Sexual Development in a Suburban Community," *op. cit.*; and Rowe, *op. cit.*

evidence of a desire to be with the particular girl and that the eventual date is more often than not the consummation of this rather focused wish. At later ages when dating itself becomes a goal, this could be expected to break down, but at this age it would be our interpretation that each step on the scale is in fact a step in the direction of greater particularism.

In non-Parsonian terms the preadolescent child could be said to be involved in a process of differentiation along two axes. On the one hand, he progressively differentiates dating behavior from the much broader repertoire of heterosexual behavior involved in "being married," (i.e., division of labor, being together, etc.) Simultaneously, he progressively differentiates one particular girl from the pool of females in general. From what we know about development during adolescence, it would seem that ultimately he begins to reintegrate his behavior toward girls, bringing the various components together in a series of global relationships. At the same time he continues the process of differentiating out a particular girl from the whole field of eligibles, in the process we call court-ship.

Whether this analysis is correct or not, however, it does appear, based on these data, that an orderly pattern of progression is discernible during these preadolescent years and that success or failure in each step has consequences for more advanced stages of heterosexual development.

Chapter 5

Courtesy the Peace Corps by Ray Witlin

An Overview of Human Life and Growth

All of existence is continuous and related. A search for beginnings and causes of life reveals psychological, physiological, biological, biochemical, and physical structures built upon and of each other.

Every organism and its environment have dynamic, reciprocal relationships. Affecting each other and being affected by each other, neither can be understood without the other, nor can either be what it *is* without the other. The cool air under the tree does not exist without the tree, nor would the tree exist without air. An

269

interesting interaction between plants and landscape can be seen in coastal areas where conservation projects are carried out. A beach which was washed away by a hurricane now stretches smoothly into the Atlantic, backed by sand dunes built by plants. The plants were dead Christmas trees stuck into the sand and then reinforced by living plants which, finding nutrients and moisture enough in the sand, sent down a network of tough roots, which held the sand in the dunes.

More remarkable even than the building of beaches is the interaction of the human baby with his environment, his family. A human baby grows into a human child as he lives in a human family, calling forth maternal and paternal responses from two adults whose behavior could not be parental if he were not there.

Varieties of Interaction Between the Individual and His World

The story of child development begins with the interactions of a small package of DNA and ends with an adult human being living in a complex social network. Everyone has some beliefs and hypotheses as to how these many changes take place. Nobody has explained it all in a comprehensive theory, but many theorists have described and explained parts of it. A theory depends first of all on the point of view from which the observer looks at the human scene and consequently on the phenomena which he observes. Theories of growth and development usually have a biological flavor. Learning experiments may suggest the influence of physics. Research in social relationships often involves sociology and perhaps anthropology. This chapter deals with six types of interactions which represent different ways of looking at human phenomena. They are: equilibration, growth and development, learning, maturation, evolutionary adaptation, and heredity.

Equilibration

The organism constantly regulates its life processes so as to maintain physical and mental states within certain limits.

Homeostasis

Homeostasis is a balance which the organism maintains within itself during the processes of living and as environmental influences affect its internal conditions. Since the balance is continually upset and re-created, through a complex of interactions, it can be called a dynamic equilibrium. Through activities that are mostly unconscious, the individual keeps his blood sugar at a definite level, his water content within a given range, his oxygen content just so. Breathing and heartbeat speed up or slow down from their average rates to restore disturbed balances. The mechanisms of homeostasis regulate sleeping and waking states, activity and rest. Pressures and depleted tissues may register consciously as felt needs, leading to such purposeful interactions with the environment as eating, drinking, and eliminating.

Looming large in the life of a newborn infant, the problems of homeostasis dwindle throughout infancy and childhood. By about 3 months of age basic physiological processes are well controlled. At any time throughout the life span, however, when the balance is seriously threatened, when biological demands become crucial or urgent, the individual drops his higher-order activities, such as giving a lecture or playing tennis, in order to restore the balance within his body.

Psychological Equilibrium

The search for balance occurs in the mental realm as well as in the physical. Equilibration is the process of achieving a state of balance. Sooner or later, the state of equilibrium is upset and a new one must be created. Equilibration includes selecting stimuli from the world, seeking this or that kind, more or less, paying attention to some of them and using some in more complex mental operations. When you consider all the sounds, sights, tastes, and other perceptions available, it follows that a person could not possibly attend to all of them at once. There must be ways of selecting stimuli and avoiding or reducing psychological conflict. In Walter's words: ". . . there are mechanisms within the brain which act like traffic cops for information and actually damp down and modify the action of the receptors themselves. It has been shown that the information which is allowed to reach the brain from the outside world is a function of its novelty and significance. The level of the receptor itself, the actual eye or ear, is cut down, as though the central nervous system were to say: 'I'm not interested in what you're sending me'" [48, p. 109]. What Walter is describing is very much akin to homeostasis of physiological functions, the maintenance of satisfactory internal conditions.

Equilibration is one of Piaget's principles of mental development [34, pp. 5–8]. Action can be provoked when equilibrium is upset by finding a new object, being asked a question, identifying a problem; in fact, by any new experience. Equilibrium is reestablished by reaching a goal, answering a question, solving a problem, imitating, establishing an effective tie or any other resolution of the difference between the new factor or situation and the mental organization already existing. Equilibration results in the successive stages of intelligence which Piaget describes.

Equilibration, in Piaget's theory, includes two complementary processes through which the person proceeds to more complex levels of organization—*assimilation*, which is the taking in from the environment what the organism can deal with and *accommodation*, the changing of the organism to fit external circumstances. Just as the body can assimilate foods and not other substances, so the mind can take in certain aspects and events in the external world and not others. Existing structures or *schemas* incorporate experiences which fit them or which almost fit them.

A schema is a pattern of action and/or thought. A baby develops some schemas before he is born and has them for starting life as a newborn. With simple schemas, he interacts with his environment, working toward equilibration. He achieves equilibrium over and over again, by using the schemas available to him at the moment. For example, a baby has a furry toy kitten which he knows as *kitty*. When given a small furry puppy he calls it *kitty*, strokes it and pats it, assimilating the puppy to an existing schema. A new little horse on wheels requires accommodation, since it is too different to be assimilated into the schema for dealing with *kitty*. It looks different; it feels different; it is not good for stroking and patting, but something can be done with the wheels which cannot be done with *kitty*. A new pattern of action is required. The child accommodates by changing and organizing existing schemas to form a schema for dealing with *horsey*. Thus the child grows in his understanding of the world and his ability to deal with his experiences in meaningful ways. Assimilation conserves the structural systems that he has while accommodation effects changes through which he copes more adequately with his environment and behaves in increasingly complex ways.

When homeostasis presents no problems, such as hunger, thirst, or fatigue, a person looks for something to do, something interesting, a new experience. If equilibrium were completely satisfying in itself, then surely he would sit or lie quietly doing nothing. In looking for action, the child seems to be trying to upset his state of equilibrium, as though equilibration were fun! And so it is. Activity is intrinsic in living tissue, brain cells included. Curiosity, exploration, competence, and achievement motivation are all outgrowths of the human propensity for enjoying the process of equilibration. The first stage of the process, perception of a problem, an incongruity or discrepancy, involves tension and a feeling of incompleteness. Something is missing or something is wrong.

The baby pushes himself forward to grasp a toy that is out of reach. The 4-year-old makes a mailbox which is necessary for his game of postman. The first grader sounds out a new word. Each child reduces a feeling of tension as he creates a new equilibrium. The equilibration (achievement of new balance) makes him into a slightly different person from what he has been, a person who can move forward a bit, a person who has made his own mailbox and can therefore make other things, a person who can read another word. Thus equilibration is a way of describing behavior development. New and more complex behavior occurs as it is demanded by the person's relationship with his surroundings.

When a person's schemas are adequate to deal with the situation in which he finds himself, he reacts automatically. For example, the response of a hungry breast-fed baby of 3 months would be quite automatic when offered his mother's breast. A 10-year-old would automatically answer the question "What is two times two?" When the schemas are not quite adequate to the situation, the child uses what he has, changing them slightly into actions which do solve the problem. For instance, the baby would change his behavior sufficiently to cope with a bottle and the 10-year-old with "$2x = 4$. What does x equal?" The change which takes place at the same time within the child is the development of a new behavior pattern or schema. A pleasant feeling of curiosity and satisfaction accompanies successful adjustments to demands for new behavior.

A person feels uneasy when he encounters a situation in which his resources are very inadequate. In order to provoke uneasiness, the problem must be somewhat similar to those which a person can solve, but not similar enough for him to succeed with. Such a problem for the baby mentioned might be a cup of milk. For the 10-year-old it might be an equation such as $5x - 49/x = 20x/5$. If the situation is so far removed from a person's past experience that his schemas for dealing with it are extremely inadequate, then he will have no reaction to it. He will not notice it. He will not select from the environment the stimuli which would pose the problem. The baby will not try to drink out of a carton full of cans of milk. The child won't attempt to solve $xY - x5 - 144 = 1062 + 2300$.

Familiar objects in unfamiliar guise produce unpleasantness, uneasiness, or even fear. (Chimpanzees are afraid of the keeper in strange clothes, an anesthetized chimp, a plaster cast of a chimp's head. Human babies are afraid of strangers.) In order to be frightened or to get the unpleasant feeling, the subject must first have residues of past experience with which to contrast the present experience. Thus does incongruity arise, with its accompanying unpleasant feeling tone. If the individual can cope with the situation successfully, he achieves equilibration and its accompanying pleasant feeling tone. Stimuli preferred and chosen are those that are slightly more complex than the state of equilibrium that the individual has already reached. Thus he moves on to a new state of equilibrium [36].

Growth and Development

The child's body becomes larger and more complex while his behavior increases in scope and complexity. If any distinction is made between the two terms, growth refers to size, and development to complexity. However, the two are often used interchangeably and this is what we have done. The terms *growth* and *development* were borrowed from the physical field, but they are commonly understood in connection with mental and personality characteristics. One can say, "He has grown mentally," or "He has developed mentally." The statement means "He is now functioning on a more complex intellectual level." Or one can speak of growth of personality and development of attitudes. Listening in on second grade and fifth grade classrooms in the same school building will reveal differences in subject matter interests and in mode of thinking.

Growth or development can be shown to have taken place either by comparing younger and older individuals at the same moment of time or by comparing the same individuals at two different points of time. When the measures of some characteristic of a number of individuals are averaged by age groups, the averages of the successive age groups show what growth has taken place. If each individual is measured only once, that is, if there are different people at each age, the study is *cross-sectional*. If the same individuals are measured at each successive age, the study is *longitudinal*. If some individuals do not remain available for continued study and new ones are added, the study is called *mixed longitudinal*. In a cross-sectional study, growth status at each age is investigated, and inferences regarding growth are drawn from *differences* between any groups. *Change* in status from age to age can be inferred only if the individuals at the two ages can be assumed to be comparable in all relevant ways. In a longitudinal study both growth status at each age and change in status from age to age can be investigated more precisely, because the same individuals are involved and actual growth patterns are established for individuals.

Principles of Growth

There are a number of generalizations about growth which are more apparent with respect to physical growth but which, as far as research can show, are also true for psychological growth. We will elaborate on nine such statements about growth at this point, some of them with subheadings.

Variation of Rates. Rates of growth vary from one individual to another, and they vary within one individual. An organism grows at varying rates, from one time to another. The organs and systems grow at varying rates, at different times. There is a sex difference in rates and terminals. Various group differences can be shown. It is no wonder that comparisons of growth require facts obtained by highly controlled methods.

An organism and its parts grow at rates which are different at different times. The body as a whole, as measured by height and weight, shows a pattern of velocity that is fast in infancy, moderate in the preschool period, slow during the school

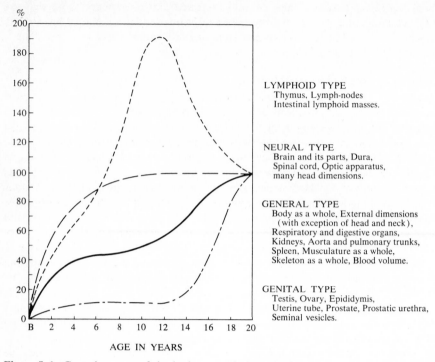

Figure 5–1. Growth curves of the body as a whole and of three types of tissue. Values at each age are computed as percentages of values for total growth.

SOURCE: Reproduced by permission from J. A. Harris, C. M. Jackson, D. G. Paterson, and R. E. Scammon, *The Measurement of Man*. Minneapolis: University of Minnesota Press, 1930.

years, and fast in the beginning of adolescence. Figure 5–1 illustrates growth velocities of different types of tissue, expressed as percentages of maturity for each age. The general type of growth, which represents not only height and weight, but muscles, skeleton, and most of the internal organs, is illustrated by a sigmoid curve, an elongated S. The brain and related tissues grow in a different pattern of velocity, very fast during the first 2 years, moderately until about 6, and very little after that. The growth curve for genital tissue is almost the reverse of that of neural tissue. The genital system grows very little during infancy and childhood and very fast in adolescence. The fourth curve in Figure 5–1 represents the lymph system which grows rapidly throughout infancy and childhood, reaches a peak just before puberty, and then decreases in size throughout adolescence.

Rates of growth vary from one individual to another. Some children are fast growers, some moderate, and some slow in regard to the number of years taken to reach maturity. Periods of fast and slow growth vary as to when they occur and for how long. One child begins the pubescent growth spurt earlier or later than another, grows faster or slower during the spurt, and finishes sooner or later.

There are sex differences in rates. Early in fetal life, girls show evidence of maturing faster than boys, especially in skeletal development. At birth, girls are four weeks ahead of boys skeletally. Boys' skeletal development is about 80 percent of that of girls' from birth to maturity [44, p. 43]. Girls are ahead of boys in dentition, as measured by eruption of permanent teeth. Although sex differences in height and weight before the preadolescent growth spurt are very slight, favoring boys, sexual maturity and its antecedent growth spurt occur in girls about two years before they do in boys. Therefore, there is a period of about two years when girls are taller and heavier than boys. At all ages, girls are more mature physiologically.

Individual Differences in Terminals. It is obvious, yet it is essential in understanding growth, to recognize that for different people maturity comes at different points. You have only to walk down the street to observe that some people grow until they are over 6 feet tall, others stop at 5 feet, and most people stop in between. Measurable mental growth stops at different times for different individuals too. The average girl reaches height and weight terminals before the average boy. Little is known about mental growth terminals.

Dynamic Interrelations in Growth. It would be surprising if different measures of growth were not related to each other. A tremendous number of studies have probed into the question of interrelationships of growth-controlling and regulating mechanisms.

Correlations between measures of growth can be between measures in the same field (physical–physical, mental–mental, and so on), or in different fields (physical–mental, mental–emotional). Skeletal development, assessed by X rays of the wrist, is at present the best indicator of physiological maturity, although if body proportions could be quantified and scaled in some manageable way, this might prove even more useful. Fat thickness in childhood is also a measure of general physiological maturity [16]. Sexual maturity and eventual height can be predicted with good accuracy from measurements of skeletal maturity. A general factor of bodily maturity operating throughout the growth period influences the child's growth as a whole, including his skeleton, size, physiological reactions, and possibly intelligence. Influencing factors of more limited scope operate independently of the general factor and of each other. One of these limited factors controls baby teeth, another permanent teeth, another the ossification centers in the skeleton and probably several others regulate brain growth. This is why various measures of physical growth have low positive correlations with each other. If there were only one controlling factor, then the different measures would presumably all correlate highly or even perfectly with one another [44].

Studies of the relation between physical and mental growth show a small but consistent positive correlation, bearing out the hypothesis of a general factor which influences all growth processes. This relationship has been studied from age 6½ onward, comparing the mental ages or academic achievement, or both, of early maturing youngsters with those of late maturers [1, 24, 39, 40, 42]. A study of children at the extremes of distributions of mental traits showed gifted boys to be significantly ahead of retarded boys in measures of physical growth [24]. A small positive correlation between mental ability and size is also found in adults [45]. As an example of the relationships between growth and personality, there is good evidence that early maturers feel more adequate and more comfortable about themselves than do late maturers [23, 31].

Optimal Tendency. An organism behaves as though it were seeking to reach its maximum potential for development in both structure and function. Even though growth is interrupted, such as in periods of inadequate food supply, the child (or organism) makes up for the lean period as soon as more and better food is available, returning to his characteristic pattern of growth. Only if the deprivation is severe, or if it occurs throughout a critical period, will he show permanent effects from it.

During the deprivation period, the organism adapts by slowing growth and cutting down on the use of energy.

All sorts of adaptive arrangements are worked out when there are interferences with the normal course of development, as though the child is determined to reach his best potential by another route when one is blocked. The child with poor eyesight seeks extra information from his other senses. Babies with a tendency toward rickets drink cod liver oil freely if permitted to, selecting their own diets from a wide variety of simple foods [7]. For northern white children, the characteristics of the home were found to be most important in determining how well the child did at school, but for southern black children the characteristics of the school were more important than those of the home. "It is as if the child drew sustenance from wherever it was available. When the home had more to offer, it became more determining; but when the school could provide more stimulation than the home, then the school became the more influential factor." [5, p. 106].

"Every breach in the normal complex of growth is filled through regenerative, substantive, or compensatory growth of some kind. . . . Insurance reserves are drawn upon whenever the organism is threatened. . . . Herein lies the urgency, the almost irrepressible quality of growth" [18, p. 165]. This principle has been recognized as working in physical realms as well as organic, where there seems to be a self-stabilizing or target-seeking property of certain systems [49].

Differentiation and Integration. From large global patterns of behavior, smaller, more specific patterns emerge. Later the small, specific patterns can be combined into new, complicated, larger patterns. For example, a photographic study of human beginnings shows an 11½ weeks' fetus reacting to being stroked on the right cheek [18, p. 25]. The fetus contracted the muscles of his neck, trunk, and shoulder, causing his whole body to bend away from the stimulus and the arms and hands to move backward. When a newborn infant is stroked on the cheek he turns toward the stimulus, pursing his lips and opening his mouth when his lips touch something. Thus he shows a new, specialized response pattern which involves a small part of his body instead of the whole. As he grows older, the rooting response changes and becomes integrated with other behavior patterns. Instead of turning toward food when he is touched near the mouth, he turns toward the breast or bottle when he sees it. His hands come into play in guiding food toward his mouth. Later he uses a knife and fork. He is integrating behavior patterns of eyes and hands with the rooting pattern, forming a smoothly functioning whole.

Examples can also be taken from purely intellectual fields, such as mathematics. There is a stage of maturity at the end of infancy when a child knows *one, two* and *a-lot-of*. At 5, he has differentiated *three* and *four* out of *a-lot-of*. By 6, numbers up to ten have true meaning. Using these differentiated concepts, he next combines them in addition and subtraction to form new and more complicated concepts. Conceptual differentiation and integration are at work as the student moves up through algebra and geometry into higher mathematics. There remains an undifferentiated sphere where each person stops in his progress in mathematics.

Developmental Direction. Certain sequences of development take place in certain directions, in reference to the body. The motor sequence takes two such directions, cephalocaudal (head to tail) and proximodistal (midline to outer extremities). Like all animals, the child grows a relatively large, complex head region early in life, whereas the tail region or posterior is small and simple. As he becomes older, the region next to the head grows more, and finally, the end region grows. Coordination follows the same direction, the muscles of the eyes coming under control first, then the neck muscles, then arms, chest, and back, and finally the legs. The motor sequence illustrates the proximodistal direction by the fact that the earliest controlled arm movements, as in reaching, are large movements, controlled mostly by shoulder muscles. Later the elbow is brought into play in reaching, then the wrist, and then the fingers.

Normative Sequence. The sequence of motor development has long been noticed and understood as one of the ways of nature. "A child must creepe ere he walke."

As the structures of the body mature in their various sequences, they function in characteristic ways, provided that the environment permits appropriate interaction. The resulting behavior patterns appear in an orderly sequence. Sequences have been described for locomotion, use of hands, language, problem solving, social behavior, and other kinds of behavior [6, 19, 20]. During the decade of the thirties, the bulk of research in child development was normative, delineating sequences of development and designating average ages for the patterns observed. The classic viewpoint, exemplified by Gesell, stressed normative sequences as an unfolding. While some lip service was paid to the necessity of an environment, development was thought of largely as an inner process. Today interaction between organism and environment is recognized as basic to development. The change in viewpoint has come about to some extent because of the broadening of areas of child study to include a variety of cultures, at home and abroad. Although child development continues to take place in orderly sequences, exceptions can be found [8]. Hence normative sequences cannot be considered as universal, but must be understood as occurring in particular kinds of environments.

Epigenesis. Growth takes place upon the foundation which is already there. New parts arise out of and upon the old. Although the organism becomes something new as it grows, it still has continuity with the past and hence shows certain consistencies over time. Through interactions with the environment, the organism continues to restructure itself throughout life, being at each moment the product of the interaction which took place in the previous moment between organism and environment. A toddler's body results from interactions of a baby's body with food, water, and air. The motor pattern of walking is derived and elaborated from creeping and standing. Writing is built from scribbling.

Critical Periods. There are certain limited times during the growth period of any organism when it will interact with a particular environment in a specific way. The result of interactions during critical periods can be especially beneficial or harmful. The prenatal period includes specific critical periods for physical growth. The first three months are critical for the development of eyes, ears, and brain, as shown by defects in children whose mothers had German measles during the first three months of pregnancy. Apparently those organs are most vulnerable to the virus of German measles when they are in their periods of rapid growth.

Experiments on vision with human and animal infants reveal critical ages for the development of visual responses, times when the infant will either show the response without experience or will learn it readily [14]. If the visual stimulus is not given at the critical age (as when baby monkeys are reared in darkness), the animal later learns the response with difficulty, or not at all.

Psychological development also shows critical periods in the sense that certain behavior patterns are acquired most readily at certain times of life. Critical periods in personality development include the period of primary socialization, when the infant makes his first social attachments [38] and develops basic trust [11]. A warm relationship with a mother figure is thought to be essential among the experiences which contribute to a sense of trust [4]. This type of critical period is probably not so final and irreversible as is a critical period for the development of an organ in the embryo. If the term "critical period" is applied to the learning of skills such as swimming and reading, then it should be understood that it signifies the most *opportune* time for learning and not the only one [30].

Stage Theories of Development

The last three principles of growth are incorporated in theories of child development which present growth occurring in stages. Each stage is created through epigenesis, behavior patterns being organized and reorganized in an orderly sequence. Thus past, present, and future development are related and can be understood as an ongoing process. Small pieces of behavior can be interpreted in terms of the stage when they occur instead of being invested with one meaning. For example, crying at 1 month of age was seen to be an active attempt to overcome interference with sucking, whereas crying at 1 year of age was found to be a passive mode of response to environmental frustration [26]. Stage theories encourage research which establishes ways of predicting future development [22].

This book is organized in stages of development, leaning heavily on two stage theories: Erikson's theory of personality growth, and Piaget's theory of the growth of intelligence. The ages which correspond with the various stages are only approximations or rough landmarks. While it is useful to be able to anchor stage concepts to some sort of chronology, it is important to realize that stages are only age-related and not age-determined. The growth principle, *variation of rates*, applies here.

Erikson's Stages. Erikson's theory might be called epigenetic in a double sense. Not only does it portray epigenetic stages, but it was built upon Freud's theory and yet is a new organization and a unique creation. Freud proposed psychosexual stages of development, each of which used a certain zone of the body for gratification of the id (the unconscious source of motives, strivings, desires, and energy). The ego, which mediates between the demands of the id, the outside world, and the superego, "represents what may be called reason and common sense, in contrast to the id, which contains the passions" [15, p. 15]. The superego or ego ideal corresponds roughly to *conscience*. Freud's psychosexual stages are: *oral*, when the mouth is the main zone of satisfaction, about the first year; *anal*, when pleasure comes from anal and urethral sensations, the second and third years; *phallic*, the third and fourth years, a time of pleasure from genital stimulation; *oedipal*, also genital but now, at 4 and 5 years, the child regards the parent of the opposite sex as a love object and the same-sex parent as a rival; *latency*, from 6 to around 11, when sexual cravings are repressed (made unconscious) and the child identifies with the parent and peers of his own sex; *puberal* when mature genital sexuality begins.

Erikson uses Freud's concepts in his theory of psychosocial development, adding to the complexity of each stage and also adding three stages above the puberal, thus dealing with adulthood as a time for growth. Progress through the stages takes place in an orderly sequence. In making his stages psychosocial as well as psychosexual, Erikson recognizes the interaction between individual and culture as contributing to personal growth. While Freud's theory has a great deal to say about pathology, Erikson's offers a guide to both illness and health of personality. For each stage, there are problems to be solved within the cultural context. Thus each stage is a critical period for development of certain attitudes, convictions, and abilities. After the satisfactory solution of each crisis, the person emerges with an increased sense of unity, good judgment and capacity to "do well" [12, p. 92]. The conflicts are never completely resolved nor the problems disposed of forever. Each stage is described with a positive and negative outcome of the crisis involved. The stages are [11, pp. 247–274]:

1. *Basic trust versus basic mistrust.* Similar to Freud's oral stage, the development of a sense of trust dominates the first year. Success means coming to trust the world, other people, and himself. Since the mouth is the main zone of pleasure, trust grows on being fed when hungry, pleasant sensations when nursing, and the growing conviction that his own actions have something to do with pleasant events. Consistent, loving care is trust-promoting. Mistrust develops when trust-promoting experiences are inadequate, when the baby has to wait too long for comfort, when he is handled harshly or capriciously. Since life is never perfect, shreds of mistrust are woven into the fabric of personality. Problems of mistrust recur and have to be solved later, but when trust is dominant, healthy personality growth takes place.

2. *Autonomy versus shame and doubt.* The second stage, corresponding to Freud's anal period, predominates during the second and third year. Holding on and letting go with the sphincter muscles symbolizes the whole problem of autonomy. The child wants to do for himself with all of his powers: his new motor skills of walking, climbing, manipulating; his mental powers of choosing and deciding. If his parents give him plenty of suitable choices, times to decide when his judgment is adequate for successful outcomes, then he grows in autonomy. He gets the feeling that he can control his body, himself, and his environment. The negative feelings of doubt and shame arise when his choices are disastrous, when other people shame him or force him in areas where he could be in charge.

3. *Initiative versus guilt.* The Oedipal part of genital stage of Freudian theory, 4 and 5 years, is to Erikson the stage of development of a sense of initiative. Now the child explores the physical world with his senses and the social and physical worlds with his questions, reasoning, imaginative, and creative powers. Love relationships with parents are very important. Conscience develops. Guilt is the opposite pole of initiative.

4. *Industry versus inferiority.* Solutions of problems of initiative and guilt bring about entrance to the stage of developing a sense of industry, the latency period of Freud. The child is now ready to be a worker and producer. He wants to do jobs well instead of merely starting them and exploring them. He practices and learns the rules. Feelings of inferiority and inadequacy result when he feels he cannot measure up to the standards held for him by his family or society.

5. *Identity versus role diffusion.* The Freudian puberal stage, beginning at the start of adolescence, involves resurgence of sexual feelings. Erikson adds to this concept his deep insights into the adolescent's struggles to integrate all the roles he has played and hopes to play, his childish body concept with his present physical development, his concepts of his own society and the value of what he thinks he can contribute to it. Problems remaining from earlier stages are reworked.

6. *Intimacy versus isolation.* A sense of identity is the condition for ability to establish true intimacy, "the capacity to commit himself to concrete affiliations and partnerships and to develop the ethical strength to abide by such commitments" [11, p. 263]. Intimacy involves understanding and allowing oneself to be understood. It may be, but need not be, sexual. Without intimacy, a person feels isolated and alone.

7. *Generativity versus self-absorption.* Involvement in the well-being and development of the next generation is the essence of generativity. While it includes being a good parent, it is more. Concern with creativity is also part of it. Adults need to be needed by the young, and unless the adults can be concerned and contributing, they suffer from stagnation.

8. *Ego integrity versus despair.* The sense of integrity comes from satisfaction with one's own life cycle and its place in space and time. The individual feels that his actions, relationships, and values are all meaningful and acceptable. Despair arises from remorseful remembrance of mistakes and wrong decisions plus the conviction that it is too late to try again.

Figure 5–2 shows the normal timing of Erikson's stages of psychosocial development. The critical period for each stage is represented by a swelling of the rope which stretches throughout life. The ropes indicate that no crisis is ever solved completely and finally, but that strands of it are carried along, to be dealt with at different levels. As one rope swells at its critical period, the other ropes are affected and interact. Solutions to identity problems involve problems in all the other stages. The metaphor of the rope can also be extended by thinking of the personalities of a family's members as being intertwined ropes. When the parents' Generativity strands are becoming dominant, the infant's Trust strand is dominant. The two ropes fit smoothly together, indicating a complementary relationship between the personalities of infant and parents.

Piaget's Stages. Figure 5–2 shows Piaget's stages in the development of intelligence. Piaget is concerned with the nature of knowledge and how it is acquired. His studies of infants and children have revealed organizations of structures by which the child comes to know the world. The structural units are *schemas*, patterns of action and/or thought. As the child matures, he uses his existing schemas to interact, transforming them through the process of equilibration. Each stage of development is an advance from the last one, built upon it by reorganizing it and adapting more closely to reality. Reorganization and adaptation go on continuously, but from one time to another the results differ from each other. Piaget has broken this series of organizations of structures into units called periods and stages. There are three periods, each of which extends the previous one, reconstructs it, and surpasses it [35, pp. 152–159]. Periods are divided into stages which have a constant sequence, no matter whether the child achieves them at a slow or fast pace. Progress through the periods and stages is affected by organic growth, exercise and experience, social interaction or equilibration. The periods are:

1. *Sensorimotor.* Lasting from birth until about 2, sensorimotor intelligence exists without language and symbols. Practical and aimed at getting results, it works through action-schemas [35, p. 4]. Beginning with the reflex patterns present at birth, the baby builds more and more complex schemas through a succession of six stages. Figure 5–2 lists the names of the stages. During this period the baby constructs a schema of the permanence of objects. He comes to know

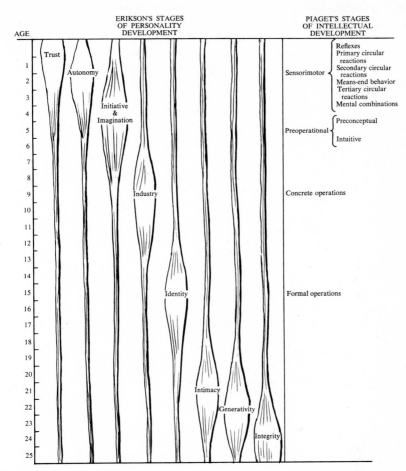

Figure 5–2. Schematic representation of Erikson's stages of psychosocial development, with names of Piaget's stages of the development of intelligence.

that things and people continue to exist even when he cannot see them and he realizes that they move when he is not looking. He learns control of his body in space. He begins to use language to imitate and to make internal representations of reality.

2. *Preoperational.* Sometimes this period, from about 2 to 7, is considered a sub-period of the whole time from 2 to 11. It is distinctly different, however, from the sensorimotor period and the period which comes around 7, the period of concrete operations. Two stages, preconceptual and intuitive thought, are included. The preoperational period is marked by the *semiotic* function and imitation. The semiotic function, often called symbolizing, is the use of an indicator or sign as distinct from the object or event to which it refers [35, pp. 52–91]. For example, the bell that announces dinner is perceived as distinct from the food but as indicating food. Achievements show much use of his new representational abilities, in deferred imitation (imitation starting after the

model has disappeared), symbolic play, drawing, mental images, and verbal representation. The child thinks that names are essential parts of the objects to which they refer. When he gives a reason, it is in terms of how he wants things to be. He sees no need to come to the same conclusions as anyone else because he does not realize the existence of viewpoints other than his own. Throughout this stage the child becomes more flexible in his thinking, more able to use past experience and to consider more than one aspect of an event at a time.

3. *Concrete operations.* The period from about 7 to 11 years of age is essentially the time when the child can think about real, concrete things in systematic ways, although he has great difficulty in thinking about abstractions. He orders, counts, classifies, and thinks in terms of cause and effect. He develops a new concept of permanence, called *conservation*, through which he realizes that amount, weight, volume, and number stay the same when outward appearances of objects or groups are changed. Although he finds it difficult to change his hypotheses, he learns to take other people's points of view and comes to feel that his reasoning and his solutions to problems should check with other people's. His thinking has become socialized.

4. *Formal operations.* The period of formal operations or logical thought begins at about 11 and continues to develop until about 15, when the individual has the mental operations for adult thinking. Instead of having to think about concrete objects, he can think and reason in purely abstract terms. He can think systematically, combining all factors in a situation so as to exhaust all possibilities. He makes hypotheses and tests them. This type of thinking is basic to logic and to the scientific method. The limitation of this stage is a confusion of what could and should be with what is practically possible. The adolescent resists the imperfections in the world when he can construct ideal arrangements in his mind.

Learning

Learning occurs when behavior changes as a result of experience. Experiments on newborn infants have demonstrated learning. As children grow older and their behavior more complex, the variables which influence behavior also increase in number and complexity. Thus different types of learning are described.

Conditioning

Conditioning, or learning by association, is the establishing of a connection between a stimulus and a response. In *classical conditioning*, the kind made famous by Pavlov, a neutral stimulus is presented with another stimulus which elicits an innate response. After several such presentations, the neutral stimulus is given without the other stimulus and the response occurs. Pavlov sounded a buzzer when he gave food to his dog. Eventually the dog salivated at the sound of the buzzer.

Operant, or instrumental, conditioning is done by rewarding the desired response whenever it occurs. Operant conditioning techniques have been developed for use in a wide variety of situations, with animal and human subjects. By rewarding small pieces of behavior, complex patterns can be built up, thus "shaping" or modifying the behavior of the subject. This technique has proved very useful in treating behavior disorders in infants, children, retardates, and the mentally ill.

Conditioning has been used to explore the abilities of infants and to show that newborn babies do learn [27]. Papoušek taught newborn babies to turn their heads to the sound of a buzzer by using a combination of classical and operant conditioning methods [32]. A bell was sounded and if the infant turned to the left, he was given milk. If he did not turn, head-turning was elicited by touching the corner of his mouth with a nipple. Then he was given milk. Newborns were slow to condition, taking an average of 18 days, whereas at 3 months, only 4 days were required and by 5 months, 3 days. Two-month-old infants learned to operate a mobile by means of head-pressing on their pillows [49]. Until recently, the problem for experimenters was to find a way of delivering rewards which would be contingent on a response that the infant was able to make. The ingenious arrangement of the mobile and an activating device in the pillow revealed not only that infants could learn instrumentally (by operant conditioning) but also that they showed enormous involvement and pleasure in the process of controlling stimulation.

Reinforcement

One of the laws of learning which Thorndike formulated in 1905 is the law of effect: "Any act which in a given situation produces satisfaction becomes associated with that situation, so that when the situation occurs, the act is more likely to recur also" [46, p. 203]. This principle is the basis of learning through reinforcement or rewards and punishment. Rewards and punishments, or positive and negative reinforcements, can be given to oneself or to others. It is not always possible to predict what will be rewarding and punishing, since previous experience and the state of the person at the time contribute to the meaning the particular reinforcement has. Havighurst has shown that rewards and punishments change with the age and maturity of the individual and that the development of the reward-punishment system varies from one culture to another [21]. These findings have important implications for educating children from minority subcultures.

Different schedules of reinforcement have different effects on learning by operant conditioning. Response strength is measured by the number of nonreinforced trials required to extinguish the behavior. Intermittent (random) reinforcement results in a much stronger response than does continuous reinforcement. This finding has practical implications for parents and teachers. For example, if the child finds that whining is never rewarded, he will soon stop whining, but if his parents give in occasionally and reward him with what he wants, then whining will be strengthened [41].

Punishment can be very effective in controlling children's behavior, but used without understanding of its complexity, punishment can have undesired effects. Important variables are timing, intensity, relationship between agent and recipient, cognitive structure (reasoning), and consistency [33].

Verbal Mediation

After the child acquires language, he grows in the ability to use words in solving problems and learning. By 5 or 6 years, the ability can be demonstrated by the child's solution of problems which are most easily done with the aid of a principle such as "Always choose the big one" or "It's the color that counts in finding the answer."

Observational Learning

Children learn many behavior patterns through watching and listening and then patterning their behavior according to what they have observed. Social learning, especially, is facilitated by modeling or imitating. Bandura and his associates have done many experiments to show the conditions under which children will learn through observation. One important finding is that children will imitate without any external reinforcement being given. That is, modeling is its own reward. Bronfenbrenner [5] has summarized information on factors affecting the modeling process, under three headings:

Characteristics of the Subject. The child must be able to perceive and to perform the actions and to be interested in observing and imitating.

Characteristics of the Stimulus Act. It is easier to imitate a complex action if it is broken into a series of components and labeled. The child then takes part in increasingly complex interactions.

Characteristics of the Model. The power of the model to induce imitation increases as:

1. The child sees the model as competent, high in status and controlling resources.
2. The child has already experienced the model as rewarding and nurturant.
3. The model is an important source of the child's comfort and support, such as parents, peers, and older children.
4. The child sees the model as similar to himself.
5. Several models show the same behavior.
6. The behavior demonstrated is typical of a group to which the child belongs or wants to belong.
7. The child sees the model rewarded for his behavior. (If he sees the model punished, he is likely not to imitate the behavior unless he gets into a situation where he does not anticipate punishment for performing the actions.)

Bronfenbrenner points out that the Soviets employ all of these principles of modeling in their educational system, where great use is made of the peer group for inducing adult-approved behavior in children. The teacher serves as a competent, high-status, resource-controlling model. The other characteristics of potent models are exemplified by peers.

Social Learning

When a child learns how to think, feel and behave as a member of a certain group, or in a particular role, the process is called social learning. *Socialization* refers to the teaching done by members of the groups or institution in order that social learning may occur in the child. Social learning occurs in people of all ages, but much of it takes place in childhood, as the individual learns appropriate values, attitudes and behavior patterns. Parents are the primary socializers. Siblings and other family members also teach. Teachers and peers are important socializing agents, and then other members of the community.

Socialization refers to both the present and the future. The child learns to behave appropriately as the child he now is, but he also learns attitudes, values and skills that he will use in the future. From interacting with his father, he learns the father role as well as the son role. Similarly, he observes his various socializers as worker, manager, host, citizen, teacher, and in all the many roles that they play in his society. His socializers make varying use of the different methods of teaching implied by the types of learning sketched above. The child learns some specific information and skills, as well as values and attitudes. Thus he is gradually socialized into his family, community and nation through a process which maintains the values and behavior patterns of that group.

Maturation

As the child's bodily structures grow, they change in size and complexity, becoming more and more the way they will be in the mature state. Bodily functions likewise change as the structures do. The whole process is called maturation. Although maturation is controlled by hereditary factors, the environment must be adequate to support it. The growth principle of normative sequence is reflected in maturation, since structures and functions mature in an orderly, irreversible sequence. Since maturation is little affected by experience, its effects are the same throughout a species. An impoverished environment slows the process of maturation more than it changes quality or sequence.

Certain behavior patterns are due to maturation more than to learning because they are relatively independent of experience. Many developmental processes involve both maturation and learning. Examples of processes which are largely maturational are the motor sequence and the emergence of language. In all but the most abnormal environments, infants go through regular sequences of raising the head, raising the chest, sitting, creeping, standing with support, and so on.

Some theories of development stress the role of maturation in determining behavior. Gesell is one of the best known of these theorists, since his writings had a great deal of influence on parents and child care authorities of his time. Gesell's descriptions of behavior stages led many parents to feel that they could do little to influence their children's behavior and that they must enjoy his good stages and wait patiently while he grew out of unattractive, annoying, or disturbing stages. While Piaget recognizes the importance of maturation, he also stresses the necessity for the child to interact, explore, and discover for himself in order to build his mental structures. Mental growth cannot be forced or hurried, however, since its counterpart is physical maturation. "Mental growth is inseparable from physical growth: the maturation of the nervous and endoctrine systems, in particular, continues until the age of sixteen" [35, p. vii].

Evolutionary Adaptation

The behavior patterns which develop through maturation can be traced back in the history of the species or the phylum. These fixed action patterns evolved as the animal adapted to a certain environment. *Ethology* is the study of the relation between animal behavior and environment. Ethology has influenced the study of human development, offering insight into certain kinds of behavior which cannot be explained as learning or fully understood as maturation. Lorenz pointed out the implications of ethology for understanding certain forms of human behavior [28]. Bowlby has integrated psychoanalytic theory with ethology [4]. Ainsworth [2] has done extensive research on attachment behavior, the main focus of the ethological approach to human development.

The adaptive behavior pattern becomes fixed in form, appearing as an innate skill in every member of a species, even though he has not had opportunities to learn [9]. A specific stimulus from the environment activates the particular behavior pattern, as though it were a key, unlocking the mechanism. Thus the behavior is sometimes called an *innate response mechanism*, or IRM. For example, a toad's catching response is released by a small, moving object, a 9-week-old gosling gives an intense fear reaction to his first sight of a hawk, and a stickleback fish will attack a red spot that resembles the red underbelly of another stickleback.

Bowlby points out that the environment to which a species is adapted is the environment in which it evolved into its present form [4, p. 59]. Most likely, when man first emerged as a distinct species, he lived by hunting and gathering in a savannah environment, much like today's most primitive societies and not unlike the ground-dwelling primates [2]. Mother–infant reciprocal behavior was adapted to protecting the infant so as to insure his survival. The baby's unlearned, spontaneous patterns of crying, clinging, and sucking brought him (and still bring him) into contact with the mother. Other aspects of attachment behavior, maturing a little later, serve to maintain and strengthen the contacts with the mother, who was (and still is) adapted or genetically programmed to respond with specific action patterns. In the urban environment of today, close physical contact of mother and baby is not necessary for protecting the baby from predators, but babies still behave as though it were and mothers still respond to their infants' behavior with innate action patterns. Closeness of mother and baby has other advantages, however, in terms of normal development.

Human behavior is largely labile, with relatively few fixed action patterns. The individual can make many adaptations, can learn a great deal. He is equipped with a few innate behavior mechanisms, such as attachment behavior and certain patterns of fear behavior, which have various kinds of value.

Heredity

While most students of child development will study the mechanisms of heredity in a biology course, we include a brief account here. After all, the mechanisms of heredity are what start the child developing and what control the course of development.

Biological Inheritance

The human being is composed of two main types of cells. By far the larger number of cells are the *body* cells. These are the cells which compose the skeleton, skin, kidneys, heart, and so on. A minority of cells are the *germ* cells. In the male, germ cells are called *spermatazoa* (the singular is spermatazoon), usually shortened to *sperm*: in the female, the germ cells are *ova* (the singular is *ovum*).

Each body cell is composed of several different parts, the most important of which for our present discussion are the *chromosomes*, of which there are 46, arranged in 23 pairs. The sizes and shapes of the chromosomes can be determined by viewing a prepared cell through an electron microscope. Twenty-two of the pairs of chromosomes are composed of two highly similar chromosomes, though each pair differs in certain respects from every other pair. These 22 pairs are similar

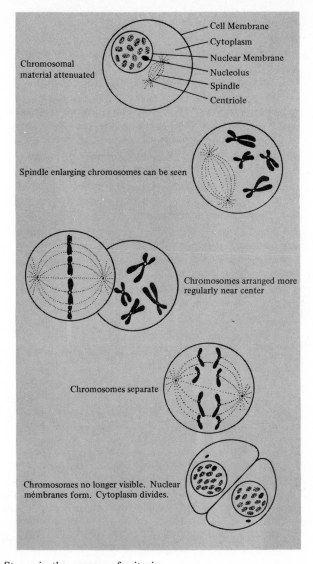

Figure 5–3. Stages in the process of mitosis.

Source: Adapted from P. A. Moody, *Genetics of Man*, Figure 3.2, p. 28. W. W. Norton, 1967.

in males and females. In males, the twenty-third pair is composed of two chromosomes which are unequal in size. The larger one is an *X chromosome*; the smaller is a *Y chromosome*. In females, the twenty-third pair is composed of two X chromosomes. When, in the course of growth, a body cell divides to form two new cells, it goes through the process of *mitosis*. The result of mitosis is that each of the new cells has exactly the same kind and number of chromosomes as the first cell had before it divided. Figure 5–3 shows the process of mitosis.

DNA, a substance in the chromosomes, is the carrier of the genetic code which transmits characteristics from one generation to the next. Figure 5–4 shows a

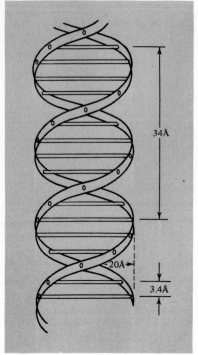

Figure 5–4. DNA takes the form of a double helix.

SOURCE: Adapted from G. W. Burns, *The Science of Genetics*. New York: The Macmillan Company, 1969, Figure 14–9, p. 258.

model of the DNA molecule, in the shape of a double helix or spiral ladder. The genes, carriers of specific instructions for growth, are arranged in linear order on the spirals. The two spirals can come apart like a zipper. Then each half produces another half.

Dominant and Recessive Genes. A recent story [43], which might be called *science prediction* rather than *science fiction*, went like this: a young couple had been quietly holding hands in a secluded corner of the campus. Then one of them said, "Let's match cards." Each pulled out a printed card containing a few holes. They put one on top of the other. None of the holes matched. They embraced happily. Like most human beings, each carried a few dangerous recessive genes out of the thousand or more which can cause birth defects. Since it takes a recessive gene from each parent to produce a characteristic which does not show in either parent, the young couple could safely plan to have children. Or if not with complete assurance, at least they would know that they were not endangering their future children as far as their own dangerous recessives were concerned. Suppose two of the holes had matched. Each of the couple was carrying a recessive gene for cystic fibrosis. For each conception, chances would be one in four for a child with two recessives and hence having cystic fibrosis, two in four for a child carrying one recessive, like the parents, and not showing the defect, and one in four for a normal child with two normal genes. And suppose they conceived a defective embryo. It could be diagnosed early in pregnancy and aborted, if they so chose.

Although at the moment when this is being written, the story is only prediction, the technology on which it is based is of the present. Many physical characteristics, including a large number of defects, are inherited according to simple Mendelian law, as illustrated in our story. Some other defects, such as color-blindness, are sex linked, which means that they are dominant in the male and recessive in the female. A male shows the defect when he carries only one gene for it, but the female does not suffer unless she has two such genes.

Heredity works in more complicated ways, also. Genes work in concert with one another and with the environment. The mechanisms of *crossing over* and *independent assortment* add enormously to the variety of genetic combinations possible. Genes "turn on" and off at various times during the life cycle. For example, the control of sexual maturation is considerably influenced by heredity.

Gene Blends. Many characteristics are the results of more than one pair of genes. Skin color in human beings is such a characteristic. It is not determined in all-or-none way, as is seed color in peas. Rather, in spite of popular belief to the contrary, a child's skin color is almost never darker than the skin of the darker parent, nor lighter than the skin of the lighter parent. If the child's skin is darker than either parent's, it is only a shade darker. At least two pairs of genes are considered to be active in determining skin color; there may be three or more.

Standing height is another human characteristic which is the result of many different genes working at least in part in a literally additive way, although blending of the kind which determines skin color may also be operating. A human being's height is the sum of the lengths of many different bones and many pieces of cartilage. Each bone's length is probably determined by one or more genes, and varies somewhat independently of the length of every other bone. Height is therefore a *polygenic* trait. (In addition, of course, the variation in heights of a group of individuals is affected by environmental factors such as diet and disease.)

Meiosis. Although each individual receives the chromosomes from germ cells of the parents, the offspring of the same parents do not receive identical chromosomes. The explanation of this difference between brothers and sisters lies in the process of *miosis*, the formation of germ cells, sperm, and ova.

Figure 5–5 shows the development of sperm which contain only 2 single chromosomes, since to show 23 would be unnecessarily complicated. In the diagram the primordial germ cell, the *spermatogonium*, is shown as containing two pairs of chromosomes. In the process of meiosis, the spermatogonium divides into two cells called *secondary spermatocytes*, each of which has one of the members of each pair of chromosomes. Each chromosome is composed of two *chromatids*. Each spermatocyte divides into two *spermatids*, each of which has one of the chromatids from the eight chromatids which are shown to have been in the original spermatogonium. From each spermatid develops a sperm. Therefore, from each male primordial germ cell result four sperm, each containing 23 single chromosomes.

The development of each ovum is similar to the development of each sperm, except that from each female primordial germ cell (called an *obgonium*) there result not four ova, but one. But it, like each sperm, contains 23 chromatids from among the 92 chromatids present in the obgonium. Since the obgonium begins meiosis with two X chromosomes, every ovum contains an X chromosome. The spermatogonium, which begins meiosis with one X and one Y chromosome, results in four sperms, two of which contain an X apiece and two a Y. If an X-bearing sperm fertilizes an ovum, the new individual will have two X chromosomes, and will be female. If a Y-bearing sperm fertilizes an ovum, the new individual will have one Y chromosome and one X chromosome, and will be a male.

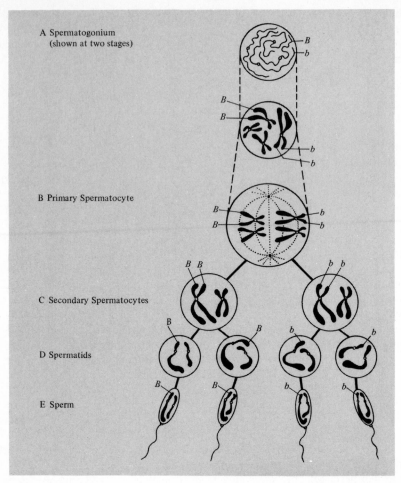

A Spermatogonium
(shown at two stages)

B Primary Spermatocyte

C Secondary Spermatocytes

D Spermatids

E Sperm

Figure 5–5. Meiosis provides the mechanism by which a heterozygous male produces sperm of two kinds: half of them containing the dominant gene, *B*, half of them containing its recessive allele, *b*.

Source: Adapted from P. A. Moody, *Genetics of Man*, Figure 3.7, p. 34. W. W. Norton, 1967.

In the same way, if one parent has two genes for any trait, each offspring will receive from that parent the same kind of genetic material as any other offspring. But if a parent has unlike genes for a trait, half of the offspring (other things being equal, which they often are not) will receive one kind of gene (e.g., the dominant gene) and half will receive the other. The process of meiosis explains part of the genetic difference between brothers and sisters, including the fact that a given father and mother are likely to have both sons and daughters.

Behavior Genetics

Not only are body form and coloration inherited from generation to generation, but different kinds of functioning are, also. The ability to roll the tongue is one of these functions. One of the authors of this book (MSS) can roll her tongue; RCS cannot. All three of their daughters can. Since this ability is known to be a dominant characteristic, we know that RCS is homozygous recessive. Some of our grand-children may turn out to be like Grandpa. Our daughters are heterozygous for this characteristic. If their husbands are also heterozygous, we could predict that our grandchildren will be tongue-rollers in the ratio of 3:1.

(Incidentally, the genetic ratios hold only for large populations, not for small samples. Since we expect that the total number of our grandchildren will be six, they might all be tongue-rollers.)

The inheritance of certain defects in mental functioning can be described in terms of chromosomes [29]. Down's syndrome (Mongolism), a type of mental retardation accompanied by distinctive physical anomalies, occurs when an extra chromosome is attached to the chromosome numbered 21, making a total of 47 instead of the normal 46 chromosomes. Klinefelter's syndrome, incomplete sexual development along with lowered intelligence in males, involves two X chromosomes in addition to a Y. Turner's syndrome, in which females have only one X chromo-some, includes defective spatial abilities. Males with an XXY condition are more likely than normals to be tall, aggressive, and mentally defective.

The transmission of all-or-none traits, such as tongue-rolling and Down's syn-drome, can be explained by basic rules of genetics. When many genes are involved and when the characteristic is highly complex, such as intelligence or emotional stability, *heritability* is studied by *quantitative genetics*. Heritability of a charac-teristic can be estimated by comparing correlations between groups of known genetic similarity. Since the heredity of animals can be controlled, they can be used for experimental work in heredity. In working with humans, investigators have to use groups which vary in known degrees, from identical twins to unrelated persons. Results of many studies on inheritance of intelligence and personality indicate that there are indeed significant hereditary components in both [47].

Intelligence. Figure 5–6 shows median (average) sizes of correlations between measured intelligence of persons of different degrees of genetic similarity [13]. Unrelated persons living apart show no correlation (− .01). Identical twins reared together are very similar (.87). Identical twins reared apart are more closely correlated than those in any other relationship group (.75). Intelligence of parents and children correlates significantly (.50). Heredity components have been found in the following intellectual abilities, listed in order of weight of influence by heredity: word fluency, verbal ability (including spelling and grammar), spatial ability, clerical speed and accuracy, reasoning, number ability, and memory [47].

Personality. There is evidence for heritability of several dimensions of per-sonality, the main ones of which are usual activity level; expression of emotions frankly in interpersonal relationships; degree of planning ahead rather than behaving impulsively [47]; extraversion–introversion [37].

Age Trends. Correlations between intelligence of children and parents are low negative in early infancy, zero at around a year, low positive at the end of the second year, and moderate (.5) in early childhood and thereafter [10]. This pattern is true of children and parents living apart, as well as of those living together. Correlations between stature of parents and children also increase throughout the early preschool years [16].

Sex Differences in Heritability. There is evidence that girls are controlled by heredity more than boys are, most likely because the X chromosome, of which girls have two and boys one, carries more hereditary material than does the Y

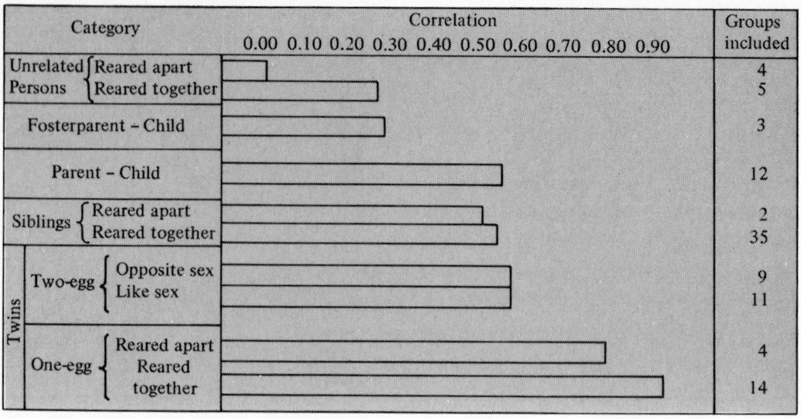

Category	Correlation 0.00 0.10 0.20 0.30 0.40 0.50 0.60 0.70 0.80 0.90	Groups included
Unrelated Persons — Reared apart		4
Unrelated Persons — Reared together		5
Fosterparent – Child		3
Parent – Child		12
Siblings — Reared apart		2
Siblings — Reared together		35
Twins — Two-egg — Opposite sex		9
Twins — Two-egg — Like sex		11
Twins — One-egg — Reared apart		4
Twins — One-egg — Reared together		14

Figure 5–6. Median correlation coefficients for intelligence test scores showing degree of similarity between performances of people of varying degrees of relatedness under different and similar environmental conditions.
SOURCE: Data from L. Erlenmeyer-Kimling and L. F. Jervik. *Science*, 1964, **142**, 1477–79.

chromosome. After age 13, measurements of stature correlate more highly for father–daughter than for father–son and for mother–daughter than for mother–son [17]. Data from the Berkeley Growth Study indicated that girls' intellectual functioning is more genetically determined than boys and that the impact of the environment is greater upon boys than upon girls [3]. High school boys and girls, studied by a twin control method, showed stronger heritability for girls than for boys on a battery of tests of achievements and aptitudes [25].

Summary

A baby, like all organisms, interacts continuously with his environment. He and his parents influence each other and change each other. Child development is described from different theoretical viewpoints, offering different ways of interpreting and understanding. Six types of interaction are described briefly in this chapter.

Equilibration is a process of regulation which the organism carries on in physical and intellectual modes. Homeostasis is the maintaining of the organism within certain physical limits such as those of chemical content and temperature. Psychological equilibrium involves regulating stimulation to an optimal level and also progressing toward more complex levels of mental organization. Piaget's notion of equilibration includes two complementary processes, accommodation and assimilation. Assimilation is the taking in and using of material from the environment; accommodation is changing the schemas to adjust to reality as it is experienced. Equilibration is enjoyable, as shown by children's curiosity and exploration, looking for problems and incongruities to be solved.

Growth and development, terms which can be used interchangeably, refer to increasing size and complexity of structure and function. The following principles or generalizations hold for many kinds of growth and development: variation in rates between individuals, between sexes, within the organism and of the organism in time; individuals differ in time of reaching maturity; measures of growth are interrelated; organisms behave as though they were seeking to achieve maximum potential, searching for substitute sources of nurture when the usual ones are not available; specific patterns of behavior are differentiated out of larger, global patterns, and then specific patterns are integrated into larger, complex patterns; certain sequences of physical and motor development take place in directions (cephalo-caudal and proximo-distal) in relation to the body; certain behavior patterns mature in orderly sequences; growth is based on a foundation, the organism interacting with the environment to transform itself; critical periods are specific times when the organism will interact with the environment in specific ways which may be harmful or beneficial.

Stage theories, including Erikson's and Piaget's, explain development as proceeding epigenetically, being reorganized on more and more complex levels which occur in an orderly sequence. Erikson's psychosocial theory uses Freud's psychosexual stages as a base and develops a theory of the healthy personality. The eight stages of man's development involve the development of basic trust versus basic mistrust; autonomy versus doubt and shame; initiative versus guilt; industry versus inferiority; identity versus role diffusion; intimacy versus isolation; generativity versus self-absorption; ego integrity versus despair. Piaget shows how children develop intelligence in the process of dealing with the world and coming to know it. His sensorimotor period, spanning infancy, is subdivided into six stages. The preoperational period, from around 2 to 7, includes the stages of preconceptual and intuitive thought. The period of concrete operations comprises the school years, and the period of formal operations (logical thought), adolescence.

Learning is the change in behavior due to experience. Different methods of learning include classical conditioning, when a neutral stimulus becomes associated with a response due to pairing of the neutral stimulus with a stimulus which normally elicits the response; operant conditioning, when a response is established as a result of rewarding it, a method used widely for shaping behavior; verbal mediation, the use of words in problem solving or self-instruction; observational learning, a complex process of imitating some of the behavior of other people, according to the characteristics of the child himself, the stimulus, and the model. Reinforcement includes rewards and punishments, both of which operate in complex ways.

Maturation is the growth toward maturity of the body, its structures, and functions—growth which is relatively independent of experience. Most developmental processes involve both maturation and learning.

Evolutionary adaptation accounts for certain behavior patterns which mature quickly into a complex and relatively fixed form. The environment to which a species is adapted is the one in which it emerged in its present form. Attachment behavior in the human infant is most easily understood in terms of evolutionary adaptation.

Hereditary characteristics in human beings are sometimes the result of single pairs of genes, but often of numbers of genes working together. Most human beings carry several dangerous recessive genes, which will do no harm unless matched with the same dangerous genes from the partner in reproduction. Birth defects can be predicted on a chance basis, and some with certainty. An ovum contains an X chromosome, a sperm either an X or a Y. The source of sex differences is in the X and Y chromosomes, including differences in heritability, females being more influenced by heredity. These functions include intelligence and many of its components and also certain personality dimensions. Correlations between physical and mental measurements of parents and children increase during the preschool period.

References

1. Abernethy, E. M. Relationships between physical and mental growth. *Mono. Soc. Res. Child Devel.*, 1936, **1**:7.
2. Ainsworth, M. D. S. Object relations, dependency and attachment: A theoretical review of the infant–mother relationship. *Child Devel.*, 1969, **40**, 969–1025.
3. Bayley, N., & Schaefer, E. S. Correlations of maternal and child behaviors with the development of mental abilities: Data from the Berkeley growth study. *Mono. Soc. Res. Child Devel.*, 1964, **29**:6.
4. Bowlby, J. *Attachment and loss.* Vol. I: *Attachment.* London: Hogarth, 1969.
5. Bronfenbrenner, U. *Two worlds of childhood.* New York: Russell Sage Foundation, 1970.
6. Bühler, C. *The first year of life.* New York: Day, 1930.
7. Davis, C. M. Self-selection of diet by newly weaned infants. *Am. J. Dis. Child.*, 1928, **36**, 651–679.
8. Dennis, W. Causes of retardation among institutional children: Iran. *J. Genet. Psychol.*, 1960, **96**, 46–60.
9. Eibl-Eibesfeldt, I. Concepts of ethology and their significance in the study of human behavior. In H. W. Stevenson, E. H. Hess, & H. L. Rheingold (Eds.), *Early behavior.* New York: Wiley, 1967, pp. 127–146.
10. Eichorn, D. H. Developmental parallels in the growth of parents and their children. In *Newsletter of Division on Devel. Psychol.*, Washington, D. C.: *American Psychological Association*, Spring, 1970.
11. Erikson, E. H. *Childhood and society.* New York: Norton, 1963.
12. Erikson, E. H. *Identity, youth and crisis.* New York: Norton, 1968.
13. Erlenmeyer-Kiling, L. K., & Jarvik, L. F. Genetics and intelligence: A review. *Sci.*, 1964, **142**, 1477–1479.
14. Fantz, R. L. The origin of form perception. *Sci. Am.*, 1961, **204**, 66–72.
15. Freud, S. *The ego and the id.* New York: Norton, 1962.
16. Garn, S. M. Fat thickness and developmental status in childhood and adolescence. *J. Am. Medic. Assoc.*, 1960, **99**, 746–751.
17. Garn, S. M. Body size and its implications. In L. W. Hoffman & M. L. Hoffman (Eds.), *Review of child development research.* Vol. 2. New York: Russell Sage Foundation, 1966, pp. 529–561.
18. Gesell, A. *The embryology of behavior.* New York: Harper, 1945.
19. Gesell, A., & Thompson, H. *The psychology of early growth.* New York: Macmillan, 1938.
20. Halverson, H. M. An experimental study of prehension in infants by means of systematic cinema records. *Genet. Psychol. Mono.*, 1931, **10**, 107–286.
21. Havighurst, R. J. Minority subcultures and the law of effect. *Am. Psychol.*, 1970, **25**, 313–322.
22. Hunt, J. M., & Bayley, N. Explorations into patterns of mental development and prediction from the Bayley scales of infant development. Paper presented at the Fifth Minnesota Symposium on Child Psychology, Minneapolis, May 2, 1970.

23. Jones, M. C., & Mussen, P. H. Self-conceptions, motivations, and inter-personal attitudes of early- and late-maturing girls. *Child Devel.*, 1958, **29**, 492–501.

24. Ketcham, W. A. Relationship of physical and mental traits in intellectually gifted and mentally retarded boys. *Merrill-Palmer Quart.*, 1960, **6**, 171–177.

25. Klinger, R. Sex differences in heritability assessed by the Washington pre-college test battery of achievement/aptitude measures. Paper presented at the meeting of the Society for Research in Child Development, Santa Monica, Calif., March 27, 1969.

26. Lewis, M. The meaning of a response, or why researchers in infant behavior should be oriental metaphysicians. *Merrill-Palmer Quart.*, 1967, **13**, 7–18.

27. Lipsitt, L. P. Learning in the human infant. In H. W. Stevenson, E. H. Hess, & H. L. Rheingold (Eds.), *Early behavior.* New York: Wiley, 1967, pp. 225–247.

28. Lorenz, K. *King Solomon's ring.* New York: Crowell, 1952.

29. McClearn, G. E. Behavioral genetics: An overview. *Merrill-Palmer Quart.*, 1968, **14**, 9–24.

30. McGraw, M. B. Major challenges for students of infancy and early childhood. *Am. Psychol.*, 1970, **25**, 754–756.

31. Mussen, P. H., & Jones, M. C. The behavior-inferred motivations of late- and early-maturing boys. *Child Devel.*, 1958, **29**, 61–67.

32. Papoušek, H. Experimental studies of appetitional behavior in human new-borns and infants. In H. W. Stevenson, E. H. Hess, & H. L. Rheingold (Eds.), *Early behavior.* New York: Wiley, 1967, pp. 249–277.

33. Parke, R. D. Effectiveness of punishment as an interaction of intensity, timing, age, nurturance and cognitive structuring. *Child Devel.*, 1969, **40**, 213–235.

34. Piaget, J. *Six psychological studies.* New York: Random House, 1967.

35. Piaget, J., & Inhelder, B. *The psychology of the child.* New York: Basic Books, 1969.

36. Sackett, G. P. Effects of rearing conditions upon the behavior of rhesus monkeys (Macca Mulatta). *Child Devel.*, 1965, **36**, 855–868.

37. Scarr, S. Social introversion-extraversion as a heritable response. *Child Devel.*, 1969, **40**, 823–832.

38. Scott, J. P. Early experience and the organization of behavior. Belmont, Calif.: Brooks/Cole. 1968.

39. Shuttleworth, F. K. The physical and mental growth of girls and boys age six to nineteen in relation to age at maximum growth. *Mono. Soc. Res. Child Devel.*, 1939, **4**:3.

40. Simon, M. D. Body configuration and school readiness. *Child Devel.*, 1959, **30**, 493–512.

41. Stevenson, H. W. Learning and reinforcement effects. In T. D. Spencer & N. Kass (Eds.), *Perspectives in child psychology.* New York: McGraw-Hill, 1970, pp. 325–355.

42. Stone, C. P., & Barker, R. G. Aspects of personality and intelligence in post-menarcheal and premenarcheal girls of the same chronological age. *J. Comp. Psychol.*, 1937, **23**, 439–455.

43. Sullivan, W. If we master the gene. *New York Times*, June 14, 1970.

44. Tanner, J. M. *Education and physical growth.* London: University of London Press, 1961.

45. Tanner, J. M. Relation of body size, intelligence test scores and social circumstances. In P. Mussen, J. Langer, & M. Covington (Eds.), *Trends and issues in developmental psychology.* New York: Holt, Rinehart and Winston, 1969.
46. Thorndike, E. L. *The elements of psychology.* New York: Seiler, 1905.
47. Vandenberg, S. G. Human behavior genetics: Present status and suggestions for future research. *Merrill-Palmer Quart.*, 1969, **15**, 121–154.
48. Walter, G. Comments in J. M. Tanner & B. Inhelder (Eds.), *Discussions on child development.* Vol. I. New York: International Universities, 1953.
49. Watson, J. S., & Ramey, C. T. Reactions to response-contingent stimulation in early infancy. Unpublished paper. University of California at Berkeley, 1970.

Readings in
An Overview of Human Life and Growth

In an earlier and possibly in some ways happier time, man was considered the final and triumphant item of creation, the master and user of other living things. Even the early evolutionary biologists considered that man stood at the apex of evolution; they did not seem aware of the possibility that the process of evolution might continue, resulting in the appearance of new species. They seemed even less aware of the possibility that the evolutionary process of man resulted in a creature who had within him the seeds of his own destruction, like the sabre-toothed tiger, whose overdeveloped canine teeth prevented him from ingesting his prey.

Ecology is the branch of biology which studies the relationship of living things to their environment, including other living things. Recently ecologists have included man as the subject of their study. In general the results of their investigations have been frightening. Especially in North America man is seen as a fouler of his environment—air, water, and soil—to such an extent that ecologists say that if present trends go unchecked, man may make his continued existence impossible.

In the first article in this chapter William W. Ballard, a biologist, describes some of the facts about man's evolutionary development and speculates about the future. He makes the important distinction between man as a species and men as individuals who together make up the species. Each individual has characteristics of the species which have arisen during the course of evolution, but each individual has his own personal history, during which he has learned some ways of behaving that may be, in the long run, maladaptive for the species.

Lawrence K. Frank, the author of the second article, gave form, direction, and impetus to the field of child development. Frank's genius provided a flow of ideas for research, education, and theory. He was responsible for establishing child development centers, the parent education movement, and interdisciplinary research. In the article presented here, Frank shows his characteristic warmth and wonder while analyzing the growth processes at work in infants. He shows how the child elaborates his individuality through interaction. In the terms used by Ballard in the first article, Frank shows how the "second computer" begins, based on the beginnings of the "first computer."

Erikson and Piaget, the authors of the third and fourth selections, are also primarily concerned with the development of the "second computer." But both are explicit in their statement that their theories are based on biology. Although both are dealing with psychological material, they start from biological characteristics of man.

The epigenetic theory of Erik H. Erikson is represented by the next essay, taken from his book Identity, Youth and Crisis. *An artist, teacher, and philosopher thoroughly trained in Freudian psychoanalysis, Erikson has made enormous contributions to the field of child development. His theory is built upon Freudian theory, which he extends and develops into a way of understanding and describing the healthy personality throughout life. Erikson describes stages of personality growth, showing for each one a relation of personality to bodily development and to interaction with the culture. Each stage is derived from and built upon the one preceding it. The organization of this book is shaped by Erikson's stages in childhood and adolescence. The content is influenced by his thinking.*

Jean Piaget, the world-famous Swiss psychologist, is the author of the fourth piece in this section. Piaget is primarily a genetic epistemologist, a scientist-philosopher who investigates the production of knowledge. He has developed a comprehensive theory of the mental structures through which human beings build their concept of reality and deal with it. Piaget has stimulated psychological research all over the world. Americans have produced hundreds of studies in response to his theories and findings. Like Erikson's theory of personality development, Piaget's account of the growth of intelligence is epigenetic and interactional. Piaget's theory is very compatible with a child development point of view, because the child's mind is seen as resulting from biologically given beginnings, actively engaged with the environment.

In the concluding selection in this chapter, Myrtle McGraw admonishes students of child development, particularly students of the development of very young children, that those who study growth need to be aware of the complexity and interrelatedness of their subject matter. To those who make applications of research knowledge about children she makes a plea for the careful consideration of terms, the continuous viewing of the child as a multifaceted organism, and the importance of adult guidance which changes synchronously with the child's development.

The Rise and Fall of Humanity

William W. Ballard

The reading which follows is the last part of a lecture titled "The Rise and Fall of Humanity." In the first part Ballard summarizes the development of living things during the course of 4 billion years of earth history, the accelerating growth of knowledge in the last few thousand years, and the serious threats to man's continued existence which have stemmed from this knowledge. Basically, Ballard says, the present crisis has arisen because there are too many people on the earth and they are demanding more than the earth can provide. These things have happened because man as a species of animal is composed of men as individuals.

To maximize the amount of life that can be supported in a given ecosystem, a large number of species of plants, animals and decomposers are brought into

Reprinted from *Dartmouth Alumni Magazine*, 1970, 62 (6), 60–64. By permission of the author, the Dartmouth Alumni College, and the *Dartmouth Alumni Magazine*.

balance, each occupying its own niche and following its own instructions to make the best of the things available to it while contributing to the flow of energy and the recycling of materials. If one species in the ecosystem gets out of balance the whole community develops an instability that may either result in an irreversible change in its character, or in the control or rejection of the destabilizing element.

The human species has been manipulating its environment since the invention of agriculture, favoring the plants and animals that serve it for food, repressing or even exterminating others. Where this was overdone—e.g., Mesopotamia, the Near East, Yucatan—ghost cities and records of dead cultures remain to show how powerfully nature can strike back. Quite recently we have begun to use the treasure trove of fossil fuels to grow the food to satisfy the multiplying demands of our own population, and we congratulate ourselves on having temporarily freed ourselves from the normal restrictions of the natural world. It is a dangerous game we are playing.

No good asking why the human *species* takes these risks. A species is an invention of the mind, a generalization. Only human *individuals* actually walk and breathe and make decisions and it is the collection of individuals who have been doing what I say the species has been doing. What went wrong with human individuals, that they have gotten their species and their environment into such a mess? The other face of this question is, what is an individual supposed to be doing, and within what limits is he supposed to be held?

The Primary Computer   To simplify, I shall restrict the latter question to animals rather than plants or decomposers. I shall pick animals that are not on a rampage, animals that have (so far as we can tell) no conscious reasoning ability, no thoughts, loyalties, hopes or faiths. Some kind of earthworm or some frog will do. I assume that whatever one of these animals does, any choice that it makes, is determined by its inherited computer system. It receives from its ancestors a scanning mechanism which reports what all the circumstances around and inside it are at the moment. This information is checked against an inherited memory encoded in its central nervous system. The computer then not only orders up the strategy and tactics that had met that sort of situation successfully before, but directs what every cell, what every organ, what the whole earthworm or frog must be doing to contribute to that response. (Directions for unsuccessful responses are not encoded in this primary computer, because they simply are not inherited.)

To see what this genetic computer requires the individual worm or frog to do, let us follow his life history, watching him obey and reconstructing from what he does the nature of the commands.

1. As a member of a bisexual species he (or she) starts as a fertilized egg, a single diploid individual with unique heterozygous genic individuality. First, *he develops*. Since the fertilized egg is insulated to a degree from the outside world, his computer works at first mostly on internal information. It refers to the inherited memory in the chromosomes and brings out instructions of various intricate sorts to the ultrastructures of the cell, programmed so that the cell divides into two, then four, then eight cells . . . until the word gets back to the multiplied computers in the multiplied cells that it is time to activate their

inherited instructions for differentiation. Tissues and organs are formed, in such sorts and such patterns as have enabled the species to survive so far. The new individual acquires the sensory and neural apparatus for bringing in more and more information from the outside, and this is referred to the more and more specialized computer developing out of the inherited instructions, in a central nervous system (in the case of a frog, a brain and spinal cord). He begins to move about, respire, feed, excrete, defend himself, in directions and at rates calculated to be appropriate to the sensed state of affairs from moment to moment. This is quite a trick for a self-built computer to bring off, and as an embryologist I wish I understood more of how it is done.

2. The young earthworm or pollywog, having broken loose from its protective envelopes and used up its dowry of yolk, is next under orders to *reach adulthood*. He recognizes dangers and opportunities by continually referring the information flowing in from his sensory apparatus to his inherited memory. He certainly has not learned his behavioral responses from his parents, never having met them. It is the inherited computer which tells him what to do from one millisecond to the next. He survives or not, partly by luck but also partly according to whether his own inherited variant of the species-specific computer will deliver the right answers to the problems of his own day and place. (The *species* survives by offering up enough varieties so that some individuals will have what the new situations demand, the wastage of the other individuals being a necessary part of the cost. No other way has yet been discovered for meeting the demands of an unpredictable future, i.e. winning a game the rules for which have not yet been written.)

3. Our earthworm or frog, if lucky, finds himself a sexually mature individual, with his instructions to reproduce now turned on. These instructions, activated by seasonal or other environmental signals, operate upon particular genes, particular cells, particular organs, and particular behavioral mechanisms set off through the nervous system. Without knowing it, much less knowing why, the animal seeks out a mate, copulates, and shares in the production of fertilized eggs that bring us again to phase 1 of the cycle.

4. Having blindly and without thought followed his instructions to (1) develop, (2) make do, survive, gain strength, and (3) reproduce, our earthworm or frog subsequently (4) *dies*. It is the ancient law. So far as the interests of the individual are concerned, it is absurd.

But now how about man? How unique is he? Does he not learn by experience and education, manage his own life, consciously determine what jobs he shall tackle, what ends he shall serve? My argument that he too is run by an inherited computer program rests partly on the observed fact that (1) he develops, (2) he makes every effort to reach maturity, (3) if lucky enough he sets the cycle going again, and (4) he dies. There is nothing unique about that. Experience, learning, individual preferences serve only for minor embellishments.

I select one case to illustrate that an animal's program is mostly inherited. Four to six weeks after fertilization (depending on temperature) a salamander embryo will have used up its yolk and must by then have acquired an elaborate repertoire of locomotor, hunting-sensory, food-grabbing and swallowing behavior to keep itself fed and growing. Does the individual learn this behavior by trial and error? No. Starting a day before any of his muscles were mature enough to contract, you can rear him in a dilute anesthetic solution until he has reached the feeding stage. Put him back into pond water, and in twenty minutes the anesthetic will have worn off and he is swimming, hunting, grabbing and swallowing like a normal tadpole. One is seeing here the computer-controlled maturation of a computer-controlled behavior. No practice, no learning. The individual within which this remarkable apparatus matures is an expendable pawn, and the apparatus is not for his enjoyment of life, it is to keep the species going.

The Secondary Computer   There is such an inherited program in the human individual, but there is much more. The baby does not so much learn to walk as to develop the inherited capacity to walk; but then he can learn a dance that no man has ever danced before, he can paint a picture with a brush clasped between his toes. During late fetal life and his first six or eight years he gradually matures a second computer system superimposed on, controlling and almost completely masking the ancient frog-type computer. The evolutionary history of this new device is traceable back to, and in some respects beyond, the time of origin of the modern mammals 70 million or more years ago. It has progressed farthest in particular mammalian orders—the carnivores, hoofed animals, bats, whales and primates, and least in the egg-laying mammals and marsupials.

The new trend has worked certain real advantages, and has been kept under reasonable control, in the higher mammals, but it is my strong suspicion that its over-development in man is the root of our trouble. Like the dinosaurs, we contain in our own structure the reason why we will have to go. Robinson Jeffers[1] said it: "We have minds like the fangs of those forgotten tigers, hypertrophied and terrible."

Up to a point, the development of brain and spinal cord follows the same course in frog and man. Sense organs, cranial and spinal nerves, principal subdivisions of the brain, basic fiber tract systems, all form in strictly comparable fashion in both. But the adult human brain is a far different thing from the adult frog brain. It continues the multiplication and interconnection of neurons during a far longer growth period, and adds to the elementary or frog-type apparatus two principal complicating tissues that far overshadow the earlier developments. One is often called reticular substance, the other is the cerebral cortex.

The reticular substance is so called because it is an interweaving of small centers of gray substance with short bundles and interspersed mats of axons (the white substance), quite different from the simple contrast between gray and white substance seen in primitive animals and in early embryos. The frog brain is not without this sort of tissue, but in the brains of advanced vertebrates like the teleost fishes, the reptiles and the birds, it becomes indescribably complex. The modern mammals push this development to still higher orders of magnitude.

Although neurological science is not yet ready with answers to most specific questions about what happens where in the central nervous system, the

[1] R. Jeffers, "Passenger Pigeons," in *The Beginning and the End.*

new techniques of exploration within the brain suggest that in and through the reticular substance the connections for integrating sensory information with the devices for evaluation and for making decisions and coordinated responses are multiplied exponentially.

Thus, an electrode planted within a single neuron in the reticular substance of the hindbrain can give startling evidence that this one cell is receiving and reacting to sensations reported from widely scattered parts of the body, and sending out coded pulses as a calculated response. Your own brain contains hundreds of millions, probably billions of such cells, every one individually a computer.

The neurologists can now stimulate chosen localized areas through implanted electrodes, either hooked up to wires dangling from the cage ceiling or activated through miniaturized transmitters healed in under the scalp and controlled by radio transmission. In such experiments, stimuli delivered to many parts of the reticular substance cause the animal to react as though he were flooded with agreeable sensation. If the cat or rat or monkey learns how to deliver the stimulus to himself by pressing a pedal, he will do so repeatedly and rapidly, until he falls asleep exhausted. As soon as he wakes up, he goes to pounding the pedal again.

There are other reticular areas which have the reverse effect. If the stimulus comes at rhythmical intervals and the animal discovers that he can forestall it by pressing the pedal, he quickly learns to regulate his life so as to be there and step on it just in time. What kind of sensation such a stimulus produces in him can only be guessed by the experimenter. One might suppose that these areas of reticular substance which have such opposite effects are there to add into the computer's analysis of the situation at the moment a go signal or a stop signal for particular alternative choices, or a sense of goodness or badness, satisfaction or distress, urgency or caution, danger or relaxation. A value judgment, in other words.

It is not difficult to see the survival value of such a device. No doubt the basic mechanism exists in the brains of fishes and frogs, though I am not aware that experiments have been done to locate it. In the reticular substance of mammals, however, we see it hugely developed. The result of overdoing this might produce an awareness of the good and bad features of so very many facets of a situation as to delay and perplex the individual in calculating his single coordinated response.

Mammals are also conspicuously good at remembering experiences from their own lives as individuals, and these memories are loaded with value judgments. There is still no clear answer as to where or in what coded form these new personal memories are stored. But an animal with all this added to the ancestral memory, enhanced with perhaps casually acquired and unwisely generalized connotations of goodness and badness, might predictably be endowed with excessive individuality, prone to unnecessarily variable behavior, chosen more often for self-satisfaction than in the interest of species survival.

The other evolutionary development, the formation of the cerebral cortex, is almost unknown in vertebrates other than mammals, and is feeble in some of these. Cerebral cortex is a tissue of awesome complexity, and our techniques for analyzing what happens in it are still highly inadequate. Stimulation of willing human subjects, in chosen spots exposed surgically, or radio stimulation of these areas through permanently installed electrodes operated by healed-in transistor devices, evoke feelings referred to a particular part of the body, or cause normal-appearing localized movements, e.g. the flexion of an arm or a finger, time and again, upon repetition of the signal. Other areas produce more generalized sensory or motor or emotional or physiologic effects. The patient, his brain exposed under local anesthesia, does not know when the stimulus is applied. When the electrode touches a particular spot of his cortex he may report that he is suddenly remembering a scene identifiable as to time and place, but the memory blacks out when the current is off. Stimulation of other areas may elicit emotions of sexual attraction or anxiety or rage graded according to the intensity of the signal.

More wide-ranging experiments with cats, monkeys or barnyard stock, singly or in groups, free to move in large caged areas, show the possibility of turning on and off a great range of complex emotions, behavior, and even personality traits, by local stimulation.[2] The effect produced through a permanently planted electrode is area specific. Though not predictable before the first stimulus is given, the response is repeated with each stimulus, many times a day or over periods of months or years.

In subjective comparison of mammals with greater or less personal individuality one gets the impression that the degrees of freedom of choice, of imaginative recognition of possible ways to react to situations, of storage capacity and retentiveness of memory, and the richness of association, are correlated with the intricacy and amount of the cerebral cortex and reticular substance. Animals highest on both scales include porpoises, elephants, cats and dogs, apes, and people.

One cannot underestimate the effects on the human species of other evolutionary trends that came to a climax in us, for instance the development of upright posture that frees the hands, the reshaping of the fingers for grasping and manipulating, the perfection of binocular vision that can bring into focus either the hands or the far distance at will. Far more significant than these was the development of speech, made possible by and controlled in a particular small area of the new cerebral cortex. This expanded the powers of the human secondary computer by orders of magnitude, even in comparison with that of close relatives like apes.

We no longer communicate with each other by baring teeth, raising hackles and flaunting rumps, but in symbolic language. We can make abstractions and generalizations and artificial associations. Through speech we can feed into the recording apparatus of each other's secondary computers not only the vast and rather accidental store of individually acquired and long-lasting memories of our own experience, but also the loads of approval or disapproval which we deliberately or unwittingly put upon them. We increasingly remove ourselves into created worlds of our own, calculating our choices by reference to a memory bank of second-hand ghosts of other people's experiences and feelings, prettied up or uglified with value judgments picked up who knows where, by whom, for what reason.

[2] J. M. R. Delgado, 1969, *Physical Control of the Mind.*

Language gave a fourth dimension to the powers of the secondary computer, and writing a fifth dimension. We can now convince each other that things are good or bad, acceptable or intolerable, merely by agreeing with each other, or by reciting catechisms. With writing we can color the judgments of people unborn, just as our judgments are tailored to the whim of influential teachers in the past.

Symbols have given us the means to attach a value judgment to some abstract noun, some shibboleth, and transfer this by association to any person or situation at will. We invent, we practice, we delight in tricks for saying things indirectly by poetry and figures of speech, that might sound false or trite or slanderous or nonsensical if we said them directly. A more normally constructed animal, a porpoise or an elephant, mercifully spared such subtleties, might well look at human beings and see that each one of us has become to some degree insane, out of touch with the actual world, pursuing a mad course of options in the imagined interest of self rather than of species.

The primary computer is still there, programmed in the interest of species survival. With his new powers, man should do better than any other animal at understanding the present crisis and generating an appropriate strategy and tactics. Instead, the effort is drowned out in the noise, the flicker-bicker, the chattering flood of directives from the personalized secondary computer. In pursuit of his own comfort and his own pleasure, man wars against his fellows and against the good earth.

The frame of each person is like a racing shell with two oarsmen in it, back to back, rowing in opposite directions. The one represents the ancient computer system, comparing the personal situation of the moment with an inherited value system and driving the person to perform in such a way that the species will survive, irrespective of how absurd his own expendable life may be. The other represents the secondary computer system, probably located in reticular substance and cerebral cortex, surveying chiefly the memories of childhood and adult life, and deciding how to act according to the value-loaded store of personal experience.

It is this runaway evolutionary development of our superimposed second computer that has produced our inventors, our artists, our saints and heroes, our poets, our thinkers. Our love and hate, ecstasy and despair. The infinite variety of human personalities. It has also atomized the species into a cloud of ungovernable individuals. We split our elections 48 to 52, make laws to break them, and either ignore community priorities or establish them by political blind-man's-buff in frivolous disregard of real emergencies. Six experts will come violently to six different decisions on how to meet a crisis because their personal histories lead them to weight the same data differently. Each of us can see bad logic and conflicts of interest affecting the judgment of most of our associates; it is more difficult to detect them in ourselves. Our individually acquired prejudices have been built into our secondary computers.

Yet it is a glorious thing to feel the uniqueness, the power of decision, the freedom of being human. Who would prefer to be even so wonderful a creature as a dog, an elephant, a horse, a porpoise? I believe nevertheless that just this ungovernable power of the human individual, the essence of our humanity, is the root of our trouble.

The California biologist Garrett Hardin, in a famous essay called "The Tragedy of the Commons," showed that this accounts for practically all the facets of our apocalyptic crisis, from the population explosion to runaway technology.[3] He is referring to the community pasture where anyone may feed his animals. Overgrazing will bring erosion and irreversible deterioration in it. Each herdsman, calculating the advantage and disadvantage to himself of putting out one more animal to graze, balancing his small share of the possible damage against his sole ownership of the extra income, adds another animal in his own interest, and another, and another. All do, and all lose together. The tragedy is the inescapable disaster when each herdsman pursues his own advantage without limit, in a limited commons. This is the tragedy that leaves us with too many human mouths to feed, soil impoverished and washed or blown away, forests skinned off, lakes ruined, plastic bottles and aluminum cans scattered over the countryside, rivers clogged with dead fish, bilge oil spreading on public waters, streets and highways made obscene with advertisements. It is what gives us choking smog, the stink and corruption below paper mills and slaughter houses, the draining of one well by another in a falling water table, the sneaking of radioactive wastes into the air and the oceans.

All these, Hardin makes clear, are problems with *no technological solution.* To be sure, the technology stands ready, but the trouble starts with some individual, you, me, whose response to a situation is to give highest priority to his personal chance of profit, or his family's, or his country's. He has a vivid sense of the value to himself of his own freedom, but the total effects of all such freedoms on the species and on the natural world which supports it is invisible or far out of focus. The technology might just as well not exist.

Some of these problems that will not be solved by technology alone can indeed be brought under control by compacts, treaties, and other agreements between willing groups, or by laws imposed by the majority upon a minority in the common interest. Hardin, however, puts the finger on the population problem as the worst example of the worst class of problems, in which all of us must restrict the freedom of all of us, when none of us want to. He is properly skeptical of conscience or altruism as forces for uniting the community when nearly all of us are still daring to gamble on the continued capacity of the commons to withstand collapse. What is needed, he says, is a fundamental extension of morality.

My way of agreeing with him is to say that human nature is our chief enemy because the species-preserving function of our primary computer has not yet been built into the secondary computer which generates our human nature. It is by now clear that our nature as individuals is not so much inherited as learned by babies as they grow into people, in and from their individual, accidental and culture-bound experiences. We need to incorporate into the decision-making apparatus that will really control them a new survival morality, a system of values the principal axiom of which is that anything which threatens the welfare of the species is bad, anything that serves to bring the species into harmony with its environment is good. We must, each of us, because of this inner drive, regulate our numbers and our selfish wants as rigorously as the

[3] G. Hardin, 1968, *Science* 162: 1243. The Tragedy of the Commons.

forces of natural selection would have done had we not learned how to set them aside.

Do we know how to create a human nature that can keep the species going without undue sacrifice of the privilege and joy of being human? How much freedom must we give up? Do we want to? Is there time?

Basic Processes in Organisms

Lawrence K. Frank

If we are to understand the infant as a persistent, but ever changing, organism, we need to think in terms that are dynamic, which calls for a recognition of the ongoing processes by which the infant grows, develops, matures and ages while continually functioning and behaving. As a young mammalian organism, the human infant lives by much the same basic physiological processes as other mammals.

The recognition of process has come with the acceptance of such recently formulated conceptions as that of self-organization, self-stabilization, self-repair and self-direction which are characteristic not only of organisms but of various man-made machines such as computers and systems designed to operate a planned sequence of activities with the use of positive and negative feedbacks. (Wiener 1961; Von Foerster and Zopf 1962). The organism may be said to be "programmed" by its heredity but capable of flexible functioning through the life cycle.

Moreover, it must be re-emphasized that each infant differs to a greater or lesser extent from all other infants, exhibiting not only individual variation but also displaying a considerable range of intra-individual variability, or continually changing functioning and physiological states, especially during the early months of life when the infant is not yet fully organized or capable of adequate self-stabilization.

Since most of our knowledge of infancy and childhood is derived from observations and measurements of selected variables, responses to stimuli, at a given time or a succession of times, we do not gain an adequate conception of the continuous, dynamic processes of living organisms, especially since we tend to focus upon the outcomes, without recognizing the processes which produce them. Accordingly, some account of these basic processes and how they operate may provide a conceptual model for understanding the multidimensional development of infants during the first year of life. Whatever is done to and for the infant, what privations, frustrations and deprivations he may suffer, what demands and coercions he must accept, what spontaneous activity and learning he displays, may be viewed as expressions of his basic functioning processes.

Every experience in the life of an infant evokes some alteration in these

From *The Importance of Infancy*, by Lawrence K. Frank. Copyright © 1966 by Random House, Inc. Reprinted by permission.

organic processes whereby he manages not only to survive but to grow and develop, to learn while carrying on his incessant intercourse with the surrounding world. Thus, by focusing on the organic processes we may discover what is taking place when we speak of adjustment, learning, adaptation, and the transitions encountered at critical stages in his development.

The concept of mechanism indicates or implies a deterministic relationship between antecedent and consequent, usually as a *linear* relationship in which the consequent is proportional to the antecedent. The concept of *process* involves a dynamic, *non-linear* operation, whereby the same process, depending upon where, when, how, and in what quantities or intensities it operates, may produce different products which may be all out of proportion to that which initiates or touches off the process. For example the process of fertilization and gestation operates in all mammals to produce the immense variety of mammalian young. But different processes may produce similar or equivalent products, an operation which has been called "equifinality" by Bertalanffy (1950).

A brief discussion of the six basic processes operating in organisms will indicate how the infant organism is able to persist and survive by continually changing and is thereby able to cope with the particular version of infant care and rearing to which he is subjected.

These six processes are: The Growth Process, The Organizing Process, The Communicating Process, The Stabilizing Process, The Directive or Purposive Process and The Creative Process. (Frank 1963.)

The Growth Process   The infant who has been growing since conception continues, with a brief interruption and often some loss of weight, to grow incrementally, adding gradually to his size and weight. His growth may be slowed down by inadequate or inappropriate feeding, by some difficulties in digesting and assimilating whatever foodstuff he be given, or by a variety of disturbances and dysfunctions. A continuing upward trend in weight is expected as an expression of normal development, although recent cautions have been expressed on the undesirability of too rapid increase in weight and the vulnerability of a fat, waterlogged infant.

This incremental growth in size and weight indicates that the infant is maintaining an excess of growth over the daily losses through elimination of urine and feces, through skin and lungs, and also in the replacement of many cells that are discarded. Thus, millions of blood corpuscles are destroyed and replaced each day, the iron of those destroyed being salvaged and reused. Likewise, cells of the skin and lining of the gastrointestinal tract, of the lungs, kidneys, liver, indeed of almost all organ systems, except the central nervous system and brain, are continually being replaced at different rates.

Probably more vitally significant but less clearly recognized is the continual replacement of the chemical constituents of cells, tissues and bony structures, like the skeleton and the teeth in which different chemicals are discarded and new materials are selected out of the blood stream to replace them. Here we see a dramatic illustration of the statement that an organism is a configuration which must continually change in order to survive, a conception which is wholly congruous with the recently formulated assumption of the world as an aggregate of highly organized complexes of energy transformations.

Growth, incremental and replacement, is a major functioning process, gradually producing an enlarging infant as the growing cells differentiate, specialize and organize to give rise to the varied tissues and organ systems in the developing embryo and fetus. In this prenatal development the creative process is also operating to produce the unique, unduplicated human infant along with the operation of the organizing process.

The Organizing Process   Only recently has the process of self-organization been recognized in scientific thinking as basic to all organisms which start with some kind of genetic inheritance and undergo multiplication and duplication of cells with differentiation and specialization of components that become organized into a living organism. (Von Foerster and Zopf 1962.) Thus the initial development of an infant takes place through the operation of the growth and the organizing processes which continue to operate throughout its life, maintaining the organism as it undergoes various transitions and transformations and copes with the many discontinuities encountered in its life cycle.

Since the normal infant arrives fully equipped with all the essential bodily components and organ systems, the growth process and the organizing process operate to incorporate the intakes of food, water and air into its ever changing structure-functioning. Most of the highly organized foodstuffs, proteins, fats and carbohydrates, are progressively broken down, disorganized and randomized, and the products of these digestive operations are then circulated through the blood stream from which the constituent cells, tissues and fluids select out what they need for metabolism and organize these into their specialized structure-functioning components. The recent dramatic findings in molecular biology show how this organizing process operates within the cell as the DNA (the carrier of the genetic information) of the genes directs the production of the various proteins and the utilization of the minerals and vitamins for the growth and multiplication of cells and the maintenance of their functioning.

Also of large significance for the understanding of organic processes are the sequential steps in the utilization of food stuffs for metabolism involving many steps and numerous specialized enzymes and catalysts. Unfortunately some infants suffer from so-called metabolic errors when one or more of these steps in the metabolic sequence is missing or inadequate and therefore his growth and development and healthy functioning are jeopardized.

In the self-organizing organism we encounter circular and reciprocal operations in which every component of the organism by its specialized functioning, gives rise to, and maintains, the total organism of which it is a participant; concurrently, the total organism reciprocally governs when, what and how each of these components must function and operate to maintain the organized whole. This capacity for self-organizing arises from the autonomy of each component of an organism which over millions of years of evolution has developed its own highly individualized and specialized functioning within the total organic complex but functions according to the requirements of the organism in which it operates.

Communication Process   Obviously, these autonomous components which give rise to growth and organization must continually communicate, internally and with the external "surround." The infant has an inherited communication network in his nervous system, his circulatory system, and his lymphatic system. Through these several channels every constituent of an organism continually communicates with all others, directly or indirectly, and with different degrees of speed in communication. Each component continually sends and receives messages whereby its functioning operations are regulated, synchronized, articulated and related to all others, with greater or less immediacy. The infant is born with most of these internal communications already functioning, having been in operation for varying periods of its prenatal development but with the central nervous system still immature. The infant also has the sensory apparatus for various inputs, of light, of sound, touch, taste and smell, also for pain, heat and cold, and for gravity and for atmospheric pressure changes. But the infant is also initially prepared for dealing with the varying intensities and durations of these intakes and impacts, gradually increasing his capacity for filtering, buffering, mingling and transducing these inputs whereby he may monitor these sensory communications according to his ever changing internal, physiological states and the kinesthetic and proprioceptive messages by which he continually orients himself and gradually achieves an equilibrium in space.

The infant must carry on this incessant intercourse with the world more or less protected by adults from too severe or hazardous impacts and provided with the food and care required by his helpless dependency. But the infant often must try to defend himself from what his caretakers try to impose on him or compel him to accept, as in feeding, toilet training, etc. Under this treatment much of the infant's energies may be expended in these efforts to maintain his stability and integrity against unwelcomed and uncongenial treatment which may interfere with his normal functioning and compromise his growth and development and learning as a unique organism. Thus we may say that the growth and organizing processes contribute to and are dependent upon the communication process, which operates through the inherited receptors of the infant which may become progressively altered, refined, and increasingly sensitized through learning. Quite early the infant may become receptive to nonverbal communications such as tones of voice, smiling, tactile comforting, or painful treatment.

Stabilizing Process   Since the world presents so many different and continually varying messages and impacts, organisms must be able to cope with the ever changing flux of experience and maintain their integrity and functional capacities by monitoring all their organic functions. While all other organisms have evolved with their species-specific range of sensory awareness and capacity for perception and for living in their ancestral life zones, the human infant, and a few other mammals are able to live in a wide variety of climates and habitations and maintain their internal world within fairly close limitations upon intra-organic variability. This becomes possible through the operation of the stabilizing process.

The stabilizing process operates through a network of physiological feedbacks, both negative and positive, to maintain a dynamic equilibrium and is not limited to the concept of homeostasis which Cannon used to describe the maintenance of the fluid internal environment. The stabilizing process main-

tains continually changing physiological states. At birth it is not fully developed
or operationally effective and hence the infant needs continual care, protection,
and appropriate nutrition. But as he grows and develops he increasingly regulates his internal functioning by responding appropriately to the various inputs
and outputs, intakes, and outlets. Obviously an infant who must grow, both
incrementally and by replacement, cannot tolerate too stable an internal environment which might prevent or limit such growth and adaptive functioning.
With his increasing exposure to the world the infant learns to calibrate all his
sensory inputs and increasingly to "equalize his thresholds," as Kurt Goldstein
(1939) has pointed out.

Not the least significant and often stressful experience under which an
infant must maintain his internal stability are the varying practices of child
care and feeding, the efforts of parents to regularize his functioning and compel
him to conform to whatever regimen of living they wish to establish. Clearly the
stabilizing process is essential to the infant's survival and to his continuing
growth and development and the variety of learning which he must master.
Happily, most infants achieve a progressive enlargement of their capacity for
living and for self-regulation and self-stabilization to assume an autonomy
expressing their integrity in the face of often uncongenial treatment and
surroundings.

The Directive or Purposive Process   With the achievement of motor coordination and locomotion, by creeping and crawling, and then assuming an
erect posture and learning to walk, the infant enlarges the purposive or goal
seeking process which involves continual scanning, probing and exploring the
world and developing his selective awareness and patterned perception, and
especially the ability to ignore or to reject what may interfere or distract him
in his endeavor to attain remote or deferred goals. Obviously, the purposive
process cannot operate effectively until the infant has achieved a considerable
degree of internal stabilization and of neuro-muscular coordination, and the
ability to cope with a three dimensional, spatial world.

Since the child initially is attracted or impelled by whatever he may become
aware of or has an impulse to seek, to handle, to put into his mouth, or otherwise to manipulate, the purposive process is frequently blocked and the child
may be severely punished in his attempts to develop his autonomous mastery of
his small world. Thus the purposive process operates differentially in each
infant who is likely to be attracted by and responsive to different dimensions of
his environment at different times; these early explorations provide an endless
sequence of learning experiences which involve, not only the actual world of
nature, but the wide range of artifacts and of highly individuated personalities
with whom he is in contact. With language the infant learns to deal with
people and verbal symbols of language for goal seeking.

The Creative Process   As noted earlier, the creative process begins to
operate early in gestation to produce a unique infant as a human organism with
the same basic organic functions and similar or equivalent components which,
however, are different in each infant. From birth on, therefore, each infant is
engaged in creating a highly selective environment or a "life space" that is as

congenial and appropriate for his individualized organism, with its peculiar needs and capacities, as is possible under the constraints and coercions imposed by others upon his growth, development, functioning, and learning. In infancy and childhood the individual is more creative than in any other period in his life cycle, but this creativity may be either ignored or discouraged by those who are intent upon making the child conform as nearly as possible to their image or ideal of attainment.

Within recent years the purposive and creative processes have become major foci in the studies of early child growth, development and education, but it must be remembered that the purposive and creative processes cannot operate independently because they are inextricably related to and dependent upon the other four basic processes which reciprocally contribute to the operation of these two processes.

Most of the training and education of the infant and young child involves curbing, regulating, focusing, and patterning, and also evoking the communicating and stabilizing and directive processes which are more amenable to intervention and control by others. Through supervision and regulation of these processes the child is largely molded, patterned, and oriented into the kind of organism-personality favored by his parents and appropriately prepared for living in his cultural and social order. As he grows older the infant is expected to learn the required conduct for group living and to master the various symbol systems by which he can relate cognitively to the world and negotiate with other people. It appears that learning as an expression of the purposive and the creative processes may be compromised and sometimes severely distorted or blocked when the child is expected or compelled to alter the organizing, communicating, and stabilizing processes, as required by his parents and other more experienced persons.

In the discussion of humanization we will see how the young mammalian organism is transformed into a personality for living in a symbolic cultural world and for participating in a social order, through the various practices of infant care and rearing that are focused upon, and directly intervene in, the operation of these six basic organic processes. But each infant is a highly individualized organism who develops his own idiosyncratic personality through the development and utilization of his basic organic processes.

Bibliography

BERTALANFFY, L. VON, "Theory of Open Systems in Physics and Biology," *Science*, CXI, 1950, pp. 27–29. See also Yearbooks of Society for General Systems Research.

FRANK, L. K., "Human Development—An Emerging Discipline," in *Modern Perspectives in Child Development*, In honor of Milton J. E. Senn, Eds. Albert J. Solnit and Sally Provence, New York: International Universities Press, 1963.

———. "Potentiality: Its Definition and Development," in *Insights and the Curriculum*, Yearbook, Association for Supervision and Curriculum Development, Washington, D.C.: National Education Association, 1963.

GOLDSTEIN, KURT, *The Organism*, New York: American Book Company, 1939.

VON FOERSTER, HEINZ, and ZOPF, JR., GEORGE W., Eds., *Principles of Self Organizing Systems*, London: Pergamon Press, 1962.

WIENER, NORBERT, *Cybernetics*, Cambridge and New York: M.I.T. Press and John Wiley and Sons, Inc., 1961.

The Life Cycle: Epigenesis of Identity

Erik H. Erikson
HARVARD UNIVERSITY

Whenever we try to understand growth, it is well to remember the *epigenetic principle* which is derived from the growth of organisms *in utero*. Somewhat generalized, this principle states that anything that grows has a ground plan, and that out of this ground plan the parts arise, each part having its time of special ascendancy, until all parts have arisen to form a functioning whole. This, obviously, is true for fetal development where each part of the organism has its critical time of ascendance or danger of defect. At birth the baby leaves the chemical exchange of the womb for the social exchange system of his society, where his gradually increasing capacities meet the opportunities and limitations of his culture. How the maturing organism continues to unfold, not by developing new organs but by means of a prescribed sequence of locomotor, sensory, and social capacities, is described in the child-development literature. As pointed out, psychoanalysis has given us an understanding of the more idiosyncratic experiences, and especially the inner conflicts, which constitute the manner in which an individual becomes a distinct personality. But here, too, it is important to realize that in the sequence of his most personal experiences the healthy child, given a reasonable amount of proper guidance, can be trusted to obey inner laws of development, laws which create a succession of potentialities for significant interaction with those persons who tend and respond to him and those institutions which are ready for him. While such interaction varies from culture to culture, it must remain within "the proper rate and the proper sequence" which governs all epigenesis. Personality, therefore, can be said to develop according to steps predetermined in the human organism's readiness to be driven toward, to be aware of, and to interact with a widening radius of significant individuals and institutions.

It is for this reason that, in the presentation of stages in the development of the personality, we employ an epigenetic diagram analogous to the one employed in *Childhood and Society* for an analysis of Freud's psychosexual stages.[1] It is, in fact, an implicit purpose of this presentation to bridge the theory of infantile sexuality (without repeating it here in detail) and our knowledge of the child's physical and social growth.

In Diagram 1 the double-lined squares signify both a sequence of stages and a gradual development of component parts. In other words, the diagram formalizes a progression through time of a differentiation of parts. This indicates (1) that each item of the vital personality to be discussed is systematically related to all others, and that they all depend on the proper development in the proper sequence of each item; and (2) that each item exists in some form before "its" decisive and critical time normally arrives.

Reprinted from *Identity, Youth and Crisis*, Copyright © 1968 by W. W. Norton & Company, Inc., pp. 92–96. By permission.

[1] See Erik H. Erikson, *Childhood and Society*, 2nd ed., New York: W. W. Norton, 1963, Part I.

DIAGRAM 1

	1	2	3	4	5	6	7	8
VIII								INTEGRITY vs. DESPAIR
VII							GENERATIVITY vs. STAGNATION	
VI						INTIMACY vs. ISOLATION		
V	Temporal Perspective vs. Time Confusion	Self-Certainty vs. Self-Consciousness	Role Experimentation vs. Role Fixation	Apprenticeship vs. Work Paralysis	IDENTITY vs. IDENTITY CONFUSION	Sexual Polarization vs. Bisexual Confusion	Leader- and Followership vs. Authority Confusion	Ideological Commitment vs. Confusion of Values
IV				INDUSTRY vs. INFERIORITY	Task Identification vs. Sense of Futility			
III			INITIATIVE vs. GUILT		Anticipation of Roles vs. Role Inhibition			
II		AUTONOMY vs. SHAME, DOUBT			Will to Be Oneself vs. Self-Doubt			
I	TRUST vs. MISTRUST				Mutual Recognition vs. Autistic Isolation			

313

If I say, for example, that a sense of basic trust is the first component of mental vitality to develop in life, a sense of autonomous will the second, and a sense of initiative the third, the diagram expresses a number of fundamental relations that exist among the three components, as well as a few fundamental facts for each.

Each comes to its ascendance, meets its crisis, and finds its lasting solution in ways to be described here, toward the end of the stages mentioned. All of them exist in the beginning in some form, although we do not make a point of this fact, and we shall not confuse things by calling these components different names at earlier or later stages. A baby may show something like "autonomy" from the beginning, for example, in the particular way in which he angrily tries to wriggle his hand free when tightly held. However, under normal conditions, it is not until the second year that he begins to experience the whole critical alternative between being an autonomous creature and being a dependent one, and it is not until then that he is ready for a specifically new encounter with his environment. The environment, in turn, now feels called upon to convey to him its particular ideas and concepts of autonomy in ways decisively contributing to his personal character, his relative efficiency, and the strength of his vitality.

It is this encounter, together with the resulting crisis, which is to be described for each stage. Each stage becomes a crisis because incipient growth and awareness in a new part function go together with a shift in instinctual energy and yet also cause a specific vulnerability in that part. One of the most difficult questions to decide, therefore, is whether or not a child at a given stage is weak or strong. Perhaps it would be best to say that he is always vulnerable in some respects and completely oblivious and insensitive in others, but that at the same time he is unbelievably persistent in the same respects in which he is vulnerable. It must be added that the baby's weakness gives him power; out of his very dependence and weakness he makes signs to which his environment, if it is guided well by a responsiveness combining "instinctive" and traditional patterns, is peculiarly sensitive. A baby's presence exerts a consistent and persistent domination over the outer and inner lives of every member of a household. Because these members must reorient themselves to accommodate his presence, they must also grow as individuals and as a group. It is as true to say that babies control and bring up their families as it is to say the converse. A family can bring up a baby only by being brought up by him. His growth consists of a series of challenges to them to serve his newly developing potentialities for social interaction.

Each successive step, then, is a potential crisis because of a radical change in perspective. Crisis is used here in a developmental sense to connote not a threat of catastrophe, but a turning point, a crucial period of increased vulnerability and heightened potential, and therefore, the ontogenetic source of generational strength and maladjustment. The most radical change of all, from intrauterine to extrauterine life, comes at the very beginning of life. But in postnatal existence, too, such radical adjustments of perspective as lying relaxed, sitting firmly, and running fast must all be accomplished in their own good time. With them, the interpersonal perspective also changes rapidly and often radically, as is testified by the proximity in time of such opposites as "not letting mother out of sight" and "wanting to be independent." Thus, different capacities use different opportunities to become full-grown components of the ever-new configuration that is the growing personality.

Equilibrium

Jean Piaget
UNIVERSITY OF GENEVA

The psychological development that starts at birth and terminates in adulthood is comparable to organic growth. Like the latter, it consists essentially of activity directed toward equilibrium. Just as the body evolves toward a relatively stable level characterized by the completion of the growth process and by organ maturity, so mental life can be conceived as evolving toward a final form of equilibrium represented by the adult mind. In a sense, development is a progressive equilibration from a lesser to a higher state of equilibrium. From the point of view of intelligence, it is easy to contrast the relative instability and incoherence of childhood ideas with the systematization of adult reason. With respect to the affective life, it has frequently been noted how extensively emotional equilibrium increases with age. Social relations also obey the same law of gradual stabilization.

An essential difference between the life of the body and that of the mind must nonetheless be stressed if the dynamism inherent in the reality of the mind is to be respected. The final form of equilibrium reached through organic growth is more static and, above all, more unstable than the equilibrium toward which mental development strives, so that no sooner has ascending evolution terminated than a regressive evolution automatically starts, leading to old age. Certain psychological functions that depend closely on the physical condition of the body follow an analogous curve. Visual acuity, for example, is at a maximum toward the end of childhood, only to diminish subsequently; and many other perceptual processes are regulated by the same law. By contrast, the higher functions of intelligence and affectivity tend toward a "mobile equilibrium." The more mobile it is, the more stable it is, so that the termination of growth, in healthy minds, by no means marks the beginning of decline but rather permits progress that in no sense contradicts inner equilibrium.

It is thus in terms of equilibrium that we shall try to describe the evolution of the child and the adolescent. From this point of view, mental development is a continuous construction comparable to the erection of a vast building that becomes more solid with each addition. Alternatively, and perhaps more appropriately, it may be likened to the assembly of a subtle mechanism that goes through gradual phases of adjustment in which the individual pieces become more supple and mobile as the equilibrium of the mechanism as a whole becomes more stable. We must, however, introduce an important distinction between two complementary aspects of the process of equilibration. This is the distinction between the variable structures that define the successive states of equilibrium and a certain constant functioning that assures the transition from any one state to the following one.

There is sometimes a striking similarity between the reactions of the child and the adult, as, for example, when the child is sure of what he wants and acts as adults do with respect to their own special interests. At other times there is a world of difference—in games, for example, or in the manner of reasoning. From a functional point of view, i.e., if we take into consideration the general motives of behavior and thought, there are constant functions common to all ages. At all levels of development, action presupposes a precipitating factor: a physiological, affective, or intellectual need. (In the latter case, the need appears in the guise of a question or a problem.) At all levels, intelligence seeks to understand or explain, etc. However, while the functions of interest, explanation, etc., are common to all developmental stages, that is to say, are "invariable" as far as the functions themselves are concerned, it is nonetheless true that "interests" (as opposed to "interest") vary considerably from one mental level to another, and that the particular explanations (as opposed to the function of explaining) are of a very different nature, depending on the degree of intellectual development. In addition to the constant functions, there are the variable structures. An analysis of these progressive forms of successive equilibrium highlights the differences from one behavioral level to another, all the way from the elementary behavior of the neonate through adolescence.

The variable structures—motor or intellectual on the one hand and affective on the other—are the organizational forms of mental activity. They are organized along two dimensions—intrapersonal and social (interpersonal). For greater clarity we shall distinguish six stages or periods of development which mark the appearance of these successively constructed structures:

1. The reflex or hereditary stage, at which the first instinctual nutritional drives and the first emotions appear.

2. The stage of the first motor habits and of the first organized percepts, as well as of the first differentiated emotions.

3. The stage of sensorimotor or practical intelligence (prior to language), of elementary affective organization, and of the first external affective fixations. These first three stages constitute the infancy period—from birth till the age of one and a half to two years—i.e., the period prior to the development of language and thought as such.

4. The stage of intuitive intelligence, of spontaneous interpersonal feelings, and of social relationships in which the child is subordinate to the adult (ages two to seven years, or "early childhood").

5. The stage of concrete intellectual operations (the beginning of logic) and of moral and social feelings of cooperation (ages seven to eleven or twelve, or "middle childhood").

6. The stage of abstract intellectual operations, of the formation of the personality, and of affective and intellectual entry into the society of adults (adolescence).

Each of these stages is characterized by the appearance of original structures whose construction distinguishes it from previous stages. The essentials of these successive constructions exist at subsequent stages in the form of substructures onto which new characteristics have been built. It follows that in the adult each stage through which he has passed corresponds to a given level in the total hierarchy of behavior. But at each stage there are also temporary and secondary characteristics that are modified by subsequent development as a function of the need for better organization. Each stage thus constitutes a particular form of equilibrium as a function of its characteristic structures, and mental evolution is effectuated in the direction of an ever-increasing equilibrium.

We know which functional mechanisms are common to all stages. In an absolutely general way (not only in comparing one stage with the following but also in comparing each item of behavior that is part of that stage with ensuing behavior), one can say that all action—that is to say, all movement, all thought, or all emotion—responds to a need. Neither the child nor the adult executes any external or even entirely internal act unless impelled by a motive; this motive can always be translated into a need (an elementary need, an interest, a question, etc.).

As Claparède (1951) has shown, a need is always a manifestation of disequilibrium: there is need when something either outside ourselves or within us (physically or mentally) is changed and behavior has to be adjusted as a function of this change. For example, hunger or fatigue will provoke a search for nourishment or rest; encountering an external object will lead to a need to play, which in turn has practical ends, or it leads to a question or a theoretical problem. A casual word will excite the need to imitate, to sympathize, or will engender reserve or opposition if it conflicts with some interest of our own. Conversely, action terminates when a need is satisfied, that is to say, when equilibrium is re-established between the new factor that has provoked the need and the mental organization that existed prior to the introduction of this factor. Eating or sleeping, playing or reaching a goal, replying to a question or resolving a problem, imitating successfully, establishing an affective tie, or maintaining one's point of view are all satisfactions that, in the preceding examples, will put an end to the particular behavior aroused by the need. At any given moment, one can thus say, action is disequilibrated by the transformations that arise in the external or internal world, and each new behavior consists not only in re-establishing equilibrium but also in moving toward a more stable equilibrium than that which preceded the disturbance.

Human action consists of a continuous and perpetual mechanism of readjustment or equilibration. For this reason, in these initial phases of construction, the successive mental structures that engender development can be considered as so many progressive forms of equilibrium, each of which is an advance upon its predecessor. It must be understood, however, that this functional mechanism, general though it may be, does not explain the content or the structure of the various needs, since each of them is related to the organization of the particular stage that is being considered. For example, the sight of the same object will occasion very different questions in the small child who is still incapable of classification from those of the older child whose ideas are more extensive and systematic. The interests of a child at any given moment depend on the system of ideas he has acquired plus his affective inclinations, and he tends to fulfill his interests in the direction of greater equilibrium.

Before examining the details of development we must try to find that which is common to the needs and interests present at all ages. One can say, in regard to this, that all needs tend first of all to incorporate things and people into the subject's own activity, i.e., to "assimilate" the external world into the structures that have already been constructed, and secondly to readjust these structures as a function of subtle transformations, i.e., to "accommodate" them to external objects. From this point of view, all mental life, as indeed all organic life, tends progressively to assimilate the surrounding environment. This incorporation is effected thanks to the structures or psychic organs whose scope of action becomes more and more extended. Initially, perception and elementary movement (prehension, etc.) are concerned with objects that are close and viewed statically; then later, memory and practical intelligence permit the representation of earlier states of the object as well as the anticipation of their future states resulting from as yet unrealized transformations. Still later intuitive thought reinforces these two abilities. Logical intelligence in the guise of concrete operations and ultimately of abstract deduction terminates this evolution by making the subject master of events that are far distant in space and time. At each of these levels the mind fulfills the same function, which is to incorporate the universe to itself, but the nature of assimilation varies, i.e., the successive modes of incorporation evolve from those of perception and movement to those of the higher mental operations.

In assimilating objects, action and thought must accommodate to these objects; they must adjust to external variation. The balancing of the processes of assimilation and accommodation may be called "adaptation." Such is the general form of psychological equilibrium, and the progressive organization of mental development appears to be simply an ever more precise adaptation to reality.

Reference

CLAPARÈDE, E. *Le développement mental*. Neuchâtel: Delachaux et Niestlé, 1951.

Major Challenges for Students of Infancy and Early Childhood

Myrtle B. McGraw
BRIARCLIFF COLLEGE

It is not possible to pinpoint any particular ideologies or theories that have given rise to the present interest in early childhood development. The forces were many; they were complex and intertwined. Sputnik shocked the nation out of a state of educational complacency. The disparity of educational opportunities and achievements of children from differing socioeconomic and ethnic groups was brought to light. Then it was determined that children from less favorable environments entered school with their educational handicaps already established. To alleviate this situation, the federal government set up Head Start programs. The outcome of the Head Start programs has led to the claim that even the pre-kindergarten period is too late—education begins in the cradle. Furthermore, since the body of knowledge doubles every 10 years, the amount of knowledge one must master favors an early beginning.

Clearly, the goal of this current wave of concern is to develop the optimum potentials of all children. The pressure is on learning, early learning. It seems clear that the infant and toddler are capable of learning a great deal, *if* the opportunities for learning are properly presented. It also seems evident that the principles of learning derived from laboratory studies of animals or college students are inadequate when it comes to dealing with rapid behavior development of the human infant. The prevailing notion is that these goals can be achieved by manipulation of the environments in which the child lives. To some extent these ideas are reinforced by experiments of the effects of "sensory deprivation," "prolonged isolation," and the comparative effects of "enriched and impoverished" environments. Such studies have been conducted on animals, children, and adults. Once again, the emphasis seems to be shifting to the environmental side of the scale, but it is not locked in with the old heredity-environment dichotomy. It is generally recognized now that nature-nurture are interdependent forces, and to try to separate them clouds inquiry. A few studies (Fowler, 1962; McGraw, 1935; Moore, 1960) have demonstrated that the performances of the young *in particular activities* can be advanced beyond normal expectancy. But we have not as yet learned how to develop to the maximum *all potentials of the growing child.* To do this we shall need new theories or concepts of development that transcend the established principles of learning.

1. *Challenge for the Researchers of Growth*   The present corps of growth scientists are the legatees of a vast body of concepts, theories, and research strategies inherited from the "psychological establishment." Of course, the growth scientists will be drawn from many disciplines and from diverse areas of psychology, other than developmental. Already it is apparent that some

Reprinted from *American Psychologist*, August 1970, *25*, 754–756 by permission of the American Psychological Association.

dyed-in-the-wool experimentalists are selecting the human infant in preference
to animals for special investigations. The challenge for all the students of growth
—regardless of their scientific expertise and theoretical orientation—is to
scan their legacy of knowledge and skills and to have the courage to rule out
those theories and techniques that are not applicable to the study of a complex,
ever-changing phenomenon, such as growth. Many experimentalists fail to
take into account that their own preconceptions may operate as uncontrolled
variables within a particular situation. Will the experimentalist, skillful in the
manipulation of the variables and instruments of measurement, become able to
recognize that the way the infant is held or positioned may also be a factor in
the results obtained? Will the examiner be so focused on the toddler's response
to the items set before him that he fails to detect that the child's wiggling and
climbing off the chair and running toward the door is his way of saying that
there is pressure on his bladder? Will researchers trained to use the IQ or just
chronological age be able to devise strategies to evaluate a multiplicity of
systems constantly in flux, each system influencing another and in different
degrees? All growth and development is not in the form of accretion. The growth
scientists will need to design methods that reveal the rises and falls, the pulsations and rhythms manifest in the growth of a given function. An understanding
of these pulsations and rhythms may become promising guidelines for the development of optimum potentials of the growing child. Strategies developed in
other disciplines (e.g., communication theories) may provide suggestive models
for evaluating constantly changing phenomena, such as rapid growth during
the early years. There is evidence that many of the current investigators (Endler,
Boulter, & Osser, 1968) are alert to the problem, and that is the first step to
improving methodologies.

2. *The Challenge of Cultural Acceptance of Scientific Theories*   In the past,
it has been traditional for scientists, especially those dealing with basic sciences,
to be removed from the applied aspects of their findings. They were searching
for fundamental truths, and whatever society did with it was none of their
concern. On the other hand, many atomic physicists have begun to voice a sense
of responsibility for the way society makes use of their knowledge. During this
century we have been able to see how many psychological theories have been
applied and misapplied to the matter of child rearing and education. If the
periods of infancy and the early years are as important for total development as
generally contended, then it is reasonable to expect the behavioral scientists to
take some responsibility for the way in which their thoughts and theories are
adopted into the cultural patterns of child management. Just how this can be
done is not clear because it has never been systematically undertaken by any
scientific discipline. The general public has faith in science and mass media
and is quick to announce, "Science proves thus and so." Sometimes the mis-
application of a theory may be ascribed to the use of a particular word, perhaps
a word that was originally drawn from another discipline.

Let us consider for a moment some current thoughts that have the potential
for creating parental anxiety. Take the question of "critical periods" as applied
to learning. The concept was first used by embryologists. It was reinforced by
Lorenz's (1935) study of imprinting. Recently, it has been emphasized in

author index

NOTE: Pages referring to bibliographic references are in *italics*. Pages have been given for authors who are mentioned on the text page only by reference number. In those cases, the following italic page must be consulted for the reference number. Pages in **boldface** refer to selections by the authors themselves.

A

Abernethy, E. M., 40, *53*, 275, *294*
Abravanel, E., 84, *101*
Acheson, R. M., 48, *53*
Acker, M., 129, *158*
Adams, P. A., 179, *180*
Ainsworth, M. D. S., 285, 286, *294*
Albert, J., 81, 84, *102*
Albrecht, E. J., 247, 249, *250*
Allinsmith, W., 150, *157*
Almy, M., 80, *101*
Alpert, R., 144, *159*
Amatora, M., 147, *155*
Anastasiow, N., 209, *231*
Anderson, T., 61, *62*
Andres, D., 239, *246*
Angelino, H., 188, 193, 194, *194*
Antonov, A. N., 48, *53*
Aronfreed, J., 235, 236, 239, *245*
Asch, H., 86, *104*, **117-126**
Ashizawa, K., 46, *55*
Atkinson, J. W., 131, *158*
Atkinson, R. K., 56, 59, *62*
Ausubel, D. P., 216, *228*

B

Bachtold, L. M., 96, *104*
Baker, C T., 130, *158*, 209, *232*
Baker, H. V., 223, *228*
Baldwin, A. L., 225, *228*
Baldwin, B. T., 249, *250*
Baldwin, C. P., 225, *228*
Bales, R. F., 207, *231*
Ballard, W. W., **298-306**
Bandura, A., 141, *156*, 237, 243, *245*
Barker, R. G., 135, *156*, 275, *295*
Barnes, R. H., 50, *54*
Barron, F., 92n, *101*
Bassett, E., 25, *34*
Battle, E., 172, *174*
Bayley, N., 278, 292, *294*
Bee, H. L., 209, *228*
Béhar, M., 49, 50, *55*
Bell, R. R., 202, *228*
Beller, E. K., 144, 145, 147, *158*, *159*
Belmont, L., 30, 31, *34*, 64, 65, *69*, 179, *180*
Beloff, J., 66, *69*
Bender, L., 180, *180*

subject index

Cultural influences, school, 147-151
Cultural settings, 197-204
Cultural values and motor skills, 21-22
Curiosity, 129-130

D

Developmental direction, principle of, 276-277
Differences in terminals, principle of, 275
Differentiation and integration, principle of, 276
Disadvantaged children, 117-126, 161-175
Discipline, 210-211
Diseases, 15-17

E

Ecology, 298-306
Education, 319-322
Egocentrism, 87-88, 250-261
Emotional development, 187-195
Empathy, 222
Epigenesis, 277, 312-315
Equilibration, 270-273, 315-318
Erikson's stages, 278-280
Ethnic differences, intelligence tests, 85-87
Evolution, 298-306
Evolutionary adaption, 285-286
Expressive roles, 207
Eye preference, 30

F

Fat, growth of, 11
Father, influence on child, 206-209
Fear, 134-136, 187-195
Flexibility of thought, 72
  parental influence on, 209-210
Formal operations, 282
Freud's psychosexual stages, 278
Friendships, 214-217

G

Generativity, sense of, 280
Genes, 288-289
Genetics, 298-306
Gifted children, 97-98, 114-117
Growth
  principles of, 273-278
  processes of, 306-311
  in size, 39-55

H

Hand preference, 29-32, 64-69
Handicaps, physical, psychological effects of, 20-21
Health, 15-21
Height, adult, prediction of, 7
Height tables, 2-3
Heredity, 286-292
Heterosexual development, 261-267
Homeostasis, 270-271
Humor, 92-93

I

Identification with parents, 206-208
Identity vs. role diffusion, 279, 312-315
Illnesses, 15-17
  chronic, 19
Imagination, 93-95
Immunizations, 17
Impulsivity, 81-82
Individual differences in size, 39-55
Industry, sense of, 127-134, 161-195, 279
Inferiority, sense of, 133-136, 279
Inheritance, biological, 286-290
Initiative, sense of, 279
Instrumental roles, 207
Integrity, sense of, 280
Intellectual development, 71-104, 105-126
Intelligence, Piagetian, 315-318
Intelligence tests, 95-98
Interpersonal relationships, 197-232, 233-267
Interrelationships in growth, 275